Anarchism and the City:
Revolution and Counter-Revolution in Barcelona, 1898–1937

Anarchism and the City:
Revolution and Counter-Revolution in Barcelona, 1898–1937

Chris Ealham

Anarchism and the City:
Revolution and Counter-Revolution in Barcelona (1898–1937)
© 2010 Chris Ealham
This edition © 2010 AK Press (Oakland, Edinburgh, Baltimore) in
collaboration with the Cañada Blanch Centre for Contemporary Spanish
Studies.

Published by arrangement with Taylor & Francis Books Ltd, a member of
the Taylor & Francis Group. (Originally titled *Class, Culture and Conflict
in Barcelona 1898–1937* and published in 2005. First published by
Routledge in collaboration with the Cañada Blanch Centre for
Contemporary Spanish Studies.)

ISBN-13: 978-1-84935-012-9

Library of Congress Control Number: 2010921021

AK Press	AK Press
674-A 23rd Street	PO Box 12766
Oakland, CA 94612	Edinburgh, EH8 9YE
USA	Scotland
www.akpress.org	www.akuk.com
akpress@akpress.org	ak@akedin.demon.co.uk

The above addresses would be delighted to provide you with the latest AK
Press distribution catalog, which features the several thousand books,
pamphlets, zines, audio and video products, and stylish apparel published
and/or distributed by AK Press. Alternatively, visit our website for the
complete catalog, latest news, and secure ordering.
Visit us at www.akpress.org *and* www.revolutionbythebook.akpress.org.

Printed in Canada on acid-free, recycled paper with union labor.

Cover by John Yates (stealworks.com)

For my parents, Annie and Jack
(in memoriam)

and for Bea
(for the future)

La calle no es de nadie aún. Vamos a ver quién la conquista.

The street still belongs to no-one. We'll see who conquers it.

Ramón Sender, *Siete domingos rojos*

Contents

Illustrations and Tables

Tables

Figures

Acknowledgements

I have incurred many debts of gratitude over the years in preparing the two editions of this book. I particular I wish to acknowledge the encouragement and faith shown in the project by Chuck Morse, Zach Blue and the rest of the AK Press collective.

At different times my research has benefited from the generous financial support of the Arts and Humanities Research Council, the British Academy, the Cañada Blanch Centre for Contemporary Spanish Studies (LSE), the Autonomous Catalan Government and the Spanish Foreign Ministry's Dirección General de Relaciones Culturales y Científicas. Most recently, my work has benefited from funding under the Spanish Ministerio de Educación y Cultura collective project, 'La España del Frente Popular: orden público, conflictividad sociolaboral y politicas unitarias'. I am also indebted to the assistance of by the staff at the National Archives in London, the Archivo Histórico Nacional in Madrid and Salamanca, the Centre d'Estudis d'Història Contemporania (Fundació Figueres), the Biblioteca de la Universitat de Barcelona, the Biblioteca de Catalunya and the Centre d'Estudis Històrics Internacionals (CEHI-FIES). At the Arxiu Històric de l'Hospitalet, Clara Pallarés helped me enormously. Most of all, I am grateful to the staff at the Institut Municipal de l'Història de la Ciutat de Barcelona, which for three years became my second home.

Other debts are more diffuse. As an undergraduate, Paul Heywood and, in particular, Paul Preston cultivated my early interest in Spanish history; Paul Preston went on to supervise my doctoral work and remains a continuing source of inspiration and encouragement. Numerous friends and colleagues have provided me with rich intellectual community and friendship, particularly Manel Aisa, Alejandro Andreassi, Óscar Bascuñán, Stuart Christie, Xavier Diez, Andrew Dowling, Andy Durgan, Graeme Garrard, Sharif Gemie, Eduardo González Calleja, Helen Graham, Michael Richards, Nick Rider, Paco Romero and Eulàlia Vega. I am especially grateful to all those who read and commented on earlier drafts of this manuscript, improving it along the way. José Luis Martin Ramos and Gracia Ventura helped me find photographs, while Mark Barrett helped prepare them for publication. I received tremendous assistance from anarchist veterans, who helped me ground my work. In particular, 'Juan', who sadly died several years ago, frankly and patiently dealt with my many enquires about his life and the workings of the Barcelona CNT and the FAI in the hope that his voice be heard. Federico Arcos also responded generously with his time and gave me a copy of the unpublished memoirs of his friend and comrade José Peirats.

When I started my research on the Spanish anarchist movement in its Barcelona stronghold, I was more interested in social movement itself than place. Today, after what proved to be an unexpected journey of spatial discovery, the opposite is true. Many friends helped me on my exploration of Barcelona's streets over the years, including Dick, Elena, Jofre, Mónica, Ramon, Sam, Silvia and Sonia. My family has also been a great source of support and encouragement. Finally, I owe the largest debt to Bea: her critical gaze improved the manuscript, while her unfailing support and spirit of optimism helped me bring this project to a conclusion. Although all the aforementioned improved this book immensely, any shortcomings are most certainly my own.

Chris Ealham, Madrid, January 2010

Important abbreviations and acronyms

BOC	Bloc Obrer i Camperol [Workers' and Peasants' Bloc]
CNT	Confederación Nacional del Trabajo [National Confederation of Labour]
CRT	Confederación Regional del Trabajo [Regional Labour Confederation]
CCMA	Comité Central de Milicies Antifeixistes [Central Committee of Anti-Fascist Militias]
CDE	Comisión de Defensa Ecónomica [Commission for Economic Defence]
CEDA	Confederación Española de Derechas Autónomas [Spanish Confederation of Right-Wing Groups]
CENU	Consell de l'Escola Nova Unificada [Council for the New Unified School]
COPUB	Cámara Oficial de la Propiedad Urbana de Barcelona [Chamber of Urban Property]
ERC	Esquerra Republicana de Catalunya [Republican Left of Catalonia]
FAI	Federación Anarquista Ibérica [Iberian Anarchist Federation]
FTN	Fomento del Trabajo Nacional [Promotion of National Work]
GATCPAC	Grup d'Arquitectes i Tècnics Catalans [Catalan Technicans' and Architects' Group]
GEPCI	Gremis i Entitats de Petits Comerciants i Industrials [Federation of Small Traders and Manufacturers]
IWA	International Workers' Association, the international association of anarcho-syndicalist unions
POUM	Partido Obrero de Unificación Marxista [Workers' Party of Marxist Unification]
PSOE	Partido Socialista Obrero Español [Spanish Socialist Party]
PSUC	Partit Socialista Unificat de Catalunya [Catalan Communist Party]
USC	Unió Socialista de Catalunya [Socialist Union of Catalonia]
UGT	Unión General de Trabajadores [General Workers' Union]

Prologue

by Paul Preston

Whenever a friend or colleague asks me to write a prologue to one of their books, especially if it is a book that I admire greatly, I usually try to persuade them that their book will be the stronger without such support. If that sage advice is rejected and the author insists, I proceed on the basis of my enthusiasm for the manuscript. In the case of this splendid and long-awaited work by Chris Ealham, I was delighted to accept the invitation because I have to confess to feeling in a very small way partially to blame for the book. I have known Chris Ealham for many years, as his undergraduate teacher, as his post-graduate supervisor and as his colleague. In the course of twenty years, we have become friends. Nevertheless, despite our friendship, I have never stopped nagging him to finish a book that has been many years in the making and, it should be said, the perfecting. The subject of the book would well account for the fact that it has required a huge investment of research and thought. It was no small undertaking to embark on book that deals comprehensively with labour militancy in Barcelona from the great crisis of 1898 via the revolutionary upheavals of 1917–1921, the dictatorship of General Miguel Primo de Rivera and the intense social conflicts of the Second Republic, through to the Spanish Civil War. A further reason for the delay – and indeed for my enormous admiration for the final version – has been the perfectionism and the meticulous scholarship that characterises Chris Ealham's work.

Readers in the Anglo-Saxon world have already had an opportunity to savour the remarkable investigative skills of Chris Ealham through his careful edition of José Peirats's great classic, *La CNT en la revolución española* as well as through some of the immensely innovative articles. Fortunately, the translation into Spanish of some of the important articles that have constituted stepping-stones to this remarkable book have permitted readers here to savour the extraordinary originality that Chris Ealham brings to the study of anarchism. What emerges from his articles, and of course from this book, is the fact that, although Chris Ealham is well-versed in the ideological background to the anarchist movement, he is much more concerned with the social realities of Barcelona that bore witness to the struggles of the libertarians. The ability to bring together the ideological and social backgrounds and to enrich our appreciation of both was highlighted by Chris Ealham's remarkable article "'De la cima al abismo": las contradicciones entre el individualismo y el colectivismo dentro del anarquismo español', en el libro colectivo en el cual colaboramos los dos: *La República asediada: la guerra civil española, 1936–1939* (Barcelona: Península, 1999, pp. 147–74).

In a famous phrase, General Emilio Mola when he was Director General de Seguridad in 1930 spoke of 'La gimnasia revolucionaria'. What Chris Ealham sets out to do is to show the desperation that lay behind what horrified conservatives regarded as the spontaneous extremism of 'la gimnasia revolucionaria'. He illuminates the real origins of the social struggle in terms of the daily problems of unemployment, of high rents, of the increase in food prices occasioned by municipal controls on ambulatory street vendors, of the efforts of the forces of order to clamp down on those members of the indigent working classes who were regarded as 'vagos y maleantes'. This is translated into a passionate and fascinating account of the libertarian struggle for ownership of the streets in terms of a quest for immediate self-help as well as long-term utopia. In this regard, Chris Ealham's reconstruction of the 'moral economy' of the Barcelona proletariat invites comparisons with the work of Edward Thompson.

Accordingly, we have before us a work of seminal importance within the field of contemporary Spanish history. Chris Ealham has a noteworthy combination of a remarkable capacity for finding and evaluating original material and an ability to ask new and revealing questions of that material. As his early articles have testified, his work is particularly remarkable for its innovative inter-disciplinary approach to social history, underlying its political analysis with a subtle account of many important but neglected questions such as housing, petty criminality and shopkeepers' profit margins. In this regard, he provides new and convincing explanations of worker militancy, explanations which he tempers with the persistence of traditional male attitudes towards women within the libertarian movement. Moreover, he rethinks the social history of Barcelona and its workers' movement in a way which invites comparison with the experiences of other European countries that have hitherto had somewhat more developed historiographies than Spain. It is a remarkable achievement for a foreign historian of Spain to make such an important empirical contribution at the same time as bringing to bear so many fruitful comparative insights, particularly with regard to the Communist rank-and-file in Berlin during the Weimar Republic.

Chris Ealham's book has tremendous range and depth in terms of the specific empirical reality of Barcelona while, at the same time, placing it in a comparative context and making virtuoso use of an interdisciplinary methodology which draws on theoretical insights from urbanism, sociology and cultural studies. Yet all this talk of pioneering methodology and of comparative perspectives should not give the impression of a dry academic tome. What makes utterly compelling reading of Chris Ealham's use of both his painstaking research and his theoretical framework is the sheer humanity with which he breathes life into his material. This is a book about people, people living extreme situations, and that is evident throughout whether in the vivid account of the popular jubilation with which the Republic was greeted in Barcelona or the more sombre picture of popular resistance to attempts by the Esquerra forcibly to repatriate southern immigrants back to Murcia and Andalucía. Ealham's account of the attitudes of the Barcelona bourgeoisie, both liberal and conservative, towards immigrants and the unemployed is not only subtle and well-researched, but manages to be passionate and coolly analytical at the same time. The book's wide-ranging examination of the links between poverty and public order is given an almost Dickensian reading in the contrasts between the lives of the 'desaliñados', as the local bourgeoisie referred to the poor, and the efforts of the 'republicans of order' to improve the efficacy of the police.

Accordingly, this is a book which will be of abiding interest to historians of Spain but which will also provoke the interest of non-professional readers eager to learn more of the endlessly complex origins of the Spanish Civil War. Although there exists a huge bibliography on the social history of Barcelona in the first forty years of the twentieth century, a tumultuous period of transformation in Spain and in Europe, I know of no single book that takes the story right through from the post-1898 conflicts right up to the great crisis of the Barcelona May Days, rendered a popular issue by the enduring fascination with Orwell's *Homage to Catalonia*, a fascination renewed in recent years by the success of Ken Loach's film *Tierra y Libertad*. There is no comparable study in any language although, interestingly, the book could be seen as something of a 'prequel' to Sebastian Balfour's widely praised *Dictatorship, Workers and the City. Labour in Greater Barcelona Since 1939* (Oxford: Clarendon Press, 1989).

As with the very finest local histories, this is one that casts its light far beyond the immediate boundaries of the Catalan capital. The fascinating analysis of the cultural, political and social conflicts within the city of Barcelona is carefully linked to an examination of how those conflicts were affected by the relationship with the central government. It poses all kinds of comparisons with social and urban conflicts in other Spanish cities, most notably Madrid, Seville and Zaragoza. In that regard, Ealham's work invites comparisons with the great classic on the Parisian working class, Louis Chevalier's *Classes laborieuses et classes dangereuses à Paris pendant la première moitié du XIXe siècle*. The comparisons to be made, with E.P. Thompson and with Louis Chevalier, are of the highest calibre. This suggests that, with this book, we are seeing the beginning of a major historical career.

Introduction

This is a study of class cultures, repression and protest in Barcelona during the four decades of crisis that preceded the Spanish Civil War. My central concern is with the interlocking and complementary areas of space, culture, protest and repression. Barcelona, the capital of Europe's biggest and most enduring anarchist movement, is an ideal laboratory for the study of these phenomena. During the period under analysis, this Mediterranean city was at the centre of economic, social, cultural and political activity and conflict in Spain as the most important actors and institutions in Spanish politics (the state, the working class, the Catalan industrial bourgeoisie, the professional middle classes, the CNT (Confederación Nacional del Trabajo, or National Confederation of Labour) and others) vied with one another for control of the city.

My study has been inspired by the Thompsonian tradition of writing history 'from below', an approach that has had an enduring influence on social history inside and outside universities throughout Europe.[1] Yet one of my central aims has been to avoid certain lacunae common to social history, such as the tendency to ignore the relationship between the changing rhythms of institutionalised high politics and the impulses of popular protest.[2] A linked problem is the spatial absences of some social history. Writing in 1993, José Luis Oyón lamented the absence of social perspectives on the city in Spanish historiography, which he took as 'an indicator of the infancy of urban historical research in Spain'.[3] That same year saw the publication in Spain of a highly original, thought-provoking and remarkably undervalued study of urban insurrections in early twentieth-century Barcelona by the Geographer Pere López Sánchez, the title of which was inspired by the riots in British cities during the 'hot' summer of 1981.[4] This study is intended as a contribution to the growing body of work that has rectified the spatial myopia of earlier writing on Spain's past.[5] It seeks to provide a history from below in a double sense: first, a spatialised social history of the dispossessed; and second, a history from the streets that examines the problematic of the city and the socio-political responses it inspired from below, as well as from above.

Chapter 1 explores Barcelona's economic, political and urban development from the middle of the nineteenth century into a highly contested space, and how this transformed the elite's previously utopian view of the city into a dystopian nightmare. The second chapter examines the growth of a working-class city, spatially and socially delineated by Barcelona's proletarian neighbourhoods (*barris*), assessing the everyday life of workers and their collective cultural, social and organisational responses to the deficiencies of the capitalist city up until the late 1920s. A key concern here is the expansion of a workers' public sphere inspired by anarchists and anarcho-syndicalists, which gave rise to the CNT, the largest revolutionary syndicalist trade union in the history of Europe. Chapter 3 details the birth and evolution of the Spanish Second Republic in Barcelona. The focus here is on the creation of a 'republic of order' to repress any initiatives from below to strengthen the power of the proletarian city and end the social exclusion inherited from the monarchy. This chapter is a radical rejoinder to liberal historians, who view the Second Republic through the prism of the long winter of Francoist repression, and it challenges the depiction of the Republic as a golden era of liberalism in twentieth-century Spain.[6] The next two chapters (4 and 5) focus on the CNT during the first year of the Republic, a period that, as Antonio Elorza has observed, was 'decisive' for subsequent developments.[7] Chapter 4 charts the re-emergence of the proletarian city in 1931 and the divisions between workers' leaders over the new political context, before assessing how the industrial struggles of the CNT rank and file to improve their economic situation during 1931 led to a clash with the republican authorities, culminating in the (anti-republican) radicalisation of the trade unions in Barcelona. Chapter 5 focuses on non-industrial working-class struggles: rent strikes, jobless conflicts and the broad gamut of unemployed street politics, including theft and shoplifting, which James Scott has aptly described as 'small arms fire in the class war'.[8] The radical anarchists embraced this direct action by the dispossessed, including armed robbery, and embarked upon a struggle for the streets with the republican authorities that had a profoundly radicalising impact on the CNT and contributed enormously to social and political polarisation in Barcelona. In Chapter 6, I analyse the anti-republican insurrections of 1932–33 and the split within the CNT as the radical anarchists sought to marginalise their critics inside the labour movement. This is followed by an appraisal of the 'militarisation' of CNT struggles as paramilitary groups became deeply involved in industrial conflicts and funded the union movement through armed expropriations and bank robberies. Hitherto, these expropriations have either been ignored by historians sympathetic to the libertarians[9] or simply denounced by right-wing historians as proof of the essentially 'criminal' nature of the anarchist movement.[10] Chapter 7 assesses the cultural struggle for hearts and minds waged in the daily press between, on the one hand, a coalition of urban elites, the authorities and their supporters, who depicted the radical CNT as a mafia-type 'criminal' conspiracy and, on the other hand, the radical anarchists, who inveighed against what they regarded as a 'criminal' socio-economic system. Since the radical position was in tune with the *vox populi*, they were able to preserve their influence in the *barris*. The latter part of this chapter explores the orientation of the CNT in the period up until the start of the Spanish Civil War. Finally, Chapter 8 examines the urban revolution in Barcelona at the start of the civil war, its political limitations, and the process whereby the revolution was contained by republicans and their Stalinist allies.

1 The making of a divided city

1.1 The limits of the bourgeois urban utopia

If, as has been claimed, Catalonia was, from the nineteenth century, 'the factory of Spain', then its capital, Barcelona, was Spain's industrial capital.[1] Barcelona underwent a major transformation from the 1850s as accumulated economic forces burst out beyond the medieval walls that had hemmed the city in around the port and that had long been regarded by urban elites as a physical reminder of a bygone economic system and a barrier to Catalonia's future prosperity.[2] During what could be described as the progressive phase in bourgeois urbanism, local economic and political elites revealed a determination to construct a modern capitalist city that might reflect the rising social power of the bourgeoisie. This urban vision was nourished by the unalloyed idealism of planners and architects, who postulated that the demolition of the city walls and urban growth would bring unfettered progress, which would maximise the prosperity of all its denizens.[3] The most famous of these planners was Ildefons Cerdà, a progressive social thinker whose utopian and ambitious plan for rational urban development became the blueprint for Barcelona's development in 1859.[4] Cerdà's plan sought urban renewal in the overcrowded and randomly arranged medieval streets of the Ciutat Vella (Old City), which was to be connected to the nearby industrial satellites that lay beyond the city walls. This would be achieved through the construction of an Eixample (Extension), which, for Cerdà, would become the core of a new socially inclusive, inter-class, functional city in which people from all walks of life would interact amid a new equality and civic unity.[5]

The great contradiction of bourgeois urbanism was that it invested unlimited faith in market forces. The subordination of the urbanisation process to the narrow interests of the local bourgeoisie and landowners ensured that Cerdà's egalitarian goals were a chimera. First, the Ciutat Vella landlords (a term that dignifies those who were often little more than 'slumlords') mobilised successfully against Cerdà's urban renewal programme, just as they mobilised against every subsequent reformist urban project. Although some of the old inner-city slums were sacrificed for the construction of Les Rambles, a central thoroughfare and the new vertebral column of the city, connecting the port with the Eixample, housing renewal in the overcrowded city centre was thwarted. Second, capital shortages and an investment crisis hindered the creation of the Eixample; effectively, unregulated markets, property speculation and corruption combined to distort beyond recognition the construction of what Cerdà had envisaged as a rational urban space.[6]

The failure to realise the hopes of the Cerdà Plan underscored the limits of the bourgeois urban project. Whereas the Parisian bourgeoisie, in close alliance with the French state, successfully implemented the Hausmann Plan and thus reshaped Paris in a way that reaffirmed the hegemonic position of capitalist interests,[7] the urban capitalist development of Barcelona was, from its origins, a marginal industrialisation process that underscored the weaknesses of local industrialists. While Catalonia's relatively dynamic and prosperous agrarian economy had laid the basis for industrial take-off in the early part of the nineteenth century, capital accumulation and the development of finance capital were subsequently retarded by the context of the combined and uneven development of the Spanish economy and the weak internal market provided by the vast unreformed agricultural heartland of the south and central regions of Spain.[8] This situation was further compounded by the generally indifferent industrial policies adopted during the Restoration monarchy (1875–1923), a centralist, backward-looking and repressive political system. For the most part dominated by the agrarian elite, the Madrid-based state was invariably aloof from, if not hostile to, the modernisation process occurring largely in Spain's periphery.[9] Lacking both the economic resources and the political will necessary to guide the urbanisation/industrialisation process, the Restoration authorities responded to the demands for reform emanating from the new social classes associated with capitalist modernisation with a blend of electoral falsification, stultifying centralism and physical repression. Nevertheless, the Madrid-based state could offer the Catalan bourgeoisie a degree of stability, at least during the early years of the Restoration, when most of Barcelona's employers uncritically accepted the hegemony of the central state, a number of them serving as the local representatives for the Spanish Conservative and Liberal parties, the 'dynastic parties' that alternated in power in Madrid.[10] But the alliance between Catalan big business and the Restoration political class ended abruptly after the so-called 'Disaster' of 1898, when Spain's last overseas colonies – Cuba, the Philippines and Puerto Rico – were lost. For Barcelona's industrialists, this was an economic disaster as it signalled the end of their access to lucrative protected overseas markets. For growing numbers of employers, the inability of the Spanish state to find a new 'place in the sun' for Catalan exports – and the absence of any coherent industrial policy *per se* – enhanced the feelings of isolation towards a distant central state that was increasingly accused of pampering the unproductive southern landowners to the detriment of modern capitalist economic interests. These sentiments crystallised around the bourgeois nationalist project of the Lliga

Regionalista (Regionalist League). Formed in 1901, the Lliga was the first modern bourgeois political party in Spain, and its new style of populist mass politics established a broad middle-class base that quickly broke the power – in Catalonia at least – of the clientelist political machines that had hitherto plugged into the corrupt central state.[11] In the context of the Restoration system, the Lliga was a modernising force in that it aimed to mobilise public opinion behind its plans to overhaul the backward central state and create an autonomous authority capable of reflecting the industrial requirements of Catalonia. In this way, the Lliga hoped to found a new focus for bourgeois urbanising energies and convert Barcelona into a city of capital. According to *La Veu de Catalunya*, the Lliga press organ:

> Barcelona is, for us, an extraordinary city, the unrivalled city, the city *par excellence*, the capital, the complete city, the point of radiation for all the trends in national life, whether economic or political, [the] fundamental organ of the people…heart and basis of the race.[12]

Barcelona was to become 'an immense city', 'a great European city', 'the Paris of the south', 'the ideal city' with 'an organic unity' in which class differences would be submerged in a shared nationalistic endeavour; for Enric Prat de la Riba, the main theorist of bourgeois *catalanisme*, Barcelona could then become 'an Imperial city'.[13] This cult of a 'Great Barcelona' (*Gran Barcelona*) was sponsored by the organic intellectuals of bourgeois nationalism, writers such as Eugeni d'Ors and Gabriel Alomar, who idealised the city in their dreams of 'Catalonia-city' (*Catalunya-ciutat*), with Barcelona at the centre of a fully urbanised and industrialised region. Paying lip service to Cerdà's utopian view of urbanisation as an integrating, civilising force that would nullify social conflict, these thinkers were enthralled by the prospect of urban-industrial expansion, giving little consideration to the implications of city growth for social fragmentation and conflict.[14] Rather, by invoking universalist ideals, it was asserted that urban development would establish new political freedoms and liberties.[15] Such views appealed to the more pragmatic and prosaic business and political elites, for whom the city was perceived as a physical and material measure of the industrial order and of their own economic, cultural and social power. In short, the local capitalists represented by the Lliga envisioned Barcelona (and Catalonia) as a bourgeois space, free of 'Spanish' feudal-agrarian residues, a goal that explains their advocacy of total economic and urban expansion.

When, after the 1901 local elections, the dynastic parties lost political control in the city, the Lliga had an opportunity to mobilise municipal resources behind a programme of bourgeois urbanism, not least because the other main anti-dynastic political force of the day, the demagogic and populist Partido Republicano Radical (Radical Republican Party, popularly known as the Radicals) also advocated a reformist urban project.

Notwithstanding formal political differences, which occasioned an often fierce rivalry between the conservative-Catalanist Lliga and the pro-centralist Radicals, both parties sought to use local institutions to foster urban growth, which was widely identified with social progress.[16] Accordingly, from the turn of the century plans were drawn up for the construction of Laietana Way, a long, North American-style business avenue that was built on the ruins of some of the most decrepit streets of the city centre and that greatly assisted capital movements and commerce, as well as providing office space for many of the city's entrepreneurs, financial institutions and employer's groups.[17] Urban reform gathered pace during the time of the Mancomunitat (1913–25), a Catalan authority conceded by the central state that, while being far from autonomous, brought considerable improvements in the urban transport infrastructure of Barcelona and Catalonia and, simultaneously, enhanced the movement of capital and goods.[18] Yet hopes that this essay in self-administration would foster a new bourgeois political hegemony through the planned transformation of urban life were wrecked by the centralising ethos that dominated official life during the Restoration. The limited fiscal powers of local institutions ensured that the blueprints for the transformation of Barcelona's urban morphology devised by bourgeois planners remained on the drawing board.[19] Instead, city space was reorganised by market forces in a thoroughly unplanned and chaotic fashion, principally during the speculative frenzy that preceded the World Exhibitions of 1888 and 1929[20] and during World War One, when Catalan employers exploited Spanish neutrality and the disruption in the international commercial *status quo* to trade with both belligerent camps.[21] Thus, in the period leading up to the 1930s, accelerated industrial development and economic diversification made Barcelona into a global commercial centre: the city's industrial hinterland was consolidated as many older companies relocated to newer and larger workshops in the growing urban periphery; the urban transport and energy infrastructure was also modernised consonant with this urban sprawl.[22]

However, it would be wrong to exaggerate the strengths or the stability of Catalan capitalism. After the 'Disaster' and the ensuing economic crisis, a series of shortcomings were thrown into sharp relief: the historical under-capitalisation and limited profitability of industry; the relatively small-scale nature of production, which also shaped the development of newer industries like metallurgy and transport;[23] the frailty of indigenous financial institutions; the poor international competitiveness of exports; the domination of foreign capital in the most advanced industries; and the restricted domestic market within a context of combined and uneven development.[24] These features had an enduring impact on the development of capitalism, so that while the 1929 Exhibition allowed for the emergence of several large-scale plants, textile manufacturing, an industry associated with the birth pangs of capitalism, continued to be the city's biggest employer.

However, there were no such barriers to urban population growth. Between 1850 and 1900, as the city's frontiers were swollen by the annex-

ation and industrialisation of previously independent villages such as
Gràcia, Sants and Sant Martí, the population increased by over 300
percent, only to double again between 1900 and 1930.[25] By 1930,
Barcelona was the most populated city in the Spanish state and a member
of the select band of European millionaire cities.[26] Yet because of the low
birth rate among the indigenous population and the tendency of local
workers to seek out the best jobs, there was a huge shortage of the cheap,
unskilled labour needed to occupy a front-line position in the urban-industrial economy. In order to increase the supply of labour, employers
promoted migration among Spain's rural dispossessed, stimulating an
exodus of hungry economic migrants from depressed agrarian areas, who
arrived in 'the Catalan California' in their droves.[27] In the 1880s, the first
major wave of migrant workers hailed from provincial Catalonia and
neighbouring Aragón and Valencia, but by the 1920s, in what was then the
biggest wave of immigration in the city's history, an army of landless
labourers arrived from Murcia and Andalusia. While migrants invariably
performed the most menial and badly remunerated jobs, the belief that
Barcelona offered a possible escape from the structural unemployment of a
subsistence agricultural system was enough to ensure a steady flow of
economic refugees, and by the late 1920s around 35 percent of the urban
population was non-Catalan.[28]

City growth culminated in a profound urban crisis. While all rapidly expanding
capitalist cities display signs of such a crisis,[29] the nature and scale of this crisis
was shaped by a series of local economic and political factors. At an economic
level, we must again mention Spain's uneven economic development. Simply put,
the outmoded agrarian system in the south and the low profit margins of Catalan
industry constituted an inadequate basis for funding a modern welfare state. This
resulted in what Ignasi Terrades has described as an 'absentee' state: an authority
structurally incapable of ameliorating the social problems engendered by the
urbanisation/industrialisation couplet through the provision of a social wage of
collective educational, medical and welfare services.[30] In political terms, the
prevailing authoritarian mentality within the central state apparatus, combined
with the political support offered by the Radicals and the Lliga to Barcelona's
urban elites, tended to neutralise reformist impulses. In addition, municipal
corruption stymied the effective deployment of the limited funds available to local
state institutions, thereby compounding the crisis of urban administration.[31]
Frequently, the Restoration authorities looked to the reactionary Catholic Church
to provide a basic level of public services in areas that, elsewhere in Europe, were
coming under the aegis of the state.[32] Education was a prime example. Church
schools relied on violence and fear in an effort to instil obedience and respect in
working-class children. So great was the scale of punishment and humiliation
inflicted on children in these schools that one former pupil labelled them 'the
prison-schools'.[33]

The limitations of the social wage were witnessed most starkly through
the absence of public housing for the working class. Although the 1911

Ley de Casas Baratas (Public Housing Act) committed local authorities to work with private capital to provide low-rent accommodation, by 1921 housing had been built for only 540 families.[34] In part, this can be explained by the growing political influence of Joan Pich i Pon, the leader of the Radicals, who became mayor during this period.[35] The leading light within the COPUB (Cámara Oficial de la Propiedad Urbana de Barcelona, or Chamber of Urban Property of Barcelona), the main defence organisation of the city's landlords, Pich i Pon used his considerable political influence to defend the interests of private landlords and bitterly resented any reforms that threatened profits. Yet more crucial was the fragmentation of Barcelona's under-capitalised construction companies, which, divided into an array of small firms, met no more than two-thirds of total market demand for housing after World War One.[36]

The result was a massive increase in the exploitation of working-class tenants. According to Nick Rider, landlords engaged in 'constant speculation and rack-renting in working-class housing', with rents increasing by between 50 and 150 percent during the 1920s alone.[37] Moreover, these increases occurred during a time when existing housing stock was being subdivided on a huge scale: by 1930, there were over 100,000 subtenants in Barcelona, as flats originally built for a single family were converted into 'beehives', sometimes accommodating as many as eight families. The problem of subdivision was particularly endemic in the already overcrowded tenement blocks of the Raval, the most built-up area of the Ciutat Vella: in 1930, the number of residents per building there was twice the city average, while the population density was almost ten times greater.[38] With multiple families sharing a single toilet in some tenements, the health context was appalling, and diseases such as glaucoma, typhoid, cholera, meningitis, tuberculosis and even bubonic plague were rife.[39] Despite the decline in housing conditions, economic migrants continued to flock to the Raval in search of cheap housing, thereby ensuring that overcrowding increased unchecked.[40] Homelessness was also rife in the area, notably among single, unskilled workers, who lacked the resources to secure a permanent residence. Depending on the weather and the prospects for casual labour, the homeless might sleep rough or rent cheap rooms in the *pensiones* (bed-and-breakfasts) or *casas de dormir* (doss houses), where beds were available on daily or hourly rates.[41] In some of the more rudimentary establishments workers paid to sleep on foot, leaning against a rope suspended in a large communal room. These low-budget options abounded in the Raval, especially near the port area.[42]

However, the most obvious example of the crisis in housing and urban administration was the expansion of *barraquisme* (shanty dwelling).[43] In contrast to the squatter camps on the margins of cities such as Johannesburg and Rio de Janeiro in the late twentieth century, because most land in Barcelona was in private ownership, the city's *barracas* were constructed by owners who profited from the housing crisis, charging newly arrived migrants a deposit and rent to live in the shanties.[44] Built from a range of materials, including cardboard, scrap metal and household rubbish, *barracas* normally consisted of one large room in which all family members would sleep. Lacking all basic amenities, including toilets, electricity and water, *barracas* were highly unstable structures, vulnerable to the extremes of heat and rain and occasionally collapsing during inclement weather. Yet the shanty dwellers did not necessarily occupy a marginal position within the labour market – the first *barracas* were constructed in the 1880s on the public beach in Poblenou, then the centre of Barcelona's industry, to accommodate migrant workers.[45] The *barracas* were therefore a vital complement to the urban economy, the product of the 'normal' operation of the housing market and the local capitalist economy, both of which were organised to further the economic fortunes of the industrial elite and the landlord class. Accordingly, the steady increase in shanty houses throughout the 1920s inspired socialist critics to dub Barcelona a 'barracópolis'.[46]

Figure 1.1 Repairs being made to the roof of a shanty dwelling in Poblenou,
         circa 1930
Source: L'Avenç Archive

The only significant public housing initiative in Barcelona prior to the 1930s – the construction of 2,200 *cases barates* (literally 'cheap houses'), which were built for 'humble people' – underscored the weak reformism of the local authorities.[47] In no sense did the *cases barates* signify a belated recognition by the city's elders of the need to coordinate the urbanisation process and resolve the urban crisis: the number of houses planned could never meet the genuine demand for housing. Like the Cerdà Plan before it, the *cases barates* project was also undermined by property speculation and corruption. This centred on the Patronat de l'Habitació, the housing trust responsible for implementing and administering the housing reform. A clique within the Patronat formed a construction company and, unsurprisingly, secured the contract to build a projected six groups of *cases barates*. Following much embezzlement and graft, the building programme came to a premature end with only four of the projected six groups of houses constructed.[48]

Figure 1.2 An aerial view of the *cases barates* near the Can Tunis district

Source: L'Avenç Archive

Effectively, the *cases barates* initiative was a cosmetic programme of rudimentary slum clearance, first seen in the 1900s with the construction of Laietana Way, part of a conscious strategy of the city's elders to push the workers to the margins of the city.[49] The immediate aim of the *cases barates* was the demolition of the *barracas* of Montjuïc, which marred the view of visitors to the lavish palaces that housed the 1929 Exhibition. While vast amounts of private and public money financed the construction of hotels to receive well-to-do tourists from across the world, the *cases barates* were built from cheap materials on wasteland on the semi-urban periphery of the city. The overriding desire to create the maximum number of housing units at the lowest possible cost meant that the new houses were poorly built slums in the making. The name *cases barates* was also a misnomer: they were not 'cheap' (rents were more or less comparable with those in the private sector), nor could these hastily erected dwellings credibly be described as 'houses'.[50] In addition, the social wage and urban fabric in the new housing projects were deficient: there were few or no basic amenities and services, such as schools and shops, and because the *cases barates* were located outside the metropolitan transport system, there were hidden social costs of habitation, as residents were forced to walk long distances on foot to reach tram or bus lines in order to travel to work or to shop.[51]

The *cases barates* provide us with an interesting example of how housing 'reform' can be conceived with avowedly repressive ends. Security concerns doubtless informed the highly structured design of the housing projects. Organised in uniform terraces in which the inhabitants could be easily isolated and policed, from the air the *cases barates*, with their perimeter walls, resembled the barrack buildings of army or prison camps.[52] Segregated from Barcelona by a *cordon sanitaire* of farmland, in Foucauldian terms the *cases barates* represented a new phase in the 'disciplinary order'; like Hausmann's project for Paris, the aim here was spatial closure and preventive social control: a section of the 'dangerous classes' was banished from the city centre and relocated and socio-spatially excluded in a highly circumscribed area on the margins of the city, where it constituted less of a threat to urban order and could be more easily neutralised by repressive forces. In one group of *cases barates* a police station was constructed inside the housing complex, while another group was built alongside Sant Andreu army barracks.[53]

The *cases barates* project illustrates how urban development occurs in the image of society. The subordination of Barcelona's growth to private interests resulted in the 'urbanisation of injustice' as the radical inequalities and class divisions characteristic of modern capitalism became embedded in the built environment.[54] In other words, for all the high-sounding rhetoric of the urban elites and their emphasis on progress and civic equality, Barcelona was not organised for the benefit of all of its inhabitants. Rather, the principal beneficiaries of the urbanisation process were private interests – many of which were represented politically by the Lliga and the Radicals – which profited from municipal clientilism, frenzied land speculation and rent inflation. Indeed, with local politics firmly under the domination of a coalition of the city's commercial, industrial and business sectors, landlords faced little regulation from the authorities: legislation that protected tenants' rights was frequently not implemented, and landlords enjoyed a free hand in the housing sector, frequently ignoring the law with impunity.[55]

Market-led, marginal urbanisation failed to stimulate a new civic unity. Indeed, in social terms a process of urban bifurcation was at work, according to which class divisions became inscribed in space. And so, by the end of the 1920s, the city was effectively divided in two, a trend epitomised by the stark polarities offered by the opulence and wealth of bourgeois districts and the squalor and poverty of the *barracas*, the *cases barates* and proletarianised *barris* like the Raval, spaces in which the prosperity promoted by the World Exhibitions was barely felt.[56] Bourgeois families had steadily vacated the Ciutat Vella from the 1880s, their former residences becoming subdivided for multiple occupancy by economic migrants and their families.[57] The bourgeoisie, meanwhile, moved eastwards into the Eixample, particularly its two main boulevards, the Passeig de Gràcia and the Rambla de Catalunya, thereby ensuring that the area was anything but the inter-class neighbour-hood of which Cerdà had dreamed;[58] over time, the migratory path of the bourgeoisie within the city extended further eastwards into adjoining districts like Sant Gervasi, Tres Torres, La Bonanova and, increasingly, Sarrià and Pedralbes.[59] That the zonal segregation of classes was always a trend, rather than a completed process of hermetic urban segmentation, can be seen in the presence of significant proletarian minorities in some bourgeois areas. The general process towards urban segregation was nevertheless irreversible: capitalists and proletarians were increas-ingly concentrated in distinct neighbourhoods as city space became more and more divided.[60]

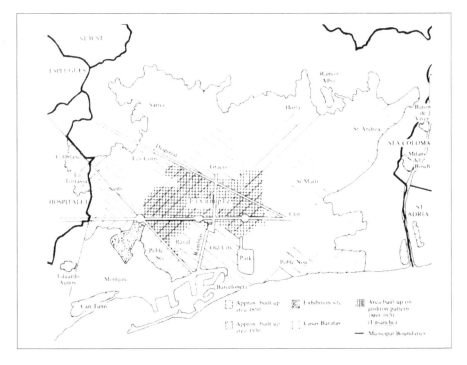

Figure 1.3 Map of Barcelona *circa* 1930

Source: adapted from David Goodway (ed.), *For Anarchism: History, Theory, Practice*, London, 1989, p.81

1.2   Bourgeois dystopia and moral panics

Barcelona fitted Manuel Castells' model of the 'wild city', a chaotic and 'raw' free-market model for urban growth, a space in which social tensions were naked and explosive.[61] As the local elite became conscious of this, utopian visions of a civilised, unified polis were eclipsed by dystopian night-mares of an uncontrollable and violent city.[62] Bourgeois confidence in the city was first rocked by a series of terrorist bombs in the 1890s.[63] Thereafter, capitalists were gripped by anxieties that the 'criminal classes' were steadily encroaching upon the frontiers of policed society. Such feelings were not assuaged by the general strikes of 1902 and 1909, both of which saw the erection of barricades, while the latter culminated in full-scale urban insurrection.[64] The terrifying image of city streets being barricaded drove incalculable fear into the 'men of property'; when insurgents took control of the labyrinthine streets of the old city in 1909, the destructive proximity of the 'internal enemy' to bourgeois social, financial and political centres was revealed. By hastening the migration of 'honourable citizens' to safe havens away from the old city centre, the 1909 uprising increased urban segregation and indicated the growing preference of the bourgeoisie for suburban life. By the 1910s, therefore, any lingering hopes for an urban utopia were eclipsed by dystopian visions, as bourgeois consciousness became predicated upon a dread of urban disorder and the desire to pacify and reconquer a city besieged by an army of proletarian barbarians. The progressive urbanism of Cerdà's day gave way to an explicitly repressive urban philosophy and the conversion of a radicalised bourgeoisie into spatial militarists.[65]

The most obvious public expression of this shift in elite consciousness was the proliferation of moral panics within bourgeois circles.[66] These moral panics increasingly emphasised the nefarious consequences of city life, identifying a series of 'outsider' groups that, it was claimed, were the cause of urban 'disorder'. Utilising a variety of mediums in the growing bourgeois public sphere, including the press, pamphlets and scientific and medical papers, in certain respects the moral panics reflected the burgeoning interest in social life that eventually gave rise to the academic disciplines of sociology and anthropology. While the moral panics were not a coherent or unified body of thought – they valued morality over sociology and presented an obscure and fragmented vision of social reality that is of little use to students of either the practices or motivations of 'outsider' groups – they are nonetheless an important elite commentary on the evolution of the capitalist city.

The first key area of elite anxiety revolved around workers' behaviour outside the workplace. Across Europe, from the 1880s onwards, there were numerous initiatives aimed at engineering the 'model' worker, whose prudent use of time and wages and rational consumption of the growing range of urban-based leisure activities would make for an obedient and efficient labourer.[67] The dream of the 'model' worker obsessed commentators from across the political spectrum, ranging from the fundamentalist Catholic Right and conservative bourgeois philanthropists across to enlightened liberal reformers. The result was a series of discourses that, although exhibiting varying degrees of Puritanism and positivist rationalism, were united in their determination to 'moralise' the working class by transforming its norms and culture.[68] At play here was a Manichean vision that contrasted the 'good' worker – respectable, abstinent, thrifty, whose 'good customs' fostered a stable family and working life – with the lot of homeless alcoholics and syphilis sufferers who were no longer able to work.

This discourse also revealed a 'moral geography' in that 'good' and 'bad' parts of the city were mapped out. New terms such as 'underworld' (*bajos fondos*) delineated places of 'darkness', an imagined moral wasteland in which crime, suicide and numerous other moral depredations were committed by a legion of unchristian 'degenerates' and under-socialised individuals, decentred or degraded by the whirlpool of urbanisation. During and after World War One, elite commentators located the 'underworld' in the area around the Raval, which was renamed 'Chinatown' (*Barri xino*), after inner-city Los Angeles.[69] Having gone into economic decline after the destruction of the old city walls and the relocation of industry to the urban periphery, the Raval's empty industrial buildings had been converted into bars, cabarets, dance halls, taverns and cafes as a new leisure industry expanded to cater to the predominantly single, unskilled, migrant labourers who constituted the shock troops of the urban industrial revolution. This, matched with the Raval's proximity to the port, gave the area a marginal, 'rough', working-class ambience that was doubtless enhanced by the geographical mobility of a significant proportion of the population who resided in the numerous cheap hostels and 'doss houses' in the area.[70] A similarly bawdy atmosphere was evident on the nearby Marquès del Duero Avenue, a wide avenue that started at the port and that was surrounded by some of the poorest tenement blocks. Known popularly as 'El Paral.lel', this street was a more down-at-heel version of Les Rambles and, by the 1920s, it had assimilated cosmopolitan European and both North and South American influences, such as jazz and tango, and it enjoyed a reputation as the 'Broadway of Barcelona'. Although a smattering of bourgeois and middle-class bohemians brought an inter-class air to Paral.lel's leisure spaces, there was a fundamental gulf between those who pursued the raw pleasures on offer in the city centre and the elite values of deferred gratifi-cation, sobriety and respectability to which the industrial bourgeoisie publicly adhered. Increasingly, 'good citizens' reviled the waterfront area bordering Paral.lel and the Raval as a zone of vice and corruption, a Dantesque inferno dominated by the criminal lairs of sexual deviants, drug barons and the lawless *classes dangereux*, which had to be placed under continual vigilance.[71]

The second focal point for bourgeois apprehension was working-class youth, or more precisely the 'aggressive' and 'insolent' adolescents who were highly visible on the streets.[72] Upper-class opinion was noticeably sensitive to the activities of 'hooligans' (*trinxeraires*), made up of homeless children abandoned by the many working-class families torn asunder by a combination of market forces and the post-1898 economic crisis, or who had left home to escape abusive parents. When these youths banded together, as they inevitably did, the 'gangs' (*pandillas*) were even more alarming, especially the much-maligned 'TB gangs', the real 'outsiders' on the streets, consisting of unemployable youths suffering from tuberculosis.[73] Lurid and sensationalist articles appeared in the middle-class press about the deviant activities of 'ungovernable' gangs of 'rebel

Figure 1.4 'Men of order' surveying Les Rambles, *circa* 1920

Source: L'Avenç Archive

youths' who were in permanent conflict with 'the fundamental institution of society…[and] the foundations of social order: tradition, family, property, law'. Increasingly, various folk devils and moral panics converged in the conservative imagination. Thus the spectre of disease was raised amid claims that hedonistic young immigrants were attracted to Barcelona by the reputation of 'Chinatown': these were errant youths who 'escaped from their homes, attracted and carried away by a bohemia which has as its epilogue a bed in a hospital'.[74] Alternatively, the street gangs were identified with crime, street disorder and the illegalities of an 'evil' and depraved 'lumpenproletarian' 'underclass'.[75] There were even concerns that 'juvenile delinquency' would be transformed into urban insurgency by the 'uncultured' and 'barbaric' inner-city mob.[76] Yet these anxieties were more than simply adult apprehension towards rowdy youthful spirits. Given that the street was the main arena for proletarian socialisation, these panics had a pronounced class content: they represented the fear of the bourgeoisie that future generations of workers would not accept their place in the industrial order.

Another source of anxiety for the local elite – again one that exhibited a clear class basis – were the 'other Catalans', the economic migrants without which rapid industrialisation and the equally speedy enrichment of the bourgeoisie would have been impossible.[77] By the end of the 1920s, these migrant workers were, along with their Catalan counterparts, concentrated in a series of proletarian ghettos; these spaces provided the main source for the dystopian nightmares of a bourgeoisie haunted by the menace posed by the proletarian city to its city. In an attempt to weaken the proletarian city and enshroud capitalist privilege in popular nationalist imagery, bourgeois ideologues vilified 'outsiders' (*forasters*) for importing alien values that they deemed to be injurious to social stability and the traditional (Christian) values of Catalan society. By drawing upon racist, social-Darwinist and colonialist discourse, migrants – and occasionally also indigenous workers – were presented as being morally inadequate, living in a state of nature or primitive barbarism, the criminal heart of darkness in the city.[78] The intonation of these denunciations made it possible for urban problems to be externalised (for instance, the first shanty communities in Poblenou were christened 'Peking', while decades later, as we have seen, 'Chinatown' became a byword for urban degeneration and crime in the conservative lexicon).[79] In addition, the new leisure forms, such as cabaret, flamenco and tango, were identified with immigration.[80] This evocation of exotic, alien 'otherness' was accompanied by a nineteenth-century medical discourse that defined social normality and stability by juxtaposing health and disease. Even liberal reformist opinion typically identified migrants with problems of 'unhygienic behaviour', providing grist to the mill of those who vilified the 'contagion' of the 'unhealthy' and the 'diseased' as a threat to the governance of the city and the freedom of all.[81] However, these themes found their apotheosis in the discourse of *catalaniste* conservative thinkers, who denounced the 'plague' of 'foreign dung' (*femta forana*) who, it was warned, would 'infect' the core values of nation and family and lead to 'de-Catalanisation'.[82] Perhaps the most extreme example of this trend was the openly racist and xenophobic writings of Pere Rossell, who emphasised the psychological, moral and religious gulf separating Catalans from 'Castilians' and the dangers of intermarriage (mental aberrations, biological degeneracy and moral breakdown).[83]

With the growth of the organised labour movement from the 1900s onwards, the multiple threats to public order outlined in the moral panics were synthesised into a single overarching challenge to the capitalist city: that of the trade unions. All conservatives, *catalanistes* and centralists alike, commonly viewed labour conflicts, particularly those of anarcho-syndicalist inspiration, as a 'provocation' caused by 'agitators' from outside Catalonia, whether the sinister foreign forces of international freemasonry and French anarchism or the migrant workers, 'a kind of tribe without authority, hierarchy or law'.[84] Yet for *catalanistes*, the emphasis was naturally distinct: 'outsiders' and 'primitive peoples' had eroded the culture of political compromise and common sense (*seny*) that had been evident throughout Catalonia's pre-industrial history.[85] This myth of a consensual, violence-free, rural arcadia allowed nationalist thinkers to attribute the violent conflicts produced by industrialisation and urbanisation to exogenous factors and 'Spanish problems', such as the agrarian crisis in the south or the permissive culture of migrant workers, thereby diminishing the importance of the contradictions of the Catalan model of unregulated economic and urban development. Thus anarchism was portrayed as an alien ideology, a 'cerebral deviation' imported by southern migrants and the 'dangerous' working class.[86] Similarly, areas such as 'Chinatown' and Paral.lel, which were already viewed as 'crime zones', were now depicted as the centre of an 'anarchic city', a 'city of bombs'. Fears were also expressed that 'disobedient' street youths would ally with the revolutionary movement and provide cannon fodder for 'wayward ideologies'.[87] These themes were given wider intellectual legitimacy by quasi-Durkheimian criminologists, sociologists and psychologists, who stressed a unitary urban value system and who contended that any behaviour that demurred from this desired value consensus reflected the dysfunctional socialisation, deviancy, personality disorder and moral disintegration wrought by rapid urbanisation. In a highly ideological discourse that permitted no analysis of power, violence or conflict, it was suggested that social conflict was not a function of collective grievances or of structural economic factors but, rather, the outcome of the 'collective crimes' of 'primitive' and 'deviant' creeds (anarchism or socialism), which connoted diseases, be they hereditary ('degeneracy'), psychological ('madness') or physical ('cancer').[88] These concerns were amalgamated into a new myth of the 'dangerous classes' in which labour activists were cast as 'professional agitators' detached from the masses, 'uneducated' and under-socialised 'troublemakers' who comprised the criminal vanguard of an offensive against the 'natural stability' of a just and otherwise harmonious social order.[89]

How then are we to assess the significance of these moral panics? First, as I mentioned above, these concerns were part of an outpouring of moral panics across Europe during the last quarter of the nineteenth century, when, in the course of the uneven but inexorable transition towards the age of mass politics, urban elites struggled to adjust to the unsettling consequences of social change. In the case of Barcelona, over the course of a few generations the city had grown massively beyond its old walls, and industrialists now faced a mass working class. With the explosion of the traditional city, social and economic modernisation had eroded traditional mechanisms of social control based on patronage and paternalism.[90] In this new situation, the moral panics were part of a hegemonic project, an ideological offensive through which urban elites sought to strengthen the bourgeois public sphere by limiting working-class access to the streets (thus the shadow of the worker was always discernible in the moral panics). In other terms, this was a language of power that allowed the urban bourgeoisie to define the streets as its own: they delineated the permissible uses of public space, castigating all resistance to the expansion of the capitalist urban order. As such, the moral panics were framed with a view towards working upon the subject by instilling a hierarchical cultural vision among workers, disempowering and dispossessing them, and by changing those aspects of working-class behaviour that, whether political or not, were deemed to be a barrier to the free circulation of goods and capital within the city or in opposition to the time discipline of industry.[91]

Yet the real importance of the moral panics was their ideological and discursive function as a language of repression. Such a language was extremely attractive for many capitalists, who, under the pressure of the historically narrow profit margins of Catalan industry, displayed what Antoni Jutglar has termed 'class egoism'.[92] Accordingly, rather than treat or compromise with organised labour, industrialists interpreted working-class demands, whether individual or collective, as a rude threat to profits and to bourgeois authority in the workplace. For the 'men of order' (*gent d'ordre*) among the bourgeoisie, the moral panics were a guide to repressive action: they profiled the 'danger' represented by 'recalcitrant' and 'diseased' groups (hence the positivist concern with classifying, cleansing and civilising), which had to be excluded from the full rights of citizenship and isolated from 'healthy' and 'respectable' individuals. They were also a justification for closing off the nascent proletarian public sphere, creating a moral and political climate that legitimated the extension of state power on the streets and the establishment of a new system of bureaucratic surveillance to regulate civil society.[93] For the angst-ridden bourgeoisie, this far-reaching project of socio-political closure of the public sphere was intensely calming, an emotional compensation for the fragility and vulnerability of the Catalan economy.

The moral panics were then historically and spatially grounded in Restoration Barcelona, a fundamental part of bourgeois culture in a given time and a given place. In the first instance, they were the product of the authoritarian cultural frames of reference that emerged within the bourgeoisie in the context of the combined and uneven development of the Catalan economy. Such reactionary ideas were able to flourish within the exclusionary political framework provided by the Restoration system, especially following the 1898 'Disaster', when themes of 'purification' and 'cleansing' became entwined with national soul searching about 'regeneration' and 'degeneration'.[94] Mostly, however, the moral panics signalled the growing frustration of the bourgeoisie at the crisis of the repressive apparatus of the Restoration state.

1.3   Spatial militarism and policing before the Second Republic

At the start of the Restoration, Catalan big business welcomed the new political system as a source of stability. Public order was the cornerstone of the Restoration state system, so while the state was 'absent' in Barcelona in terms of public welfare, from the 1870s onwards its repressive power was felt on the streets in the form of a militarised apparatus that monitored the public sphere. A new architecture of repression, consisting of army garrisons, police stations, jails and reformatories, was created, and innovations such as the introduction of police beats and street illumination enabled the authorities to extend their gaze across the expanding cityscape.[95] Day-to-day responsibility for law and order, and for monitoring the public sphere in general, rested with the Civil Governor, the institutional agent of the central state.[96]

It fell to the police to preserve urban discipline and neutralise the myriad tensions on the streets of this divided city. This project was problematised by the absence of a coherent governmental attitude towards urban policing. The fiscal crisis of the state retarded the evolution of an effective civilian police force. State expenditure on the security forces simply failed to keep pace with the growing population, and between 1896 and 1905, when the urban population rose by around 25 percent, the number of policemen in the city decreased from 193 to 170, resulting in a ratio of one policeman for every 3,200 inhabitants. Although by 1919 this ratio stood at one policeman per 700 inhabitants, the Barcelona constabulary was still small by European standards. Furthermore, chronic under-funding and poor administration hampered the operational efficiency of the police. Among the underpaid ranks of the police, demoralisation and corruption were widespread. Low pay encouraged many officers, including those of high rank, to take part-time jobs, regardless of the distractions from everyday police tasks that this presented.[97] In sum, the force was singularly ill-equipped to undertake the multifarious investigative or preventive police tasks required in an increasingly complex city.[98]

The police force compensated for its lack of professionalism and absence of roots in and intelligence about civil society with a brutal readiness to exceed its remit. In keeping with the authoritarian mentality that dominated the Restoration state, policing evolved in a highly reactive fashion, as an

Figure 1.5 Members of the Barcelona constabulary taking a cigarette break in the back of a lorry, *circa* 1930

Source: Ateneu Enciclopèdic Popular

essentially repressive response to events. This *modus operandi* resulted in frequent complaints of brutality, miscarriages of justice and violent 'third degree' interrogations from those who came into contact with the security forces.[99] Throughout the Restoration, the authorities encouraged police terror, and the judiciary remained supine before the political executive. Justice was the exclusive preserve of the upper classes. As far as policing the lower classes was concerned, an array of arbitrary and draconian practices was permitted, including detention without trial (*detención gubernativa*),[100] internal deportation (*conducción ordinaria*),[101] extra-judicial murder (*ley de fugas*)[102] and the prosecution of radical intellectuals and labour leaders, who were 'morally guilty' of inspiring the material deeds of protesters.[103] In practice, the police were deployed to limit the access of trade unions to the public sphere: trade unionists were routinely intimidated, at work, at home or in the streets, while during periods of social conflict the force protected employers and their property unconditionally.[104]

During moments of intense social or class confrontation, such as the 1902 and 1917 general strikes, the 1909 urban uprising, or the urban guerrilla struggles of 1918–23, the police proved incapable of preserving public order. At such times, the Civil Governor resorted to martial law (*estado de guerra*), whereupon constitutional guarantees were suspended and responsibility for public order passed to the captain-general of the Barcelona garrison.[105] The army, whose power was symbolised by and embodied in Montjuïc Castle, the mountain fortress overlooking the city from the south, was the last line of a system of militarised urban repression.[106] Another component of this repressive system was the Guardia Civil (Civil Guard), a paramilitary rural police force that enjoyed the status of a regular army unit and was commanded by a senior army officer.[107] The Guardia Civil played a growing role in maintaining public order in Barcelona, and the force had a number of posts and barracks in the volatile inner city, as well as in the growing industrial periphery and in one of the groups of *cases barates*. Specialising in 'preventive brutality', the Guardia Civil practised a direct form of exemplary violence against those who dared to contest the urban order.

As industrialisation continued apace and the working class grew in size and organisation, this militarised system of policing came under growing pressure and could be sustained only by increasing force. But confrontational and brutal policing tarnished the public image of the state security forces, generating, as will be seen in Chapter 2, a focus for anti-police, anti-state sentiments. In this way, rather than producing quiescence, state violence exacerbated social rebellion. And so, by the end of World War One, when economic crisis provoked a sharp rise in social protest, the repressive apparatus was in danger of being overloaded. The culture of repression that prevailed in capitalist circles also played a big part in the escalation of social protest. As we have seen, the 'men of order' possessed a very narrow conception of 'order', which consisted of little more than strict hierarchical control in the factories and a sense of security on the streets.[108] However, the irony here was that by the late 1910s the first of these goals increasingly made the latter impossible. Indeed, in the context of a mass inter-war working class, the ferocious and unrelenting drive of capitalists to maintain industrial control, coupled with the absence of any channels through which workplace conflicts could be resolved peacefully, meant that labour conflicts periodically spilled onto the streets, placing the security forces under renewed strain and thereby frustrating bourgeois sentiments of public safety.[109]

The conflict between Barcelona industrialists and the Restoration state over the issue of public order has rarely figured in explanations of the rise of bourgeois *catalanisme*.[110] Nevertheless, the fact that the Catalan bourgeoisie could not claim a state of its own, matched with its distance from the levers of political power in Madrid, amplified elite insecurities from the start of the twentieth century. In both 1902 and 1909, the 'men of order' complained of the 'general strike by the authorities' and the fact that the security forces 'disappeared', leaving the city unguarded and defenceless before 'the power of anarchy'.[111] Although the army could, *in extremis*, be mobilised to shore up the urban order, the strategic concerns of both the military top brass and the political elite sometimes limited the deployment of the armed forces on the streets. Thus, in 1909 for instance, the upper classes were irritated at what they saw as the reluctance of authorities to deploy the army to crush the urban insurrection.[112] In general terms, the fact that the Restoration state was, between 1898 and 1923, progressively weakened by a combination of cabinet instability, military rebellion, economic decline, colonial failure and rising working-class struggle did little to instil confidence among industrialists in the ability of the central authorities to structure daily life and guarantee adequate social control in the streets. In these circumstances, public order anxieties provided fertile ground for the Lliga, which projected elite resentments about the failure of the corrupt Spanish state to preserve order into its campaign for a reform of public administration.[113]

And yet the defence of the bourgeois order always preceded party political concerns. The culture of social control expressed through the moral panics provided an important (repressive) common ground for Barcelona's divided elites who, after 1898, were increasingly fragmented into monarchist, republican, *catalaniste* and Hispanophile sectors.[114] Postulating an imagined political community and assuming a single civic interest, the moral panics were a clarion call for the unity of 'citizens of good will' and the 'lovers of order' in the face of the threat of the 'dangerous', 'other' city. This was a call to arms behind a repressive minimum programme around which various bourgeois factions could unite to parry any threat to their authority. There was no scope for tolerance or sentiment; Barcelona must become a carceral city in which all 'men of order' would stand *en garde*, united and ready to repel any possible attack on the everyday life of the bourgeois urban order.[115]

In this way, public order concerns were placed at the very centre of bourgeois politics, to the extent that the defence of law and order was the *sine qua non* of successful government. By evaluating government in terms of the effectiveness of its public order policies, the bourgeoisie exerted constant pressure on the authorities for an expansion of the architecture of repression in the city. This pressure became all the greater after 1917 owing to the emergence of aggressive *nouveaux riches* capitalists during the war and to the general radicalisation of European elites in the wake of the Russian Revolution.[116] With the Restoration state entering its definitive crisis, and clearly unable to meet industrialists' demands for increased police resources, the central authorities allowed the city bourgeoisie extensive rights of self-determination in the sphere of policing. This resulted in the creation of paramilitary groups, which were mobilised alongside the state security forces in the battle against the 'red peril'.[117] The first and largest of these parallel police forces was the Sometent militia. Established as a rural militia centuries earlier, during the 1902 general strike the Sometent was deployed in Barcelona in flagrant contravention of its charter, which prohibited it from entering cities. In 1919, Sometent volunteers started to receive military training, and its charter was modified to allow it to join in the repression of urban labour protest. While the Sometent was recruited from all social classes, its explicit anti-worker role endeared it to the higher echelons of Catalan society and, in many respects, this militia represented the bourgeoisie and the petit bourgeoisie in arms.[118] Guided by its watchwords *pau, pau i sempre pau* (peace, peace, forever peace), the Sometent played a crucial auxiliary role in repressing strikes and dislocating working-class organisation. Moreover, by recruiting from within civil society, particularly among local shopkeepers and Catholic workers, the Sometent compensated for some of the shortcomings of police intelligence.[119]

Employers also protected themselves, either by carrying firearms or by recruiting small teams of gunmen and private security teams, whose services were especially important during strikes.[120] During and after World War One, the assorted adventurers, gangsters and foreign agents who decamped in neutral Barcelona bolstered these groups and, as a consequence, they subsequently acquired a more sinister and aggressive repertoire. The most notorious of these groups included the assassination team recruited by former police chief Bravo Portillo during the war, and which was financed by German secret services to eliminate employers working for the Allied war machine.[121] Another shadowy gang from this era was masterminded by the self-styled 'Barón de Koenig', a German agent and enigmatic playboy, who operated from an office on Les Rambles.[122] However, it would be wrong to exaggerate the role of foreigners in the violent labour struggles, which originated for the most part in the readiness of the 'men of order' to militarise industrial relations. Indeed, the most active and enduring of all the parallel police squads were recruited from the gunmen of the Sindicatos Libres (Free Trades Unions), counter-revolutionary, 'yellow' trade unions that included members of the Sometent.[123]

In the postwar era, these paramilitary or 'parallel' police groups crystallised within a wide network of repression designed to prop up the urban order.[124] This militarisation of space reached its zenith during 1920–22, when two army officers, General Miguel Arlegui and General Severiano Martínez Anido,[125] served as Barcelona chief of police and civil governor, respectively. During their tenure in office, Libres gunmen worked in tandem with official police and army teams in a 'dirty war' against trade union activists.[126] Leading members of the bourgeoisie were at the centre of this disciplinarian project. Publicly, many industrialists welcomed the intervention of the armed forces in labour conflicts and celebrated the robust approach to 'union problems' adopted by Martínez Anido, 'the pacifier of Barcelona'. If there were casualties or fatalities among the forces of repression of 'labour insurgency', collections for the families and dependents of the 'victims of terrorism' were expeditiously organised by businessmen. Industrialists also regularly found work for retired or wounded policemen and soldiers. Privately, however, the 'men of order' played a decisive role in the anti-union murder squads, for it was the city's employers who, both individually and collectively, bankrolled gangs specialising in extra-judicial murder.[127]

While the repressive initiatives of locally recruited paramilitaries undoubtedly assuaged elite anxieties, the very need for these auxiliary forces in the first place remained a graphic illustration of the shortcomings of existing policing arrangements under the Restoration. Thus, although the combination of formal and informal repressive agencies resisted the challenge of the trade unions in the postwar years, this was clearly not a recipe for long-term stability. Moreover, growing levels of violence could mask neither the profound crisis of the disciplinary methods of the state nor the more obvious and general crisis of the Restoration political system. Finally, in 1923, the Restoration system was overthrown by General Miguel Primo de Rivera, a former army commander in Barcelona, who was fully apprised of the threat to public order in the city and whose aspirations had been encouraged by important sectors of the industrial bourgeoisie. Unsurprisingly, the 'good citizens' welcomed the military security offered by Primo de Rivera's dictatorship (1923–30), the 'iron surgeon' who, they hoped, would improve the business climate by eliminating 'terror and crime' on the streets and liberate the bourgeoisie from the threat of the unions.[128]

The support offered by the Lliga to Primo de Rivera highlighted the contradictions of the bourgeois *catalaniste* project, compressed as it was between a militant working class and a central state that, while distant and backward, nevertheless remained the ultimate guarantor of order. It also reveals how the 'social question' always came well ahead of the 'national question' in the priorities of the Lliga.

Yet the loyalty of Barcelona's industrialists towards the Madrid-based state was always conditional and, during the Primo de Rivera dictatorship, as occurred during the Restoration, leading groups within the Barcelona bourgeoisie moved from a position of support to a stance of controlled opposition towards their erstwhile knight protector. This estrangement can in part be attributed to the gulf between the *catalaniste* sentiments of a fraction of the bourgeoisie and Primo de Rivera's centralising tendencies, as well as the failure of the dictator's monetary policies to guarantee economic growth. Yet what is often ignored is the extent to which the bourgeois 'men of order' reacted against what they perceived as the failure of the dictatorship to satisfy their everyday security requirements.[129] For all the efforts of both the bourgeoisie and the authorities to assert their control over the cityscape in the 1920s (witness the drive to dominate space symbolically via the architectural monumentalism of the dictatorship), the urban elite repudiated a regime that, it believed, had failed to preserve public order within the city. The root of the problem for the bourgeoisie consisted in the ongoing failure of police expenditure to keep pace with a rising population.[130] Indeed, elite concerns centred on the massively expanded proletarian neighbourhoods such as the *cases barates*, and particularly Collblanc and La Torrassa in l'Hospitalet, the main destination for the legions of unskilled migrant labourers who arrived prior to the 1929 Exhibition. The extent of elite disquiet was summed up by two petitions sent to the local authorities in l'Hospitalet in April and September 1930, in which the 'lovers of order' and 'right-thinking individuals' complained that public order was dangerously reliant on volunteers from the Sometent and on the speedy arrival of mobile police units from Barcelona.[131] In short, because of 'a shortage of representatives of the civil authority' and the fact that the Barcelona constabulary was often busy, l'Hospitalet was effectively at the mercy of 'evil doers' (*maleantes*), a point underlined by numerous 'regrettable incidents' that occurred in the city. The predictable conclusion of these petitions was that the future prosperity of Barcelona's southern neighbour hinged upon the creation of a new Guardia Civil barracks in the La Torrassa–Collblanc area.[132]

We must now turn our attention to the proletarian city that aroused such trepidation among the 'men of order'.

2 Mapping the working-class city

This chapter explores the emergence of working-class space in the city. This rival, 'other' city, which was violently opposed by the elites as a mortal danger to bourgeois Barcelona, was nevertheless a direct creation of the capitalist city that established new conditions of sociability for hundreds of thousands of workers in the proletarian *barris*. For the city's workers, the *barris* were a total social environment: they were spaces of contestation and hope,[1] the starting point for resistance against the bourgeois city, a subversive struggle that earned Barcelona notoriety as the revolutionary capital of Spain and as a 'red' city of international repute. Before exploring the layers of culture, practice and organisation that allowed for the reproduction of proletarian Barcelona during the years before the Republic, it is first necessary to map out the various coordinates of the increasingly uniform socio-urban context in the *barris*, since it was these that produced the series of cultural frames through which workers made sense of the urban world and which, in turn, exerted a profound influence on the collective and political identity of the city's labour movement.[2]

As we saw in Chapter 1, from the last part of the nineteenth century urban industrial expansion resulted in a process of bifurcation, as class divisions became embedded in the cityscape. By the start of the twentieth century, a number of clearly defined proletarian neighbourhoods had emerged, such as Poblenou, the 'Catalan Manchester', the Raval, Poble Sec, Sants and Barceloneta.[3] There were differences within the city of the proletariat. The Raval, a waterfront district with many recruiting places for casual labour, was home to a picaresque proletariat of sailors, dockers and itinerant workers, and it exuded a pronounced bohemian and marginal ambience, far different to the annexed industrial villages of Sants and Gràcia. Similarly, there were contrasts between the rapidly developed periphery of the city, which was very much a product of the postwar industrial development, and the older *barris*, which retained a higher degree of social diversity, the most extreme case being the old village of Gràcia, a neighbourhood in which better-paid or skilled workers resided in close proximity to members of the middle and even upper classes. Yet by the late 1920s Gràcia was a rare exception among the city's *barris*, as the growing trend was for workers to live alongside other workers in or close to centres of industry in socially homogeneous and segregated districts, and there were few contacts between workers and employers outside the workplace.[4]

The 1920s saw the expansion of a second ring of proletarian districts, principally l'Hospitalet to the south and Santa Coloma, Sant Andreu and Sant Adrià del Besòs in the north. In these peripheral areas, new neighbourhoods appeared almost overnight. For instance, the contiguous La Torrassa and Collblanc districts, the most northerly neighbourhoods of l'Hospitalet, experienced a population increase of 456 percent in the 1920s caused by the arrival of around 20,000 economic migrants from southern Spain.[5] In all the newly developed *barris*, the urbanisation process was totally uncoordinated, and collective urban services failed to keep pace with the expanded population. In essence, the new *barris* lacked centrality: the city, understood in terms of an urban infrastructure of cultural, educational, medical facilities and public housing, simply did not exist. Many streets were without pavements and lighting; drainage, water and electricity were luxuries.[6] Housing was no better: some crudely constructed dwellings lacked basic foundations and collapsed during inclement weather. Although the local authorities recognised the 'health risks' in these rapidly developed areas, the Catalan-speaking urban elite that dominated municipal politics was far removed from the realities facing the migrant labourers crammed into the *barris* and lacked the political will to improve their lot.[7]

Even though the proletarian city was not a monolith, it would be wrong to draw too sharp a distinction between urban conditions in the rapidly developed outer ring of *barris* and the older working-class districts. Given the underdevelopment of the local state, the symptoms of the urban crisis were registered throughout the working-class city and, whether in the tenement slums of the Raval and Barceloneta, in the sprawling peripheral areas like the *cases barates*, in the jerry-built housing of Santa Coloma or in the *barracas* scattered across the city, workers experienced a low social wage and the under-provision of collective services, such as hospitals and schools.[8] In fact, despite the growth in white-collar employment after World War One, it is possible to point to a growing convergence in working-class lifestyles and a relatively homogenised proletarian experience. Indeed, the expression of the *barris* in the 1920s heralded the consolidation of an overarching structure of material coercion that touched upon the everyday lives of most of Barcelona's 330,000 workers.

As far as its socio-professional status was concerned, by the end of the 1920s the working class was predominantly un- or semi-skilled, with few bargaining resources. Like many other large port cities, Barcelona had long offered numerous opportunities for casual labourers on the docks. In addition, the two biggest and oldest industries in the city – textiles and construction – relied heavily on unskilled and casual hands.[9] Over time, these characteristics were reproduced among the workforce in newer sectors of the local economy, such as the metal and transport industries, which employed large numbers of 'sweated' semi- and unskilled workers. The trend towards deskilling received a new impetus with the advent of the so-called 'second industrial revolution' during and after World War One, which created a 'new' or mass working class from the legions of unskilled economic migrants from the south of Spain and the 'proletarianisation' of skilled workers, who were unable to resist technological advances, particularly due to the favourable political conditions offered by Primo's dictatorship. By the end of the 1920s, therefore, many of the occupational factors that previously separated the skilled worker or the artisan from the unskilled had been eroded.[10]

A further element within the common context of working-class life was the danger of industrial accidents. The limited profit margins of the city's industry discussed in Chapter 1 instilled a cavalier attitude among employers towards workplace safety, and Barcelona province topped the Spanish league table for industrial accidents every year between 1900 and 1936.[11] Even among traditionally 'aristocratic' sectors of the workforce, like the printers, or in the city's most advanced workshops, such as the Girona metal works, working conditions and safety records were abysmal. However, it was the largely unregulated construction sector, the main source of employment for unskilled migrants, which claimed the highest number of accidents.[12] So great were the dangers of industrial injury that *La Vanguardia*, a conservative newspaper with no reputation for concern for workers' welfare, sometimes denounced factory conditions.[13] Despite the danger of injury, workers were utterly unprotected, without social welfare, accident insurance or sickness benefits. Labour therefore offered very few certainties, other than those of hard work and paltry wages in dangerous and degrading circumstances.

The generalised working-class experience of inequality and discrimination can similarly be charted in the consumption sphere, where workers saw their wages devoured by rampant inflation. As we saw in Chapter 1, during the years between the two World Exhibitions, landlords systematically exploited housing shortages to increase rents and, with home ownership the preserve of a minority of skilled and white-collar workers, nearly 97 percent of all workers were at the mercy of the private rented sector.[14] The burden of rent payments was even greater for migrant workers, since they normally spent most of their savings on the journey to Barcelona and could seldom afford a deposit for a flat. Meanwhile, the unskilled, the low-paid and those in irregular employment (which is to say most migrant workers) had difficulties making regular rent payments, and evictions were 'very frequent'.[15] The cost of food presented a further set of strains for most of the city's workers. Although food prices had soared across Spain after the 1898 crisis, inflation was greatest in Barcelona, and the cost of meat in the city was higher than in most north European cities, where workers enjoyed higher wages. This situation was compounded by the 'subsistence crisis' (*crisis de subsistencias*) during World War One, which saw the cost of living increase by 50 percent in the *barris* between 1914 and 1919.[16] With growing public concern across Spain at the rising cost of living, even the elitist Restoration politicians finally conceded that the economic distress that had long shaped everyday life for the working class required legislative action. Typically, however, the anti-inflationary measures implemented by the authorities were contradictory: there was no action against the deviant culture that prevailed among those sections of the commercial class that cheated consumers by doctoring weights and adulterating foodstuffs, and prices soared throughout the 1920s as shopkeepers and traders profited from the *crisis de subsistencias*.[17]

In the light of this everyday structure of material coercion, even those workers in regular employment encountered financial difficulties. By the end of the 1920s, a childless working couple could barely generate a significant surplus.[18] With female wages far inferior to those of men, a short period of unemployment would have plunged the couple into what moralists described as the 'sunken classes'. It is not surprising, therefore, that most workers bore few of the outward signs of 'respectability' associated with the skilled working class, with many workers relying on the many pawn and second-hand clothing shops that thrived in the Raval. Moreover, the working-class family economy was so precarious that it depended on contributions from all family members. Consequently, since employers were free to ignore the social legislation that outlawed child labour, generation after generation of working-class children were robbed of their innocence by economic compulsion, and throughout the 1910s and 1920s it was the norm for young boys to start work between the ages of 8 and 10, whereupon they were used as a cheap source of 'sweated' unskilled labour and subjected to brutal forms of discipline by foremen and employers.[19]

Figure 2.1 A fairly typical working-class family, probably of migrant origin

Source: L'Avenç Archive

2.1   Proletarian urbanism

For all the poverty that prevailed in the *barris*, and notwithstanding elite denunciations of disorderliness, the proletarian city did have an order: it was a rough,
aggressive and increasingly assertive order, a complex social organisation
moulded by dense social networks and reciprocal forms of solidarity, what
Raymond Williams termed the 'mutuality of the oppressed'.[20] This collective
reciprocity was the fundamental structure in the *barris*: it offered workers a
degree of stability and security and fostered integrative relationships, offsetting
the material disadvantages of everyday life.[21] Conversely, because mutual aid
could be withdrawn from those judged to be in defiance of communal norms,
reciprocity could also operate as a means of coercion.[22]

The working-class family structure played a central role in the development of these reciprocal practices, forming the hub of a series of overlapping
social structures and community networks through which workers responded
to the material problems of everyday life 'from below'.[23] In a certain sense,
the 'family economy' was embedded in a form of collective reciprocity rooted
on kinship. Yet reciprocity also flowed through and across families; an
example of this was the manner in which families were bound together
through the practice of selecting 'godparents' (*compadres*) for newly born
children from among neighbours and friends. Although, as one worker
pointed out, this was an informal relationship ('there was no involvement of
the Church or the local authorities'), this arrangement provided 'an ever-
lasting family tie' with people from a similar social background who, most
importantly of all, were always willing and ready to offer material help in
times of need.[24] If a family encountered privations, neighbours routinely
offered assistance, whether providing meals or taking in the children of the
family concerned.[25] In addition, neighbours organised community-based
childcare systems so as to allow local residents to maximise their earning
potential.[26] This communal reciprocity compensated for the deficient social
wage. As one worker explained:

> In those days there was no unemployment benefit, no sickness benefit or
> anything like that. Whenever someone was taken sick, the first thing a neigh-
> bour with a little spare cash did was to leave it on the table.... There were no
> papers to be signed, no shaking of hands. 'Let me have it back once you're
> back at work'. And it was repaid, peseta by peseta, when he was working
> again. It was a matter of principle, a moral obligation.[27]

The scale and flow of neighbourhood reciprocity is best understood in terms of
the exceptional degree of sociability in the *barris*. Unlike many other large
European cities, where factories were increasingly located in industrial zones
that were distant from residential spaces, Barcelona's spatial-industrial development was such that, right up to the 1930s, the factory remained the key
organising force in many *barris* in which life occurred within an intimate

social geography. Not only did workers tend to live near to factories, the majority of the city's workers travelled to and from work on foot.[28] Sociability was further conditioned by the symptoms of the urban crisis, such as the city's overcrowded and appalling housing stock, which served as a brake on the privatisation of everyday life and prevented the erection of barriers between the private and public sphere.[29] Throughout the *barris*, diverse loci for working-class sociability were established in collective spaces in which people entered into a high degree of face-to-face contact. The most important of these were the streets, which were largely free of cars and were generally viewed as an extension of the proletarian home, all the more during the summer months, when large parts of neighbourhood life were conducted there. The other most significant spaces of working-class socialisation were neighbourhood cafes and bars, which acquired the status of the living rooms of the poor. There were then numerous opportunities for individual workers to discuss their experiences – both individual and collective – with other workers, whether on the way to work or during leisure time.

Reciprocity, and indeed sociability, also depended upon 'serial' or 'chain' migration, a pattern of settlement that shaped the growth of working-class Barcelona during the years between the two Exhibitions and that saw migrants from the same town or province cluster in specific neighbourhoods, streets and even tenement blocks.[30] These networks, based on kinship and pre-existing loyalties from the migrant's place of origin, were of inestimable assistance to newcomers in their search for work and accommodation, enabling them to become grounded in the city very quickly.[31]

Despite the undoubted importance of these pre-existing social networks for migrants, they did not present a barrier to the emergence of working-class identity and consciousness.[32] Indeed, the proletarian city was essentially democratic: none of the *barris* in which the migrants resided were ghettoised, and there were numerous opportunities for newly arrived workers to interact with migrants from other regions and with Catalan workers, whether in the streets and tenements of the *barris* or in the workplace. Furthermore, while many migrants may often have ended up in the worst jobs in the city, the relatively uniform socio-material context and the limited opportunity structure that conditioned working-class life ensured that the experiences and the lot of migrant workers were not that different from those of the rest of the working class. This relatively high degree of 'class connectedness' fostered a nascent consciousness of class that overlaid all other identities.[33]

Consciousness formation was very complex, molecular and dynamic, whereby individual and collective experiences of the social and spatial orders were accumulated and refined through a process of reflexive engagement. In this way, the practical, sensuous experiences of material realities and the everyday struggle to survive within a determinate space were converted by workers into a series of collective cultural frames of reference.[34] The result was a communal reservoir of class-based experiential knowledge, a refraction of everyday urban practices, the product of the sharp learning curve of everyday oppression and exploitation. This

Figure 2.2 United in the workplace: workers at the 'El Aguilar' beer factory pose for the camera

Source: Ateneu Enciclopèdic Popular

Figure 2.3 Class hierarchies in the street

Source: Ateneu Enciclopèdic Popular

was, then, a situated form of local consciousness: a social knowledge of power relations within a specific locale, a vision of the world embedded in a specific time and place, constructed on the ground, from below.[35] In its most elementary form, this sense of class was more emotional than political: it represented a powerful sense of local identity, an *esprit de quartier*, stemming from the extensive bonds of affection generated by the supportive rituals, solidarities and direct social relationships of neighbourhood life. It was in essence a defensive culture, a radical celebration of the local group and the integrity of its lived environment predicated on the assumption that everyday life was constructed in favour of 'them' to the detriment of 'us'.[36]

Even if this localised culture was cognisant of class differences, in practical terms it rarely engendered more than an untheorised dissatisfaction with the 'system' and should not therefore be confused with class or revolutionary consciousness.[37] Nevertheless, the culture of the *barris* was central to reproducing and extending a collective sense of identity among workers, a nascent sense of class that was preserved in and propagated through a series of social practices, modes of behaviour and communication and that provided valuable raw material for the labour movement. It was a relatively autonomous form of culture, enabling workers to comprehend the social world in which they lived; it sustained the web of communal attitudes, values, shared ideological formulations and egalitarian norms, which Paul Willis described as 'alternative maps of social reality'.[38] Moreover, this culture of solidarity penetrated elite ideology: it sponsored class responses – workers' reciprocity being just one example – to collective problems; it was the world view of a propertyless class that had little if any respect for the property of others and that advocated an alternative and distinctly anti-capitalist form of proletarian urbanism: housing was seen in terms of social need, not profit, while the streets were perceived as an extension of the home and were to be used as their occupants desired, whether for leisure, for solidarity or for protest.[39]

One such spatial practice legitimated by this culture was street trade, a form of proletarian 'self-help' and one element in a larger informal economy.[40] In the main, street trade was the preserve of newly unemployed workers and the wives of the low-paid, who invested the few savings they could muster in a small amount of merchandise, which they sold on the streets near established shopping areas and markets in what was the humble commerce of the needy designed to make their poverty a little more bearable.[41] This, combined with the fact that the street traders had no overheads and could undercut market traders and shopkeepers, meant that in areas such as the Raval, the *cases barates* and La Torrassa, they were enormously popular with working-class consumers, and their commerce became an integral part of local consumption patterns.[42]

Other aspects of this proletarian urbanism clashed frontally with the juridico-spatial logic of the state and capitalism. An early example of this was the 1835 'La Bonaplata riot', which saw workers threatened by new technology destroy the plant that endangered their jobs. In the absence of any institutional channels through which workers could express their grievances, these direct action protests had a clear political dimension – they were the pursuit of politics by other means. Thus workers were fully apprised of the important role played by the control of space in social protests, and the streets were used for a broad range of protest functions: they could be occupied in order to express popular demands to the authorities, as in the case of demonstrations; they could be used to identify social transgressors, as occurred during protests at the homes of unpopular shop-keepers or landlords; or, more emphatically, the streets could be used to subvert bourgeois power, as witnessed in acts of public defiance. The ongoing political disenfranchisement of the working class ensured that 'traditional' forms of street protest retained considerable attraction for workers right into the twentieth century.[43]

There was a strong material justification for the endurance of this direct action protest culture. In the light of the precarious existence facing much of the urban working class, any deterioration in economic conditions might elicit a violent response. Thus, in 1903, when the local council imposed new taxes on foodstuffs entering the city, impoverished female street vendors rioted, smashing the shop windows of wealthier traders.[44] Often, these direct action protests were combined with some kind of self-help strategy. For instance, throughout the nineteenth century, in both rural and urban Spain, there was a popular tradition of forced requisitioning of foodstuffs, a type of mobilisation that gave notice to the authorities of the economic problems facing the lower classes and that provided participants with much needed comestibles. This form of redistribution of wealth from below was revived during the economic crisis after the 1898 'Disaster' and again during the hyperinflation of World War One, when it was common for mass raids, frequently by women, to be launched on shops and vehicles transporting foodstuffs.[45] There was also a vast constellation of individual and small group illegality, including pilfering and petty depredations in workplaces, eating without paying in restaurants and the seizure of foodstuffs from country estates.[46] While much of this illegality was the preserve of poorly paid or unemployed workers, there is evidence that some of it was perpetrated by gangs of young workers, a number of whom had apparently rejected the work ethic in favour of an alternative lifestyle outside the law; their activities sometimes extended to more modern and organised practices, such as armed robbery.[47]

This 'economic' or 'social crime', which has often been defined by criminologists as 'victimless crime', was validated by a working-class culture that provided ample justification for law breaking in order to make ends meet. Such attitudes received a new impetus after World War One, when the more respectable working-class culture of the artisan gave way to a rougher proletarian culture. Thereafter, illegal practices were increasingly accepted within the moral code of the fluctuating but invariably large swathe of the local working class that eked out an existence on subsistence wages. In normative terms, low-paid workers presumably had few problems in justifying the appropriation of the property of their employers as a 'perk' or as a compensation for poor pay; similarly, the frequent armed robberies directed at tax and rent collectors were unlikely to concern workers. Moreover, since the working class was essentially a propertyless class, these illegal practices rarely impacted upon other workers.[48]

There are other ways in which this illegality reaffirmed the socio-spatial independence of the working class. Illegality drove a sharp wedge between the working class and commercial sectors, such as shopkeepers, market traders and small farmers, who lived in relatively close proximity to the working class and whose property was the target of this illegality.[49] The urban middle classes were bitterly opposed to proletarian street practices. In particular, shopkeepers and market traders felt threatened by street trade, which they regarded as a mortal threat to their business. Yet it would be difficult to argue that street trade was the root cause of the tensions between the working and middle classes, which can be traced back to rocketing inflation after 1898 and during and after World War One. The readiness of the commercial middle class to profit from inflation – or at least the perception that this took place to the detriment of the urban working class – doubtless left many workers feeling little sympathy for those who were inconvenienced by either street trade or illegality.

Street practices similarly sealed the separation of the working class from the state and its laws and from those entrusted with their enforcement. Such a divergence was largely inevitable, for the preservation of the urban *status quo* was one of the objective functions of the state, and several of the urban self-help strategies violated the judicial order. Other practices, meanwhile, such as street trade, although not necessarily illegal, were periodically criminalised by the authorities. Moreover, the fact that street trade was repressed only after vociferous campaigns by the commercial middle class made it easy for many workers to conclude that the laws, like the police who defended them, were anything but neutral and that they were motivated by the concerns of the moneyed classes and enforced to the detriment of the interests of the dispossessed. Consequently, the *vox populi* held that the state, the law and the police were alien to the moral order of the *barris*, a perception that was left unchallenged by the inactivity of the authorities in the realm of public welfare.[50]

Popular opposition to the state was most commonly witnessed in terms of resistance to the police, which was popularly viewed as the vanguard of state power on the streets. Anti-police feelings flowed ineluctably from the institutional role of the police as the regulators of social space and their responsibility for structuring everyday life in the capitalist city. One of the most important police functions, for example, was the 'modification' and 'management' of working-class behaviour in the streets, especially when workers were not subject to the time discipline of the factory. In addition to repressing 'unlicensed' street vendors, the police might be called upon to confront women protesting at food prices, groups of unemployed workers discussing the job situation, or teenage street gangs. Police repression affected working-class life irrespective of gender, place of origin and age. Young workers, whose socialisation occurred through play in the streets, routinely came into conflict with the police. As far as many migrant workers were concerned, their previous experiences of the security forces would have been largely limited to the Guardia Civil, a force that was widely viewed by landless labourers as an army of occupation. Their subsequent experiences of policing were unlikely to alter these perceptions: for many migrants, their first encounter with the Barcelona constabulary often came on the outskirts of the city, where agents greeted the buses bringing labourers from the south to ensure that all newcomers to the city paid a council-administered tax.[51] Since many migrants could not afford the tax and therefore did not register with the municipal authorities, they had a firm aversion to all contact with the police.[52]

The external danger represented by the police inspired an extensive anti-police culture and practice in the *barris*. Fed by the collective memory of police repression and transmitted by a strong oral tradition, this was a highly inclusive culture, uniting young and old, migrant and non-migrant, male and female alike, and affirming a profound sense of community identity. Even working-class street gangs, whose activities sometimes bordered on anti-communitarian behaviour, were regarded as 'inside' the community and were unlikely to be betrayed to the authorities.[53] Anti-police culture also delineated the limits of community through the identification of 'outsiders'; there is evidence, for example, that policemen (and their children) residing in the *barris* were ostracised and excluded from community life.[54] Equally, because auxiliary paramilitary groups that emerged through class struggle, such as the Sometent, were heavily involved in the repression of popular illegality, 'outsider' status was conferred upon its members, who were seen as part of an array of forces rallied against the working class.[55] Finally, fears of community disapproval and/or physical sanctions doubtless dissuaded those who might have cooperated with the police from doing so.

More than anything, however, popular anti-police culture was a culture of action; it championed the rights of 'we', the community, to determine the way in which the streets were to be used; it was a struggle for neighbourhood self-reliance, self-governance and freedom from external authority; a defence of a set of popular urban practices revolving around personal face-to-face ties against the bureaucratic agencies of social control and authority (the police and the courts) and impersonal market forces. Drawing on long traditions of direct action mobilisations, it was an aggressive culture that justified the use of all possible means to resist the efforts of the security forces to regulate life in the *barris*. This resulted in a perpetual battle for the streets between the urban dispossessed and 'the coppers' (*la bòfia*), as the police were pejoratively known.[56] This struggle was notably protracted in areas with large groups of street traders and unemployed, where even low-key police activity could result in the formation of large, hostile groups that readily disrupted police activities, preventing arrests, physically assaulting the police and, when possible, divesting them of their arms.[57] Anti-police practices relied heavily upon community solidarity: successful anti-police actions were celebrated as a sign of neighbourhood strength and reinforced the sense of local identity. Overall, then, the struggle with the police had a galvanising effect on working-class districts, making them more cohesive, resilient and independent, so that by the end of the 1920s, many *barris* were akin to small republics: organised from below and without rank or privilege, they constituted a largely autonomous socio-cultural urban order; they were relatively free spaces, virtually impenetrable to the police, in which the authority and power of the state were weak.[58]

We thus see that, notwithstanding the tendencies towards domination and spatial militarism, in the course of their everyday life the excluded were still able to create cultural, ethical, psychological, social and physical spaces of contestation, spaces that, as we will see, provided the bedrock for a powerful working-class resistance to capitalism and the state. Yet for the widespread hostility felt towards the 'system' to be converted into a more enduring and transforming resistance, this existing (local) culture had to be distilled and imbued with more universal concerns, which required the organisation of a proletarian public sphere.

2.2   The anarchist-inspired workers' public sphere

From the 1860s onwards, it is possible to trace a libertarian communist tradition in Barcelona as anarchists, and later anarcho-syndicalists, were at the forefront of attempts to create new political, social and cultural spaces within civil society. The prestige of anarchism was helped by the fact that its social-democratic rival was weak, especially after 1899, when the UGT (Unión General de Trabajadores or General Workers' Union), the socialist trade union formed in Barcelona in 1888, moved its executive to Madrid. Thereafter, the city's workers tended to view social democracy as a distant movement with an ideology that was largely irrelevant to their concerns, and the anarchists were relatively free to consolidate a space for themselves in the workers' movement, although periodic state repression meant that this was by no means a linear development.[59]

The main vehicle for anarchist practice was the *grupo de afinidad* (affinity group), which consisted of between four and twenty members who were bound together by personal affinity and mutual loyalty. Committed to raising consciousness and structuring everyday life according to libertarian principles, the *grupistas* prized the attributes of individual rebellion and heroism, generating a culture of resistance to the work ethic and the daily rituals of capitalist society. While the more scholarly affinity groups might meet at a theatre or bookshop, others pursued a bohemian existence in cafes and bars, defying economic imperatives as far as possible and mixing with 'outsider' milieu and excluded groups, such as gypsies.[60] The aim was generally the same: the cultivation of 'cerebral dynamite',[61] a rebellious spirit reflected in the names of *grupos* like Los Desheredados (The Disinherited), Los Indomables (The Uncontrollables) and Els Fills de Puta (The Bastards). Although their cell structure and *esprit de corps* afforded a high degree of protection from police infiltration, by the 1890s traditional anarchism based exclusively on small groups of devotees had reached an impasse owing to a mixture of state terror and the isolation of most *grupos*, which usually operated in extra-industrial locations and had few if any points of connection with the wider community of workers.

In response to this situation, from the turn of the century some anarchists drew inspiration from French anarcho-syndicalism, an ideology that appealed to class motifs and that prioritised the importance of the proletariat as a force for social transformation. Anarcho-syndicalism promised a new urban rhythm: in the short term, it advocated a struggle for 'the three eights' (*los tres ochos*): an eight-hour working day, eight hours for sleep and eight free hours for leisure, entertainment and education; however, this was a stage on the journey towards the ultimate objective: the destruction of capitalism and the state and the birth of a classless society. This aggressive trade unionism was recognised by the dispossessed as a suitable expression of their everyday needs and desires. Inevitably, anarcho-syndicalism entered into conflict with bourgeois 'class egoism' and state power, resulting in a cycle of mobilisation and repression. In February 1902, a series of partial economic strikes culminated in Barcelona's first general strike of the twentieth century, to which the authorities responded with militarism: martial law was declared, and hundreds of labour leaders were jailed, while street fighting between pickets and the army left seventeen dead and forty-four injured. Yet the determination of workers to improve their living conditions guaranteed that union organisation not only survived the employer–state offensive but emerged strengthened. In 1907 Solidaridad Obrera (Worker's Solidarity) was created, a city-wide union federation that laid the foundation for the CNT, a new national grouping formed in Barcelona in 1910. Through organised in national, regional and local committees operating across a series of distinct spatial scales, the CNT wanted to coordinate change at national level through a range of actions rooted in the social networks of the *barris*. Indeed, many of its unions shared premises with community groups and were part of the infrastructure of neighbourhood life.[62] The CNT was a decentralised, loosely structured body, a model that, its animators hoped, would militate against bureaucratic tendencies and better enable it to stand up to repression. Similar fears of bureaucratic conservatism saw the CNT disavow all strike funds and arbitration, preferring instead to prosecute strikes on the basis of organised reciprocity, whereby unions came to the help of striking unions, and through 'direct action' tactics, such as 'active picketing', which entailed sabotage and violence against those 'scabs' (*esquirols*) who refused to heed union orders.

The direct action protest culture of the anarcho-syndicalists fitted within the traditions of popular protest in a city in which street fighting with the police and barricade construction were all inscribed in the history of urban protest from the nineteenth century. Part of the CNT's appeal stemmed from its readiness to erect a militant organisation around these rich and rebellious working-class cultural traditions. In this way, CNT tactics like boycotts, demonstrations and strikes built on neighbourhood sociability: union assemblies mirrored working-class street culture, and the reciprocal solidarity of the *barris* was concretised and given organisational expression by the support afforded to confederated unions. Equally, the independent spirit of the *barris* was reflected in revolutionary syndicalism and its rejection of any integration within bourgeois or state political structures. On the other hand, the exclusionary tendencies of the *barris*, such as the sanctions of ostracism imposed on those who defied communal values, were now extended to 'scabs'. In this way, the independent traditions of the *barris* helped to define the *modus operandi* of the CNT, and although the rise of union organisation brought with it a more 'modern' and disciplined culture of protest, the anarcho-syndicalists developed a broad 'repertoire of collective action', which accommodated many of the 'self-help' strategies that had evolved in the *barris*.[63] Firm believers in the spontaneous self-expression of the masses, and in strict opposition to the socialists, who maintained a sharp distinction between the revolutionary and the 'criminal', the libertarians emphasised the inalienable right of the poor and the needy to secure their existence, 'the right to life', by whatever means they saw fit, whether legal or illegal. They also encouraged popular illegality, such as eating without paying in restaurants, an activity that became very popular with the unemployed and strikers.[64] At the same time, the CNT sought to refine popular urban protests: whereas the largely spontaneous street mobilisations brought temporary control of the streets, the CNT desired a more permanent control of the public sphere and a revolutionary transformation of space. Nevertheless, the streets remained an important focus for protest and insurrection. As *Solidaridad Obrera* explained, 'the revolution will have the street as its theatre and the people as protagonist'.[65] The anarcho-syndicalists were therefore happy to articulate the myriad tensions and energies that developed outside the workplace, establishing new fronts in the struggle against oppression and new spaces of resistance. And this was made more likely by the reluctance of employers to reach an accord with the unions and by the underdevelopment of institutional mechanisms for the peaceful resolution of labour disputes, which meant that strikes frequently spilled out of the factories and onto the streets, where the tactically flexible anarcho-syndicalists combined their 'modern' modes of mobilisation with 'traditional' protest forms. For instance, the CNT supported consumption protests, demanding cuts in rents and food prices as well as providing armed escorts for groups of working-class women who requisitioned food from shops.[66]

This commingling of 'modern' and more 'traditional' protest cultures became a recurring feature of urban struggle and electrified conflicts in the city. An illustration of this came during the 1902 general strike, when an industrial stoppage was followed by collective attacks on bakeries and markets by groups of workers who requisitioned foodstuffs. In addition, full vent was given to popular hostility towards the police, who came under attack from groups of workers trying to liberate pickets. Later, when the security forces moved in to the *barris* to quell street protests, the community rallied to repel them, bombarding the police and Guardia Civil with missiles, which rained down on them from the balconies of flats.[67] This same hostility towards the police was witnessed during the 1909 general strike, which began as a 'modern' protest organised by the unions, who then lost control of a mobilisation that culminated in a riot far more 'traditional' in flavour than the 1902 general strike. Prior to the rioting, crowds had gathered on the streets chanting 'death to the police' before setting off to attack and loot the homes of several policemen. There were also reports of isolated protests at the homes of employers and landlords.[68] This collective custom of taking grievances to the homes of individuals perceived to have transgressed communal norms has its origins in pre-modern times and highlights the confluence of distinct protest cultures. Meanwhile, the transformation of the 1909 strike into a full-scale urban insurrection was accompanied by a brief essay in proletarian urbanism: workers reshaped the built environment, barricaded streets and organised the destruction of vast amounts of Church property.

The combination of 'modern' and 'pre-modern' modes of struggle was particularly evident with regard to unemployed protests, in the course of which organised demonstrations easily ended in violence, rioting and looting. The unemployed also favoured popular traditions of touring workshops *en masse* in search of work, a practice that carried with it a strong element of intimidation, particularly when large numbers were involved, and that frequently resulted in clashes with the police. This violence is best understood not as a collective descent into barbarism or a function of ignorance but as the outcome of the everyday conflict between desire and the absence of means. In other words, with neither a political voice nor any channels through which popular grievances could be addressed, the unemployed made politics by other means, 'collective bargaining by riot' to cite Eric Hobsbawm's famous expression.[69]

Besides building upon popular practices, the anarcho-syndicalist CNT also borrowed from the vibrant collective identity of the *barris* and the rich and diverse cultural frames of reference of the local working class. It did this by affirming the direct experiences of many workers in the peculiar set of historical, social, political and cultural circumstances in Restoration Barcelona: the connivance of politicians with the economic elites; the readiness of local politicians such as Cambó and Pich i Pon to use their influence to enhance their own financial interests; the decades of political stasis; the untrammelled inflation and unchecked exploitation by shopkeepers, landlords and employers; the sacrifices made by workers for the state in terms of military conscription, especially during times of war; the dearth of public services and welfare provision; the experience of the state exclusively in terms of police and army repression; the curfews and martial law that

Figure 2.4 Barcelona skyline, July 1909, as Church buildings burn across the city.

Source: Francesc Bonamusa, Pere Gabriel, Josep Lluís Martín Ramos and Josep Termes, *Història Gràfica del Moviment Obrer a Catalunya*, Barcelona, 1989, pp.172–73

Figure 2.5 Members of the community grouped around a barricade in the Raval, July 1909

Source: Francesc Bonamusa, Pere Gabriel, Josep Lluís Martín Ramos and Josep Termes, *Història Gràfica del Moviment Obrer a Catalunya*, Barcelona, 1989, p.169

affected the freedom of movement of all workers in the city; the complicity of the authorities with a reactionary Church; the refusal of the authorities to offer meaningful legal protection for workers and the complicity of officialdom in the violence of the Sometent or the Libres, which did not always differentiate between those who were active in the unions and those who were not;[70] and the closure of the reformist path and the absence of any real prospect of legal or peaceful change.

Demonstrating the degree to which everyday social and material experiences shape class and urban struggles,[71] the 'stocks of knowledge' accrued in the *barris* favoured the expansion of a specifically anarchist counter-culture: because the experience of the repressive state was undiluted by social welfare initiatives, most workers had little desire for a political campaign to conquer the state – rather, the state was seen as a mortal enemy that had to be crushed. The alienation inspired by years of political corruption provided a context for anarchist anti-politicism, and the widespread view that politics could not resolve the everyday problems facing workers made direct action attractive; the resistance of employers to any loosening of their authority in the workplace lent credibility to claims that working-class needs could not be satisfied by local capitalism and that revolutionary trade unionism was the only salvation for the masses, who had to trust in their own autonomous struggle to destroy the vast repressive coalition that structured everyday life against them; and the experiences of the clergy, especially the 'despotism of the teachers'[72] in Church schools, generated a body of latent anti-clerical sentiment. Anarchism offered workers a degree of moral superiority alongside a bourgeois class that was widely perceived as 'criminal'. A profound sense of 'we' emerged around these cultural frames and shaped collective action, providing a positive awareness of potential allies along with a negative awareness of enemies. In sum, capitalist oppression, state repression, clerical tyranny and the immiserisation of the proletariat were more than simply abstractions propounded by ideologues. They were experienced on a daily basis by workers, and this lived experience confirmed the central tenets of libertarian ideology: that the law and the police were not neutral entities but the tools of the state and propertied classes to structure everyday life in favour of capital; that the state was the main barrier to change, which, if it was to come, could not come gradually or legally through reform but instead demanded violent action by the dispossessed.

While the world vision advanced by the CNT was rooted in the experience of a social group in a specific time and space, for the Confederation to achieve its revolutionary goals the essentially local identity of the *barris* had to be refined into a more mature and radical working-class culture. To a certain extent, this occurred in the course of CNT struggles for common interests and goals. More formally, anarcho-syndicalist ideology provided a language of class that brought new meaning to lived experiences and social practices in the *barris*, making it possible for existing cultural frames to be overlaid with universal symbols. In this way, as we will see, the CNT was able to anchor its mobilisations on community strengths and grievances while appealing more generally to the working class as a whole on the basis of class allegiance.

It was no surprise that the CNT quickly became embroiled in a violent struggle with the state and employers. Shortly after its birth, the Confederation was driven underground, only to surface during World War One on a wave of militancy, buoyed up by the political crisis of the Restoration state and by wartime industrial growth, which laid the basis for a more united working-class practice. During 1918–19, the CNT became the lodestar of the dispossessed, its national membership doubling from 345,000 to 715,000; in the Barcelona area alone, the CNT claimed a membership of over 250,000, making the Catalan capital one of the most, if not the most, unionised cities in Europe. Such was the growing power of the CNT that its unions began to impose a degree of restraint over the city's otherwise rapacious industrialists and, in some cases, for the first time, win strikes.

This upturn in the fortunes of the CNT was made possible by the adoption of a new union structure at the 1918 national congress, held in Barcelona's Sants *barri*.[73] Aware that the spatialised power of the recently expanded *barris* represented a powerful foundation for organised resistance to capital and the state, CNT strategists established grassroots *comités de barriada* (district committees), which were located in new union centres (*sucursales*) in the main working-class neighbourhoods.[74] In the words of one activist, the local *comités* were 'the eyes and ears of the union in any given neighbourhood',[75] the connecting point between the *barris* and the Barcelona local federation, which determined the orientation of the unions. While the CNT remained a national confederation of segmented community-based unions and neighbourhood groups, the new structure allowed for a more unified and powerful union at city level. Making full use of improvements in the transport system and the growing availability of bicycles, and backed by the Barcelona CNT's paper, *Solidaridad Obrera*, which played an essential auxiliary role, advertising union meetings, talks and social activities across the city, the local federation could receive feedback from, and send instructions to, the *comités* with great speed. This enabled the CNT to respond swiftly to events on the ground and generally mount a more sustained and coordinated opposition to capitalism.

The most famous and dramatic mobilisation of the reorganised CNT of the post-World War One era was the 1919 strike at the Ebro Irrigation and Power Company, an Anglo-Canadian concern known locally as 'La Canadenca'. The conflict began in early 1919, when a handful of CNT white-collar workers were sacked. In reply, CNT power workers – blue- and white- collar alike – walked off the job and appealed to the local federation for solidarity, transforming a fairly insignificant conflict over union rights into a protracted struggle between a vast coalition spanning the city and state authorities and national and international capital, on the one hand, and the confederal working class in the Barcelona area, on the other. Much of the state's repressive arsenal was mobilised; martial law was implemented, and following the militarisation of essential services, soldiers replaced strikers and up to 4,000 workers were jailed. Nevertheless, cuts in the energy supply paralysed most industries in Barcelona province for forty-four days. Amid food shortages, power cuts and torchlit army patrols at night, the Catalan capital seemed like a city at war. Finally, the authorities forced the La Canadenca management to bow to the CNT's demands, which included pay rises, the payment of the strikers' lost wages and a complete amnesty for pickets. In an attempt to forestall further class conflict, the government became the first in Europe to legislate the eight-hour day in industry. This triumph heralded the coming of age of the CNT – it had arrived as a major player in the industrial arena and a central reference point in working-class life.

A great strength underpinning the CNT's collective actions was the degree of confluence between its organisational networks and those of the *barris*. The district committees permitted the CNT to penetrate workplaces and neighbourhoods like never before, allowing it to become enmeshed within a web of communal, kinship and reciprocal networks, on the basis of which it organised powerful mobilisations rooted in mutual aid and class solidarity.[76] At the same time, the CNT bolstered pre-existing dynamics of sociability and community energy, attributing to them a new meaning and symbolism.[77] The CNT advanced an alternative urban blueprint: its street politics heightened community consciousness and the spirit of local autonomy; the impenetrability and independence of the *barris* were also reaffirmed by the CNT's organised hostility to policing; and its conception of participatory democracy from below solidified existing social networks.[78] For the revolutionary anarchists in the CNT, direct democracy would fortify the *barris*, converting them into collectively run liberated zones, the raw materials for the Kropotkinian autonomous, stateless communes.

The nexus between the CNT and the *barris* depended greatly on its activists. One of the great paradoxes of the CNT was that, despite its huge membership in the city, the number of union activists was relatively small. The majority of *cenetistas* participated little in the internal life of the unions, attending union meetings rarely, if at all, and paying union contributions only sporadically. Nevertheless, the CNT had a mobilising power that was hugely disproportionate to the number of its activists.[79] In part, this reflected the dynamism and selflessness of many CNT militants, who risked recriminations arrest and even death to keep the union alive. Equally important was the fact that militants, like the leaders of the organisation, were workers themselves. (Unlike in Russia, another European country with a sizeable anarchist movement, few intellectuals were attracted to the ranks of Spanish anarchism, even less so when revolutionary syndicalism grew in popularity.) Yet besides their higher degree of class consciousness – activists were commonly known as 'the ones with ideas' (*los con ideas*) – there was nothing in their dress, lifestyle, behaviour, experiences, speech or place of residence to set them apart from the rest of the workers and, whether at a public meeting, a paper sale, in the factory or the cafe, activists could convey and disseminate ideas in a way that workers found both convincing and understandable.[80] Militants were frequently highly respected members of the community: they were exemplars for less or non-militant workers and the young, and neighbours often turned to *cenetistas* for answers to their problems. As one worker explained, 'those of the CNT were the best....They most understood the cause of the worker'.[81] The standing of activists in the community was extremely important for an organisation like the CNT that addressed workers who were frequently illiterate and who did not have access to the radio at home. In these circumstances, the success or failure of mobilisations often hinged on activists' ability to draw neighbours and friends into protest actions through face-to-face contacts in the streets. CNT militants also benefited from the informal culture of the *barris*. CNT paper sellers habitually approached acquaintances to buy their papers, and activists intervened in the frequent and fervent discussions of local events on the streets, especially during times of strike activity or social protest.[82]

The direct experience of *cenetistas* of the everyday problems facing workers allowed them to respond to collective problems with practical and viable solutions that were firmly grounded in the social fabric of the *barris*; as one rank-and-file militant put it, 'they [the activists] came to feel the cause of the workers more'.[83] This sensitivity to the realities of the *barris*, which was encouraged by CNT decentralisation, cemented the bonds between the community and the Confederation, endowing its unions with a strong local feel and assisting it in achieving its goal of addressing 'all the problems of everyday life'.[84] From here it is possible to appreciate another of the great strengths of *cenetismo*: its ability to organise around occupation and address everyday material issues and problems of subsistence in the *barris*, such as the *abaratamiento* campaign against wartime inflation. Another example of this community-based trade unionism came in 1918, when the CNT formed a Sindicato de Inquilinos (Tenants' Union), the main demands of which were a 50 percent cut in rents and an improvement in housing stock.[85] A few years later, in 1922, after considerable grassroots agitation in the housing sector, the Sindicato de Inquilinos launched a rent strike, which had the full support of the Builders' Union.[86] Given workers' limited bargaining and mobilising resources, this represented an extremely coherent protest strategy, because popular protests and forms of class struggle in defence of the general material interests of the community, what Edward Thompson famously dubbed the 'moral economy',[87] tended to be mass mobilisations that were nourished by dense social networks. The CNT was therefore able to channel the multiple solidarities derived from daily interactions, a point well summed up by one worker, who explained: 'People knew one another better in the neighbourhoods and, since everyone was exploited the same as the next person, there was an atmosphere of rebellion, of protest'.[88] Because solidarity is greater when it can appeal to a collective identity firmly based on concrete experience, these protest actions and subsistence-related conflicts typically drew in whole neighbourhoods, which in turn emerged politicised and with their group identity strengthened. The reliance of the CNT on community networks brought enormous stability to its unions, and during times of repression, local solidarity compensated for its lack of formal organisation and minimised the dangers to protesters of police action: not only was repression dispersed across a wide network of individuals but powerful community ties, combined with collective pressures and the danger of sanctions for non-participants, such as ostracism or violence, reduced the impact of the so-called 'free rider' problem, whereby members of a social group might receive the general benefits of protest without experiencing the material costs of mobilisation.[89] In view of this, contrary to those who have perceived social protest as the 'politics of envy' of the socially dislocated, we see that urban mobilisations were rooted in a fairly extensive social integration at community level. In short, the CNT was then very much a product of local space and the social relations within it: its unions made the *barris* feel powerful, and workers felt ownership of what they regarded as 'our' union.

The CNT was also very much concerned with creating the united front of all the dispossessed within a common revolutionary project. Reflecting the anarchist aim of mobilising all those who were marginalised by capital, and in sharp contradistinction to both the exclusionary culture of the bourgeoisie and to social-democratic culture, with its stress on sobriety and respectability, the Confederation attempted to attract 'deviant' elements. In prisons and jails, *cenetistas* rejected the institutional categories that labelled inmates as either 'political', 'social' or 'common' prisoners, dedicating time and energy to teaching other prisoners to read and write in an attempt to make revolutionary converts.[90] The CNT was an integrating force in the *barris*, successfully incorporating a number of subgroups that might have been a brake on working-class organisation and solidarity. One such case is provided by the street gangs of working-class youth, several of which were brought within the orbit of the unions.[91] The CNT also successfully appealed to the many thousands of migrant workers in the city. While some of the migrants had some previous contact with the organised labour movement, many more were leaving behind a landscape of rural misery that bred resignation and despair rather than protest. Nevertheless, the CNT recognised that migrants were a potent democratising force, and it was the only body prepared to accept the newcomers for who they were and to channel their hopes and aspirations. As the hegemonic and most important labour union, the CNT became a powerful magnet for unskilled migrants. For many newcomers, the CNT provided a point of entry into the city; CNT union centres were spaces of socialisation, places where migrants received important practical help and local knowledge about employment and housing patterns in an unfamiliar and sometimes hostile new environment.[92] Through their exposure to the rituals and practices of the labour movement, migrants assimilated new urban values and became firmly established in the social fabric of the city.

The inclusive culture of the CNT ensured that groups like the unemployed, who might have felt excluded from the unions and who could have been susceptible to the appeal of demagogic politicians, remained within the labour movement. Not only did the unions offer the unemployed the chance of future employment, CNT centres were a safe haven for the unemployed, who often had nowhere else to go and faced police harassment on the streets.

Nor was the CNT weakened by generational divisions or by a rival youth culture. As Dolors Marin has recognised, the workers' public sphere was based on a respect for the older generations.[93] The unions drew life from the kinship networks in the *barris*, successfully incorporating young workers into their ranks, many of whom were frequently attracted to the unions by family members, principally fathers and brothers and other powerful male role models, such as uncles.[94] In such circumstances of early politicisation, there were cases of boys as young as ten belonging to both the CNT and an anarchist group.[95]

However, the mobilising strategy of the workers' public sphere was not flawless. This is relevant in the case of women workers, whose dissident potential was not always maximised. The unions were essentially masculine spaces, and men tended to go to union meetings either alone or with their sons, leaving their partners at home.[96] There were also very few female union leaders, and women were frequently underrepresented in the union member-

Figure 2.6 Revolutionary play: children with their barricade and flag, July 1936. Besides the clenched fists, note the youth in the centre wearing the uniform of the workers' militia

Source: Ateneu Enciclopèdic Popular

ship, even in industries such as textiles, the main source of employment for working women. Instead, women workers played a secondary, supporting role within the union movement and, even when women shared the ideas of their partners, their contribution to the movement was limited to the domestic sphere, reproducing the rebellious power of their partners, children or brothers and making sacrifices in the home in order to sustain male militancy, especially when partners were in jail or on the run from the authorities.[97] Certainly, the contribution of these women to the CNT was important and should not be undervalued, but it could have been greater, principally if we consider that when women participated in conflicts in the subsistence sphere, such as the *abaratamiento* campaign and rent struggles, they behaved with much radicalism and militancy.

Yet the CNT was just one element in Barcelona's growing proletarian public sphere, an alternative grassroots social infrastructure comprising newspapers, cultural associations and social clubs. The other key institution was the *ateneu* (atheneum), a popular cultural and social centre modelled on bourgeois clubs.[98] Like the CNT, the *ateneus* filled a genuine need in the working-class city and, between 1877 and 1914, seventy-five were formed in Barcelona. Each *ateneu* provided its members with a range of urban services and facilities, and some of the larger ones had a cooperative shop, offering foodstuffs at reduced prices.[99] During a time when there were very few affordable forms of leisure, the *ateneus* organised a wide choice of leisure activities, such as theatre, choral and musical groups. Sociability and entertainment were always combined with social agitation, and the plays performed in the *ateneus* were normally of a radical, leftist or anti-clerical persuasion.[100] Another important area of activity was the sporting and excursion clubs, which organised hiking, camping and rambling trips in the surrounding countryside and coastal areas.[101] Hiking, much in keeping with the anti-urban strain within anarchist ideology, became a highly popular non-commerical recreational activity that allowed workers to escape briefly into nature and leave behind the overcrowded and cramped *barris*, which possessed few open spaces or playing fields.[102] In political terms, excursion clubs had an important propagandist function, providing workers with an opportunity to discuss ideas and writings away from repressive urban structures and return to the city with their consciousness raised. Naturist groups also went to the countryside to find freedom from the artificial conditions of urban life and attain a more balanced relationship with the natural world, away from the restrictions and conventions of the bourgeois order.

Yet the overriding objective of the *ateneus* was cultural empowerment. The pride of any *ateneu* was its lending library, which would contain a broad selection of the classics of European post-Enlightenment political and literary writing, ranging from Marx and Bakunin across to radical bourgeois writers such as Ibsen and Zola. In addition, there would be a reading room, places where groups could hold discussions, an auditorium for more formal debates and public talks, and a cafe. Reflecting the strong emphasis placed by the anarchists on pedagogy and their conviction that capitalist hegemony could be eroded through education and the cultivation of the intellect, the *ateneus* organised day schooling for working-class children and evening classes for adult workers, providing tuition in grammar and writing skills and a more general education in mathematics, literature, geography and foreign languages, as well as in more engaged subjects, such as history, sociology and political theory.

From the turn of the century, the efforts of the *ateneus* to meet the popular demand for education were assisted by rationalist schools, which were either union-funded or part of the 'Modern School' (*Escola moderna*) movement of Francesc Ferrer i Guàrdia. In what was a radical departure from the repressive practices of clerical educationalists, the rationalist schools encouraged spontaneous expression, experimentation and a spirit of equality in the classroom, placing good-quality education within the reach of most working-class budgets.[103] Consequently, the *ateneus* and the rationalist schools were the fulcrum of the social and cultural fabric in the *barris*.[104]

Figure 2.7 Biology class at the l'Hospitalet Rationalist School (1928–29 academic year). Josè Peirats, then a brick maker and future historian of the anarchist movement, is first from the left

Source: Gracia Ventura Archive

Like the CNT, the *ateneus* and the rationalist schools rested on existing community structures and sociability. The myriad social and cultural activities of the *ateneus* attracted whole families and, with crèche facilities for the very young, all members of the community, irrespective of age, were able to participate.[105] Because most *ateneus* had specific youth sections, the generational divide was breached and enduring friendships were established by adults and children under the umbrella of these institutions.[106]

The *ateneus* reinforced the spirit of autonomy of the *barris*; they dignified and gave meaning to the neighbourhood experience and, because they were often opened only after a huge collective sacrifice, they were a source of much local pride, encouraging a belief in the common possession of the wealth of the community.[107] In general terms, then, *ateneu* culture reinforced class divisions, deepening the ties between the *barris* and the activists of both the CNT and the libertarian movement. In this way, the *ateneus* cemented the links between workers' everyday aspirations and those of the movement, establishing a new frame of reference for community discontents and making it possible for existing workers' culture to be overlaid with a more coherent ideology of protest, thereby converting the 'spontaneous sociology' of the *barris* into anarchist ideas and practice. One migrant explained this process:

> I'm Andalusian and I moved to l'Hospitalet when I was nearly 10 years old. I learnt everything I know from the anarchists. I was 14 or 15 and I didn't know how to read or write. I learnt at the night school organised by the libertarians.[108]

Owing to its ties with the *ateneus* and the rationalist schools, the CNT was able to influence an oppositional working-class culture and help to mould a relatively autonomous proletarian world view during a time when, elsewhere in Europe, the advent of new forms of mass culture, such as football and music halls, was beginning to erode and dilute socialist consciousness. In particular, the *ateneus* and the rationalist schools propagated an anti-clerical culture that challenged the obscurantism of Church education and the received hierarchies of state learning, thereby making an inestimable contribution to the class culture of the CNT by educating successive generations of activists and leaders, many of whom went on to write for the labour and anarchist press.[109] Simultaneously, the *ateneus* conveyed a culture of action and mobilisation, and even when concerned with cultural activities, they still encouraged a kind of activism that could later lead to other activities and campaigns for local services. Meanwhile, during times of collective protest, the *ateneus* sometimes played a key supporting role, mobilising and bringing their members onto the streets for a big rally, demonstration, meeting or strike action.[110]

However, it is noteworthy that the patterns of gender discrimination that we witnessed earlier with regard to the CNT were replicated in the more ideological and politicised spaces of the *ateneus* and the anarchist groups that operated within them. Signalling the failure of alternative culture to break completely with official culture, women were frequently restricted to offering moral and material support for the masculine group, finding meeting places and offering logistical support; on excursions, women were predominantly involved in tasks of food preparation![111]

Nevertheless, it is possible to conclude that by the end of World War One there was a vibrant alternative public sphere, a kind of counter-spectacle with its own values, ideas, rituals, organisations and practices, or, in Gramscian terms, a counter-hegemonic project.[112] This proletarian public sphere conquered new spaces for ideas and for protest movements within urban civil society and was a direct challenge to an already weak bourgeois sphere, which, as we have seen, was bereft of institutional mechanisms such as schools through which official ideology could be conveyed. Consequently, the authorities were keen to limit or impede the expansion of this rival public sphere, and any opportunity was exploited to clamp down on this alternative educational network.[113]

However, following their vertiginous expansion during and after World War One, it was the unions that were regarded by the 'men of order' as the biggest threat to the social order. Alienated from a central state that, in the eyes of the most radical employers, had capitulated to the CNT by legalising the eight-hour day, the militant wing of the city bourgeoisie rallied to break the power of the unions. This led, in November 1919, to a three-month employer lockout of *cenetistas*, who faced daily harassment from the Sometent militia, which patrolled workplaces in search of union activists. Ironically, despite their vocal defence of a 'law and order' agenda, the eager-ness of the 'men of order' to close off the proletarian public sphere resulted in numerous infringements of the civil rights of workers, so while workers were theoretically free to join the union of their choice, including the CNT, which was not a proscribed organisation, the Sometent frequently stopped and searched workers for CNT cards and, if found, workers could expect to be assaulted, fired and blacklisted. Similarly, the Sometent prevented CNT organisers from collecting dues from union members and supporters, ille-gally confiscating union money and 'roughing up' activists.

When these measures failed to cow the CNT, the radical wing of the Catalan bourgeoisie, which sought a military solution to industrial conflict, became more active. During 1920–22, these militant industrialists courted Generals Arlegui and Martínez Anido, who, while serving as chief of police and civil governor, respectively, became notorious for organising the selective assassination of *cenetistas*. The descent into terrorism reflected the worsening structural-political crisis of the Restoration state. If, during the early phase of the Restoration, the deployment of institu-tional force, the 'politics of the Mauser' as it was known to contemporaries, could be seen as one of the strengths of the monarchical state following the structural changes brought about by World War One, the dependency of the state on violence mutated into its most glaring weakness. While violence might be efficacious insofar as it temporarily reclaimed the streets for the authorities, it could not bolster the already weak political authority of the state and served only to raise questions about the long-term survival of the Restoration and swell the ranks of the anti-monarchist opposition.

The anti-union terror of the Libres did little to shore up an already fragile urban order; rather, repression raised the stakes in the struggle for the streets. Certainly, repression could not finish with the CNT, which, in the postwar era, was able to rely on the cover provided by the durable community networks in the *barris* to survive the clampdown on its organisation and activists. However, the ferocity of the postwar anti-union offensive did have a profound impact on the internal balance of forces within the CNT. At the start of the repression, there were three main factions within the CNT: anarcho-syndicalists, anarchists and the 'communist-syndicalists', who supported the Bolshevik revolution.[114] The anarcho-syndicalists predominated within the CNT National Committee. Preoccupied with issues of national union strategy and recruitment and expansion, the anarcho-syndicalists were keen to develop mass trade unions and the myriad bodies that made up the workers' public sphere as a necessary prelude to the revolutionary transformation of society. However, this project foundered on employer intransigence, which closed off most of the channels for collective protest, lessening the attractiveness of the anarcho-syndicalist strategy within CNT circles. Moreover, as the most visible and public face of the organisation, the anarcho-syndicalists paid a very high physical price, and many of their number were either jailed or assassinated. With confederal institutions forced underground, the social context became radicalised; the arguments of militant anarchists were seemingly confirmed, while moderate voices within the CNT increasingly went unheard. Marking the start of a period known as *pistolerisme* (gun law), the initiative passed to the advocates of armed struggle against capital and the state.[115]

Organised in *grupos de afinidad*, the anarchist urban guerrillas favoured clandestine forms of organisation, placing great store on the values of individual or small-group violence. The *grupistas* fulfilled a range of tasks, forming 'defence squads', which provided bodyguards for prominent activists, and organising armed collections for the unions in workplaces and on the streets, a hazardous task that carried the risk of confrontation with either the official or parallel police. In return, the union committee would compensate the *grupistas* financially for lost working days, meeting their expenses if they had to flee the country and, if apprehended, supporting their relatives. Aware that the *grupistas* could emerge as an elite within the organisation or become removed from the realities of working-class life, the 'expropriators' were remunerated at the wage rate of a skilled worker. Adopting ever more robust and direct action tactics, the *grupistas* defended the right of the CNT to the streets by force of arms. The 'action groups' also took the 'social war' to the bourgeoisie, sending threatening letters (*anónimas*) to employers and applying *lex talionis*, 'bringing justice' (*ajusticiamiento*) in the parlance of the *grupistas*, hunting down members of the Libres and the Sometent and those industrialists and politicians who funded the repression of the CNT. (One such 'action group', Metalúrgico (Metallurgical), which was based in the Metalworkers' Union, assassinated Prime Minister Dato in 1921.) Another important sphere of anarchist activity was in the *comité pro-presos* (prisoner support groups), which were responsible for the legal costs of militants awaiting trial for union activities, such as picketing, and for the welfare of the dependents of detained and deceased activists. By the end of 1921, spiralling repression had caused the expenditure of the prisoners' support groups to rise exponentially. This was a dangerous situation for the CNT: with its unions starved of funds and on the brink of collapse, the Confederation's principles of active solidarity were seriously compromised. *Grupistas* responded with a series of audacious armed expropriations, targeting banks and payrolls and handing over the requisitioned money to the CNT. Although these 'men of action' were a small minority among the anarchists, their readiness to risk their lives for the movement gave them a status within CNT circles that far exceeded their numbers.

During this period, some of the more anarchist-oriented 'action groups' started funding themselves through expropriations, thereby guaranteeing themselves an autonomous existence.[116] This was the case with Los Solidarios (The Solidaristic), which emerged as one of the most important *grupos de afinidad* and to which some of the most sensational expropriations and assassinations were attributed.[117] While the leading figures in Los Solidarios were Buenaventura Durruti, Francisco and Domingo Ascaso, Aurelio Fernández, Ricardo Sanz and Juan García Oliver, the ambitious range of activities undertaken by *grupos* of this nature required anything between ten and twenty auxiliary members, who provided vital logistical and practical support. The better-organised groups like Los Solidarios were also known to have sympathisers near the Pyrenees, whose local knowledge of mountain passes facilitated the smuggling of weapons into Spain and enabled *grupistas* to flee to France away from persecution.[118] Similarly, in a big city like Barcelona, 'safe houses' would be organised to help *grupistas* to evade the police.

In terms of the social background of its members, Los Solidarios was typical of the new, unskilled working class that emerged during and after World War One. In 1920, the key members of the group were single males, between 19 and 25 years of age; all had experience of unskilled, casual labour, poor working conditions and job insecurity (Durruti and Fernández were mechanics, Francisco Ascaso and García Oliver waiters). Some of the group had arrived in Barcelona to work (e.g. García Oliver); others (Durruti and the Ascasos) were lured by the city's revolutionary bohemian reputation, which was much enhanced by *pisto-lerisme* and which made the Catalan capital a strong pole of attraction for anarchists from all over the Spanish state.[119] All had come into contact with the anarchist and/or union movements at an early age and, at one time or another, all had been victimised by employers for their energetic interventions in social struggles. After a bitter strike in his native León, Durruti's militancy saw him disciplined by management and union alike: he was sacked by his employers and expelled by the UGT for committing acts of sabotage. Their everyday experience as unskilled workers with few bargaining resources and equally few prospects of gradual change doubtless shaped their practice: they abhorred politics, which they believed changed nothing, and they were intensely critical of the anarcho-syndicalist wing of the CNT and its emphasis on union mobilisation, which they regarded as little short of 'reformist'. As self-styled 'avengers of the people', Los Solidarios prioritised armed struggle above all else, believing that freedom had to be fought for, gun in hand. Indeed, they had an essentially military conception of the revolution: for them, the starting point of anarchist activity was not the theoretical consciousness-raising measures that occupied so many other *grupos* but violent action, the 'rebel gesture' that would incite an insurrection.[120]

Although the era of *pistolerisme* was brought to an end by Primo de Rivera's military coup of September 1923, it had a profound legacy, and many CNT militants, not to mention the *grupistas*, preserved the habit of carrying arms. Primo's seizure of power also highlighted some of the tactical limitations of *grupismo*. In the prelude to the coup, the *grupistas* were trapped in a cycle of violence with the security forces and right-wing militia groups; this, along with the succession of armed expropriations and attacks on banks, created a widespread feeling of insecurity in elite circles, which did much to prepare an ambience that favoured the military takeover. In short, the *grupistas* lacked a coherent project for social and political transformation, so while they might assassinate a detested politician or an unpopular employer, the power structure survived and the deceased would quickly be replaced by new 'enemies of the people', possibly more repressive than their predecessors. The *grupistas* were fighting an essentially defensive, rearguard campaign. There was no doubting their courage when it came to confronting employer-sponsored gunmen, but they failed to develop a political strategy capable of mobilising large numbers of workers. Certainly, many workers celebrated the struggle of the *grupos* against 'them' (the Sometent, the Libres and the police), the result of which was that *grupista* actions were at least tolerated and would never be betrayed. In a more positive light, workers viewed the *grupos* as a source of local pride and strength, and the deaths of hated policemen and capitalists were viewed as acts of proletarian vengeance. Nevertheless, the struggle of the *grupos* was that of an armed elite, with its own unique *esprit de corps* and *modus operandi* that kept the *grupistas*, who probably never numbered more than 200, relatively aloof from the bulk of the working class. Consequently, not only was the relatively small number of *grupistas* no match for the military, they were also unable to bring large numbers of workers onto the streets to oppose Primo's coup. Nor were the unions in a position to organise a collective response. The employer offensive, the victimisation of militants in the workplace and the campaign of assassination on the streets had taken its toll. (During 1919–23, in addition to the hundreds who had been wounded, 189 workers, the majority of them *cenetistas*, had been killed in Barcelona and l'Hospitalet alone, along with twenty-one employers.[121]) Although CNT transport workers brought city life to a halt between May and July 1923, this stoppage was a pale imitation of the 1919 'La Canadença' strike and probably served only to convince employers of the need to finish with revolutionary syndicalism once and for all. When the coup came, therefore, the CNT could organise only a token response.

Upon acceding to power, Primo gave a high degree of freedom to right-wing and reformist unions while attempting to close off much of the CNT-related proletarian public sphere. However, because this alternative workers' sphere had become heavily embedded in the rich civil society of the *barris*, its eradication required a fierce repression, the scale of which exceeded Primo's plans. Therefore, not only did many *ateneus* continue to function, but many exclusively anarchist *ateneus* were established during what was a period of tremendous cultural activism and politicisation in the *barris*.[122] These *ateneus*, along with excursion and hiking groups, provided much-needed cover for activists who organised meetings in the great outdoors.[123] Alternatively, activists retreated into other spheres of popular sociability, such as bars and cafes, which had been used by anarchist and anarcho-syndicalist militants as meeting places for decades.[124] Therefore, despite a formal ban on the Catalan CRT (Confederación Regional del Trabajo, or Regional Labour Confederation) from November 1924, *cenetistas* continued to organise in the *barris*, preserving clandestine structures in workplaces and operating within both the legal and clandestine spaces in the *barris*.

An important forum for CNT activity during the dictatorship was the cooperative movement. Joan Peiró, a leading CNT strategist, encouraged *cenetistas* to work within workers' consumer cooperatives, which, he believed, should be used to help fund anarcho-syndicalist cultural and propagandistic ventures.[125] Typical of these initiatives was a cooperative established in Sant Adrià, a rapidly expanded working-class settlement on Barcelona's northern outskirts. The project began when CNT activists organised a collection among the community. Once enough money had been raised to purchase the necessary building materials, members of the community and volunteer carpenters, bricklayers and plasterers constructed the building that housed the cooperative. Consisting of a shop and bakery where members could purchase a range of goods and foodstuffs at cost price and of the same or better quality than those sold in shops and markets, the cooperative protected working-class consumers from exploitative commercial sectors.[126] The cooperative also played an extensive social and cultural role in the local community: it had a library, a bar with a billiard table and a cafe, and it organised a special section for local youth as well as a host of cultural activities, evening classes, lecture programmes, plays, musical recitals and excursion clubs.[127] In general terms, therefore, the cooperatives helped to preserve the proud, independent spirit of the *barris* and the culture of seeking practical collective solutions to the collective problems of everyday life. The cooperative also fulfilled several less overt functions, such as organising collections for imprisoned *cenetistas* and their families.[128] Moreover, with decisions in the cooperative taking place on the basis of direct democracy, a new generation of workers was socialised in the democratic culture and practices of the CNT.[129] Furthermore, even if workers were not mobilising in the streets, the associational life in the cooperatives provided an experience of self-organisation and autonomous activity.

Through their involvement in cultural associations and consumers' cooperatives, *cenetistas* retained multiple connections with the *barris* and the nexus between the union and community therefore survived. As the dictatorship went into decline at the end of the 1920s, the changing political circumstances allowed workers to mobilise and networks of solidarity were converted into networks of resistance. These networks were strengthened by the urban-industrial growth produced by the dictator's programme of public works in Barcelona, which had increased the potential constituency of the CNT. It was this that prompted the chief of state security, General Emilio Mola, to reflect in 1930 that 'Barcelona was the heart of the CNT'.[130] As we will see in Chapter 3 and beyond, the scene was set for a new phase in the struggle between the workers' public sphere and the state.

3 The birth of the republican city

This chapter will first explore the period in which the monarchist dictatorship disintegrated and was replaced by the Second Republic. It will then examine in more depth the main features of republican policy insofar as they affected the regulation of public space in Barcelona.

Primo de Rivera's dictatorship succeeded only in temporarily suspending the conflicts stemming from the legitimation crisis of the Spanish state. By September 1929, and with the collapse of international financial markets, important groups within the hegemonic bloc, including sections of the traditional political and economic elites (the Crown, the clergy, the *latifundistas*, the industrial bourgeoisie and the armed forces), were distancing themselves from an increasingly unpopular regime. Finally, in January 1930, Alfonso XIII replaced Primo de Rivera with the 'soft dictatorship' (*dictablanda*) of General Dámaso Berenguer, whose mission was to prepare the political conditions for new elections in a revived constitutional monarchy. In Barcelona, the main supporter of this project was the bourgeois Lliga, which hoped to emerge as a key force in a future parliamentary monarchy. Like much of the Barcelona grand bourgeoisie whose interests it expressed, the Lliga was keen to safeguard the 'principle of authority' during this period of change and regarded the monarchy as the main power structure in Spain.[1] Underscoring the *de facto* alliance between the party of Catalan big business and the Spanish Crown, in February 1930 Alfonso XIII appointed the Lliga's Count Juan Antonio Güell mayor of Barcelona.[2]

Yet the Lliga, like many Spanish conservatives, ignored the fact that by trampling on the 1876 constitution in 1923, the king had stymied any prospect of recreating a constitutional monarchy in the 1930s. Not only had the dynastic parties that sustained the fiction of 'Restoration democracy' been abolished, but many monarchist politicians viewed the king as a meddling opportunist. Meanwhile, important groups within the army officer corps, the midwife and executioner of the Restoration, were offended at what they saw as the king's disloyalty and ingratitude towards Primo de Rivera. During 1930–31, erstwhile monarchists in the officer corps were prepared to countenance a new political compact and joined with liberal republican soldiers in forging links with the opposition. The growing ambivalence of the king's 'praetorian guard' would prove fatal to a monarchy that, having relied on repression for so long, possessed few ideological mechanisms through which it could shore up its power.

Nor did the economic context favour Berenguer's planned restoration of civil and political liberties. Although Spain's limited integration into the global economy muted the aftershocks of the Wall Street crash, the abrupt end of Primo de Rivera's ambitious public works schemes increased unemployment significantly, as did the closure of the 1929 Exhibition, which left the Barcelona construction industry in turmoil. Moreover, the social impact of unemployment was magnified by the underdeveloped welfare system described in Chapter 1. By early 1930, the limited poor relief offered by state, Church and municipal bodies could not meet the needs of the growing number of jobless workers.[3] Consequently, the reopening of legal spaces, such as when Berenguer legalised the CNT in April 1930, was immediately followed by social dissent. The unskilled and the unemployed were in the vanguard of these protests. In September, CNT building workers launched a general strike in Barcelona, and there were numerous street demonstrations by jobless workers, several of which resulted in violent clashes with the police. Unemployed self-help strategies, such as street trade and illegality, were also much in evidence, especially in and around the groups of *cases barates*, the Raval and parts of l'Hospitalet.[4] Finally, following a surge in inflation and renewed social protest, Berenguer clamped down on the CNT in February 1931.[5] Unable to steer a path between reform and repression, he resigned that same month, being replaced by Admiral Aznar, who formed what would be the last monarchist government.

CNT protest during 1930–31 was part of a wider set of mobilisations that underscored the growing isolation of the monarchy. Nowhere was this more graphically seen than in the revival of republicanism, a political movement of the liberal and progressive middle classes against the monarchy. The central message of republicanism was that the 'people' (a moral community comprised of the middle and working classes of urban and rural Spain) should unite to overthrow the corrupt governments of the monarchy, which ruled on behalf of a narrow clique of oligarchs, and replace it with a representative system of governance based on full political democracy and the extension of civil liberties and universal suffrage to the whole of society. Enfranchised and armed with the rights of citizenship, the 'people' would express their democratic desire for social reform and limit the power of the egoistic oligarchy, creating a just and fair society.[6]

Although republicanism was popular in Barcelona for a brief period at the start of the twentieth century, its influence had been undermined by the rise of autonomous working-class organisations. Thereafter, revolutionary syndicalism emerged as the most steadfast opponent of the monarchy.[7] However, the political conditions during the dictatorship presented the organised labour and republican movements with a common enemy and a shared sense of purpose. During the early part of the dictatorship, exiled anarchists and

republicans organised a series of armed plots aimed at replacing the dictatorship and the monarchy with democracy. Undeterred by the failure of these
actions, the labour and republican movements adopted more gradualist
tactics. This culminated in the San Sebastián pact of August 1930 and the
establishment of the 'Revolutionary Committee', backed by a broad coalition
of the myriad republican groupings and the reformist, social-democratic wing
of the labour movement.[8] Although, true to its formal anti-politicism, the
CNT refused to sign up, it vowed to work towards the aims of the San
Sebastián pact from the streets, agreeing to support a general strike against
the monarchy.[9]

The announcement of municipal elections for 12 April 1931 provided the
monarchists and the supporters of the San Sebastián pact alike with a chance
to test public opinion: for the former, favourable results would pave the way
for a general election and the establishment of a constitutional monarchy; for
the latter, the April elections were a plebiscite on the future of the
monarchy.[10] Prior to the elections, in Barcelona the most energetic and
dynamic opposition party was the ERC (Esquerra Republicana de Catalunya,
or Republican Left of Catalonia), which expected a future Spanish republic
to allow home rule for Catalonia. Founded in March 1931 on a wave of anti-
monarchist, pro-nationalist feeling stimulated by the dictatorship, the ERC,
which would dominate Catalan politics in the years leading up to the civil
war, was an electoral coalition of various small radical *catalaniste* and
republican groups and is often regarded as typifying the 'new' republicanism
of the 1920s and 1930s.[11]

The ERC's great strength was its populism, which allowed it to tap into
the manifold discontents of the diverse political and social sectors alienated
by the dictatorship. Its radical nationalist right wing exploited the disintegration of the Lliga's old support base following its compromises with the
monarchy. This faction included a small group of Catalan xenophobes such
as the notorious racist Pere Màrtir Rossell and the crypto-fascists Miquel
Badia and Josep Dencàs, who despised what they saw as a 'de-Catalanised'
working class. But the key figure inside the ERC was the septuagenarian
Francesc Macià, popularly and affectionately known as L'Avi (The
Grandfather). From a conservative aristocratic family, Macià attained the
rank of colonel in the Spanish army before resigning in protest at anti-
Catalan sentiment within the officer corps.[12] Thereafter, he embodied
Catalan resistance to the dictatorship and the monarchy, establishing a proud
record of militant opposition, organising abortive armed conspiracies for
which he sought (and found) allies in the anarchist and communist movements. Sensitive to the injustices perpetrated against the 'popular classes',
including migrant workers, Macià and the 'workerist' left wing of the ERC
made overtures towards the labour movement, promising to abolish the
comités paritarios (parity committees), Primo de Rivera's corporate labour
courts, which were the antithesis of *cenetista* traditions of direct action.
Some ERC members even talked of 'workers' democracy'.[13]

It was no coincidence that the ERC's founding conference took place in the working-class *barri* of Sants. Aware of the widespread distrust of politicians in the *barris*, where *catalanisme* was often identified with the bourgeois Lliga, the ERC presented itself as 'the true anti-dynastic force' that would 'harmonise the idea of Catalonia with the repair of social injustices'.[14] Although committed to an electoral strategy, the ERC attempted to tap local revolutionary traditions, defining itself as 'the party of the revolution' that would initiate 'the liberation of the nation, not only from the interference of the Church, but also from capitalist control'.[15] The ERC made a specific commitment 'to legislate especially for the working class', which would receive 'the right to live with complete security and dignity'.[16] Concrete measures were proposed to alleviate the immediate misery of the most downtrodden sections of the working class, including anti-inflationary legislation linking wages to the cost of living, a minimum wage, health and welfare reforms, and a cut in the working day, with a six-hour day in industries ravaged by unemployment.[17] Besides a pledge to increase public services, the ERC vowed to bring culture to the urban working class through an ambitious school-building programme.[18] The party also promised a revolution in housing, as summed up in Macià's famous pledge to establish a 'garden city' and provide workers with 'houses with gardens' (*la caseta i l'hortet*).[19] In short, the ERC proposed a democratic republican city.

All these promises would be enshrined in law. Thus, in contrast to the monarchy, when the state impeded the efforts of the labour movement to defend the interests of its members, the Republic would offer 'effective legal protection', including the 'freedom and right to strike' for the unions.[20] In its 'Programme of Government', the ERC committed itself to a range of other civil liberties and 'individual and collective freedoms': the full freedom of the press, an end to censorship, the right to free and compulsory education, and 'equality before the law'. Police reform figured prominently in the ERC's priorities. There would be an end to the 'governmental terrorism' of monarchist policing, which saw the security forces 'pitted against honourable people' through 'infamous' practices like internment without trial; the ERC even suggested that it would disband the police and replace it with a democratically controlled 'civic guard'.[21] Central to the ERC's reformist programme was its radical commitment to renounce the debts incurred by the 'thieves of the Exhibition' (the coalition of local politicians, landowners, businessmen and property speculators) who ran the council during the dictatorship. By enriching themselves, these 'gangsters of Barcelona' had 'impoverished the city', leaving the council saddled with a mammoth deficit equivalent to the Portuguese national debt: in 1930, 44 percent of the municipal budget went on loan repayment.[22] Clearly, if the ERC honoured the debts of previous administrations, the public spending that lay at the heart of its vision of a democratic republican city would be impossible.[23]

This reform programme was widely disseminated in working-class circles through the press and radio and by word of mouth at meetings and rallies. Macià, in particular, was an important link between the masses and the ERC, his direct and passionate form of oratory conveying a sense of trustworthiness and concern for workers that had rarely been seen before in politicians. Yet the ERC's appeal to working-class voters is best understood in terms of its relationship with the CNT. Founding members of the ERC, such as the lawyers Lluís Companys and Joan Casanovas, enjoyed considerable prestige among the Barcelona CNT leadership from the period of *pistolerisme*, when they defended *cenetistas* in the courts and experienced monarchist repression, including deportation and the threat of assassi-nation.[24] Later, during the dictatorship, republicans, radical separatists and *cenetistas* occupied the same oppositional space, whether in jail, in exile in Paris or Brussels or in the clandestine struggle in Barcelona. One ERC activist, Dr Jaume Aiguader, the 'people's physician', who became the first mayor of repub-lican Barcelona, had flirted with anarchism in the 1920s when he allowed his Sants surgery to be used as a clandestine meeting place for republicans and *cenetistas* alike.[25] CNT activists were also attracted by the ERC's promise of a new judicial framework for industrial relations. Of all the parties contesting the elections, it was most committed to dismantling the *comités paritarios*; this vocal commitment to trade union freedoms was enough to convince even the most anti-political CNT organiser that the labour movement would at least be able to fight for working-class interests regardless of whether the Esquerra delivered on its promised social reforms.[26]

The CNT therefore created a pro-ERC climate in the *barris* before the April elections. Besides advertising ERC meetings in *Solidaridad Obrera*, as the elections drew close, many leading *cenetistas* – anarcho-syndicalists and anar-chists alike – addressed meetings alongside Esquerra activists to protest against governmental repression and call for an amnesty for social and polit-ical prisoners.[27] While *cenetistas* did not publicly endorse a vote for the ERC, the fact that they shared a platform with its activists, some of whom were elec-toral candidates, could only have been interpreted as an endorsement of the ERC's candidacy. The CNT press also contributed to the growing cult surrounding Macià, registering its 'admiration' of the 'idealism' and 'clean political history' of the 'apostle of Catalan freedom'.[28] As well as praising the ERC as the party of 'the most distinguished men of Catalan democracy', *Solidaridad Obrera* denounced its rivals: the 'corrupt' Radicals, the 'social-fascist' PSOE (Partido Socialista Obrero Español, or Spanish Socialist Party) and the 'fascist' Lliga, whose leader, Cambó, was 'the father of the terrorists of the Sindicato Libre'.[29]

It would be incorrect to conclude that the CNT masses or their leaders were somehow seduced by the ERC's populist politics. Rather, CNT support for the ERC derived from the CNT's traditional apoliticism. As we saw in the previous chapter, in keeping with anarcho-syndicalist orthodoxy, the CNT opposed conventional politics as another means of enslaving the working class and normally called on workers to abstain from the 'electoral farce'. However, in the spring of 1931, the pressure of circumstances (the need to abolish the *comités paritarios* and attain an amnesty for its jailed activists) and a set of rational calculations based on these factors dissuaded CNT leaders from advocating an electoral boycott, an option that would probably hand power to the Right, leaving the monarchy intact, the prisoners in jail and the CNT facing an uncertain legal future.[30] Although the CNT leadership did not call on people to vote in the elections, it adopted the ambiguous stance that the elections were a matter of conscience, effectively allowing workers to vote for the republicans as a 'lesser evil'.[31] Consequently, on election day, there was frenzied activity in the main working-class districts, especially the Raval, where *Las Noticias* observed 'extraordinary excitement' outside polling stations.[32] As was later explained by Peiró, Catalan CRT secretary at the time of the elections, 'the masses felt an irresistible urge to change the political decor of the state'.[33]

Two days after the elections, on 14 April, the hopes of the anti-monarchist opposition were confirmed. In urban areas, where the elections could not be rigged with the same success as during the Restoration, an overwhelming majority of voters had backed the parties of the San Sebastián pact. In Barcelona, thirty-eight of the fifty council seats went to pro-republicans, the monarchist Lliga winning the remaining twelve.[34] The undisputed victor was the ERC, gaining 31 percent of the vote and twenty-four seats. Interestingly, the biggest and best-organised parties in the San Sebastián pact, the Radicals and the PSOE, the two most important parties during the Second Republic, fared badly in Barcelona, winning only twelve seats (ten for the Radicals and two for the PSOE).

When news of the triumph of the anti-monarchist parties broke, Barcelona's factories emptied and thousands of people, many of them *cenetistas* and workers, poured onto the streets. There were pro-republican demonstrations in even the most proletarian of the *barris*.[35] In l'Hospitalet, workers downed their tools and sang 'La Marseillaise' in the streets.[36] Underscoring the hopes that had been invested in the Esquerra, as well as the opprobrium felt for the Lliga, a common chant of the crowds was 'Visca Macià! Mori Cambó!' ('Long live Macià! Death to Cambó!').[37] Although Cambó found it prudent to flee Spain, the mood was one of collective revelry rather than retribution.[38] By lunchtime, jubilant crowds from the *barris* had converged on the city centre and, as the clamour from the streets grew, republican politicians finally acted: shortly after 1pm, Macià appeared on the balcony of the Generalitat, the former seat of Catalonia's medieval parliament in central Barcelona, where he proclaimed the 'Catalan Republic within the Spanish Federal Republic'.[39] The Republic had yet to be proclaimed in Madrid, where the more cautious members of the Revolutionary Committee sought the assent of the military. Only when the army high command made it known that it would not defend the monarchy did the Revolutionary Committee discover the fortitude needed to proclaim the Republic.[40]

As news of events in Madrid filtered back to Barcelona, a democratic fiesta was already underway on the streets. A huge crowd gathered outside the

Figure 3.1 A vast crowd greeting the proclamation of the Second Republic outside the
         Generalitat and Barcelona Council buildings, 14th April 1931. The square
         would soon be renamed Republic Square.

Source: L'Avenç Archive

Generalitat in Sant Jaume Square, soon to be renamed 'Republic Square', and
greeted Macià with 'La Marseillaise'.[41] The street celebrations drew in the
popular masses in the broadest sense and were characterised by intermingling of
the middle and working classes.[42] At the foot of Les Rambles, crowds of
workers waved red flags and sang 'The Internationale' as they mixed with
groups carrying republican flags. In a new spirit of fraternity, bus and tram
conductors allowed people to travel free around the city.[43] More significantly,
the discipline of the security forces was partially broken, as members of the
police and cavalry joined in the street celebrations, which continued into the
early hours of the next day.

Notwithstanding the outpouring of collective joy at the coming of the
Republic, there were indications on the streets that the masses were impatient for change. Soon after the proclamation of the Republic, *cenetistas*
marched on the Model Jail to release their comrades; prison records were
also destroyed in a very orderly two-hour operation. Shortly afterwards,
women prisoners were released from the Amàlia Street jail near the Raval,
which, in keeping with the prevailing mood, occurred peacefully and
prompted another street celebration involving demonstrators, newly freed
prisoners and members of the community.[44] However, there was evidence
that the accumulated hatred of decades of monarchist repression might lead

to violent conflict on the streets. During 15–16 April, the Guardia Civil defended the Barcelona Law Courts against crowds protesting outside the headquarters of the political police, seeking to destroy judicial records. Also on 15 April, members of a crowd protesting outside the headquarters of the political police, the Brigada Policial especializada en Anarquismo y Sindicalismo (Anti-anarchist, Anti-Trade Unionist Police Unit), were lucky to escape without injury after officers unexpectedly opened fire from inside the building.[45]

In order to secure the loyalty of the masses in the *barris*, it was imperative that the republicans take immediate action to meet, at least in part, some of the popular aspirations that they had aroused prior to the elections. Concretely, the material needs of the most disadvantaged sections of the working class had to be addressed, and the streets had to be policed in such a way as to alter popular perceptions of authority. Macià initially – and naively – hoped to achieve this by bringing the CNT into a government of national unity, something that was anathema to even the most moderate *cenetistas* and that promised to split the union.[46] Consequently, only the reformist Left, the tiny Fabianesque USC (Unió Socialista de Catalunya, or Socialist Union of Catalonia) and the UGT, which had no influence whatsoever in the *barris*, entered Macià's cabinet.[47]

Another barrier facing Macià's political project was the split between the republicans of Barcelona and Madrid over the question of Catalan devolution. By declaring the 'Catalan Republic within the Spanish Federal Republic' on 14 April, Macià had exceeded the agreed objectives of the San Sebastián Pact and thereby presented the republicans in Madrid with a genuine dilemma: they could not afford to allow the traditionally centralist military to identify the birth of the Republic with the apparent dissolution of the state. And so, on 15 April, a government delegation arrived in Barcelona with the aim of persuading Macià to change tack. Despite his day-old pledge to lay down his life for the Catalan Republic, Macià accepted the proposal by Fernando de los Ríos, a wily Andalusian socialist with an extensive knowledge of Catalan history, that the power of the central state be reinstated, whereupon it would be devolved gradually to a revived Generalitat government. Macià accepted the suggestion out of 'republican solidarity', and on 21 April the new Generalitat was officially recognised by the Madrid provisional government: the ephemeral Catalan Republic, like Macià's freedom of manoeuvre, lasted a mere three days.[48] Incredibly, Macià extracted no real concessions from the central government in return for his *volte-face*, nor did he secure any guarantees over the speed of devolution, which was to be determined by the more conservative republicans in Madrid at an unknown date in a far from certain political future. In the interim, the only source of power for the ERC was in Barcelona city hall and in a string of council chambers throughout Catalonia, local political spaces that had been systematically debilitated by successive central administrations over the preceding 100 years and that were no basis for reforming urban public services. The Esquerra was also forced to renege on its earlier commitment to annul Barcelona Council's debts, following pressure from central government and international financial institutions concerned about what would constitute a *de facto* confiscation of bank capital. Indalecio Prieto, the PSOE finance minister, revealed an obsessive desire to appease domestic and international financiers by balancing the budget and repaying the debts of the monarchist governments of yesteryear.[49] Moreover, Prieto was extremely suspicious of the ERC's reformist posture and froze all loans and state funding to Barcelona Council and the Generalitat, thereby guaranteeing that these bodies operated with a budget deficit throughout the coming years.[50]

The prioritisation of budgetary control meant that the republican authorities in Madrid and Barcelona were unable to honour their public commitment to a 'new deal' of benefits and public works for the unemployed. Even when new bodies were set up to deal with unemployment, such as the Caja Nacional para el Paro Forzoso (National Unemployment Fund) created by the Madrid government in 1931, these were beset by financial constraints and were little more than an indication of good intent.[51] Meanwhile, Prieto's centralist instincts ensured that the Madrid government refused to free already scarce resources to offset joblessness and social exclusion in Barcelona.[52] According to Albert Balcells' study of unemployment in Catalonia, in February 1933, nearly two full years after the birth of the Republic, only 2.4 percent of the jobless received any kind of state benefit, and this expired after a fixed period.[53] The ERC's main initiative on behalf of the unemployed was to create the Comissió Pro-Obrers sense Treball (Unemployed Workers' Commission). Although prior to the first democratic elections in June 1931 the ERC had described unemployment as 'one of the most imposing problems which the Republic has been presented with',[54] afterwards, doubtless having attracted many votes from those out of work, the party and its supporters adopted a different stance: Serra i Moret, the USC head of the Comissió Pro-Obrers sense Treball, told journalists that 'unemployment is not such a big problem'. The ERC also denied any responsibility for unemployment, portraying it as an unfortunate inheritance from the monarchy. In practical terms, the ERC offered little more than soup kitchens, food vouchers and allotment schemes, justifying its *volte-face* on the question of unemployment benefit in democratic discourse by declaring that a subsidy was 'immoral' and would produce 'a new caste' among the unemployed and within the working class.[55]

In effect, the republicans believed that democratic legality was coterminous with reform. Reflecting the preponderance of lawyers in their ranks, they exuded a judicial utopianism, a fixation with legal processes and forms and the judicial aspects of equality. The republicans lacked a coherent theory of state power and assumed that the state and its laws were essentially neutral entities that could be mobilised on behalf of all citizens and administer justice for everyone. This was reflected in the slogan of *La Calle*, a Barcelona republican paper: 'Republic, law, justice'.[56] Whereas the monarchist state was immoderate and brutal, unchecked by the law, the republican state would provide judicial protection for civil society, thereby creating a new balance between repressive and conciliatory mechanisms of power. Accordingly, the republicans hoped to reconstitute and rationalise authority, thus ending the crisis of state power, which would be imbued with popular legitimacy. Article 1 of the new constitution, which defined Spain as 'a republic of workers of all classes', highlighted the vague abstractions of the republican mind. Although the constitution presupposed the parity of rich and poor before the law, the emphasis was firmly on formal not substantive equality, and throughout the republican period, successive governments, both with and without socialist representation, pursued traditional liberal economic policies. The republicans, therefore, naively assumed that rank and privilege would not affect the legal process, believing that chaotic and disorderly market forces could be reorganised through the endeavours of enlightened public agencies without limiting the freedom of private interests. In doing so, they ignored the fact that the structural inequalities and class power system inherited from the monarchist period might undermine legislation. By maintaining the fiction of legal equality, republican law effectively reinforced the socio-economic *status quo* and became the guarantor of these very inequalities. Thus, while the Republic signified a limited increase in civil and political freedoms, social inequality and the everyday economic compulsion that weighed down on the working class remained essentially unchanged.

3.1   The 'republic of order'

There was a clear divergence between the discourse and practice of republicanism in opposition to the monarchy, when it appeared as a socially progressive, even radical, political force that placed the accent of its discourse on 'freedom', and republicanism in power, when it pursued the middle-class dream of order.[57] This emphasis on order was evident at the very birth of democracy, when Macià announced: 'Anyone who disturbs the order of the new Catalan Republic will be considered an *agent provocateur* and a traitor to the nation'.[58] Later in the afternoon, at the first session of the 'revolutionary republican city hall', newly appointed Mayor Aiguader defined the central task of the council as the 'defence of order in the street'.[59] These themes were later developed by Companys, Barcelona's first republican civil governor, who emphasised the need for 'discipline' within a 'republic of order', promising 'strong measures' against those who represented 'the negation of authority'. It was, in Companys' opinion, imperative to expand the police in order to guarantee 'social peace' and avoid 'mob rule in the city'.[60] Such concerns were greater still among the more conservative members of central government, such as Miguel Maura, a neophyte republican and once a fanatical monarchist. Alarmed by what he saw as the 'pre-revolutionary ambience' and the 'dangerous alternative' presented by the revolutionary Left, Maura joined the government, becoming the first republican interior minister, in order to quell what he saw as the 'popular rage' and the 'din' (*bullicio*) in the streets.[61] According to Manuel Azaña, prime minister from 1931 to 1933, Maura was obsessed with 'subversion' and 'vomited draconian decrees' in cabinet meetings. Azaña nevertheless agreed with Maura on the need for an 'energetic policy to make the Republic feared'.[62]

However, it would be wrong to conclude that, after 14 April, the republicans cynically relegated freedom in favour of the more convenient quest for order. Rather, following the collapse of the First Republic in discredit and political turmoil in 1873, order became a hallmark of traditional republican culture, only to be understated or obscured by the anti-oligarchic nature of much republican propaganda during the final stages of the struggle against the monarchy. The re-emergence of 'order' as an overriding political priority was perhaps most graphically seen in the case of the ERC, arguably the most radical faction within the republican movement. Although superficially the ERC's 'new' republicanism may have appeared more dynamic and original than 'historic' republicanism, it displayed traditional republican traits: the idealisation of bourgeois democratic freedoms and the legal process, which, it assumed, would be a panacea for all the injustices and problems of the past;[63] the belief in the essential harmony of society, with all citizens contributing to the well-being of the social organism;[64] and the modernist vision of the city as a democratised, non-hierarchical space, equally accessible to all citizens. Under closer scrutiny, we see that the ERC's nationalism far outweighed its social reformism. In substantive terms, its project for modernisation and national reconstruction bore many similarities to that of the Lliga. Indeed, the ERC was infused with the typical idealism of the nationalist middle-class intelligentsia of this era, evincing a blind faith in the recuperative properties of national self-determination and the utopian expectation that independence would *ipso facto* end national and class oppression.

However, what was unique about the ERC was its populist rhetoric, which reflected its desire to integrate the working class into a flexible, socially inclusive bourgeois democracy based on a market economy. At a rhetorical level, the ERC combined the yearning for prosperity of the middle class with the desire for order of the bourgeoisie and the sentiments of equality associated with the working class. Accordingly, the ERC saw itself as a force that would arbitrate between the two main classes of Catalan society. In practice, though, for all its promises of reform, the ERC, including its left wing and its socialist allies in the USC, was mainly concerned with the political reintegration of previously disaffected and dissident groups in Catalan society. Thus both the ERC and the USC viewed 'problems' such as industrial conflict and anarchist violence as impediments to the evolution of a rich civic culture and the 'progress' of Catalonia.[65] Equally, the ERC's concern with improving the everyday life of the dispossessed revealed much of the haughty pomposity of the philanthropists of the 1880s: the working class was assumed to be in need of assistance, which could best be provided by the middle classes, which would civilise the unenlightened through reform and education. Social problems such as violence, poverty, alcoholism and sexual licence were regarded, therefore, as essentially working-class problems that could be resolved with the integration of all citizens into the republican nation.[66]

Several historians have seized upon the complex social basis of the ERC as evidence that the party was an inter-class organisation.[67] Certainly, owing to Catalonia's distinct urban and rural social structure, the ERC was able to secure a larger mass base than the 'historic' republican groups. Nevertheless, a close analysis of the ERC's social basis and its politics reveals that it represented definite interests and had clear foci of support among the intermediate sectors of urban and rural Catalonia: the *rabassaires*, the staunchly nationalist tenant farmers who looked to it as a counterweight to the Lliga, the political representative of the large Catalan landowners, and intermediate urban sectors, small property owners and shopkeepers, who had previously felt excluded by the elitist nationalism of the Lliga. Certainly, the ERC had friends among industrialists, businessmen and smaller factory owners, but these were a minority of its supporters. The same was true of its working-class support, which was largely limited to white-collar workers, clerks and shop workers.[68] This is confirmed by the social geography of the ERC's *casals* (nationalist clubs) in Barcelona, the largest and most active of which were in districts, such as Gràcia, which were more popular than proletarian.[69] Conversely, in the working-class heartlands like the Raval or La Torrassa, Esquerra-affiliated centres had few members and a rather tenuous existence.[70] As far as the ERC's leadership was concerned, it fitted the profile of the 'historic' republican parties more closely: it was recruited from the petite bourgeoisie, the urban middle class and, in particular, the intelligentsia of intermediate professional and technocratic sectors (lawyers, industrial engineers, doctors and civil servants), who were not directly involved in the class struggle but who had close ties to industry and were concerned with 'progress' and 'order'.[71]

Unlike in the monarchy and the dictatorship, when state repression served the interests of narrow economic elites, the republican ideology of order was, according to its advocates, democratic. 'Order' and 'freedom' were an inseparable couplet within the republican project, the main axiom of governance being that the consolidation of democracy and reform by perspicacious politicians was impossible without order.[72] As one prominent ERC activist stated, 'if the monarchy represented disorder, the Republic must signify order'.[73] This would allow the elected representatives of the people to determine the rate of change from above, unimpeded by the mobilisation of the working class, who must patiently and passively await the reforms enacted by educated middle-class professionals.[74] However, the danger to the Republic was that a culturally retarded section of the masses might easily confuse what was in its best interests. Consequently, the Republic must not be 'a weak regime': any resistance by 'primitive' sectors to the political and moral leadership offered by the republicans or attempts to accelerate the pace of change from below would be repressed by the democratic state.[75] Thus republican state repression would serve the interests of all society: it would preserve mass democracy ('power which is in the hands of all', as one republican newspaper explained[76]) and create the optimum conditions for reform.

The 'republic of order' can also be regarded as the political companion to the continuation of traditional economic policies. We saw in Chapter 2 how, under previous regimes, the implementation of liberal capitalist economics produced profound dynamics of contestation and conflict, which in turn resulted in spiralling state repression. This process was repeated during the Republic, although repression was invoked as part of a democratic ideology of domination. In the industrial sphere in the first months of the Republic, PSOE labour minister and UGT general secretary, Francisco Largo Caballero, established new arbitration committees, the jurados mixtos (mixed juries), to resolve the legitimate grievances of the workforce peacefully and to end the unmediated industrial conflicts that radicalised labour relations during the monarchy. Their creators hoped that the jurados would educate workers to trust state institutions and make redundant the direct action labour culture of the CNT, which republicans regarded as backward and ignorant, a product of monarchist repression and unreason. These militant syndical struggles were, in the opinion of Largo Caballero, obsolete under the Republic, where there could be 'no strikes, nor complaints nor protests. The first thing now is to consolidate the regime' and preserve 'authority' and 'discipline' in industrial affairs.[77] Any trade union demands that were not submitted to the jurados would, in the words of Maura, feel 'the full force of the law'.[78] In this way, the republicans aimed to introduce a tighter industrial discipline than that which existed during the monarchy.

This new ideology of order was most forcefully and frequently expressed with regard to the unemployed, who, having mobilised during the final phase of the monarchy and the dictatorship, and doubtless impressed by the promises of republican politicians to assist the most needy sectors of society, expected immediate relief from the new authorities. Two months into the Republic, Macià, while renewing his commitment to help jobless workers, explained that this hinged on the 'serenity', 'patience' and 'discipline' of the unemployed, which would allow the peaceful consolidation of the Republic and the establishment of the necessary legal channels to address the 'legitimate' aspirations of the out-of-work.[79] Following renewed street protests by the unemployed, the authorities embarked on a strategy aimed at criminalising any hint of dissent from the unemployed. Even Joan Ventalló, from the left wing of the Esquerra, linked joblessness with crime, declaring that unemployment was a 'problem of public order, a simple police problem'.[80] Thereafter, the repressive dimension of ERC unemployment policies was increasingly visible. From its inception, the Comissió Pro-Obrers sense Treball sought to police the jobless, repeating the republican message that the authorities could only resolve the problems of the unemployed after the stabilisation of the new regime. Until then, the unemployed were to display 'calm' and 'understanding' and avoid 'excesses' or 'any disturbance of the peace, such as attacks on banks or food shops'.[81]

Another constant feature of ERC pronouncements on unemployment was an emphasis on the nefarious consequences of migration. The ERC attributed unemployment to an excessive supply of labour (i.e. the workers who came to work in Barcelona before the 1929 World Exhibition) and advocated the repatriation of non-Catalan migrants.[82] The ERC effectively interpreted unemployment in nationalist terms. Although non-Catalans had been arriving in Barcelona on a massive scale since the 1880s, it was ironic that, with the liberal Left in power for the first time, a ruling party should define migration as 'an offensive against Catalonia' and exploit this as a political issue.[83] While this may smack of a conspiracy theory, ERC discourse was part of a deliberate strategy to divide the working class along ethnic lines and between those who worked and those who did not.[84]

This divisive strategy was enshrined in the ERC's policies in the Generalitat and in Barcelona Council. The ERC initially hoped to reduce unemployment through the voluntary repatriation of migrants. Early in the Republic, the Generalitat and Barcelona Council hired a train to return unemployed migrants to southern Spain. The trip – along with the fact that those who wished to leave Barcelona would receive free food and drink for a journey lasting over a day – was advertised on posters across the city. The authorities were delighted at the huge interest in the scheme, and a packed train set off. However, in what appeared to be an act of sabotage, the train was forced to stop at La Bordeta, where the train line was closest to La Torrassa. By the time the train was ready to resume the journey south, nearly all the migrants had fled with the food and drink provided by the local authorities.[85] Following this farce, the ERC opted for forced repatriation, a more expensive option that was similarly unsuccessful. When we consider that it might take southern rural migrants a year to save the fare for a boat or 40-hour bus trip to Barcelona, it is no surprise that repatriation met with resistance.[86] There were numerous instances of deported migrants returning almost immediately to their adopted home, aware that Barcelona's factories provided better chances of finding work than the crisis-ridden fields of southern Spain. In some instances, unemployed workers who were repatriated as 'beggars' twice in the same week managed to return to Barcelona by the weekend.[87]

Undeterred, the ERC instituted new spatial controls, even though these contravened an earlier commitment enshrined in its party statutes to respect 'the freedom of movement and selection of residence'.[88] Although the ERC lacked the authority to regulate the access of Spanish citizens to Catalonia, it was determined to change Barcelona's status as an 'open city' and halt the migrant 'invasion' because, as *L'Opinió* put it, 'nobody would tolerate an unknown individual installing themselves in their house under the pretext that it is better than their own house'. The ERC was obsessed with erecting a *cordon sanitaire* of immigration controls, which would be enforced by a new immigration police based at Barcelona's railway stations and port and along the main road entrances to the city. The ERC also favoured a 'passport' system, requiring migrants to provide evidence of a job offer or proof of savings. Taken together, these 'hard but fair' measures would, it was claimed, reduce unemployment by at least 50 percent and 'prevent [the arrival of] those who come to create conflicts'.[89]

These measures were justified through a fierce propaganda offensive against migrants that continued throughout the Republic and that grew in direct proportion to the economic crisis and social conflict, despite evidence that migrant workers had, in their droves, voted for the ERC in the April and June 1931 elections and supported the push for Catalan autonomy. The attack on migrants coincided with the ascendancy of the racist nationalist wing of the ERC within what was still a very unstable coalition.[90] Non-Catalan workers were stigmatised by an anti-migrant backlash that evoked images of a 'systematic' 'flooding' by 'outsiders' of 'our home' (*casa nostra*): 'trains arrive full of people who come [to Barcelona] to be unemployed', forming 'swarms' and 'virulent plagues' of 'undeserving' poor and an 'army' of beggars. The unemployed were frequently described in the Esquerra press in Spanish (*los sin trabajo* or *los parados*), rather than in Catalan (*els sense feina* or *els parats*), a distinction that reflected the ERC's nationalist assumption that Catalonia was a harmonious and cohesive society and that migrants 'came' to Barcelona to 'be unemployed'.[91]

Murcians were singled out in particular, even though they accounted for only a small percentage of the overall migrant population in Barcelona. According to the stereotype of 'the illiterate Murcian', migrants were an inferior tribe of degenerates, like 'backward' and 'savage' African tribesmen, the source of crime, disease and conflict in much the same way as the Irish were vilified in Victorian England. This colonial-type mentality was often glimpsed in cartoons of Murcian men and women, who appeared as ugly, subhuman beings.[92] This was emphasised by Carles Sentís, a Catalan republican journalist who published a series of reports on La Torrassa ('Little Murcia') in l'Hospitalet, in which he focused on the morally abhorrent practices and general indiscipline of the migrants. For Sentís, the migrants were a primitive race with a 'prior' culture, living in a state of nature. In particular, he argued that the promiscuity of Murcian women and a 'regime of free love' was the cause of all social problems in La Torrassa, such as trachoma and juvenile delinquency.[93] Unfortunately for the rest of the unemployed, these 'vegetating' migrants were an 'asphyxiating' burden on already stretched welfare resources: 'when they arrive in a town the first thing they ask for is the welfare office', 'robbing the bread from our Catalan children' and converting Barcelona into one vast 'poor house'. Indeed, the ERC asserted that it wanted to do more to help the unemployed; however, it feared that this would 'attract all the unemployed of Spain to Barcelona'.[94]

ERC unemployment policies were premised on a 'secular Last Judgement'[95] designed to help the 'virtuous poor' while repressing the 'dishonest' and 'vicious' unemployed in workhouses. As one local republican explained, Barcelona Council's Welfare Department assessed 'who needs assistance and who must be repressed'.[96] In many respects, this was a continuation of the nineteenth-century distinction between the 'deserving' and the 'undeserving' poor: the former were deemed capable of self-improvement and thus merited official assistance, while the latter were 'undesirables', the 'professional poor', who represented a danger to society and had therefore to be repressed.[97] Accordingly, to qualify for assistance from the Comissió Pro-Obrers sense Treball, jobless workers had first to prove that they were 'true workers' and not 'vagrants' by agreeing to accept any work they might be offered. They also had to fulfil a series of stringent conditions, providing proof of residence in Barcelona for at least five years, a clause that excluded the substantial number of immigrants who came to work on Primo's public works programmes after 1926, as well as the thousands of workers who returned to the city after the collapse of the European economy in 1929 or who were exiled during the dictatorship. The Comissió also required the unemployed to demonstrate 'good conduct', a condition that effectively excluded any worker who had played an active role in the CNT.[98] Unsurprisingly, the Generalitat *borsa de treball* (labour exchange), which offered work to the 'deserving' unemployed, was criticised for ignoring the fate of workers who had been victimised by employers for their trade union activities.[99]

ERC policies resulted in an increase in the everyday harassment of the unemployed in the streets. One example is the persecution of 'undocumented' workers. The discretion once used by police officers in their dealings with unemployed workers who could not afford to keep their identity papers in order came to an abrupt end.[100] In addition, Barcelona Council issued a new *targeta d'obrer parat* (unemployed worker's card), an identity card scheme that recorded an individual's work history; anyone who did not carry the *targeta* faced the workhouse or repatriation.[101] The council also organised specialist teams to persecute the unemployed, creating 'a special police force' within the city's Guàrdia Urbana to undertake the 'laborious task' of 'purifying' the jobless; in the words of *L'Opinió*, the aim of the Council was 'not to give to the poor, but to repatriate outsiders and round up tramps' to separate the problem of unemployment from that of "idleness"'.[102] Given the repressive and exclusive nature of official unemployment bodies, migrant workers logically remained outside, so by mid-1931 fewer than 10,000 unemployed in Barcelona were registered with the Generalitat *borsa de treball*. More tellingly, in the construction sector, the main source of employment for migrants in Barcelona, only 3,593 had registered with the *borsa* at a time when unemployment in this industry was closer to 15,000.[103]

As the gulf between republican institutions and the unemployed grew, the authorities displayed increasing paranoia on the issue of public order, a sensitivity that extended to all manifestations of popular rowdiness, whether drunken behaviour or pitch invasions at football matches.[104] Property and street crime were even depicted as anti-governmental plots by the 'so-called unemployed'.[105] Concerns were expressed about gangs of 'enemies of the Republic' with the 'mission of committing robberies to discredit the republican regime'.[106] Civil Governor Companys warned that 'malefactors' (*maleantes*) and 'undesirable elements' were 'impersonating the unemployed' and 'stirring up' the jobless to commit 'criminal acts' and 'outrages' on behalf of 'anonymous subversives' and other 'armed enemies of the people' who wished to become the 'lords of the streets'. It was widely felt in republican circles that democratic freedoms were submitted to 'intolerable' abuse by the unemployed, who could 'feel brave' to protest with 'abandon', whereas they 'didn't mutter a word during seven contemptible years of dictatorship', when 'it was more dangerous'. Since the logic of the 'republic of order' denied the jobless any legitimate right to complain about their situation, anyone who did was an 'enemy of democracy'. This, in turn, inspired the Esquerra to insist that the main problem with unemployment was the protest that accompanied it.[107]

The 'republic of order' provided much common ground between the new authorities and middle-class and bourgeois pressure groups, who had traditionally craved social order and who demanded firm authority on the streets. In particular, strong law-and-order policies were central to appeasing and retaining the support of republicanism's middle-class base. The role of the unemployed in social protest prior to the Republic had caused much concern among the propertied and commercial sectors, and repatriation of the migrant unemployed, now the cornerstone of ERC unemployment policy, was a key demand of the bourgeoisie.[108] This must have been the source of great relief for big business, which was closely identified with the Right and which, at the start of the Republic, felt vulnerable and politically exposed following the transfer of power to the reformist liberal Left.[109] With right-wing parties in disarray until mid to late 1932, elite groups made their traditional public order concerns known to the new authorities through an intense and energetic lobbying campaign, organising a series of petitions and deputations to President Macià, the civil governor's office and the Interior Ministry in Madrid.[110] In one note to the Madrid government, the Cámara de Comercio y Navegación, the Barcelona Chamber of Commerce, described the 'gravity' of the social situation in Barcelona, which, it alleged, was 'strangling economic life'.[111] The FTN (Fomento del Trabajo Nacional, or Promotion of National Work), the most powerful Catalan bourgeois pressure group, and the Barcelona landlords' association, the COPUB, played a key role here, affirming that they were apolitical, 'always pro-government, on the side of order', while also giving notice that their future support for the Republic was contingent on the preservation of 'legality and order' and respect for private property, 'the most basic guarantee of a well-organised civilisation'.[112] In precisely the same way as it did during the monarchy, the FTN exaggerated the incidence of crime, complaining that 'professional villains' and 'the unwashed' (*los desaliñados*) had taken advantage of the 'absurd tolerance' of 'anarchy and freedom' during the period of regime transition, which resulted in an 'eruption of certain forms of criminality' and 'the extension of evil'. The FTN informed the authorities that they had a choice: either strengthen the 'principle of authority' and protect the 'men of trust and order' from 'banditry' or become 'the protector of all excesses…synonymous with disorder and licence'.[113] A similar message was conveyed by the conservative press, which highlighted instances of violence and illegality to justify increasing policing in 'a Barcelona that is so chaotic'.[114] *La Vanguardia* demanded 'inflexible toughness' and 'the old implacable severity', as anything else would result in 'civil intolerance' and 'irreverence'.[115]

This pressure for a 'republic of order' was sustained by urban middle-class pressure groups, many of which had close ties with local republican groups and were therefore able to exert even greater influence on the new authorities.[116] Various groups, ranging from taxi drivers, private security guards and nightwatchmen to restaurateurs, bar owners and hoteliers, complained to the authorities that Barcelona was gaining the reputation, domestically and internationally, as a 'den of thieves' and demanded a thorough repression of law breakers.[117] With the Generalitat and the council keen to develop the local tourist industry, such calls could not fall on deaf ears.[118] Shopkeepers and market traders added to the incessant pressure for repression. The Associació per la Defensa dels Venedors dels Mercats (Association for the Defence of Market Traders) called on the authorities to eliminate street trade 'using all means necessary', warning that otherwise its members would withhold tax payments, an important source of municipal revenue. Meanwhile, the Lliga de Defensa d'Industria i Comerç (League for the Defence of Industry and Commerce) announced that its members were ready to take the law into their own hands if 'unlicensed traders' remained on the streets. Although street trade affected only the narrow interests of commercial sectors, those who felt threatened by it appealed to a general interest, arguing that the 'illegal traders' were a criminal group that formed part of a wider pattern of lawlessness.[119]

During the first few months of the Republic, therefore, a new repressive consensus emerged between the authorities, the traditional elites and urban commercial sectors. President Macià, who was keen to woo liberal bourgeois elements, nurtured relations with the business community, and from the early summer of 1931, it was clear that a new, albeit unsteady, compact had been established between the economic and political powers in Barcelona. This was evident at the regular banquets attended by local notables throughout the Republic. At the first of these, an 'exquisite dinner' organised by the council for 500 guests in June 1931, President Macià, Mayor Aiguader i Miró, Companys and Generalitat ministers rubbed shoulders with the political and economic representatives of the oligarchy from the FTN, the COPUB and the Lliga, and their armed protectors, the Barcelona chief of police and high-ranking military officials.[120] Meanwhile, during periods of social unrest, the authorities provided police protection for individual employers, and although many industrialists persisted in their criticisms of the state of law and order, elite organisations like the FTN and the COPUB prudently expressed their gratitude to the civil governor and the police chief for defending the 'principle of authority' during strikes.[121]

3.2   Policing the 'republic of order'

Another area of overlap between the 'republicans of order' and the 'men of order' among the bourgeoisie was over the need to improve the effectiveness of the police. We saw in Chapter 1 how Barcelona's capitalists became frustrated by the operational limitations of the police during the monarchy. In keeping with their desire to forge a rational authority, the republicans were committed to reforming the security forces. The new standard bearers of republican order and legality in the cities were the Guardia de Asalto (Assault Guards), a motorised rapid response force. Created by Ángel Galarza, the PSOE chief of state security, and Maura, the interior minister, the *asaltos* were part of a new economy of repression designed to meet the potential threats to public order in Spain's increasingly complex urban centres, particularly the protest movements inspired by a modern labour movement. Galarza and Maura wished to break with the brutal 'excesses' of monarchist essays in urban social control, which inflamed rather than defused street conflicts. In contrast to the Guardia Civil, which relied on long-range armaments like the Mauser rifle and whose deployment in crowded city streets inevitably resulted in large numbers of civilian casualties, the conventional arms of the *asaltos* were the revolver and a 30-inch (80cm) leather truncheon, which encouraged them to move into the thick of any street protest, where they would neutralise the threat to public order by singling out 'ringleaders' for arrest, injuring only those who dared to cross the frontier of legality. The *asaltos* therefore represented a more deliberate, focused and inexorable repression. They were the shock troops of the Republic: all recruits had to meet exacting height and fitness requirements and, in the event of a serious threat to public order, they were equipped with machine guns, rifles and mortars. In Maura's opinion, they were 'a perfect force'.[122]

Lauded by the authorities as a thoroughly democratic and professional force, since they were recruited predominantly from republican and socialist parties, the *asaltos* were nevertheless politicised. Moreover, they did not break with the militaristic and authoritarian monarchist model of policing whereby army chiefs were entrusted with training the security forces: the first head of the *asaltos* was Lieutenant-Colonel Agustín Muñoz Grandes, who imposed military values on the corps. Another similarity between the Guardia Civil and the *asaltos* was that the new force had few contacts with the local population: most of the *asaltos* stationed in Barcelona originated from Galicia, central Spain and Aragón. In the view of one

Figure 3.2 Policing the city: assault guards patrolling l'Hospitalet, 1933
Source: L'Avenç Archive

historian, 'other than their name and uniform', there was little difference between the *asaltos* and the *civiles*.[123]

The commitment to the construction of a 'republic of order' ensured that republicans missed an opportunity to win the loyalty of the masses through a radical reform of the police. This was starkly revealed in the refusal of the new authorities to disband the Guardia Civil, even though republicans were fully apprised of the scale of popular hatred for a force that had been at the forefront of domestic repression during the Restoration.[124] From the start of the Republic, workers' groups argued that the disbandment of the Guardia Civil was central to the peaceful evolution of the regime, if not its survival.[125] (When General Sanjurjo, commander-in-chief of the Guardia Civil, launched a military coup in August 1932, this prophecy proved most apt.) Yet Maura, a 'fervent admirer' of the Guardia Civil, was convinced that the 'authority' and 'discipline' of the force could make it a prop for the new democratic institutions, and he 'categorically refused' to dissolve the force or reform it 'in such a way to give the impression that it had been dissolved'.[126]

There is no evidence that republican politicians were aware that the preservation of this traditionally anti-democratic and highly repressive body might imperil their goal of enhancing state legitimacy. Although Maura recognised the need to redeploy the Guardia Civil away from cities on the grounds that its methods resulted in unacceptable levels of civilian casualties, the authorities regarded Barcelona, Spain's largest city, as a special case. Guardia Civil stations and barracks thus remained within the city's boundaries, where the force was assigned an auxiliary policing role, principally when public order was under severe stress. Moreover, because the recruitment of the *asaltos* commenced only in June 1931, there was inevitably a transitional period during which the *civiles* would be responsible for public order. For instance, while the authorities rushed the first *asaltos* into service at the end of July, there were still only 800 in the city by mid-October, and in December it was reported that the political police was being deployed alongside the civil police to patrol country roads against highway robbers.[127]

In policing, as in other policy areas, the republicans had no coherent blueprint for reform and democratisation. It also seems that, given the central role accorded to the security forces in the 'republic of order', the republicans shied away from any far-reaching structural reform of the police. Even the notorious political police, the Brigada Policial Especializada en Anarquismo y Sindicalismo, a hotbed of monarchist reaction, was not purged, undergoing only a token change of name to become the Brigada de Investigación Social (Social Investigation Brigade).[128] The republicans also broke with an earlier commitment to end the internal policing function of the army, just as they failed to honour their pledge to disband the reactionary Sometent militia, the 'terror of both town and country' and the 'civic guard of capitalism', which had repressed pickets and strikers during the monarchy.[129] The piecemeal attitude of republicans in Madrid and Barcelona towards police reform was highlighted by a trip of Chief of State Security Galarza to the Catalan capital at the end of May 1931. During a number of press conferences, Galarza and Civil Governor Companys recognised that the Barcelona police force was a 'completely useless organisation', 'absolutely lacking in efficiency' and in need of 'a complete and total reorganisation'. Bizarrely, their proposal to make the local constabulary 'a more efficient instrument' and end the 'immorality' prevailing among officers consisted of removing a few 'bad eggs' while placing trusted figures in important command positions to oversee the removal of monarchists. Accordingly, Arturo Menéndez, an austere artillery captain who was indelibly marked by his military background and former member of the republican socialist Revolutionary Committee, became Barcelona chief of police.[130]

From the start of social conflict in the Republic, the limited horizons of the new democratic dawn were visible. Like during the monarchy, workers were regarded as either a real or a potential problem by the republican authorities, which failed to break with existing patterns of aggressive, anti-working class policing. This continuity reflected not so much the coherence or inconsistencies of the republican reform project; it derived rather from the imposition of a 'republic of order' on the coercive economic relations of the 1930s. When industrial disputes developed outside of the jurados Mixtos they were banned by the authorities, and the Guardia Civil employed its traditional *modus operandi* of shooting unarmed pickets and workers.[131] As was seen in the monarchy, police repression tended to deepen rather than

diminish protest cycles, and according to successive republican civil governors, the resources of the security forces were stretched to breaking point at
key moments during the Republic: the police were often unable to protect
individual industrialists, while on the streets they had to be supplemented by
Guardia Civil reinforcements from rural Catalonia and, at key moments, by
the army.[132]

Judging by the numerous incidents of police brutality towards workers, it is
easy to conclude that the unconditional support of the authorities encouraged
agents to act with impunity. Much violence was aimed at intimidating working-
class militants and those sympathetic to them. In mid-September 1931, just five
months into the Republic, the first *cenetista* died of injuries inflicted at the
Laietana Way police headquarters.[133] That same month, in an action that bore
all the hallmarks of an extra-judicial assassination, policemen escorting a group
of arrested workers to the Laietana Way station killed three and injured five
others. The police later claimed that they acted in self-defence, having come
under fire from some of the detainees and from the rooftops. The veracity of the
police version of events is open to question: not a single policeman was
wounded, and it was routine police procedure to search detainees for weapons
at the moment of arrest. The authorities nevertheless accepted the testimony of
the officers involved, and nobody was disciplined.[134] A few weeks later, in
early November, a group of prominent Barcelona anarchists were detained in
the street, taken to police headquarters and beaten up.[135] Bar owners who
allowed *cenetistas* to meet in their premises also faced regular police harassment, even the destruction of their property.[136]

A similar tolerance was witnessed in a series of shooting incidents during
the Republic involving both the security forces and armed militia like the
Sometent.[137] The tendency of the security forces was to shoot without asking
questions. Anyone who failed to stop for the police ran the risk of being
shot: in the proletarian *barri* of Clot, a youth running home during his lunch
break was shot in the back when he failed to hear a call to halt; the same fate
befell two Swedish sailors on shore leave in the Raval when they did not
respond to a police warning.[138] On the docks, an unemployed worker who
fished for food in the sea at the waterfront was killed by a policeman who
mistook him for a robber.[139] On another occasion, a group of *asaltos*
responded to the sudden backfiring of a car by opening fire and killing a
nightwatchman.[140] Meanwhile, on the estates and fields surrounding
Barcelona, where there was great concern about the theft of crops by the
unemployed, the Guardia Civil and the Sometent killed several people in
circumstances that were far from clear.[141]

Although the police were probably less corrupt during the Republic, many
officers behaved as if they were beyond the law, occasionally stealing property
during house searches.[142] Throughout the Republic, there was a steady flow of
reports of drunken violence by policemen.[143] It was not uncommon for agents
to draw their firearms, which they were allowed to carry at all times for their
personal protection, on unsuspecting members of the public. On one occasion,

a nightwatchman was threatened with a pistol when he disturbed an off-duty *asalto* having sex in a city park in the early hours of the morning.[144]

It was the unemployed, though, who bore the brunt of police repression. It has been argued, by Howard Becker and others, that in times of economic crisis, the authorities rely on the security forces and the penal system to impose social discipline on the growing numbers of workers no longer subjected to the informal, everyday fetters and coercion of the workplace.[145] This is confirmed by the creation of new police squads like the council-run Brigada per a la Repressió de la Venta Ambulant (Brigade for the Repression of Street Trade) and the teams established to rid the port of 'villainous people' and for 'rounding up beggars'.[146] Police violence towards the unemployed was directed more at imposing subservience than enforcing laws. Public spaces – the streets and parks where the unemployed spent a lot of time – were the site for this violence. Jobless workers were periodically stopped by police in the streets and beaten up.[147] One worker was arrested by an *asalto* for 'looking suspiciously' at him. In l'Hospitalet, two workers required 'hospital treatment' after 'being insolent' to the police, while a couple of workers who mocked a bourgeois on a bicycle were beaten up by the Guardia Civil for 'larking about'.[148]

The practices deployed in the consolidation of the 'republic of order' resulted in a sharp closure of the democratic polity and the erosion of civil liberties. Ironically, in their desire to impose respect for the 'rule of law', the republicans employed illegal and unconstitutional methods like detention without trial, whereby the civil governor ordered the internment of an individual for two weeks. This draconian tactic was resurrected early in the Republic, even though republicans had earlier vowed to outlaw the practice. For instance, during a strike in July 1931, the civil governor ordered that 'anyone who looks suspicious will be detained [without trial]…including [for] mere moral complicity' in the stoppage.[149] Organisers of groups of unemployed workers were also interned, sometimes for several months. There were many allegations, and much supporting evidence, that detainees, who had no access to lawyers, were frequently mistreated and beaten in the course of 'intensive interviewing' by the police.[150]

'Detention without trial' was particularly favoured by Josep Oriol Anguera de Sojo, a pious Catholic lawyer and, according to one of his close allies, 'an inflexible authoritarian', who became Barcelona civil governor in early August 1931.[151] Anguera de Sojo was obsessed with imposing the 'principle of authority' on the streets regardless of the cost and the consequences involved. He believed that 'agitators', 'individuals with bad antecedents' and anyone guilty of what he called 'public scandal' immediately forfeited their civil liberties and were therefore liable to 'detention without trial'.[152] The principal assumption behind 'detention without trial' – that social protest would disappear with the internment of 200 or so 'social delinquents' – shaped the policies of successive civil governors in republican Barcelona.[153] Thus, during the CNT general strike of May 1933, Claudí

Ametlla, himself a trained lawyer, admitted that he defeated the mobilisation 'thanks to an abuse of my legal power', which included infringing the civil liberties of 'dozens of men' who were interned and by bullying taxi drivers (he threatened the renewal of their licences, an area over which he had no authority) to place their cars at the disposal of the police. Although some internees might be held for six months and longer, such practices were justified in terms of 'sacrosanct public order'.[154]

Detention without trial was frequently combined with the police 'swoop' (*ràtzia*), a lightning raid by the security forces, sometimes backed by army units, into the *barris* which would then be searched thoroughly from house to house; all those who looked 'suspicious' or who happened to be present in a place deemed to be a 'criminal haunt', such as a bar frequented by 'malefactors', were detained, held overnight at a police station, fingerprinted, registered and photographed before their release.[155] Subsequently, whenever there was increased tension in the city, such as on the eve of a major strike or prior to the arrival of an important government figure, the police would detain the 'usual suspects' and those registered as 'dangerous'.[156]

In keeping with the republicans' prevailing legalistic mentality, and perhaps reflecting a certain discomfort or sensitivity among republican lawyers at the use of unconstitutional measures, extraordinary legislation was promulgated that rendered legal many of these draconian practices. The first example was the Ley de Defensa de la República (Law for the Defence of the Republic), a classic law of exception passed in late October 1931, which effectively castrated constitutional freedoms and was, in the opinion of Azaña, 'necessary to govern'.[157] The supporters of the new law, which was based on the 1922 German Law for the Defence of Democracy, regarded it as a defence against violent threats to the regime from both Right and Left. In practice, however, the law was used much more against 'enemies of the Republic' on the Left and reflected republican paranoia about revolutionary conspiracies. The thrust of this law was its preventive nature: as Azaña noted, it was not designed to repress an actual threat but 'to avoid the birth of that danger'. Tellingly, despite the significance of this law and its implications for the future of democracy, the Ley de Defensa was passed without any real parliamentary discussion, pushed through with the full support of PSOE deputies, most notably de los Ríos and Largo Caballero. Republicans who previously waxed democratic were converted into partisans of draconian legislation. Macià, who had once stated his opposition to such laws of exception, accepted the new law without any qualms, while Azaña's only regret was that the new law had not been introduced earlier.[158]

Directed at 'subversion', a vague category that could be applied to any protest behaviour, the Ley de Defensa established new categories of deviancy and, in doing so, created new illegalities. For example, by making it a crime to spread information likely to incite a breach of the law or bring discredit to state institutions, the Ley de Defensa had serious implications for the freedom of expression of the radical press.[159] Moreover, by giving the interior minister new powers to ban meetings and rallies by groups and unions deemed 'anti-republican', this law limited the right of association of anarchist and communist groups, who were forbidden to hold any meeting, rally or assembly without giving prior notice to the police.[160] All 'legal' assemblies, meetings and rallies were subject to the scrutiny of a *delegado gubernamental* (government agent), normally a policemen, who had powers to dissolve the gathering at any moment. The powers of the *delegado gubernamental* were open to abuse: if they believed that the rhetoric of speakers was likely to threaten public order, they could order the closing of the assembly. Meanwhile, any attempt to hold a secret meeting – be it of activists or for educational purposes – was treated as a 'clandestine' and 'illegal' gathering.[161] In the syndical sphere, the Ley de Defensa de la República reinforced Largo Caballero's labour legislation, prohibiting strikes that did not give eight days notice to the authorities or that appeared to have 'political' motives.[162] This law meant that activities such as picketing and any kind of clash with the police were treated as an attack on the Republic.

In 1933, the Ley de Defensa was superseded by the Ley de Orden Público (Public Order Act), which was drafted by Anguera de Sojo, who, after his spell as Barcelona civil governor, became attorney general. Anguera de Sojo's experience of governing Barcelona's rebellious city spaces in 1931, combined with the lively interest that he retained in the politics of a city that he visited every weekend, doubtless played a part in the drafting of this law. His Ley de Orden Público allowed curfews to be imposed on specific neighbourhoods and legalised police *ràtzies* (swoops). In what was a significant militarisation of policing, the Ley de Orden Público allowed for the suppression of the constitution in times of social unrest and its replacement by martial law and the transfer of civil power to the army high command until 'order' had been re-established. Meanwhile, in a direct imitation of monarchist crowd control tactics, Article 38 of the Ley de Orden Público allowed the authorities to 'prohibit the formation of all types of groups on the public highway. ... If orders to disperse are disobeyed, after three warning signals the security forces will use the necessary force to re-establish normality. No warning is necessary if the security forces come under attack'.[163]

Other preventive police practices were legalised in the Ley de Vagos y Maleantes (Law against Vagrants and Malefactors), also passed in 1933. Concerned not with the prosecution of criminal acts, which were already punishable under the penal code, the Ley de Vagos y Maleantes sought to help to identify and repress *homo criminalis*: those individuals whose 'state of dangerousness' (*peligrosidad*) posed a potential threat to social order and the criminal code. This was to be achieved through the creation of special police units and courts, which, suitably informed by contemporary legal and scientific principles, would detain, evaluate and classify individuals, ordering the isolation of 'socially dangerous types' in labour and concentration camps. Inspired by Luis Jiménez de Asúa, a respected PSOE jurist, this law was conceived as part of a modernising project designed to rationalise penology by introducing a more proportionate and measured system of punishment that would, in turn, enhance the credibility of the state. Ironically, beneath this veneer of modernity and the appearance of the 'neutral' application of justice, the Ley de Vagos y Maleantes was a blunt instrument of repression that legalised a much older and unjust economy of repression (internment without trial) and combined this with the additional threat of an unspecified period of incarceration.[164] (According to Ametlla, the idea for a Ley de Vagos y Maleantes was first conceived by Attorney General Anguera de Sojo, who, as Barcelona civil governor, was instrumental in reintroducing 'internment without trial' in 1931.[165])

The Vagrancy Act can be viewed as a product of the law-and-order consensus established between the old elites and the republican authorities in 1931 that 'dangerous' and 'violent' individuals were 'not real citizens' and thus did not deserve the same civil and political rights available to the rest of the population.[166] The FTN welcomed this 'excellent' law as 'vital for the defence of society', one that would halt 'the avalanche of disorder'.[167] *La Vanguardia* summed up the concerns of the traditional 'men of order', identifying the significance of a law that separated the 'dangerous' unemployed from the 'calm' ones, thus preventing 'a gang of wolves springing up extemporaneously from the depth of the mass, like in the great revolutions'.[168] The ruling parties in the Generalitat were similarly enraptured with a law that they saw as 'one of the most successful to come out of the parliament of the Republic', which could isolate the 'respectable unemployed' from the 'dangerous poor', 'hobos' and 'tramps', whom they believed to be responsible for crime, social violence, monarchist intrigues, prostitution and street trade.[169] Although the USC, the Esquerra's socialist coalition partners, reviled Hitler's detention centres, they had no qualms about establishing their own concentration camps for the unemployed in Catalonia.[170] Indeed, this law reflected the social-democratic disdain for the traditions of the 'rough' working class, a social sector that was cast as brutish, disorderly and undisciplined and whose dedication to gambling and drinking made it a mortal danger to the republican-socialist agenda for change.[171]

Although justified as a measure against pimps and drug pushers, in the hands of the police the Ley de Vagos y Maleantes added to the escalating legislative terror against the unemployed, effectively criminalising practices like street trade that were viewed as a danger to the 'republic of order'. The police used the law in a highly arbitrary fashion, and any worker who did not enjoy regular work could be stopped and searched on the grounds that they appeared 'suspicious'. In particular, the Vagrancy Act was used as an anti-nomadic device to impose a fixed and repressive spatial ordering on migrant and seasonal workers, who were interned in camps, where they were subjected to capitalist time–space discipline. Even urban workers who travelled around workshops in search of work were interned as 'vagrants'.[172] There were also several cases of workers being arrested in bars on their day off. Age and disability were no exemption from the concentration camps: an 84-year-old man was interned for begging, as was a partially sighted man who lived from tips earned by opening car doors for guests outside a posh city centre hotel.[173]

As well as repressing those who could find no place within the capitalist labour market, the Ley de Vagos y Maleantes was widely used against those who refused to work within the market and/or resisted it. Opponents of government economic and social policies, who might previously have been interned without trial, were detained under the law as 'dangerous' internal enemies of the state; these included *cenetistas* found fly posting and distributing manifestos, unemployed organisers, and Italian and Argentinian anti-fascist exiles in Barcelona. Jobless anarchists and those who had been either victimised or blacklisted were also charged under the Vagrancy Act. Several *cenetistas* who had previously been interned without trial were released and immediately jailed as 'vagrants'. There were even cases of *cenetistas* with regular employment being detained under the law, sometimes while at work. One group of Barcelona *cenetistas*, including Durruti and Francisco Ascaso, were charged with 'vagrancy' while on a CNT speaking tour in Andalusia, even though they had jobs in a textile factory which, through an agreement with their employer, were kept open during their absences on union affairs.[174]

The local urban policies developed by the Esquerra in Barcelona Council and the Generalitat provide further examples of the way in which the republican veneer of modernity occluded the survival of traditional practices. Although the local authorities renamed streets and housing projects after martyrs of the anti-monarchist struggle, for all their reformist rhetoric, housing reform, the cornerstone of municipal socialism, was largely ignored: policy options such as rent controls and the compulsory purchase of slum housing stock were untried, despite rents rising throughout the 1930s.[175] Nor were the debt-ridden local authorities able to oversee the urbanisation and sanitisation of the peripheral *barris*. Instead, the 'republicans of order' regarded Barcelona in much the same way as the monarchist 'men of order': an unruly, menacing space, a city besieged by the tyrannical mob of the Raval. The ERC attempted to resolve urban tensions with a spatial militarism that bore many similarities to the policies developed under earlier regimes. Shanty dwellers were subjected to brutal slum clearance programmes that, while ridding the city of some of the miserable *barracas* (around 1,500 remained in Montjuïc in 1932[176]), inevitably increased homelessness.[177] Meanwhile, in February 1932, the local authorities opened a fourth group of *cases barates* on the outskirts of the city, consisting of 534 housing units.[178] The ERC's reformist fanfare could not conceal the fact that this was a continuation of the exclusionary housing policies begun during the monarchy and the dictatorship.

The dichotomy between the reformist promise and the repressive practice of the ERC's urban governance were most vividly witnessed in relation to the Raval, Barcelona's oldest working-class *barri*. As we saw in Chapter 1, over the years the Raval became demonised as 'Chinatown'. The Esquerra and its supporters assiduously cultivated moral panics surrounding the petty criminals, pimps, and opium and cocaine dealers of 'Chinatown', an area they portrayed as existing outside official control.[179] From the start of the Republic, the need to defend 'public morality' from the threat of the 'Chinatown underworld' (*baix fons*) was invoked as a justification for a systematic preventive police offensive against what *La Vanguardia* described as a 'place that seems to have its own laws'.[180] There were frequent police swoops against bars and 'criminal haunts', with those unfortunate enough to be in the vicinity often interned without trial. However, it was noticeable that police repression in the Raval was directed heavily at union offices, worker activists, street traders and the unemployed as much as the 'bad people' of the 'underworld'.[181]

Growing official concern at 'Chinatown' culminated in the drawing up of the 'Plà Macià' (Macià Plan), which formed part of the Generalitat's modernist plan for rational urban development and regional planning.[182] The Plà Macià was commissioned in the spring of 1932, a collaborative venture between the *catalaniste* planning think tank, the GATCPAC (Grup d'Arquitectes i Tècnics Catalans or Catalan Technicians and Architects Group) and Le Corbusier, the Svengali of modernist urban technocratic utopias; following a meeting with Macià in Barcelona, Le Corbusier's admiration of authority obliged him to name the project in honour of the Catalan president.[183] Inspired by his maxim 'Architecture or revolution. Revolution can be avoided', Le Corbusier's ideas can be looked upon as the perfect urbanist foil to the 'republic of order'.[184] Unveiled in 1934, the Plà Macià contained the promise of modernity, of a 'new Barcelona', remapping the entire region in accordance with the most advanced principles of urban planning as embodied by the GATCPAC. The crux of the Plà Macià revolved around the demolition of the Raval, an area visited by Le Corbusier during one of his trips to Barcelona that left him appalled by its unsalubrious and dilapidated housing stock and urban density. The solution, he felt, lay in the 'mopping up' (*esponjament*) of the Raval's streets, which would give way to a series of straight roads and major thoroughfares capable of aiding the movement of goods throughout the Barcelona area.[185] In this way, the old city would be regenerated and the flow of goods and services improved, bringing 'progress' and increased industrial power to the whole of Catalonia. New housing stock for the former inhabitants of the Raval was to be created in the form of modern, Bauhaus-style multi-story blocks of dwellings in the Sant Andreu *barri*, away from the city centre. Through a system of zoning, establishing separate spheres for living, working, trading and relaxing, the Plà Macià aimed at increasing the consumption of urban services in what was a step towards a bureaucratic and technocratic society of controlled consumerism. Thus, alongside the creation of new schools and open spaces, new leisure forms were conceived, to be located in the Ciutat de repòs i de vacances (City of leisure and holidays), a coastal holiday zone south of Barcelona in the Castelldefells area.

Like so many republican projects, the Plà Macià was constrained both by budgetary problems and by the outbreak of the Spanish Civil War in 1936, after which it remained a utopian dream of Generalitat planners.[186] Commentators often interpret the Plà Macià and its radical *avant-garde* supporters in the GATCPAC as being informed by progressive, democratic and anti-fascist ideas.[187] However, this urban plan typified the repressive undercurrent of many republican reforms. Moreover, the Plà Macià was not dissimilar to the nineteenth-century Hausmannisation of Paris: both plans were appropriate to the economic and security requirements of the holders of social, economic and political power of the day, driving major roads through the narrow, winding streets of working-class districts in order to facilitate the movement of goods and, when necessary, the forces of public order.[188]

The main difference between earlier urban plans for Barcelona and the Plà Macià was that the latter was packaged as a technocratic urban utopia of the enlightened middle class.[189] However, the vision of successive generations of planners was remarkably similar: they would leave the alienating and oppressive economic structure of the city intact (the class origins of ERC planners impeded them from limiting the freedom of market forces and private property, arguably the *sine qua non* for genuine, rational planning[190]) while constructing a hierarchical, tightly controlled city in which the 'cancer' of disorder would be banished, with all classes accepting their place and function within a rational urban system. The security dimensions of the Plà Macià cannot therefore be denied. First, it aimed at reducing Barcelona's domination of Catalonia, thereby establishing a new political equilibrium based on strengthened Catalan provinces. This was to be achieved by containing the capital's growth and stimulating new foci of industrial development outside the Catalan capital, thus increasing the industrial and political importance of the bastions of popular *catalanisme* in the countryside.[191]

Second, there would be new, subtle, bureaucratic forms of repression. Central here was the reform of the social context facing the hitherto rebellious working class. A host of ERC reformers, physicians, educationalists, architects and planners, led by the mayor, Aiguader i Miró, exuded an idealistic ideology of environmental determinism: they assumed that informed public agencies could compensate for problems of urban design and transform the physical environment of the *barris*, thereby altering the social reality of the working class. Equally, traditional working-class identity and culture would be broken down by new leisure pursuits and consumerism. This new social control project hinged on the pacification of the Raval, Barcelona's most unruly space. On one occasion, Companys spoke in confidence to one of Le Corbusier's disciples of his desire to demolish the Raval 'with cannon shot'.[192] The planned destruction and 'complete sterilisation' of the Raval was merely the most recent attempt by urban elites to reconquer the old city from the 'perishing classes' and defuse many of the tensions occasioned by Barcelona's uncontrolled development, something that had been coveted by urban planners since Cerdà.[193] The Plà Macià can therefore be seen as a continuation of the obsession of nineteenth-century reformers for 'cleansing' and 'purifying' the city, for inducing a new spatial order with a surgeon's incision in a 'sick', 'diseased' space. This spatial exclusionism was glimpsed earlier with the construction of the Laietana Way and the *cases barates*, as urban elites used slum clearance to force the 'dangerous classes' out of the city centre, dispersing them far away from the centres of economic and political power. In the case of the Raval, Le Corbusier's oft-cited plan to 'kill the street'[194] meant relocating a historically rebellious community in newly designed spaces where they would be more easily contained and controlled by the security forces. Consequently, the social networks and local solidarities that had sustained anti-capitalist resistance and social protest in the Raval would be disrupted. Yet, with the Raval being the birthplace of the Barcelona working class, its demolition was an act of aggression against a local history of proletarian resistance: it signified the destruction of key historical and symbolic spaces of the local proletariat, the elimination of the sites of memory of resistance to capital, of demonstrations, riots, barricades, insurrections and a whole array of protest behaviour that had taken place since the 1830s. These spaces of hope and struggle, a source of inspiration to many workers, were to be replaced with major roads, places without history, around which new solidarities would not be possible. In this way, the authorities would redefine space, and the way it was used and experienced by those who inhabited it, in the hope that this would nullify urban contradictions and conflicts within the Raval.

3.3   Conclusion

The dependence of the 'republic of order' on draconian legislation such as the Ley de Defensa de la República, the Ley de Orden Público and the Ley de Vagos y Maleantes, and coercive urban practices such as the Plà Macià, signified a major advance on the 'normal' repertoire of state control and an important step on the road to an authoritarian, 'law-and-order state'. Faced with class struggle, the republicans effectively failed in two of the key challenges they faced: to guarantee civil liberties and to end persecutory policing. Instead, they consolidated their power like typical 'men of order', raising the costs of mobilisation by stockpiling repressive legislation, militarising public order and routinely deploying repression.[195] Rather than invest in far-reaching reform packages that might have defused social tensions, the authorities increased spending on the security forces: the complement of paramilitary *asaltos* in Barcelona grew throughout the 1930s, rising from just under 2,000 in mid-1932 to 6,000 in July 1936.[196] Although the 'republic of order' was justified in terms of the interests of a reformist future, the excluding practices and stratagems employed by the republicans eroded civil liberties and the 'rule of law', weakening an already fragile liberal-democratic public sphere. The Ley de Vagos y Maleantes, which selectively denied the rights of citizenship to the dispossessed, demonstrated the readiness of republicans to distance themselves from their previous belief in the formal equality of all citizens before the law. Equally, the legalisation of preventive imprisonment that was central to the Ley de Vagos was anathema to the classical legal 'presumption of innocence'. This metamorphosis was most clearly embodied by Jiménez de Asúa, the architect of the 1931 constitution, who by drafting the Ley de Vagos consciously circumvented core constitutional freedoms such as the freedom of circulation of all citizens throughout state territory.[197] The Republic that had promised so much for the masses had assumed a character that many workers would find as reprehensible as the monarchy that preceded it.

4 The proletarian city and the Second Republic

4.1 The reconstruction of the proletarian city

This chapter explores the response of the proletarian city to the new legal reality introduced after 14 April in Barcelona. As we saw in Chapter 3, the collective euphoria at the coming of the Republic was great in CNT circles.[1] In many parts of Barcelona, local *cenetistas* played an active role in proclaiming the Republic.[2] The CNT clearly imposed its political preferences on events. For example, shortly after the proclamation of the Republic, an armed group of *cenetistas* escorted Companys to the civil governor's building so that he could take office.[3] *Solidaridad Obrera* welcomed the Republic as a triumph of 'the will of the people' and 'the most hallowed aspirations of freedom and justice'.[4] On the day after the birth of the Republic, as a gesture of solidarity, the Barcelona CNT declared a general strike that affected all branches of industry apart from essential food and transport services. The evident goodwill of the CNT leaders towards the ERC doubtless explains Macià's attempt to bring the CNT leader Angel Pestaña into his first government as Generalitat minister for public works.[5] Since government participation was alien to CNT traditions and would almost certainly have divided the union, this came to nothing; nevertheless, a hastily convened plenum of the Catalan CRT delegated Pestaña and a colleague to liase with the Generalitat.[6] At state level, the CNT National Committee announced its 'peaceful disposition' towards the Republic.[7] Meanwhile, a joint manifesto issued by the Catalan CRT and the Barcelona local federation warned workers of the need to protect the Republic from the danger of anti-democratic military action.[8] Clearly, the CNT leadership was keen to stabilise the new regime during what it regarded as a 'new era'.[9]

Testifying to the vitality of the workers' public sphere, after April 1931 the various social, cultural and economic institutions responsible for the main improvements in the lives of Barcelona's workers during the first third of the twentieth century were reorganised. Tenants' groups and food cooperatives flourished. In particular, the CNT emerged resurgent: its militant traditions of sacrifice, struggle and solidarity attracted thousands of expectant workers, its unions becoming a receptacle for the new working class formed under the dictatorship in the 1920s, which was, for the first time, free to establish real organisational links. Badly paid and unskilled migrant workers in the rapidly developed peripheral *barris* flooded into the CNT, along with many child workers, some as young as ten and with no previous experience of union organisation.[10] In May 1931 alone, the Catalan CRT admitted 100,000 new members; by August, the Confederation could claim 400,000 affiliates in Catalonia, while the Barcelona CNT announced that it had encadred a staggering 58 percent of the city's proletariat.[11]

In many *barris*, the CNT became the dominant organising structure and there was an increasingly symbiotic relationship between the organised labour movement and closely knit working-class communities. In part, this reflected the strong sense of collective optimism and feeling of triumph in the *barris* following the demise of the monarchy; it also stemmed from the creation of new union centres and CNT district committees.[12] Thus, an alternative moral geography was established in the newly developed red belt of the city, in *barris* such as Sant Andreu and within the various groups of *cases barates*, where workers were unable to attend union offices in the city centre on a daily basis. This new, organised working-class sociability was epitomised by the expansion of the l'Hospitalet CNT, particularly the La Torrassa District Committee, where a lively, vibrant grassroots union flourished. The district committees advanced a vision of the Republic of the ghettos, a decentralised, direct form of participatory democracy that mirrored the sociability of the *barris*. Local union bodies also promised to improve the economic position of the *barris* through communal rather than individual responses to poverty, the *sine qua non* for the formation of a self-sufficient working-class economy designed to withstand the impositions of the market.

The development of *ateneus* was no less dramatic. Throughout the dictatorship in the 1920s, many anarchists and anarcho-syndicalists had immersed themselves in cultural and educational activities. Although the illiteracy rate in 1930s Barcelona (15 percent) was well below the Spanish average (32 percent), educational facilities in the *barris* were inadequate: for example, in Poble Sec, in January 1931, there were school places for only 200 of the estimated 7,000 children in the district.[13] Illiteracy was unevenly distributed across Barcelona and remained far higher in the *barris*, particularly those with large concentrations of unskilled migrants such as Barceloneta, where over 50 percent of the population was unable to read and write.[14] To counter this, *ateneus* were established in the red belt of the city, becoming an important, and sometimes the sole, source of education. For instance, the Ateneo Cultural de Defensa Obrera (Cultural Atheneum for Workers' Defence) formed in the Can Tunis *cases barates* in April 1930, organised a school for 400 local children.[15] Such was the demand for their educational services that *ateneus* were periodically forced to find larger premises.[16] One of the most important of these schools was the Escuela Natura in the Clot *barri*. Financed by the Textile Union, the Escuela Natura, which also organised a popular summer camp in a country house in the Pyrennean town of Puigcerdà, had around 250 pupils, including many of the children of leading *cenetistas*. Educated by a team of teachers under the supervision of rationalist pedagogue Juan Puig Elías, all punishments were eschewed in favour of reason.[17] Besides enriching pedagogical and artistic life in the *barris*, the *ateneus* transmitted the alternative values of a rebel, anti-capitalist, anti-hierarchical culture that laid the basis for contestation and protest.[18]

The development of the *ateneus* inevitably deepened connections between the anarchists and the masses in the *barris*, particularly the youth. This helps to explain the development of a new element in the working-class sphere of 1930s Barcelona: the FAI (Federación Anarquista Ibérica or Iberian Anarchist Federation). Formed in Valencia in 1927 as a pan-Iberian anarchist secret society, the FAI was barely organised at state level by 1931, although its members had already established themselves in some *barris*.[19] Since the 1920s, clandestine anarchist *grupos de afinidad* had become more grounded in local society and, while these remained, perforce, relatively closed groups, they increasingly drew on multiple family, community, workplace and spatial loyalties, meeting regularly in neighbourhood cooperatives, *ateneus*, cafes and bars.[20] Perhaps the most famous of these bars was La Tranquilidad (described by one anarchist habitué as 'the least tranquil cafe' in the neighbourhood) on Paral.lel, where Durruti and his *grupo* established themselves for much of the Republic.[21] Run by a former CNT militant, this bar, where non-consumption was tolerated and tap water provided for those unable to purchase drinks, was extremely popular with workers and anarchists alike as a space for discussion and debate. So, while Barcelona had long attracted anarchists from across the Spanish state and beyond, the consolidation of an exclusively anarchist network of sociability in the late 1920s and early 1930s made it possible for newly arrived anarchists to find out where *grupos* met and integrate themselves quickly into the city. This was timely, because the establishment of dictatorships in Italy, Argentina, Uruguay and Cuba during the same years resulted in the exile of many anarchists, a large number of whom took refuge in Barcelona. Some of these anarchists, for instance Fidel Miró, a Catalan expelled from Cuba, and Sinesio García Delgado (aka Diego Abad de Santillán), a Spaniard forced out of Argentina, would become leading figures in the FAI.[22]

4.2   The divisions in the CNT

As the proletarian public sphere re-emerged, so too did the divisions within it. Primo de Rivera's coup effectively neutralised the CNT's internal divisions, quite possibly preventing a split within the union. In 1931, the largest of the factions inside the Catalan CRT was the anarcho-syndicalists, who effectively controlled the Confederation at state level and in Barcelona during the transition from monarchy to Republic. The two most prominent anarcho-syndicalists were Pestaña and Peiró, both of whom had previously been anarchist *énragés*.[23] The anarcho-syndicalists regarded the revolution as an essentially constructive exercise that required union organisation to be perfected and stable workplace committees that would eventually assume responsibility for running the post-revolutionary economy to be created.[24] Many of the anarcho-syndicalist leaders were older militants who had lived through the postwar repression of *pistolerisme* and dictatorship; their experience of leading the CNT during the *dictablanda* had apprised them of the need to navigate a path through the limited freedoms offered by capitalist society and of the importance of having friends in the democratic camp. The prioritisation by the anarcho-syndicalist CNT leadership of practical trade unionism over their ultimate revolutionary objectives inclined them towards a reformist praxis of coexistence with the Republic.

At the start of 1931 this pro-republican stance was not the source of significant political division within the CNT. The dominant feeling in CNT ranks, even among most of the 'pure' anarchists, was that the unions needed time to regain their former strength before advancing along the revolutionary road. Even inside the Builders' Union, the union that had the strongest anarchist component, there was a strong feeling that the birth of the Republic had to be assisted.[25] This republican intoxication extended to the most radical factions among the anarchists. *El Luchador*, the weekly newspaper of the Montseny family, the self-styled purveyors of anarchist propriety, praised President Macià and called on the working class to be ready to defend the Republic against monarchical restoration.[26]

Only a minority of anarchists were opposed to the Republic from its birth, yet this was a theoretical or strategic opposition rather than a practical one. This position can be traced to Nosotros ('Us'; formerly Los Solidarios) *grupo de afinidad*, whose members feared that a stabilised republican democracy might seduce workers at the ballot box and domesticate the CNT. According to García Oliver, a prominent Nosotros member, this could be best avoided through 'insurrectionary pendulum actions': violent mobilisations perpetrated by small groups of activists designed to help the masses to 'overcome the complex of fear they felt towards repressive state forces, the army and the police'. Because they were intended to provoke violence from the state and the Right, supporters of these 'revolutionary gymnastics' hoped that they would create a spiral of protest capable of attracting broad sections of the masses until they provided the spark for a revolutionary fire that would devour the Republic.[27] Alternatively, should these insurrectionary exercises fail to produce the revolution, they would at least force the authorities to employ draconian measures, thereby impeding the institutionalisation of the proletariat within the Republic. This perspective, which was rooted in a late nineteenth-century concept of anarchist insurrectionism, ignored the greater repressive capacity of the modern state. Nevertheless, this strategy was consistent with the experiences of the seasoned *grupistas* from the period of *pistolerisme*, activists who typically conflated traditional direct action with small group violence and who possessed a rather simplistic, militaristic mentality that located complex political problems in terms of relations of force. The promise of impending revolutionary action also appealed to younger activists, many of whom were captivated by the accelerated pace of political change during 1930–31 and who were optimistic that the Republic would, sooner rather than later, suffer the same fate as the dictatorship and the monarchy.[28]

While Nosotros had little influence within the Confederation at the start of the Republic, it did manage to secure one of its main objectives at the CNT National Plenum held in Madrid at the end of April 1931, where it was agreed that *comités de defensa confederal* (confederal defence committees) should be formed. These paramilitary formations, comprised of union militants and anarchists, would be on a permanent war footing, ready to defend the CNT from aggression by either the employers or the state.[29] Whereas the anarcho-syndicalists viewed the defence committees as a reserve force, capable of augmenting the struggle for trade union control of society, the radicals regarded this parallel structure as 'the armed wing of the violent revolution'[30] or, in the words of Antonio Ortiz, another Nosotros member, 'a vanguard which had to channel [*encauzar*] the revolution'.[31]

However, it would be a mistake to conclude that the radicals were spoiling for a fight with the new authorities. Nosotros, like the moderates in the CNT, had invested hope in the Republic: Durruti, frequently seen as the embodiment of intransigent anarchism, praised Macià for his 'inherent goodness' and his 'purity and integrity'.[32] Moreover, while the insurrectionary position adopted by Nosotros later became identified with the FAI, it is worth bearing in mind that, at the start of the Republic, Nosotros was not affiliated to the FAI and that many anarchists were critical of the vanguard role they ascribed to a small, dedicated minority, which they denounced as 'anarcho-Bolshevism'. Certainly, the FAI was the radical wing of the anarchist movement, but it was a heterogeneous body, consisting of a variety of groups, including pacifists, Malthusians, Esperantists, naturists, educationalists, artistic groups and theatre troupes, all of which were united only in their opposition to reformism and communism within the CNT.[33]

Only the dissident communists – the smallest of the three factions within the CNT – appreciated in April 1931 that conflict between the unions and the Republic was inevitable. Organised politically within the BOC (Bloc Obrer i Camperol, or Workers' and Peasants' Bloc), these anti-Stalinist communists voiced the concerns of a tiny minority within the working class that believed in the need for genuinely revolutionary politics and argued that exogenous socio-political forces, such as the middle-class republicans, could not be trusted. Devoid of the democratic illusions that prevailed among the CNT leadership and in anarchist circles, the *bloquistas* expected no benevolence from the new regime: 'the republican government can never be on the side of the workers, nor can it be neutral. It is a bourgeois government and, as such, it must forcefully defend the bourgeoisie against the proletariat'.[34] The prescience of this prophecy would soon be evident.

4.3   The 'hot summer' of 1931

From July throughout the summer, there was a veritable explosion of trade union conflicts in Barcelona as workers took advantage of their new-found freedoms to launch disputes that affected individual workshops and entire industries, including vital sectors of the economy, such as Barcelona docks, and the Telefónica, the main communications company in Spain. These mobilisations peaked in August, when there were forty-one strikes in Barcelona alone, including a successful stoppage of 40,000 metalworkers, who stayed out for the whole month.[35] Indicative of the upsurge of militancy, two separate disputes over working practices and victimisation culminated in factory occupations.[36]

Figure 4.1 Thousands of strikers and CNT supporters occupy Republic Square after a demonstration during the telephone workers' strike, summer 1931

Source: Francesc Bonamusa, Pere Gabriel, Josep Lluís Martín Ramos and Josep Termes, *Història Gràfica del Moviment Obrer a Catalunya*, Barcelona, 1989, p.255

While the summer wave of strikes was unprecedented in the history of Catalan industrial relations, exceeding even the mobilisations that followed World War One, contrary to the conspiracy theories that prevailed in republican circles, it was neither a revolutionary attack on the state nor an attack on the Republic. Rather, to comprehend the reasons for the strikes, we need to recall that, from the advent of industrialisation in Catalonia right up until the 1930s, employers had more or less continuously enjoyed the upper hand in labour issues. Only briefly, after World War One, did the CNT manage to limit the freedom of capital before being driven underground by Primo de Rivera's labour-repressive dictatorship. Meanwhile, during 1930–31, working-class living standards deteriorated further owing to the growth of unemployment and inflation of basic foodstuffs and rents.[37] As we saw in Chapter 3, the republican authorities continued to impose the same liberal economic policies that had generated enormous effervescence in the *barris* during previous regimes, leaving the material basis of working-class discontent intact and, moreover, allowing the cost of public transport, which had been remarkably stable between 1907 and 1931, to rise sharply during the 1930s.[38] Interestingly, therefore, in July 1931 the British consul-general expressed his surprise at the restraint of the unions, given that 'there is no doubt that there is still a good deal of underpaid labour in Barcelona'.[39]

The open, decentralised nature of the CNT and its responsiveness to rank-and-file sentiments was a key factor in the eruption of strikes. Strikes had a very simple appeal for the union grassroots – the promise of collective improvement – and many took place through the CNT but were not necessarily under the direct control of the union, as shop stewards were either simply unprepared or unable to neutralise the groundswell in favour of action.[40] Strikes were then, primarily, part of a working-class campaign to recapture ground lost during a period when employers enjoyed *carte blanche* in the workplace.[41] Thus most CNT demands revolved around 'bread-and-butter' issues aimed at improving working conditions by increasing wages, limiting the length of the working day and abolishing intensive forms of exploitation such as piecework and child labour. Many of these demands were longstanding ambitions of the CNT and were not designed to endanger the consolidation of the Republic. For instance, one of the most common union demands in 1931 was that employers recognise the CNT *bolsa de trabajo* (labour exchange), through which the Confederation hoped to reintegrate the unemployed into the workplace and limit the untrammelled right of employers to sack workers by fiat.[42] In a more general sense, the CNT sought to regain the collective dignity of the proletariat, hence its demands for the reinstatement of workers victimised during the 1917 railway workers' conflict and the 1919 'La Canadenca' strike.

In another sense, the explosion of strikes can be attributed to the political context. First, it was inevitable that, as the political repression of the monarchy and dictatorship ended, the accumulated desire for change would result in an increase in collective social demands. Indeed, the CNT base, which was now free to organise collectively, was keen to assert its demands and flex its collective muscles following seven years of enforced slumber. Second, republican promises to break with the past and improve upon the governments of the monarchy and the dictatorship aroused enormous expec-

Figure 4.2 Workers in conversation outside their workplace during a labour dispute
during the Second Republic

Source: Francesc Bonamusa, Pere Gabriel, Josep Lluís Martín Ramos and Josep Termes, *Història
Gràfica del Moviment Obrer a Catalunya*, Barcelona, 1989, p.259

tations in the new authorities. In power, therefore, republicans faced the
dilemmas of the sorcerer's apprentice: many workers had projected their
hopes for social justice onto the republican project and expected that the new
authorities would, as a minimum, bring sweeping improvements in their
living standards; in the best scenario, they believed that the Republic would
usher in a new era of social equality. Consequently, workers believed that
the Republic provided new openings for collective demands, which many
expected to be either well received by the authorities or at least to be
received differently.[43] Thus, in the days of hope after the birth of the
Republic, the climate of branch union assemblies was one of ebullience; the
dominant feeling was that the time was ripe for change. In specific cases,
such as the Telefónica conflict, workers went on strike to achieve objectives
that some members of the first republican-socialist coalition government had
committed themselves to while in opposition.[44]

The response of employers to the new political situation was a further
factor in the strike wave. While employers spoke of the need to preserve
'authority' and 'order', their well-established practice of ignoring labour
legislation survived. Early in the Republic, at a time when bourgeois pressure
groups were calling on the government to repress 'lawlessness' without

quarter, business associations flouted new laws limiting the length of the working day and the use of child labour, as well as health and safety legislation. Moreover, employers actively victimised CNT activists who demanded the implementation of the new laws. A frequent piece of advice given by employers to sacked workers was 'Let the Republic give you work!' or 'Let the Republic feed you!'[45] Predictably, the CNT picked up the gauntlet thrown down by the employers, embarking on a series of conflicts to ensure that industrialists complied with labour legislation. With considerable hypocrisy, therefore, business groups denounced what they charged was the CNT's 'systematic campaign' of 'blackmail' and the 'morbid pleasure' that its activists derived from the 'sport' of striking.[46]

Barcelona's tense labour relations were aggravated by the manner in which the first government of the Republic set about repressing the direct action culture of the CNT rank and file. Largo Caballero, the UGT general secretary and labour minister, exploited his office to pursue the sectarian goal of fostering the small foci of socialist trade unionism in Barcelona. He hoped to achieve this through his labour courts, the *jurados mixtos*, which effectively criminalised the main practices of the CNT and, in doing so, ultimately paved the way for the rupture between *cenetismo* and the Republic. Inspired by the corporatist traditions of the skilled sections of the Madrid working class, who favoured class collaboration over mobilisation and were prepared to submit their professional demands to arbitration, the *jurados* were attractive only to a small minority of better-off workers in Barcelona. In the wood sector, artisans and some self-employed workers joined the UGT[47], while at La Maquinista, the city's biggest metal works, the few well-paid skilled and office workers were *ugetistas*, whereas the mass of the workforce was organised in the CNT.[48] Yet, overall, the *jurados* were singularly unsuited to Barcelona's industrial conditions. In the first place, the industrial courts were at variance with the structure of local capitalism, which was presided over by a confrontational bourgeoisie that had historically rejected the presence of independent workplace unions and where conflicts between capital and labour tended to be open and unmediated. Second, the *jurados* were alien to Barcelona's dominant working-class traditions of direct action, which, as we saw in Chapter 2, were at variance with social-democratic culture and its emphasis on deferred gratification. The ponderous and bureaucratic procedures of the industrial courts held little appeal for the predominantly unskilled workforce, for whom temporary contracts and low wages were the norm: they wanted an immediate improvement in their lot and appreciated that direct action was the most appropriate strategy for extracting concessions from an aggressive bourgeoisie.

Either oblivious to the consequences for the development of CNT–government relations or, more likely, as part of a strategy to weaken the UGT's rival by placing it in direct opposition to the state, in the summer of 1931 Largo Caballero drove the Confederation into a corner over the question of the *jurados*, particularly on the docks, where a vicious union war erupted.

Certainly, the CNT leaders regarded Largo Caballero's intransigence as a deliberate provocation: given his earlier connivance with Primo de Rivera in an attempt to gain an advantage over the CNT, many *cenetistas* could not help but conclude that he was now seeking to manipulate republican institutions for similar ends. In practical terms, meanwhile, it was impossible for the CNT to accept the *jurados*. CNT power had always been expressed through mobilisation: it was in the streets where activists believed that concessions were to be extracted from the employers and the state; to enter the industrial courts, which were foreign to the culture of the movement, was an unacceptable risk for CNT organisers, who had no experience of arbitration procedures. Hence, the CNT claimed that the *jurados* were a 'social and judicial monstrosity [designed] to trap the proletariat', part of a strategy from above to co-opt the movement (or its leaders) and demobilise the grassroots.[49]

The stance of the government towards CNT mobilisations was vividly seen in the strike at the ITT-owned Telefónica, a company whose labour practices had been roundly condemned by republicans and socialists during the final months of struggle against the monarchy. On the very first day of the Telefónica stoppage in July, the government declared the strike 'illegal', since the CNT had not submitted its demands to the *jurados*.[50] According to Interior Minister Maura, the conflict was 'political', an accusation that is perhaps best applied to the stance of his cabinet colleague, Largo Caballero, who was keen to build up UGT strength in the telecommunications sector and who saw the dispute as an opportunity to deal a blow to the socialist unions' main enemy in this sector.[51] By outlawing CNT struggles, union conflicts were effectively politicised and converted into struggles with the state, setting the government on a collision course with the CNT and making inter-union conflict inevitable.

As CNT strikes developed outside the *jurados*, official discourse came to resemble that of the old monarchist authorities. The republican socialist supporters of the Madrid government described the CNT as the 'open enemies of the new regime' whose 'pernicious leaders' had embarked on a conscious offensive against the Republic. Increasingly, the authorities emphasised the actions of CNT pickets, a consensus forming around the view that *cenetistas* were instigating random terror on the streets. *Crisol*, a Madrid-based left-wing republican paper, likened CNT 'violence' to that of the Nazis, while *El Socialista*, the main PSOE daily, denounced the editorial board of *Solidaridad Obrera*, then controlled by moderate anarcho-syndicalists, as 'gunmen' (*pistoleros*).[52] This was something of an irony, because there is strong evidence that, notwithstanding the UGT's public celebrations of republican legality, *ugetistas* perpetrated a significant amount of the violence in Barcelona during the first weeks of the Republic. For instance, in early June a dispute broke out at a box factory near the port after the management had victimised some CNT organisers and replaced them with UGT members. When a CNT delegation approached the factory to protest at the sackings, *ugetistas* opened fired with pistols, injuring thirteen *cenetistas*.[53] This was followed by a similar attack in Blanes, along the coast from Barcelona, which left four *cenetistas* wounded.[54]

The failure of the police to make any arrests after these acts of aggression doubtless encouraged many *cenetistas* to assume personal responsibility for their physical security and helps to explain the growing number of arms on the streets. A further factor here was evidence that former members of the right-wing Sindicatos Libres, including several of its gunmen, had joined the UGT. Indeed, during 1930–31, the Barcelona UGT became the rallying point for a mishmash of skilled and conservative workers, such as private security guards, pastry chefs and piano makers, all of whom were united by a virulent hatred of the CNT and its aggressive methods of class struggle. Moreover, it was in the service industries, a traditional source of Libre strength, where the Barcelona UGT enjoyed significant growth during the Republic.[55]

4.4   'Overrun by the masses': the radicalisation of the CNT

In keeping with its wait-and-see attitude towards the Republic, the moderate anarcho-syndicalist leadership was keen to ensure that relations between the CNT and the new authorities did not become too confrontational. Accordingly, as the summer became 'hot', the CNT leadership felt obliged to channel the frustration felt by many among the rank-and-file of the organisation at the repressive logic of the 'republic of order'. Rather than denounce the Republic *tout court*, the moderates' criticisms focused on Maura and Largo Caballero, two ministers within the republican–socialist coalition government whose 'anti-anarchist psychological make-up' most predisposed them against the CNT. The attack on Largo Caballero focused on his labour laws and the 'legal violence' of the *jurados*, while Maura, the son of Antonio Maura, the architect of the suppression of the 1909 uprising in Barcelona, became known as 'el hijo de Maura' (the son of Maura), a play on a popular expression that implied that the interior minister was of uncertain parentage. In June, the moderates began a campaign to have Maura and Largo Caballero removed from government, an initiative that was premised on the reformist assumption that the CNT could coexist happily with a Republic in which the two offending ministers did not hold cabinet positions. Largo Caballero and the rest of the government were warned that by attacking the CNT they were 'playing with fire and it is possible that this fire will consume your plans'.[56] Yet the moderates continued to hope that the government would somehow rectify its position and treat the CNT differently. *Solidaridad Obrera* even demanded that Maura be tried under republican law as a monarchist *provocateur*, while in July, when the two ministers supported the management during the Telefónica strike, the CNT denounced them as 'lackeys of US imperialism'.[57]

The CNT leaders also embarked upon a rearguard struggle against the growing militancy of the grassroots of the movement, which had expected so much from the Republic. One of the main concerns of the leadership was that an endless succession of strikes could sap proletarian energies and, possibly, provoke a wave of state repression that would endanger future revolutionary developments.[58] The moderates therefore hoped to regulate the flow of conflicts, proposing that only those unions with the most disadvantaged members be allowed to initiate strike actions, during which time other unions would be required to provide economic support. When possible, local union leaders intervened to prevent strikes, even accepting the intervention of the authorities, such as the civil governor, to avert strikes. The leadership also successfully persuaded both the textile and builders' unions to postpone strikes, forestalling conflicts that would have affected up to 100,000 workers in the Barcelona area.[59] Nevertheless, at the end of May 1931, the leadership conceded that the CNT had been 'overrun by the masses'.[60]

As the strikes grew in number, the moderate anarcho-syndicalist leadership criticised the role of the *delegados de taller* (shop stewards). These activists constituted the backbone of the CNT: they rarely spoke in public, but they were highly respected figures in the factories, where they organised the unions on a daily basis, convening meetings and collecting financial contributions. Extremely sensitive to rank-and-file opinion, the *delegados de taller* played a decisive role in articulating working-class demands. According to the moderates, the 'irresponsibility' of the *delegados de taller* resulted in premature strikes, which had few prospects for victory, an abuse of CNT federalism and a burden on the resources of the Barcelona local federation and other unions that were obliged to provide solidarity.[61]

While it is incontrovertible that some strikes were indeed badly organised, the depiction of the *delegados de taller* as a small minority of agitators was unfair, since often the workplace organisers were pushed into conflicts by a rank-and-file impatient for an improvement in their social position. Moreover, that the Builders' Union, the only union under the control of the radical anarchists at this time, pulled back from the brink of strike action in the summer of 1931 at the behest of the moderate-controlled CNT local federation, undermines suggestions that the strike wave was the work of the radicals.

But there was no diminution in the overall level of union conflict, as strike actions inevitably spilled out into the community. For the workers directly involved, and for their relatives and neighbours, strikes were highly emotional situations: the decision to withdraw one's labour signified sacrifice and possibly a trip to the pawnshop; it also intensified social life in the *barris*, increasing contact between strikers and their friends, family and neighbours. The sympathy felt for strikers fostered a new sense of community belonging, something that was encouraged by the organised solidarity of the CNT. Consequently, entire districts became radicalised, transforming the *barris* from a community of itself (objective) into a community for itself (subjective). An example of this process came during the Telefónica conflict, which was acclaimed as a heroic struggle of a 'community' of workers standing united against a coalition of hostile external forces: North American capital, the Madrid-based state and its armed executives. For many workers in the *barris*, active picketing, which appeared as coercion and intimidation to outsiders, signified a necessary imposition of the collective will.[62] *Solidaridad Obrera* encouraged 'hospital visits' for the 'scabs' that broke 'class discipline', printing their names and addresses.[63] Pickets were so fearsome that there were reports of 'scabs' crossing picket lines dressed as women. Confirming the efficacy of direct action tactics, many recalcitrant employers acceded to union demands only after intense picketing, such as during the particularly violent barbers' strike in the summer, when, following repeated attacks by pickets on salons, they agreed to wage rises and recognised the CNT and its *bolsa de trabajo*.[64]

The CNT grew during the course of the summer mobilisations, drawing in hundreds of thousands of workers who saw it as the best vehicle to pursue their day-to-day material aspirations. This underlined the extent to which CNT membership was always conditional on the ability of its unions to fight, and sometimes win, against the bourgeoisie. If the unions relented or wavered, the danger existed that concessions already won would be eroded, along with the chance to achieve future gains through direct action.

The stage was set for confrontation between the CNT and the authorities. Since the authorities were incapable of either promulgating reforms capable of placating grassroots demands or co-opting the most important community and working-class leaders in Barcelona, they were obliged to confront the strike movement. The Guardia Civil was sent to evict workers forcibly from occupied factories in Poblenou and Sants.[65] In the telephone strike, Maura issued instructions that 'energetic measures' be deployed against strikers, while Galarza, the republican security chief, informed both police and army that any pickets found to be involved in sabotage were to be shot on sight.[66] As the judicial net widened, pickets faced new persecution on the streets. Union flyers, a favoured means by which the CNT responded quickly to events and communicated with the *barris*, were declared 'illegal' on the grounds that they contained material that had not been approved by the censor, and activists who distributed or posted these news sheets were liable to arrest.[67] Similarly, strikers who used verbal persuasion to encourage workers to join the stoppage were arrested for 'threatening behaviour'. Following a clash between police and pickets in Madrid, Miss Telefónica 1931, the winner of the company's beauty pageant, was detained, while in Barcelona a group of young children was arrested in the Raval for taunting a telephonist with chants of 'Maria the scab'. The appearance of the *asaltos* on the streets during the Telefónica strike and their deployment by the authorities to guard 'scabs' and impose 'lightning bans' on union assemblies prompted violent clashes with pickets.[68]

Repression increased the costs and risks of CNT protests and raised the stakes in industrial conflict. One of the consequences of the struggle to defend strikes from state repression and from the violence of UGT members was the consolidation of the CNT defence committees, as pickets and activists asserted their right to self-defence. For instance, forbidden activi-

Figure 4.3 An artists' view of picket sabotage in the 1931 Telephone workers' strike

Source: Francesc Bonamusa, Pere Gabriel, Josep Lluís Martín Ramos and Josep Termes, *Història Gràfica del Moviment Obrer a Catalunya*, Barcelona, 1989, p.254

ties such as fly-posting and leafleting came to be performed by armed defence committees. Based on small, clandestine networks in the unions and the *barris*, these semi-formal bodies were enveloped in increasingly violent clashes with the security forces. One of the bloodiest nights was on 23 July. During 21–22 July, a CNT meeting place in Seville was subjected to artillery bombardment, and four pickets were murdered by police.[69] Tension was therefore high among *cenetistas* in Barcelona and, in the early evening of 23 July, two *asaltos* were seriously wounded after they attempted to detain a group of militants outside the CNT Textile Union offices in the anarchist stronghold of Clot. Later that night, a contingent of *asaltos* and police raided an alleged 'clandestine meeting' at the Builders' Union offices in the Raval. Doubtless fearing that the police would apply the Ley de Fugas, the activists inside the building greeted the security forces with a hail of gunfire, leading to a four-hour siege during which the Builders' Union offices were surrounded by hundreds of policemen, *asaltos* and soldiers. Eventually, the *grupistas* surrendered to the army. Six workers died, and there were dozens of wounded on both sides.[70]

The 'republic of order' had sufficient repressive capacity to block the initial push of the Barcelona CNT, even though at the peak of the strike wave it proved necessary to reinforce the security forces with Guardia Civil and military units. Thus, at the end of August, Civil Governor Anguera de Sojo requested that 400 members of the Guardia Civil be sent to the city.[71] In September, during what was, according to Anguera de Sojo, 'a critical time' in which 'we either guarantee order once and for all or suffer a setback', a further 100 civil guards arrived.[72] That same month, the Guardia Civil complement in the city was increased on two further occasions in the ongoing battle for the streets.[73] As summer turned to autumn, the collective strength of the CNT was significantly undermined by repression; strikes lasted longer and were less likely to end in victory for the unions. Sensing that they had weathered the storm of protest, the employers, who felt amply protected by Civil Governor Anguera de Sojo, went on the offensive, victimising activists and sacking workers. In the metal industry, the deal brokered by the authorities at the end of August, which saw employers accept most union demands, including an end to piecework, wage rises and the establishment of an unemployment subsidy, was wrecked in the autumn as the authorities turned a blind eye to infringements of the settlement. Even *La Vanguardia* was moved to condemn heavy-handed employers as a danger to 'civic peace'.[74]

The repression of CNT mobilisations in the summer of 1931 drove a wedge between the regime and the workers who had expected so much from it. Aggressive policing in the *barris* aimed at dislocating the structures that connected the CNT with working-class communities was seen to favour the same business sectors that prospered under the monarchy. This was bitterly resented by many workers, who experienced republican state power on the streets as little more than the police and army, a continuation of repressive, class-based policing. This was hardly surprising when we recall that the new authorities ignored CNT demands for a far-reaching reform of the police and the dissolution of the most despised branches of the monarchist security forces: the Guardia Civil, the Sometent and the secret political police.[75] Displaying extreme political subjectivity, the republicans overrated the openness of their system of governance: for many on the streets, the use of the *asaltos* and the invasion of *barris* under the cover of the Ley de Defensa de la República signified an increase in the militarisation of urban space. The contradictory efforts of Maura and Largo Caballero to change popular attitudes towards the state and authority were never likely to have much of an impact upon the views of the unskilled and underemployed sectors of the Barcelona proletariat. This was quickly acknowledged by the authorities, who appreciated the difficulties they faced in penetrating the *barris* and 'the genuine lack of auxiliary elements' who could provide much-needed intelligence.[76] Meanwhile, the logic of the 'republic of order' was inimical to republican hopes of securing the loyalty of the masses; as repression grew, plans to stabilise the regime by establishing popular state institutions were revealed to be a chimera, a utopia in the liberal republican mindset. Indeed, the *asaltos* demonstrated that they could be as brutal as the monarchist police, and it was not long before their readiness to give 'boxing lessons' to workers made them as feared as the Guardia Civil.[77] Even the right-wing *La Vanguardia* acknowledged that the majority of Barcelona's inhabitants harboured a 'general disrespect' towards the police.[78] The growing hatred of the police, who appeared as the guardians of class justice and privilege in the *barris*, led many workers to become alienated from the 'republic of order', which contrasted sharply with the 'republic of freedom' that they had expected. The republican utopia thus dissolved under the acid of working-class struggle.

The clash between the 'republic of order' and the *cenetista* grassroots radicalised the union rank-and-file and made the position of the quietist moderate union leadership untenable. Central to this radicalisation process were the *delegados de taller*, who saw their syndical ambitions frustrated by the *jurados* and the other fetters placed on the everyday activities of the CNT. Rather than being a panacea for proletarian ills, 'this lamentable Republic' bore the hallmarks of previous regimes: the republican obsession with order equalled that of the monarchist authorities;[79] employers amassed the lion's share of wealth, while workers received 'wages of misery that impede us from satisfying the most elementary necessities';[80] and the 'scabbing' by 'UGT turncoats' was again tolerated by the authorities and justified by the PSOE daily, *El Socialista*, the 'police journal' and 'official organ' of the Catalan bourgeoisie.[81] In the face of this hostile coalition of forces, the prospects for CNT mobilisations were reduced: in October, a union delegate complained at a plenum of the Barcelona local federation that union practices were effectively 'useless' because the authorities 'don't allow us to act at all'.[82]

Some historians have suggested that the FAI orchestrated a seizure of power within the CNT to oust the moderate leadership.[83] Such a view is based on a serious misjudgement about the nature of the CNT, which was a 'bottom-up' and not a 'top-down' organisation: as we saw when the moderates dominated the CNT National Committee during 1931, the union 'leadership' was never really in a position to exert control over the rank-and-file. Moreover, given the decentralised, federalist structure of the CNT, there was no organisational apparatus to seize. Meanwhile, the FAI lacked any real organisational coherence until around 1934–35 and was in no position to 'seize' control of the CNT in 1931, when it had around 2,000 activists throughout Spain.[84] At the start of the Republic, the FAI in Barcelona, the capital of Iberian anarchism, did not even possess a typewriter: anarchists stuck handwritten notes to the city's walls and copied pages from pamphlets and books and circulated them for propaganda purposes.[85]

The displacement of the moderate anarcho-syndicalists during mid to late 1931 and the ascendancy of militant anarchists and radical anarcho-syndicalists reflected the ability of the latter to channel the disaffection of the *delegados de taller* with the Republic. As state repression rendered conventional mass mobilisations difficult, the radicals and armed activists from the defence committees took the initiative, advocating, and sometimes deploying 'revolutionary violence', which, they believed, would frighten the bourgeoisie and their republican political masters into surrender. The radicals lacked a clear programme. Some were FAI members; others, such as Durruti and his *grupo*, who came to be synonymous with the radicalised CNT before the civil war, were identified with the FAI, or at least what was understood publicly to be the position of the FAI. More than anything though, Durruti and Nosotros were anarchist streetfighters who advocated a programme of action that appeared to be in tune with the needs of the moment. Their origins in a similar unskilled background to many thousands of workers in Barcelona meant that they had a language through which they could tap into and express the disenchantment of the growing number of workers, including the *delegados de taller*, who felt defrauded by the Republic. This disillusionment was not theoretical or doctrinal: it originated not from anarchist pamphlets and newspapers but from the frustration borne from the repression of the everyday trade union practices of the CNT. Nevertheless, the repressive turn of the 'Police Republic' confirmed libertarian orthodoxy – that the constituted power is always an anti-proletarian force, 'unconditionally on the side of the bourgeoisie' and the protector of the rule of capital. Accordingly, whereas CNT leaders initially vented their fury at one or two cabinet ministers, the radicals denounced the entire political class of the 'republic of jailed workers', which, they charged, was comprised of politicians no different from their monarchist predecessors, or, as *Solidaridad Obrera* put it, 'the same dogs with different collars'.[86]

The radicals took heart from the signs of mass impatience at the tempo of change after April 1931, particularly the clashes between workers and the security forces, which, they believed, were evidence that the masses were overcoming their 'complex of fear'. All that remained was to create a spark that would inspire the workers to envelop all Spain in a huge revolutionary conflagration.[87] Notwithstanding their immense revolutionary optimism, the violent guerrilla struggles advocated by the radicals in the defence committees were however, an armed politics of frustration, a symptom of the decline of the curve of social protest that began during 1930–31. These trends are more evident still when we turn our attention to the extra-industrial struggles of the unemployed.

5 The struggle to survive

Unemployed self-help and direct action during the Republic

5.1 Unemployed street politics

This chapter will explore the patterns of social and political polarisation that developed around the unemployed and extra-industrial struggles in Barcelona. As we saw in Chapter 3, the unemployed played a prominent role in the social protest of 1930–31. Following the birth of the Republic, the overriding objective of the moderate anarcho-syndicalists, then hegemonic within the CNT, was the organisation of the unemployed in union-controlled labour exchanges (*bolsas de trabajo*). These had several attractions. For instance, since the existence of a reserve army of labour endangered the authority of the unions, the *bolsas* established a vital connection between the unemployed and the labour movement, ensuring that the jobless remained under the influence of class culture. The CNT's aim was to force employers to recruit new operatives exclusively through its *bolsas*, thereby providing work for the unemployed. From a syndicalist/corporatist perspective, the *bolsas* would allow the CNT to extend its control over the supply of labour and, more generally, enhance its power over the economy and society. The *bolsas* were also schools for industrial activism: unemployed members were encouraged to undertake union activities, such as fly-posting and picketing and other tasks, which were remunerated at the daily wage rate for semi-skilled manual labourers; following the creation of the defence committees, the *bolsas* served as a conveyor belt for recruits to the paramilitary bodies inside the CNT.[1] Lastly, and perhaps most importantly, the *bolsas* enhanced militancy: strikes could begin in the knowledge that the jobless would not become a weapon in the hands of the employers.

From the start of the Republic though, most unemployed practices developed outside the unions, in the streets, and they were invariably conditioned by the memory of past survival strategies employed by the dispossessed in Barcelona. Illegality, both individual and collective, provides one such example. Notwithstanding its various forms, most illegality can be described as 'occasional' or circumstantial, a response to the precarious conditions of everyday life, rather than 'professional'. Indeed, in the absence of a developed welfare system, a significant part of the urban population was obliged to transgress the law in order to guarantee its physical and material survival.[2] Hence the regularity with which basic foodstuffs such as fruit, vegetables and bread, the fundamental components of proletarian diets, were seized from bakeries and shops. The *modus operandi* commonly employed was for a lone woman to enter a shop or bakery and order provisions as if undertaking her daily shopping. Once the groceries were packed, 'persons unknown' would enter the shop and ensure that the foodstuffs were removed. Normally, the implication or threat of violence was enough to allow the seizure of foodstuffs but, when appropriate, these were backed up with physical force.[3] Larger groups of unemployed workers sometimes joined together in more organised raids on port stores and warehouses, actions that were often conducted at night.[4] Another common way the unemployed ate was 'eating without paying' or, as it was sometimes described in the bourgeois press, *comiendo a la fuerza* (literally, 'eating by force'). This was generally the preserve of impecunious males, who, either alone or in groups, entered a restaurant or bar, ordered and consumed food, before either refusing to pay or fleeing. On one occasion, jobless workers succeeded in demanding food in the Barcelona Ritz. In a rare and hedonistic case, three unemployed men spent a night on the town in a Paral.lel cabaret before leaving in the early hours of the morning without paying a large drinks bill. More frequently, groups of unemployed workers toured hotels and restaurants demanding food from the kitchens.[5] In the peripheral *barris*, where the city met the countryside, the unemployed often seized food from nearby farms and, throughout the republican years, the estates around l'Hospitalet to the south of Barcelona and Santa Coloma to the north were raided by the jobless. So great was the problem that, according to the Sociedad de Patronos Cultivadores (Small Farmers' Association) in l'Hospitalet, a local agrarian pressure group, by the end of 1931 farmers were obliged to guard crops 'at all hours, day and night'.[6] There is also evidence that unemployed workers requisitioned valuable items, presumably with the intention of selling them to third parties, namely the regular thefts of religious icons from churches, bicycles and car parts (one unemployed mechanic was detained stripping down a luxury car in the street).[7]

In a city with a buoyant clandestine firearms market, it was not difficult for unemployed workers to acquire pistols for armed robberies. Again, this assumed a variety of forms. In inter-class spaces such as the Rambles, armed street crime was directed at rich pedestrians. More common were armed raids on apartments and villas in the bourgeois districts of Sarrià, Pedralbes and Vallvidrera, and on the weekend homes of the well-to-do scattered around the outskirts of Barcelona.[8] Another favoured location for hold-ups by lone gunmen and small groups was the isolated *carreteras* (roads) that connected Barcelona with neighbouring towns. Press and police reports reveal that on a single evening an active armed group might stop up to five cars before returning to the city.[9] Taxi drivers' purses were frequently targeted: the common practice was to hire a taxi and direct it to a suitably isolated destination, often the outlying *carreteras*, before seizing the driver's money and, sometimes, the taxi. Other popular targets of armed illegality were rent or debt collectors.[10] All this occurred alongside a constant stream of attacks on commercial establishments such as tobacconists, bars and jewellery shops and the armed bank couriers who transported money around the city.[11]

Owing to the absence of reliable crime statistics, it is difficult to gauge the extent of these practices. The crime pages of the daily press recorded illegality, but this was often exaggerated for reasons of political expediency. Equally, the victims of these attacks were often warned by their assailants not to report attacks to the police. As *La Vanguardia* noted, robberies on the *carreteras* were regularly underreported due to fear of reprisals; this was confirmed by the police, who offered full confidentiality to victims of robberies on secluded country roads, which by night were popular with rich lovers.[12]

What we can be sure about is the strong normative element contained within the practices documented above; this is perhaps clearest in the removal of collection boxes and icons from churches. Many unemployed workers were ready to justify stepping outside the law in order to survive the ravages of the recession. For example, two unemployed workers confronted by a farmer while seizing crops informed him: 'The land is for everyone!'[13] Shopkeepers and shop workers regularly reported that those who seized groceries from shops justified their actions in terms of the recession, that they were unemployed and, through no fault of their own, lacked the economic resources to purchase victuals. Similarly, those who ate without paying in bars and restaurants justified their actions in terms of their 'right to life'.[14]

Unemployed illegality was so deeply embedded in the property relations of 1930s Barcelona that it is difficult to disguise its pronounced class character. In the overwhelming majority of cases, unemployed self-help was directed at the middle and upper classes, the real possessors of wealth in the city. For instance, since car ownership was possible only for the wealthy, the hold-ups on the *carreteras* affected elite members of society exclusively. Conversely, there were very few recorded instances of intra-working class crime. While this is not easy to measure, if we recall that *Solidaridad Obrera* made every effort to reflect the everyday concerns of Barcelona's workers, from dangerous stray dogs to pollution, it is striking that reports of workers falling victim to street crime or theft were exceptionally rare. In 1931, there was one report of a worker robbed of his wages at gunpoint. The response of *Solidaridad Obrera* was both predictable and illustrative: it invited workers to take direct measures of self-defence, counselling that 'it is necessary for us workers to arm ourselves, to prevent them [i.e. criminals] from robbing us of the fruit of the sweat of our brows'.[15] Workers certainly resented those who attempted to steal from them, as was discovered by a foolhardy pickpocket (*ratero*) who infiltrated the CNT May Day demonstration in search of wallets and watches: the hapless felon was spotted by marchers and heavily beaten before police managed to protect him from the wrath of the crowd.[16]

Another practice that developed in direct proportion to unemployment was the street trade of jobless workers. These jobless traders peddled foodstuffs, which, for the most part, they purchased from wholesale markets with their savings, although it was also rumoured that some produce was seized from farms and allotments.[17] Because street traders habitually sold their wares near markets and shopping areas and had no expenses, they could undercut market traders and shopkeepers, making them very popular with working-class consumers, especially in the poorest *barris*. Such was the growth of this commerce that street traders constructed *el mercadet*, a purpose-built trading zone near the Raval, which allowed free access to all unemployed vendors and attracted working-class consumers from all over Barcelona.[18] While not a form of direct protest, street trade nevertheless reflected a popular struggle for a new proletarian economy.

This same struggle can be seen in agitation against Barcelona's high rents, which started in October 1930.[19] Shortly before the birth of the Republic, a rent strike began in the waterfront district of Barceloneta, quickly spreading to the poorest *barris*, such as the *cases barates*; localised rent protests also began in Sants, a *barri* with a large factory proletariat, and areas with concentrations of shanty houses.[20] For the most part, the rent strike was a protest of the unemployed, the unskilled and the underpaid, for whom issues of material life and consumption loomed large: for the jobless, it signalled complete liberation from the burden of rent payments; for the low-paid, it promised an immediate material gain without the hardships of an industrial stoppage. Although the rent strike demonstrates the capability

Figure 5.1 A female street trader with her wares

Source: L'Avenç Archive

of the dispossessed to assert their aspirations spontaneously, it did not occur in a vacuum: it was rooted in a multi-faceted web of relations and solidarities derived from neighbours and kinship and drew on long traditions of community autonomy. In keeping with all rent strikes, this mobilisation was strengthened by democratic grassroots decision making.[21] It was also inextricably tied to the radical mobilising culture propounded by the CNT since World War One. While the CNT did not initiate the rent boycott, it was no coincidence that it began in Barceloneta, an important union stronghold and the site of La Maquinista, Barcelona's biggest metal factory, and *cenetistas* were deeply involved in the street committees and neighbourhood groups that organised the strike.

Nor can the development of the rent strike be separated from the mass expectations aroused by republicans before and after the birth of the Republic, when they proposed a new deal for tenants and rent controls.[22] (Naturally, once the rent strike had spread across proletarian Barcelona, this quickly changed, as the republicans appreciated the size of the Pandora's Box they had opened.) With the ERC in power, many tenants doubtless wished to give notice to republicans of their earlier commitment to act on the housing question. Significantly, the rent strikers were emphatic that they did not seek to embarrass the new authorities, stressing the economic content of their aspirations, which they believed did not presuppose the bankruptcy of the property-owning class or the revolutionary abolition of landlord–tenant relationships. Thus the rent strikers announced their refusal to pay exorbitant rents, which, they insisted, had to be reduced by 40 percent, a 'modest' cut that they believed would still yield a 6–17 percent financial return to the landlord. This cut was to be applied only to rents under 100 pesetas per month, i.e. those paid by workers.[23]

Although the rent strike always belonged to the streets, radicals inside the CNT were quick to recognise its significance as an urban struggle. In particular, a group of *cenetistas* and anarchists from inside the Construction Union established close ties with the neighbourhood associations and activists who organised the strike. This was unsurprising, for this was the *sindicato* with the highest rate of unemployment of all the Barcelona unions: approximately 40 per cent of its 30,000 members were out of work in 1931, and rent payments created huge problems for its essentially unskilled, low-paid members still in work.[24] Shortly after the birth of the Republic, Construction Union activists founded the CDE (Comisión de Defensa Económica or Commission for Economic Defence) to study living costs in Barcelona.[25] Headed by two *faístas*, Arturo Parera and Santiago Bilbao, the CDE appreciated that the rent strike was an important act of economic self-defence through which the underpaid, the unemployed and the dispossessed could reappropriate space and free themselves from market domination by taking control of everyday life. In a series of meetings and notes in *Solidaridad Obrera*, the CDE welcomed the rent strike as a justified response to 'scandalous rents' and 'indecent conditions' and offered workers succinct advice: 'Eat well and, if you don't have the money, then don't pay your rent!'[26] The CDE also demanded that the unemployed be exempted from rent payments.[27] In essence, the CDE's struggle was reformist, for an increase in the social wage and collective consumption.

Another form of unemployed mobilisation was street protest. Given that the jobless have few protest resources (perforce they have no labour to withdraw), unemployed workers' movements tend to present their agenda to the authorities in the public sphere via street action and demonstrations. There were several peaceful unemployed demonstrations in the days after the birth of the Republic. On 20 April, barely a week after the fall of the monarchy, the unemployed marched on the Generalitat and the council chambers in Republic Square, in the city centre. Although there is some circumstantial evidence of activist involvement, this march and others were not intended to discomfort the new authorities. The marchers' main demands – the six-hour day in industry and public works – both figured in the ERC's programme before the April municipal elections and could hardly therefore be viewed as revolutionary. Equally, the readiness of the demonstrators to take their demands to the new authorities suggests that they had a certain amount of faith in the republicans. A delegation of the unemployed entered the Generalitat to parley with key political figures, including President Macià, Serra i Moret, the head of the Generalitat Comissió Pro-Obrers sense Treball, Civil Governor Companys and Mayor Aiguader i Miró. The unemployed representatives reported that, in their discussions, the ERC leaders offered 'not only verbal support but real assistance', assuring that 'governmental action in the form of a subsidy or unemployment insurance will undoubtedly be forthcoming', along with public works. Upon learning of this new commitment by the authorities, the demonstrators outside the Generalitat were jubilant, and they withdrew peacefully from Republic Square.[28]

However, on 31 April, a new unemployed demonstration arrived in Republic Square in a more defiant mood, and this time the protest ended in violence. According to *Las Noticias*, the marchers, 'on the whole young people', attacked nearby shops and requisitioned comestibles, one of the most elementary forms of protest available to the unemployed. When the marchers reached the Rambles, they entered La Bouquería, Barcelona's central market, seizing more food; later, a nearby warehouse in the Raval was stormed and more victuals were removed.[29] While it might appear harsh to criticise the authorities for failing to 'solve' unemployment in the two weeks they had been in power, the riot gave eloquent notice that the jobless wanted more than just platitudes and promises from the city's new rulers.

The 31 April riot occurred on the eve of the first May Day of the republican era, the most significant event in the proletarian calendar. The new authorities hoped that May Day would underline the consensus between the Republic and the labour movement. The reformist workers' organisations represented in government – the PSOE and the UGT – saw it as a 'day of peace', while the

Figure 5.2 An unemployed workers' demonstration. The banner reads 'Without Bread and Work'

Source: Francesc Bonamusa, Pere Gabriel, Josep Lluís Martín Ramos and Josep Termes, *Història Gràfica del Moviment Obrer a Catalunya*, Barcelona, 1989, p.191

ERC, in keeping with its populism, made May 1 a public holiday, 'a day of the people'.[30] Yet the May Day celebration revealed the divergent interests of the constituent parts of the 'people', as unemployment and the divisions it unleashed fractured the cross-class alliance that had ushered in the Republic. Thus the May Day demands of the l'Hospitalet CNT – the introduction of the six-hour working day and the 'disarming of all the institutions that served the monarchy, such as the police and the Civil Guard' underlined that the Republic had not gone far enough down the road to freedom and justice for the most militant sections of the working class.[31]

But the most graphic measure of proletarian identity and power was the huge May Day rally and demonstration organised by the Barcelona CNT at the Palau de Belles Arts, near the city centre, the first open show of support for the Confederation in its birthplace since the early 1920s. Highlighting the impor-tance of consumption-related issues for the CNT, as well as the inevitability of conflict with republicanism's middle-class base, the theme of the rally was 'The First of May against Unemployment, Inflation and for a Reduction in Rents'. This promise of positive action in favour of the unemployed and the unskilled attracted around 150,000 workers from the *barris*, the largest mass gathering in Barcelona since the birth of the Republic.[32] Some of the tenants' associations active in the rent strike also attended. It was clear that these community groups had established close ties with the radicals from Nosotros, who had draped a lorry in red-and-black flags from which a succession of anarchists and community leaders addressed the crowds, calling for immediate action on behalf of the jobless and the low-paid, such as rent cuts and the readmission of the unemployed into the factories.[33] At the end of the rally, the marchers set off for the Generalitat palace in Republic Square to present their demands to the authorities. By the time the front of the demonstration had reached the Rambles, its rearguard was almost half a kilometre away in Urquinaona Square, as tens of thousands of workers proceeded ineluctably towards the Generalitat, breaking everyday routines and power flows and giving notice of their intent to move from the urban margins to reclaim the city centre.

Upon learning that the massed ranks of the CNT were bound for the Generalitat, Macià revealed his lack of confidence in the security forces by ordering that the Catalan police, the Mossos d'Esquadra, were to take sole responsibility for guarding the Generalitat Palace and Republic Square. However, as thousands of demonstrators arrived in Republic Square singing the anarchist anthem, 'Los hijos del pueblo' (The Children of the People), the small contingent of Mossos was very quickly outnumbered. Fearing that his agents would lose control of the situation, the chief of the Mossos d'Esquadra made an urgent call for police reinforcements. A contingent of the Guardia de Seguridad, the state police, responded first. When these reinforcements arrived in a square packed with demonstrators, they also found themselves outnumbered and unable to reach the Mossos inside the Generalitat. The commander of the Guardia de Seguridad, who apparently believed that marchers were attempting to storm the Generalitat, ordered his men to open fire above the heads of the demonstrators. What had previously been a peaceful demonstration was suddenly engulfed in violence. As marchers ran for cover, a 45-minute gun battle ensued between the guardias and armed workers. Calm finally prevailed when the hated guardias were replaced by soldiers, who were cheered through the streets by marchers as the 'sons of the people' who, unlike the police, would not fire on workers. When the fighting ended, a policeman lay dead and two more were wounded, along with ten workers.[34]

It would be wrong to interpret the violent conclusion of the May Day march as evidence that Barcelona was on the eve of a new period of *pistolerisme*. Although the armed *faístas* and *grupistas* that provided security for the march opened fire on the police, it must be remembered that the first shots came from the Guardia de Seguridad. Moreover, and perhaps most significantly, right-wingers and former members of the anti-republican Sindicatos Libres, who had recently been banned by the new authorities, had joined the demonstration and were in Republic Square in order to provoke violence – the majority of those arrested on arms charges were ex-Libres, compared with just a solitary *faísta*.[35]

After the violence, the authorities displayed a new keenness to reduce the tensions that were developing around unemployment. However, rather than undercut social protest, piecemeal measures resulted only in further conflict. For instance, a council-run allotment scheme, which created 2,000 plots on Montjuïc on which jobless workers could grow fruit, required a permanent police guard from attack by those who did not have a plot.[36] Similarly, in early May the council began to issue food vouchers to those unemployed workers who could demonstrate that they had resided in Barcelona for at least five years. The voucher system inevitably brought new tensions to the surface: besides frustrating the many migrant workers who were not entitled to municipal welfare, it was underfunded and quickly proved incapable of meeting the needs of those unemployed who qualified for assistance. With as many as 3,000 unemployed workers converging on the office in Hospital Road, a narrow street in the Raval from where the scheme operated, it was not long before fights broke out between jobless workers and the police.[37] In June, following clashes with the police, unemployed workers stormed the welfare offices and seized food vouchers. Later, the unemployed attempted to march to nearby Republic Square and issue new demands on the authorities, only to be repelled by the police, resulting in further violence.[38]

Since the riots of 30 April and 1 May, the republican authorities had become extremely concerned about the volatility of street protests in the city centre and were now determined to deny the unemployed the right to define public space. Any attempt by the unemployed to bring their demands to the centre of the political and administrative power of the city would now meet with police repression. Yet this could not bring urban peace: by trying to deny the unemployed access to the only forum in which they could express themselves, the authorities increased the competition for public space and made it more violent. Thus, when the unemployed found their path to the Generalitat blocked, they turned back into the Raval and vented their anger on the middle class, attacking shops and entering bars and demanding food.[39]

In an attempt to avoid large concentrations of unemployed workers in the city centre, the ERC-controlled Generalitat and city council established a series of soup kitchens across Barcelona. Again, new protests developed. Besides providing free meals, the kitchens brought little relief to the unemployed, who still had to bear the burden of rent payments. On one occasion, a publicity visit by republican politicians to soup kitchens in the Can Tunis *cases barates* provoked a riot.[40] In addition to allegations of graft and corruption in the awarding of catering contracts, most criticism of the kitchens focused on the quality of the food, which *Solidaridad Obrera* described as 'slops'.[41] In early July, *La Vanguardia* reported that 'a spirit of protest' developed among the unemployed regarding the quality of the meals in the Hospital Road soup kitchens. When *asaltos* arrived to impose order, fighting erupted and a worker was shot. Carrying the bloodstained shirt of the wounded man, the indignant patrons of the soup kitchen set out to protest to Republic Square, only to be attacked by the police when they reached the Rambles. That afternoon, a second march was charged by Guardia Civil cavalry, and sporadic street battles ensued for several hours in the Raval.[42]

There was an underlying logic to these street protests. A recurring feature was the collective demand of the unemployed for access to the streets and the defence of their right to occupy public space. Thus, at the end of July, the unemployed began another peaceful march to the Generalitat. When the marchers were charged by Guardia Civil cavalry, frustrated demonstrators resisted the security forces before entering hotels to demand food.[43] The calculated attack on the property of the urban middle class, whether its seizure or its destruction, became one of the hallmarks of unemployed street politics. Another characteristic was their organisation. For all the apparent confusion that reigned in the streets, the protesting crowds revealed both coherence and structure. Depending on the opposition they met from the forces of order, protesters might withdraw, regroup and launch counterattacks on a range of selected targets, whether the security forces, shopkeepers, hoteliers or market traders.[44]

These unemployed street politics were inflected by Barcelona's long history of direct action protests, of which they formed part. These 'traditional' protest forms endured into the Republic; for instance, when, in Barceloneta, on a Sunday in late July, a tram collided with two workers, injuring one and killing the other, a crowd quickly formed on the streets and began to vent its anger on Tram Company property, overturning three trams and burning another. When the police attempted to enter the *barri* to impose order, they were forced out, only re-entering under cover of darkness. The following day, however, when the tram service recommenced, there was, according to *La Vanguardia*, a 'popular uprising' (*motín popular*), as residents – men, women and children – ripped up pavements and tram lines and blocked roads with barricades to prevent the circulation of trams and police, who were both forced from the *barri* again. Faced with this popular pressure, the council yielded to the central demand of the community – that the tram service be suspended – and introduced bus transport.[45]

A further point of commonality between unemployed street politics and working-class customs was their anti-police content, perhaps the most defining feature of jobless protests. Since the police were the guardians of state power on the streets, since the unemployed spent a lot of time in public spaces like parks, and since the streets were the main forums for unemployed protests, relations between the two were inevitably tense.[46] The struggle of the unemployed with the police was inseparable from popular traditions of resistance to authority. So great were these traditions that detainees frequently appealed to passers-by to intercede on their behalf. Crowds were often more than happy to oblige, attacking the police and attempting to free detainees whether they knew the arrested person or not.[47] For instance, in early September 1931, in a street in the heart of the Raval, a 'common criminal' arrested by the police cried for public support. In reply, residents left their tenement blocks to attack the police and attempt to free the detainee, while other neighbours bombarded the security forces with bottles, cans and rocks from their balconies. In the end, police fired warning shots into the air before removing the detainee.[48] In another case, according to a police report, in La Torrassa, when an *asalto* hit a felon in the course of an arrest, the agent was surrounded by an aggressive crowd. The swift intervention of the Guardia Civil and the police was required 'otherwise things would have turned very nasty'.[49]

The full repertoire of these complex street politics was acted out in the rent strike. By the summer of 1931, the rent campaign had been 'appropriated' by the CDE, which organised a series of mass meetings in the *barris*. The rent strike spread like wildfire. At the end of July, the CDE claimed that 45,000 tenants were refusing to pay rent in Barcelona. By late summer, over 100,000 tenants had joined the mobilisation, and in September there were reports of 'significant resistance' to rent payment in Calella, 50 kilometres to the north, and Vilanova i la Geltrú, 30 kilometres to the south, as the strike spread to surrounding towns.[50] Importantly, the CDE provided strategic leadership for the rent strike, constituting a point of liaison for a coordinated protest. In response to appeals from the authorities for the strikers to submit their demands individually to arbitration, the CDE explained at length that the campaign would continue to rely on direct action methods. First, because the urban poor needed an immediate improvement in their living standards, a panacea once advocated by the republicans – passively awaiting the conclusion of arbitration procedures – was not a realistic option. Second, the CDE had little faith in the republicans, who had reneged on their earlier commitment to act on the housing question and were now apparently prepared to tolerate the 'oligarchy of the landlords'.[51] Third, the CDE claimed that the notoriously intransigent landlord class, which was unaccustomed to any challenge to its authority, would only make concessions to tenants under pressure. In the light of the above, the CDE argued that if the rent strike ended, tenants would effectively be disarming themselves in the face of their enemies with no guarantee of any rent reduction.[52] These sentiments were echoed by the anarchist newspaper *Tierra y Libertad*, which considered the rent strike 'opportune': it 'will do more in a few months than several centuries of legislation'.[53] It also should be recognised that, given that the rent strike started independently of the CDE, it was far from obvious that it could end the mobilisation, even if it so wished.

The CDE attempted to politicise working-class awareness of consumption issues: it promised a struggle for a new urban meaning in opposition to the vision held by speculators, renters and shopkeepers and, indeed, by the republican authorities, of the city as a place for profit and exploitation. Following a visit to La Boquería market, a CDE delegation remarked that because of uncontrolled food prices, '"life" is a privilege. The people either do not eat or, at best, eat little and badly'. The CDE also denounced shopkeepers for cheating consumers by adulterating foodstuffs and doctoring weights. Days later, at a CDE meeting attended by 1,500 people in Barceloneta, where the rent strike began, CDE organiser Santiago Bilbao excoriated shopkeepers and landlords for 'robbing' the workers, after parsimonious employers had already 'pilfered' from their wage packets.[54]

The additional layer of organisation provided by the CDE was crucial given the limited protest resources of the unemployed: it allowed for the coordination of those who were individually weak, linking street and neighbourhood networks in a powerful collective resistance to the urban *status quo*.[55] By appealing to an undifferentiated working-class community, the CDE mobilised many non-unionised workers in the rent strike. The open nature of this action was of paramount importance, for agitation on living standards could only really be effective if it attracted the widest number of workers, irrespective of political creed or organisational affiliation. The only demands the CDE made of new strikers was that they register with the strike committee and subsequently act in absolute solidarity with other strikers. This resulted in a kind of united front in the streets. There was a high degree of grassroots autonomy and popular control, which enabled the CDE to mobilise far beyond its own organisational structures. At the same time, the link between the rent strike and the CDE and, by extension, with the CNT, threatened to open up a new front in the struggle for urban power, uniting the fight for community self-determination with the struggle for workers' control of industry.

For many workers, the rent strike provided a real experience of community decision making and popular democracy. Strikers discussed neighbourhood problems in popular assemblies, and the specific grievances of tenants in different *barris* were incorporated within the overall struggle for a reduction in rents. Some tenants demanded improvements in housing quality, and the unemployed demanded free public transport to facilitate their search for work, while in the *cases barates*, one of the strongholds of the strike, the rent campaign fused with longstanding demands for school provision, health facilities, street lighting and transport links with Barcelona city centre. In the Horta *barri*, the rent strikers issued an audacious series of demands for a working-class space, including the removal of the Guardia Civil from the area and the immediate closure of the local church.[56]

The resultant sense of collective ownership of the rent protest made for a profound level of solidarity, drawing on the order of the *barris* and the reservoir of community loyalties and networks. As the CDE announced, 'rather than sleep on the streets, we are ready for anything'. Accordingly, when landlords ordered the electricity or water supply to be cut to strikers, sympathetic workers reconnected them. Similarly, when landlords evicted tenants for the non-payment of rent, CDE activists, strikers and neighbours were always on hand to return tenants and their furniture to their flats. Meanwhile, when evictees could not be reinstalled immediately, there were always neighbours prepared to offer beds and temporary accommodation. This solidarity was reinforced by the relatively uniform existence and experiences of the strikers. For instance, according to one worker, the 'majority' of tenants in the *cases barates* were unemployed migrants who simply could not afford rent.[57] As the tempo of evictions intensified, the crowds became more innovative and structured in their street protests. The reinstatement of tenants increasingly assumed the form of community celebrations, drawing in rent strikers from neighbouring streets and, at crucial moments, from other districts.[58] Practices such as squatting and returning evictees to flats betrayed elements of counter-cultural ideology, a working-class view of housing not as a source of profit or property but as a social need.[59]

Collective force was integral to the strikers' resistance. During a popular protest against an attempted eviction in the Can Tunis *cases barates*, a lorry of Guardia Civil had to be dispatched to prevent the torching of the local church, which was, in the view of the residents, a symbol of oppression. Assaults on bailiffs – the quickest and most effective way of preventing evictions – became commonplace, and there were reports of bailiffs refusing to carry out evictions through fear of reprisals.[60] In late August, in l'Hospitalet, an angry crowd attempted to lynch two bailiffs.[61] On another occasion, bailiffs left their lorry behind while fleeing an angry crowd. When police squads started escorting bailiffs, violent street battles resulted, sometimes involving working-class women and children. The prominent role of women resembled 'traditional' consumption protests, and the police were frequently unable to counter female militancy and withdrew without effecting evictions. Another similarity with earlier protest repertoires was the collective marches on landlords' houses. Following the reinstallation of an evicted family in Sants, residents marched to the landlord's abode, warning him not to re-evict his tenants and announcing publicly his contravention of the moral code of the community. Some landlords reported to the police that threats had been made against them by armed rent strikers.[62] News of successes – that families had been reinstated or that evictions had been thwarted – travelled from *barri* to *barri* by word of mouth and brought added confidence to protesters.[63] Meanwhile, *Solidaridad Obrera* provided a focus for the strikers, publishing the names and addresses of those who opposed the rent protest.[64]

5.2   Repressing the 'detritus of the city'

As we saw in Chapter 3, there was no place within the 'republic of order' for any struggle that developed outside the new institutions. However, the authorities set about containing the unemployed in part because their street politics threw the antagonistic interests of the jobless and republicanism's middle-class base into sharp relief. From the start of the Republic, commercial pressure groups placed unrelenting pressure on the authorities to repress unemployed street traders, frequently accusing the police of being too 'soft' on these 'lawbreakers'.[65] The new authorities were extremely receptive to the demands of their important middle-class social constituency, especially since several Esquerra councillors were drawn from the urban petite bourgeoisie. Indeed, there was a significant overlap between the new republican political elite and the commercial associations directly affected by unemployed practices.[66] For instance, Enric Sànchez, president of the Unió General de Venedors de Mercats (General Union of Market Traders), a market traders' group at loggerheads with the street traders, had been an ERC candidate in the April 1931 council elections.[67] It was understandable then that the authorities should be sympathetic to the demands of market traders and shopkeepers for tough action against street traders.

There were also many ties between the republican movement and the landlord class. In l'Hospitalet, the president of one of the republican groups in Collblanc was head of the property owners' association, and both bodies were located in the same building.[68] Meanwhile, jurisdiction over the *cases barates*, one of the centres of the rent strike, rested directly with an ERC-controlled quango, the Comissariat de Cases Barates. But the COPUB, the main landlords' association in Barcelona, did most to encourage repression of the rent strike.[69] According to the COPUB, which had a highly idealised view of housing conditions, the 'state of insubordination of many thousands of tenants [and the] state of anarchy in Barcelona, especially in the peripheral districts' was the work of 'irresponsible elements' intent on 'harm[ing] tenants' interests' and rupturing the 'harmony between landlords and tenants'. These 'agitators' were part of an 'organised offensive against global property' designed to 'provoke conflicts' and create an 'unnecessary state of alarm' in order to 'compromise the new political institutions' and 'damage the national economy' before establishing a Bolshevik dictatorship. It was thus the duty of the authorities to adopt an 'unyielding' policy of repression, including a ban on the CDE, on behalf of the 'tenants of good faith', thereby 'maintaining the principle of authority' and 'the triumph of order and social peace'.[70] While not averse to threatening that its members would withhold taxes if the authorities did not crush the rent strike, for most of 1931–32 the COPUB relied on the perssure that its longstanding president, Pich i Pon, as leader of Barcelona's Radical Party, a party represented in central government, was able to put on ministers, both by writing letters and by organising delegations of COPUB members to Madrid.[71]

The republicans in power in Barcelona and Madrid, who already believed that the consolidation of the new regime required the appeasement of the middle classes, were not prepared to watch impassively as a key part of their support base came under attack. Increasingly, therefore, the authorities criminalised unemployed practices, drawing a sharp contrast between *provocateurs* and the rest of the jobless. Mobilisations were successively attributed to 'outside elements', 'undesirables', 'professional layabouts' and 'picturesque criminals who pass as unemployed workers' but were not 'the real unemployed'. In a sharp radicalisation of republican discourse, 'agitators' were described as 'the enemy within': 'reactionaries' and 'enemies of the republic' who 'stirred up' the 'detritus of the city', paying them 'ten pesetas' to cause 'disturbances' and 'outrages' while eroding 'the already limited appetite for work which exists in this country'. Even street trade, an integral part of the culture of the *barris* since the turn of the century, was depicted as part of the Barcelona 'underworld', an 'attack' on the Republic by those who wished to create 'an anarchic city'.[72] Similarly, the rent strike was blamed not on an acute housing crisis but on the 'coercion' and 'violent practices' of 'a minority of tenants' and 'professional agitators', 'a few hundred spoilers' and 'irresponsible loudmouths' whose base 'manoeuvres' and 'disgraceful protests' were 'a danger and a discredit to the city'.[73] In a further attempt to isolate the rent strike organisers from their potential supporters, republicans spread black propaganda, alleging, for instance, that rent strikers from the *cases barates* profited from the dispute by subletting their flats while they rented luxurious villas on the Catalan coast or started small businesses.[74] Recreating the nineteenth-century distinction between the 'deserving' and 'undeserving' poor, and expanding the latter category to include 'subversives' such as unemployed organisers and street vendors, the republicans announced that only the 'morally healthy', those 'honourable and dignified workers [who] remain at home' would receive assistance, in recognition of their 'social discipline'.[75] The 'genuine unemployed' were implored to ostracise 'subversives', who made it difficult for the authorities to address the problems facing 'genuine unemployed workers'.[76] The logic of this discourse was unswervingly repressive. If, as was claimed, a small group of 'troublemakers' in the *barris* were to blame for protest, the 'republic of order' would benefit from the incarceration of 'subversives', 'professional scroungers' and 'volunteer vagabonds'.[77]

Republican politicians were energetic in their deployment of state institutions in defence of their middle-class constituency. The ERC, which controlled the council-organised police, the Guàrdia Urbana, and the Generalitat-run Mossos d'Esquadra, deployed all the police resources it could muster against the street traders. From August 1931, Lluís Puig Munner, a shopkeeper and ERC councillor in the Raval, led the newly formed Brigada per a la repressió de la venta ambulant (Brigade for the Repression of Street Trade), a 'special security service' created by the city council to remove unemployed traders from the streets.[78] Following a series of violent clashes between police and street traders, council police squads were accompanied by *asaltos* or the Guardia Civil on incursions into hostile proletarian districts.[79]

Yet state power was most fiercely directed at the rent strike and the CDE. Unemployed struggles such as the rent strike typically fail to achieve their objectives because they are either co-opted or repressed. In the circumstances of 1931, with the authorities determined to demobilise the masses and stabilise the political situation, and with the COPUB making incessant demands for repression, the latter was always more likely. The authorities went on the offensive in early August, after Anguera de Sojo became civil governor. The interior minister had already informed a COPUB delegation that the government was prepared to crush the rent strike, recognising that any compromise would serve as a spur to new demands and 'signify the destruction of authority and its substitution by anarchy, chaos and national misery'.[80] Anguera de Sojo's arrival in office coincided with the peak of the rent mobilisation, and he was deter-mined that anyone involved in the 'absurd' rent strike should be made to 'comply with the law'.[81] The paramilitary *asaltos*, who started supervising evictions from the end of July, were increasingly deployed as the authorities strove to demoralise the strikers by forcing them onto the streets.[82] There was increasing cooperation between the authorities and the COPUB, which now provided free legal advice, lorries and men to enable its members to effect evic-tions and compiled a detailed blacklist of rent strikers and other tenants evicted for rent arrears. Meanwhile, Anguera de Sojo moved to decapitate the rent strike by pursuing the COPUB's central demand and banning the CDE. Although the CDE had not committed any offence, it faced growing harass-ment: its meetings and rallies were banned capriciously by the civil governor, who appeared determined either to provoke the CDE or drain its resources – the CDE relied on post-meeting collections among supporters to pay the cost of renting meeting places. Following complaints from CDE activists, Anguera de Sojo imposed a blanket ban on its meetings. He then demanded a list of the entire CDE membership from the Barcelona CNT and, when the latter failed to comply, slapped a heavy fine on the organisation.[83] Lastly, Anguera de Sojo, who, like the COPUB, regarded the rent struggle as the 'manoeuvre' of a 'pernicious minority', resorted to internment without trial, ordering the arrest of prominent rent strike organisers, even though they had committed no crime. In a graphic illustration of the limits of social and political inclusion during the Republic, Bilbao, one of the founders of the CDE, was dragged from his bed by police and placed in the Model Jail, along with many other *cenetista* and anar-chist activists involved in the CDE and the rent strike.[84]

5.3   Resisting the 'dictatorship in Barcelona'

The CNT and the FAI could not ignore this escalation of repression, which led to the internment, among others, of Parera, another founder of the CDE who had recently been appointed secretary of the Catalan CRT, and Durruti and García Oliver, two of the most important anarchists in Barcelona. In early September, several dozen *cenetistas* who had been interned without trial in the Model Jail for several weeks began a hunger strike under the slogan 'Freedom or Death'. The Barcelona CNT declared a general strike in solidarity with the internees and in protest at state repression on 4 September. The stoppage, which spread to the industrial hinterland of Manresa, Mataró, Granollers, Sabadell and Terrassa, lasted for 72 hours and affected around 300,000 workers in Barcelona. Convinced that the CNT had to be taught a lesson, Anguera de Sojo, with the full backing of central government, made no attempt to negotiate a solution with moderates in the unions. Instead, in response to what he saw as a 'conspiracy', he prepared for 'the final battle' (*pugna definitiva*) with the CNT and detained *cenetistas* in their droves, an act that he believed would forestall 'great unrest' by elim-inating the mobilising agents connecting the movement to the grassroots.[85]

The radicals in the CNT, meanwhile, saw this as an opportunity to test the insurrectionary waters and announced a 'nationwide revolutionary general strike for the triumph of anarchist communism'. With the armed squads from the defence committees already in the streets, the FAI ordered its *grupos* to take the offensive. Barricades were erected in the proletarian belt of the city and in the Raval, and the middle classes responded with panic buying of foodstuffs, which quickly sold out. However, this was an inauspicious baptism of fire for the FAI *grupos* and the defence committees, whose poorly armed activists were unable to engage the security forces in anything more than sporadic guerrilla actions.[86] In a show of strength, martial law was declared: two warships were moored in Barcelona harbour, and hundreds of Guardia Civil reinforcements, including cavalry, arrived in the city. At the end of the strike, sixteen workers were dead, three of whom had been summarily shot while in police detention. A further 300 workers were arrested, and the jails were so full that half of these were interned on prison ships in the harbour.[87]

In the new climate of repression after September, the authorities placed further restrictions on the access of the unemployed to the streets.[88] Police swoops on areas favoured by street traders became commonplace. In mid-September, on the orders of the council, *el mercadet*, the centre of street trade in central Barcelona, was destroyed in the presence of a detachment of *asaltos*, local ERC politicians and representatives from market traders' associations, as embittered street vendors looked on. Later, *asaltos* occupied Republic Square to repel possible protests by unemployed traders, while a succession of delegations of market traders arrived to congratulate the municipal authorities on demolishing *el mercadet* 'for the good name and prestige of the city and the businesses of Barcelona'.[89] In the rent strike, highlighting the extent to which the authorities viewed this protest as a frontal challenge to state power, the Ley de Defensa de la República was invoked the day after it became law in an attempt to rupture networks of militants and the connections between the CNT and the *barris*. Thereafter, rent strikers who opposed evictions or who re-entered flats were interned under the Ley de Defensa, undermining a great deal of the solidarity that had characterised the rent protest until this point, much to the satisfaction of the COPUB, which thanked the central government for this new weapon against 'acts of rebellion'.[90] In the peripheral *barris*, where the rent strike was especially solid, the law allowed the authorities to limit the space available to dissenters and, in operations that resembled those of a foreign army of occupation in hostile territory, entire neighbourhoods were invaded by the security forces, which searched houses and workers' centres. Meanwhile, the authorities used the law to sever the connections between the rent strike and the CNT, effectively banning the Builders' Union, from where the CDE had emerged.[91]

State violence was never entirely successful in curbing practices that were socio-economic in origin. To no small extent, this reflected the determination of the unemployed to defend, often with violence, their right to public space.

Hence, the unemployed traders remained on the streets throughout the Republic.[92] There were numerous instances of collective resistance by street traders to the security forces. Members of the local community often intervened to defend street traders from the police, who responded by using extra violence, even against female and child street traders, in an attempt to make arrests quickly before hostile crowds could form. One *asalto* explained to a journalist that this often involved using truncheons against women: 'Nothing annoys me more than those women who let themselves get involved in disturbances caused by rabble rousers'.[93] Street traders sometimes reacted to police repression by attacking market traders, whom they knew implored the authorities to drive their unemployed competitors from the streets. In the last quarter of 1931, police persecution of street traders resulted in two major riots at markets in which angry jobless vendors and members of the local community destroyed stalls and seized food and goods.[94] Perhaps in an effort to avoid a recurrence of these riots, the local authorities apparently tolerated a limited amount of street trade, although, as one republican journalist noted, the repression of the unemployed vendors increased prior to local and general elections, when the Esquerra was especially keen to please its middle-class electoral base.[95]

Figure 5.3 Street trade, 1936

Source: Francesc Bonamusa, Pere Gabriel, Josep Lluís Martín Ramos and Josep Termes, *Història Gràfica del Moviment Obrer a Catalunya*, Barcelona, 1989, p.318

Nor was repression successful in ending the rent strike. A combination of material need and the dense fabric of social networks in the *barris* ensured the continuation of the rent protest in some neighbourhoods throughout the Republic. This was particularly so in l'Hospitalet and the *cases barates*, where strikers resisted the authorities and the landlords despite police harassment and, in some cases, without electricity and water.[96] Such community-based defensive struggles against the most palpable manifestations of oppression and exploitation highlighted the innovative capacity of the *barris* for self-activity and self-expression and their desire to seize control of their destiny and their local space. These mobilisations may have lacked the focus of protests by formal organisations, but they were nevertheless powerful and dramatic. An example of this came at the end of 1932 when, following an increase in the harassment of rent strikers in La Torrassa, the police came under a fierce attack from an angry crowd, which seized some of their weapons before attempting to burn down the local COPUB office.[97]

The repression of industrial and extra-industrial struggles inspired by the local material needs of the *barris* constituted a steep learning curve for ordinary workers and radical activists alike. The experience of repression produced a collective awareness of the limits of 'freedom' under the Republic and a prevailing sense of exclusion. In the absence of the promised reform package, many workers in the *barris* came to view the republican state as little more than intrusive welfare agencies, the police and army.[98] A highly conflictive law-and-order situation developed. Following sustained criticism of the jobless in the republican press, it was reported that unemployed activists had visited newspaper offices and 'threatened' journalists.[99] Policemen in l'Hospitalet, one of the most contested spaces, received written death threats, and there were numerous assaults on members of the security forces and private guards.[100] The sense of political alienation in the *barris* could only have been intensified by revelations of the huge salaries received by members of the new political elite, doubtless giving rise to the public perception that republican politicians were much the same as their monarchist predecessors.[101] The gulf between the Republic and the *barris* was underscored when a member of l'Hospitalet Council was beaten up and robbed in the working-class district of Collblanc.[102] The growing sensitivity of the local political elite to urban conflict impelled a succession of republican politicians to apply for gun licences from the late summer of 1931 onwards.[103] While, obviously, the Republic was different in various ways from the monarchy, this was less evident to those who experienced aggressive republican policing on the streets, particularly the unemployed, who, more than anyone, were acutely sensitive to the same continuing dynamics of exclusion and repression of protest.[104] Over and above the failure of the republicans' timid reform of the security forces, the ongoing police–people conflict was rooted in the structural inequalities of the urban economy, which ensured that a significant proportion of the working class would clash with authority, either through their individual efforts to survive or through their collective endeavours to improve their social conditions. Hence the uninterrupted street war between the police and unemployed workers, who by the very conditions of their existence were forced to live outside the law.

5.4   Street politics and the radicalisation of the CNT

The war on the streets was central to the radicalisation of the Barcelona CNT and the displacement of the moderate union leadership. The September general strike coincided with the publication of the so-called 'Treintista manifesto', issued by thirty prominent moderate *cenetistas*, for the most part older anarcho-syndicalists such as Peiró and Pestaña, who held important positions within the CNT.[105] While the *treintistas* reiterated their ultimate revolutionary objectives, in the short term they sought a period of social peace, an armistice with the authorities that would allow the unions to function more freely. Rather than criticise the republicans for raising popular expectations and failing to deliver upon their reform programme, the *treintistas* blamed street violence on radicals and 'an audacious minority', a clear reference to the FAI, which they charged was committed to 'the violent deed' and 'riots'.[106]

Given the march of events since the birth of the Republic, the hopes of the *treintistas* were naive in the extreme. They ignored the fact that the authorities were never likely to create the political and legal conditions for the CNT to expand its organisation. Indeed, such was the commitment of the republicans to clamping down on the Confederation, particularly after the September general strike, that there was little scope for any rapprochement with the moderate *cenetistas*. Ongoing repression limited the *treintistas'* room for manoeuvre and diminished the credibility of their message. Towards the end of October, the prison population in Barcelona continued to rise, and increasing numbers of 'social' prisoners and 'common' offenders were kept on a prison ship in the harbour,[107] while in early November, Bilbao, the rent strike organiser who had been interned without trial for three months, denounced what he saw as 'the dictatorship in Barcelona'.[108]

The influence of the radicals in the defence committees and the prisoners' support committees grew in direct proportion to republican repression, giving rise to fierce denunciations of the 'white terror of the Republic', which included 'monarchist techniques' like internment without trial to decapitate 'the rebellion of the CNT'.[109] Further evidence of the 'Mussolini-type methods' employed by the 'republican dictatorship' came in mid-October, when Anguera de Sojo declared the FAI an illegal organisation, forbidding its meetings and banning its press (*Tierra y Libertad* continued to publish after shedding the FAI logo, which it had sported since its foundation). In the view of *Tierra y Libertad*, the ban was a declaration of war by the authorities, who 'from above, from positions of power, are provoking a social war that we must enter until its conclusion'. All peace was impossible, because underground, the 'clandestine and anonymous action' of the FAI 'will be more radical and more violent'.[110] The FAI called its *grupos* into action, 'ready to give up their lives for freedom', and meetings of the ruling Catalan and Spanish republican parties began to be attacked. In early November, a meeting of various republican and socialist groups in Montjuïc was, according to *Solidaridad Obrera*, 'converted' into a demonstration in support of 'social' prisoners. The mere mention of Companys' name 'produced a wave of revulsion in the auditorium', while a speech by Victoria Kent, the director of prisons, was jeered as 'popular fervour took over the meeting'. The following month, at an ERC meeting in Poblenou, protests against intern-ment without trial led to violence as *grupistas* armed with coshes and iron bars overpowered stewards. This was followed by more attacks on ERC meet-ings across Catalonia.[111]

This context militated against a reasoned discussion of the Treintista manifesto and strengthened the claims of the radicals that the moderates were 'traitors' prepared to capitulate in the face of state power. Certainly, the moderates surrendered to their radical critics inside the CNT. Overcome by events in the streets and facing sustained attack within anarchist and anarcho-syndicalist circles, instead of holding their ground and answering their detractors, leading *treintistas* relinquished key positions, which were then filled by their radical opponents. Thus, in September, moderates resigned from the editorial board of *Solidaridad Obrera* and the following month, at a Catalan CRT plenum in Barcelona, a new radical-controlled editorial board was elected, including García Oliver and Montseny and with Felipe Alaíz as editor.[112]

The spread of unemployment and jobless protests helped the radicals to strengthen their position inside the CNT unions and among the rank-and-file. When the *treintistas* were at the helm of the CNT, they failed to take the challenge of unemployment seriously. As we saw earlier in this chapter, at the start of 1931 the CNT leadership had an essentially corporatist approach to unemployment, organising the out-of-work through the union *bolsas de trabajo*. Also, during many of the strikes from April to September, the moderate anarcho-syndicalists placed anti-unemployment measures at the centre of CNT demands; hence, the frequent calls for work-sharing arrangements, employer-funded unemployment subsidies, cuts in the working day without wage cuts, an end to redundancies, and the aboli-tion of piecework and other intensive forms of labour. However, once the authorities and the employers had rallied to check the power of the CNT, the effectiveness of this trade union-oriented approach was exposed. To be sure, the majority of employers opposed the CNT *bolsas* as a challenge to their freedom to hire and fire, fearing that otherwise their factories would be overrun by rabble-rousing anarchists encouraging free love instead of increasing productivity. (Ironically, the few far-sighted employers who accepted the *bolsas* and gave work to some of the most feared CNT mili-tants, those with histories of assassinations, bank robbery and industrial sabotage, enjoyed, in return, extremely tranquil industrial relations in the

1930s.[113]) The moral code of the *treintistas* was placed under genuine strain by mass unemployment. The anarcho-syndicalist conception of proletarian dignity was essentially a radical version of the bourgeois conception of the 'good worker', an 'honourable' wage earner living exclusively from labour. According to this schema, while it was legitimate for workers to break the law during a strike, whether by beating up 'scabs' or engaging in 'active picketing' and sabotage, extra-industrial illegality, which became increasingly common as unemployment increased, was regarded as 'crime', totally inappropriate for 'disciplined' workers.[114] Not only did the moderates fail to develop an alternative strategy for the unemployed, they sometimes veered towards reactionary positions, such as limiting female access to the labour market and the adoption of immigration controls. (In April, in the heady days after the proclamation of the Republic, Pestaña, increasingly seen as the reformist *bête noire* of the radicals, was an observer at the historic gathering of the Generalitat's Unemployed Workers' Commission, which had first decided to repatriate the immigrant unemployed.[115]) Moreover, after the rupture between the CNT and the republicans, Pestaña continued to write for the republican press, such as *La Calle*, a paper that actively demonised the unemployed.[116]

The radicals, meanwhile, always willing to embrace conflicts in the streets as well as in the factories, rode the crest of a wave of unemployed protest and accused their enemies in the CNT of betraying the interests of the unemployed. The first two unions to fall under the influence of the radicals – the Construction and Wood Workers' unions – had the highest unemployment rates. By consolidating their influence in the *ateneus*, community and union centres of the *barris*, the radicals channelled the growing anti-republicanism of the streets, where they established an everyday presence standing on street corners or on boxes reading from the workers' and anarchist press, addressing groups of workers and discussing politics with them. Sources both hostile and sympathetic to the workers' cause insist upon the vibrancy and excitement on the streets, where political events were fervently discussed, particularly in *barris* with high unemployment.[117]

Repression and socio-political exclusion presented the radicals with an opportunity to appeal to new radicalised constituencies beyond the factory proletariat, articulating the voices of the dispossessed and all those excluded by the Republic. In the case of the street traders, while the CNT had spoken of their 'right to the streets' during the monarchy,[118] once the republicans started repressing the unemployed vendors, *cenetistas* organised them as a section within the Barcelona Food Workers' Union.[119] Radicalised by its experience of state repression, the l'Hospitalet CNT Street Traders' Union announced at the end of October that 'the transition from monarchy to Republic was nothing more than a change in names and personnel, while the procedures, ambience and mentalities of the authorities have remained the same'.[120] The same anti-republicanism was found among the rent strikers, who had their own sense of what was 'fair' and recognised that this was anathema to the authorities, who allowed rents to rise and offered 'aid [to] the owners' by interning strikers and their leaders without trial.[121] A similar process occurred with thousands of migrant workers alienated by the ERC's exclusionary policies and stereotyping of migrant workers as 'Murcians'. The most notorious manifestation of the sense of exclusion of migrant workers was the erection of a sign announcing '¡Cataluña termina aquí, aquí empieza Murcia!' ('Catalonia ends here! Murcia starts here!'), on the border of Barcelona and l'Hospitalet's Collblanc *barri*, whose predominantly migrant population was vilified by the authorities, nationalist groups and employers' associations throughout the Republic. While the CNT had always recruited workers irrespective of their place of origin, and indeed continued to do so, the radicals channelled the hostility of migrant 'outsiders' to the authorities, and militant *cenetistas* and anarchists defined themselves as 'Murcian' in solidarity with a community under attack.[122] Large numbers of migrants therefore looked on the radicals as the only people prepared to accept them unconditionally and, throughout the 1930s, the newly developed *barris* on the outskirts of the city that had the largest concentrations of migrant workers, such as La Torrassa and the *cases barates*, became anarchist and CNT strongholds in the vanguard of social protest. (In the Santa Coloma *cases barates*, 74 percent of all residents were migrants, and over 30 percent of these were from Murcia.[123]) These migrant workers joined CNT protests not because they were alienated or isolated individuals, as was suggested by the authorities. Instead, their protest was firmly located within a supportive network of organised social relations that provided mobilisation resources and protection from external threats.

The mass resistance to the state fomented an enabling spirit of community self-determination, transforming many *barris* into an active social force for struggle and change. The closest contemporary equivalent to the simmering urban insurrection in the *barris* is the Intifada in the Palestinian refugee camps. There was increasing evidence that the radicals and the anarchists were prepared to project and channel anti-police traditions, giving them new layers of meaning. As *Solidaridad Obrera* insisted: 'The republican police is like the monarchist police, just as republican tyranny is the same as that of the monarchy. The police is unchanged, nor will it change. Its mission was, is and will continue to be the persecution of workers and the poor'.[124] In practical terms, CNT activists could rely on the support of the streets; so, when police detained a *cenetista* in La Torrassa, he implored members of the public to liberate him before showing up at a union office to have a set of police handcuffs removed by a CNT metal worker.[125]

In keeping with its characterisation as a 'guerrilla organisation',[126] the stridently anti-republican FAI and its radical supporters adopted an insurrectionary approach to unemployment. From the end of 1931 until the outbreak of the civil war, the radicals asserted that capitalism was in a condition of irrevocable collapse and that unemployment could only be solved 'after the revolution', which would bring 'the final solution': the destruction of 'an economic order that cannot guarantee a life for all'. Thus, welfare benefits and public works were denounced as 'denigrating' state 'charity' that humiliated the proletariat before the authorities and might weaken the insurrectionary appetite of the masses. Instead, the radicals advocated 'profoundly revolutionary tactics, concordant with our revolutionary identity'. As the Builders' Union explained, if workers are sacked, 'the struggle has to be pursued to its logical conclusion...up to the seizure of the factories and workshops'.[127]

The combination of state repression and anarchist tactics resulted in a shift away from mass struggles, such as the rent strike and the struggle for recognition of the *bolsas*, towards modes of conflict based on more irregular, non-institutionalised small-group resistance in the streets. In the view of the radicals, the unemployed would participate in their own 'revolutionary gymnastics'; by 'throwing the jobless onto the streets' to disrupt public order and open up a new front in the war with the state, the unemployed would be transformed into insurgent shock troops.[128] The unemployed guerrilla struggles advocated by the radicals were all firmly rooted in the existing constellation of popular street practices, which the anarchists embraced as a subversion of dominant urban rhythms. For instance, building on the traditional jobless practice of touring factories to look for work, the Construction Workers' Union called for the jobless to storm workplaces and demand work.[129] Spurred on by *cenetistas*, there were reports of up to 300 workers paying visits to employers. If CNT branch unions discovered that management was offering overtime instead of employing jobless workers, they sent along out-of-work members to demand work in what *cenetistas* called 'union placements' (*imposiciones sindicales*). The unemployed also put themselves to work in factories and then demanded to be paid by management at the end of the day. In a bid to generate employment, groups of jobless builders began ripping up paving stones around the city. There was much action among the new proletariat in the peripheral *barris*. In Sant Andreu and Santa Coloma, the CNT invited the unemployed to seize all unused land. The unemployed also continued to enter estates to requisition foodstuffs, particularly in l'Hospitalet. Inevitably, these practices resulted in continuing clashes with the police.[130] There is also evidence of militants ('persons unknown', according to a police report) encouraging street traders to attack the security forces.[131]

Perhaps the most innovative and controversial feature of the radical anarchists' support for unemployed street politics was their endorsement of popular illegality, what they called 'social crime' or 'proletarian appropriation'. *Solidaridad Obrera* and the anarchist press frequently published articles imploring the unemployed to 'take radical measures' to satisfy their needs, 'one way or another'. Following a riot by unemployed workers in Sant Andreu in April 1933 in which shops and the local market were looted, *Solidaridad Obrera* applauded the propaganda value of 'the rebel gesture': 'the only way to make Capital and the State recognise that there is hunger and that it was necessary to do something about it'.[132] Illegality was also justified as the 'conquest' of the 'right to life' by 'unfortunates pursued by hunger, who rob because hunger is killing them'. *Solidaridad Obrera* noted that 'not only do we understand [them], we also excuse [them], because responsibility lies with the egoistic and brutal society that oppresses us'.[133]

Unemployed illegality was fully validated by radical anarchist counter-culture. As *Tierra y Libertad* mused: 'robbery does not exist as a "crime"....It is one of the complements of life'.[134] Meanwhile, *Solidaridad Obrera* called on the dispossessed to 'assert their right to freedom and to life, seizing "illegally" the wealth that the official robbers hoard under the protection of the state'.[135] At a basic level, this was a spontaneous, defensive struggle of the jobless, whose 'last remaining dignified option' was 'to associate with other unemployed to conquer the right to live by force'.[136] This ideology of action led to a disdainful attitude towards beggars. One evening, Durruti brought a shocked silence to the La Tranquilidad bar when he responded to the plea of a beggar for money by reaching inside his jacket pocket to fill the hand of the appellant with a huge pistol, offering the advice: 'Take it! Go to a bank if you want money!'[137]

For the anarchists, 'proletarian appropriation' was pregnant with political meaning: it was an attack on the law, the values and the property relations of the existing social order, the first glimmer of rebellion, a sign of the spirit of self-determination of the dispossessed and a prelude to revolutionary action. Thus anarchists concluded that illegality was 'anarchist and revolutionary': it could 'wear down the capitalist system' and play a pivotal role in the class struggle, itself an act that perforce occurs outside the judicial framework of bourgeois society.[138] All that was required was to politicise illegal self-help strategies and unify the war of 'our brothers', the 'criminals', with the 'subversive spirit' of the anarchist struggle against the state. Ever ready to mobilise beyond the factory proletariat, the radicals applauded street gangs as a vanguard force in the fight against the police.[139]

In practical terms, there is ample evidence of *cenetistas* and radical anarchists helping to organise 'proletarian shopping trips'; these ranged from the small-scale requisition of foodstuffs from local shops, bakeries, lorries and warehouses to well-planned mass raids on markets and farms. In one dramatic dawn raid, a group of eighty people entered the Born market, in the city centre, and tied up market staff and lorry drivers before making away with a huge amount of fruit and vegetables.[140] There was also much evidence of activist participation in armed illegality. A clear illustration of this came during the 1932–33 wood workers' strike, when pickets organised 'proletarian appropriation' against employers who opposed the strike, frequently seizing their cash boxes and raiding their safes.[141] Many CNT unemployed activists, whose subculture of resistance impelled them to resist poverty, were implicated in 'proletarian appropriation'. A gang detained during an attempted robbery on a train included two anarchist brothers from l'Hospitalet, both of whom were activists in the local unemployed committee.

Three unemployed *cenetistas* from La Torrassa arrested while holding up cars on the outskirts of the city were believed by police to be the perpetrators of a series of highway robberies. A number of unemployed activists detained for eating without paying in restaurants were also found to have been involved in armed 'appropriations'.[142] Besides the unemployed, armed illegality was favoured by activists who found themselves blacklisted due to their militancy.[143] An important group of armed illegalists was foreign anarchists fleeing Italian and German fascism and the dictatorships in Portugal, Argentina and Uruguay, most of whom were already leading an illegal, clandestine existence in Barcelona, where they faced the constant threat of deportation.[144] While the International Refugees Support Committee offered some assistance for the *émigrés*, organising collections and offering legal advice, there were few opportunities for work. Moreover, the tasks of the International Refugees Support Committee were hampered by the republican authorities, which showed little hospitality towards proletarian anti-fascist exiles.[145] Of the foreign anarchist 'expropriators', the Italians, some of whom had met Spanish and Catalan exiles in Paris and Brussels during the Primo years, excelled themselves. The most celebrated of the Italian illegalists was Giuseppe Vicari, leader of the so-called 'Vicari Gang', which carried out a series of armed raids on shops and chemists.[146]

Armed illegality was not always economic in inspiration. For some anarchists, the 'rebels opposed to all laws',[147] it was often tactical, a new version of the 'propaganda of the deed' that would inspire the rebellion of the unemployed. Thus one group of unemployed anarchists admitted in court that they had launched an armed robbery in the hope that it might help the unemployed to shake off their servile spirit. Armed illegality sometimes acquired theatrical features, such as when, during an armed raid on a cinema box office, a gang member patiently explained to bystanders that he and his colleagues were not 'robbers' but unemployed workers 'tired of living with hunger'.[148] Illegality also became a way of life for some around the libertarian movement. This was especially true of the 'conscious illegalism' of anarcho-individualists, who worshipped the free life of bandits and outlaws and saw crime as a glorious virtue.[149] These anarcho-illegalists were most candid about their motivations under police interrogation. As one member of a group of individualists detained during an armed robbery proudly told stupefied police agents: 'I'm a pure anarchist and I rob banks, yet I'm incapable of robbing the poor, like others do'. Another of his associates admitted: 'I go into banks to withdraw with the pistol, while others withdraw using cheque books. It's all a matter of procedure'.[150] So convinced were they of the righteousness of their cause that a few individualists attempted to convert policemen to anarchism.[151]

It is perhaps from within the radical youth of the anarchist movement that we find those who most avidly embraced armed illegality. Guided only by their counter-cultural values and their alternative morality, these anarchist youths set out to pursue an autonomous lifestyle within an intentional community of rebels, a mini-society comprised of 'free individuals' consciously living outside the law in defiance of social regimentation, conventional moral values such as the work ethic, and traditional hierarchies. Belying the depiction of anarchists as secular saints, these youths embraced 'rough' working-class values, and a number of them, doubtless attracted by the black legend of 'Chinatown', were habitués of the taverns and bars of the Raval, where they attempted to expose criminals to anarchist ideas and culture and imbue their actions with a new consciousness. The extent to which these young activists permeated the 'underworld' milieu of the city was revealed by a police report in December 1934. During a series of raids on bars in the Raval, the police arrested 'a mixture of anarchists and robbers', twenty 'individuals who led an abnormal way of life (*vida irregular*), the majority of them young and already on file as anarchists'. One of the detainees was wanted by police for questioning about the murder of an employer. Nine of those arrested resided in the same Raval bed-and-break-fast. A subsequent raid on a bar frequented by young anarchists in Sants yielded over 300 gold watches and a quantity of stolen radios.[152] (This open-ness to those that other labour groups might describe as 'deviant' did provide the anarchist movement with some important militants, such as Mariano 'Marianet' Rodríguez Vázquez, secretary of the Barcelona Builders' Union before the civil war and CNT secretary-general after July 1936, a former internee in the Asil Durán.[153])

However, there was a major flaw in the radical strategy towards the unemployed: their sectarianism. For all their flexibility in channelling the protests of the dispossessed and the jobless, the radicals ignored the fact that resolute action on behalf of the unemployed presupposed the broadest possible unity within a powerful and massified CNT. This was clearly inim-ical to the radicals' aim of an anarchist trade union. The radicals' sectarianism was first glimpsed in the rent strike. Although the rent strike organisers appealed to all workers irrespective of their ideological affinity, radical anarchists increasingly sought to exploit the mobilisation for their own ends. Thus, at a mass CDE rally in July, Parera, one of the founders of the CDE, attacked what he called 'the extreme Bolshevik Left', asserting that the unemployed would only find work after 'the installation of anar-chist communism'. When Marxist-communists in the audience demanded the right to answer these claims, fighting broke out.[154] Equally, although the CNT had agreed to organise unemployed workers' committees – a 'life or death' issue for the unions – this was always secondary to the unrelenting anti-communism of the radicals. For instance, during a discussion on the organisation of the jobless at a meeting of the Barcelona CNT local federa-tion, the radical delegate from the Metal Workers' Union opposed the creation of an unemployed committee due to the influence of the BOC among the jobless in his industry, indicating that the jobless committees that existed were 'completely communist'. In other words, for the radicals, it was preferable to leave the unemployed unorganised rather than see them fall under the sway of rival factions from within the CNT.[155] Anarchist *grupistas* also hindered attempts by communists to organise the unemployed: in l'Hospitalet, for instance, meetings were disrupted by armed anarchists.[156] Later, the radicals made no attempt to establish broad, collective struggles similar to those initiated by the CDE in 1931. Accordingly, the struggle of the BOC to forge proletarian unity within its 'Workers' Alliance against Unemployment' (Aliança Obrera contra el Atur Forçós) was opposed as a 'communist plot'.[157] This was no isolated case: not only did the radicals believe they alone could best organise the unemployed, they were also convinced that they could make the revolution themselves.

6　Militarised anarchism, 1932–36

6.1　The cycle of insurrections

In what constituted the beginning of a series of armed insurrections, on 18 January 1932 anarchist-led miners in Figols disarmed members of the security forces and raised the red-and-black flag of the CNT over official buildings before proclaiming libertarian communism.[1] The rising lit a tinderbox in the worker colonies of the Llobregat valley, which had been radicalised by a series of recent trade union struggles involving textile workers and miners for better wages and working conditions.[2] The Barcelona CNT, which had clearly not been forewarned, learned about the rising on the afternoon of 19 January; a further 24 hours elapsed before activists from the local federation met delegates from the regional and national committees to plan support actions that might open up a second front of struggle.[3] Even then, instead of preparing an immediate solidarity strike, union militants, including *faístas*, 'went home to bed'. Finally, before what it called the 'consummated act', the Catalan CRT 'agreed to make the movement its own'. However, it was not until the weekend that local CNT leaders called a general strike, which, timed as it was, had an impact only on a few factories and on the service and transport sectors. Consequently, only on Monday, a full week after the start of the Figols rising, was the strike felt in the Barcelona area, when the defence committees entered the fray, setting up barricades in Clot and Sant Andreu in north Barcelona and engaging the *asaltos* in a number of gunfights, particularly in La Torrassa, where an *asalto* was killed.

The January strike demonstrated that the defence committees were still far from operational. Revealing considerable naivety, Durruti and Francisco Ascaso were arrested by police in La Tranquilidad on Paral.lel, a popular anarchist meeting place.[4] It was later revealed that the *grupistas* in the streets lacked weaponry because the 'quartermaster', who knew of their whereabouts, had been arrested. Unarmed, the *grupos* could not hold the streets: by the end of the first full day of the Barcelona general strike over 200 arrests had been made, and heavily armed *asaltos* were dispatched to occupy the *barris*. In Figols, meanwhile, isolated and outnumbered, the insurgents surrendered to the army.[5]

The authorities were far from conciliatory. In an attempt to decapitate a radicalised labour movement, 104 anarchists were deported without trial to Spanish Africa under the Ley de Defensa de la República; several of the deportees, including Durruti and Francisco Ascaso, had played no part in the rising.[6] The clampdown on revolutionary groups was so far-reaching that even groups like the BOC, which opposed the rising, had its offices closed and some of its activists interned without trial. Yet the CNT bore the brunt of the repression: *Solidaridad Obrera* was banned for several weeks and all CNT unions were closed, providing employers with an opportunity to victimise militants. The scale of the repression inhibited any effective protest against the deportations. When, at a meeting of the CNT local federation, the Builders' Union called for a 24-hour general protest strike, the Transport and Railway Workers' unions revealed that any such stoppage was impossible because the CNT 'has lost control of the workers' owing to 'the disorientation that exists within our class following the recent mobilisation'.[7] The only protest registered against the deportations was paramilitary: the defence committees replied with a campaign of armed propaganda, including a series of bomb attacks against official buildings, such as the council chambers, and against workplaces where militants had been victimised.[8]

The January action and its aftermath brought the tensions inside the CNT to a head. The *treintistas* and the BOC argued that the chaotic putsch exemplified the limitations of the libertarians.[9] The radical anarchists, meanwhile, mythologised the rising as a blood offering to anarchy, deflecting attention away from the inadequacy of their insurrectionary preparations with a fierce campaign against the 'cowardice' of their enemies.[10] Increasingly, the radical line held sway within the CNT. Thus, the Barcelona local federation blamed the failure of the 'revolution' on 'reformists', even though, as one of the moderates pointed out, they, like the radicals, had failed to seize the initiative.[11]

The highly charged atmosphere inside the CNT following the deportations precluded any reasonable discussion of tactics, and critics of the radical line were simply denounced as 'counter-revolutionaries'.[12] At the April 1932 Catalan CRT plenum in Sabadell, the BOC-inclined unions, including the local federations from Girona, Lleida and Tarragona, along with a number of individual *cenetistas* from Barcelona, were expelled. Not content with expelling communist heretics, *grupistas* attacked BOC meetings, resulting in bloody skirmishes.[13] But the greatest vitriol was reserved for anarcho-syndicalists. Peiró, a *treintista* and former CNT secretary-general who had devoted his entire life to the unions, was denounced as a 'police agent'.[14] Faced with increasingly personal attacks, Pestaña and his lieutenant Emili Mira resigned from the national and regional committees, respectively, in March 1932 and were duly replaced by *faistas*. With the *treintistas* now almost totally isolated in the CNT committee structure, the *treintista*-controlled Sabadell unions were expelled in September. This coincided with what moderates described as an 'uncivil war', in which *treintista* activists were physically assaulted by *grupistas* in the streets, at work and at union meetings.[15]

The split precipitated a staggering membership crisis. From its high point of 400,000 in August 1931, membership of the Catalan CRT fell to 222,000 in April 1932. However, with most of the membership losses in provincial Catalonia, the position of the radicals in their Barcelona stronghold was secure. Indeed, during the first year of the Republic, the CNT lost under 50,000 members in the Barcelona region (approximately one-quarter of the overall losses of the Catalan CNT), and with nearly 150,000 *cenetistas* in Barcelona province, the expulsion of the dissident communists and the anarcho-syndicalists enhanced the Barcelona local federation's importance within the regional organisation.[16] Nevertheless, a combination of the split and the increased tempo of repression eroded the mass mobilising capacity of the unions, a trend noted by the British consul in Barcelona, who observed that, by late May 1932, 'the bulk of the working people are failing to respond to [CNT] propaganda as readily as before'.[17]

Undeterred and, moreover, unrestrained by any organised internal opposition to the 'revolutionary gymnastics', the radicals substituted their own violence for mass union struggles. Accordingly, 1933, which was welcomed by *Solidaridad Obrera* as 'the year of the social revolution', began and ended with anti-republican anarchist uprisings.[18]

The second insurrectionary putsch began on Sunday 8 January 1933, almost a year after the Figols rising. While this action had a greater impact in Barcelona and in a few other key areas of anarchist influence, it nonetheless revealed that few improvements had been made in either revolutionary strategy or organisation.[19] By launching the rising on a Sunday, it was clear that the insurgents trusted exclusively in armed power and had scant interest in incorporating larger numbers of trade unionists in their struggle. Although the insurrectionists hoped that a general strike of railwaymen would coincide with their mobilisation, they viewed the strike in purely military terms, as a measure that might impede troop movements. Moreover, the revolutionaries ignored both UGT strength on the railways and the divisions among the CNT railway workers, who eventually aborted their stoppage at the eleventh hour. Nevertheless, the rising went ahead, in no small part due to the influence of members of Nosotros, eight of whom were represented on the Catalan CRT Defence Committee.[20] García Oliver, the secretary of the Catalan CRT Defence Committee, successfully prevailed upon Manuel Rivas, the *faísta* general secretary of the CNT and secretary of the National Defence Committee, to endorse the action.[21]

The element of surprise, along with much-needed weaponry, was lost in the days before the rising when police discovered a number of bomb factories in the *barris* and intercepted *faístas* as they ferried supplies of arms and explosives around Barcelona. A police raid on the Builders' Union offices on Mercaders Street yielded a large haul of ammunition, and there was much press speculation that a rising was imminent. Finally, following the accidental explosion of a bomb factory in Sant Andreu, the date of the rising had to be brought forward. The signal for the insurrection was the detonation of a huge bomb placed by CNT sewage workers in the drains beneath the main police station on Laietana Way, an act that almost killed García Oliver and other anarchists held in the cells there. Armed mainly with homemade, yet quite reliable, hand grenades, the insurrectionaries lacked firearms and, unsurprisingly, therefore, the putsch was a short-lived affair. The first major action by the insurgents – a two-pronged attack on the Law Courts and the nearby Sant Agustí barracks, on the edge of the city centre – ended after a 15-minute gunfight; having failed in their bid to procure much-needed weaponry, a hundred *grupistas* retreated into Poblenou. An attempt by around fifty *grupistas* to storm the Atarazanas barracks, at the port end of the Rambles, was thwarted, but only after a two-hour gunfight on the Rambles and the neighbouring streets in the Raval, which left two members of the security forces and a *faísta* dead. With the city centre relatively quiet, the arena of combat shifted to the *barris*. In the anarchist stronghold of Clot, insurgents erected barricades, seized cars from the rich and held the *barri* for several hours, clashing fiercely with the Guardia Civil and killing a policemen. There was also much fighting in Poblenou and l'Hospitalet. However, by the end of the following day, despite some sporadic gunfire in and around the Raval, the rising had run its course.

The January 1933 rising was most memorable for the repression that followed. Detainees were viciously beaten in the Laietana Way police station. It appears that members of Nosotros were singled out by the police: García Oliver was left with a cracked skull and broken ribs, while Alfons Piera had his face beaten and his nose broken with a rifle butt.[22] However, the most notorious example of repression came in the village of Casas Viejas in Andalusia, where local anarchists rose in the belief that the insurrection had succeeded everywhere else in Spain. Fearing that the Casas Viejas rising might be copied elsewhere, Arturo Menéndez, director-general of internal security, who had served as Barcelona police chief during the first months of the Republic, ordered that the rising be quelled as quickly and forcefully as possible.[23] This order was interpreted by the *asaltos* as an invitation to apply the Ley de Fugas: twenty-two civilians died, including several women and children; as a macabre lesson to the rest of the villagers, the charred bodies of the dead were left on display before burial.[24]

Within the logic of 'revolutionary gymnastics', the January 1933 putsch and the rise in state brutality made it a greater success than the January 1932 rising insofar as it stymied the political incorporation of the working class. The CNT, meanwhile, had its own problems incorporating workers and continued to shed members. By March 1933, the Catalan CRT membership was under 200,000, around half the total two years earlier. The CNT in the Barcelona area had lost 30,000 members in under a year, although with around 110,000 members, the Barcelona CNT could still hold sway over the Catalan CRT and the National Committee.[25] The radicals were unmoved in their voluntarist conceptions that they could give the revolutionary process a push without the communists, socialists or even the anarcho-syndicalists.

Thus, just one month after the suppression of the January 1933 putsch, the FAI Peninsular Committee affirmed that 'we have no doubt the social revolution will soon come'.[26]

The final insurrectionary essay was the culminating point of the 'Huelga electoral' ('electoral strike') called by the CNT and the FAI during the November 1933 general elections. This was a decisive moment in the political history of the 1930s, as the quasi-fascist CEDA (Confederación Española de Derechas Autónomas, or Spanish Confederation of Right-wing Groups) threatened both the parliamentary majority of the reformist Left and the very future of the Republic.[27] In sharp contrast to the benevolent apoliticism of 1931, the anarchists attempted to mobilise around the resentments that had accumulated during the first two republican years, the social policy of 'police stations, prisons and courts', which 'converted the nation into a prison' and the Ley de Vagos y Maleantes, a 'fascist experiment with a democratic label'.[28] Playing an ultra-leftist, divisive role that had much in common with the German Communist Party (KPD) prior to Hitler's electoral triumph, the radical anarchists argued that there was no difference between the various electoral options, even suggesting that fascism was already in power. Accordingly, Macià, the 'leader of the Catalan bourgeoisie', who 'betrayed' the Spanish Revolution in 1931 with his 'false promises as friend of the poor', represented, for the anarchists, the 'initial premise' of Catalan fascism and the 'guarantor of the bourgeois political order'.[29] Also like the KPD, the CNT and the FAI blocked united anti-fascist action, directing their fury against what they regarded as the 'fascism' of their enemies, be they *treintista*, socialist, republican or *bloquista*, all of whom were regarded as variants of authoritarianism. Meanwhile, the radicals downplayed the danger of the far Right, suggesting that the quintessential 'libertarian spirit' of the Iberian people would thwart fascism, unlike in Germany, where Hitler's triumph reflected the authoritarianism 'at the heart of every German'.[30]

Typically, the radicals exaggerated their own strength, warning that, if the elections 'opened the door to fascism', the 'iron front' of the CNT–FAI would destroy fascism and the Republic. Equally, a high level of abstention in the 'political comedy' would be interpreted as a mandate for the 'anarchist revolutionary experience'. These themes were reiterated at a series of monster CNT rallies, some of which were the biggest ever seen in 1930s Barcelona, which took place immediately before and after the elections. In Clot, a crowd of 90,000 workers heard Durruti, recently released from jail for his part in the January 1933 rising, launch an impassioned plea for the amnesty of the 9,000 workers imprisoned in Spain. Days later, a rally organised by the anarchist weekly *Tierra y Libertad* attracted over 100,000 people, who heard Francisco Ascaso announce that 'the hope of the international proletariat and the disinherited of the world' was that the CNT pass a 'death sentence' on the state and make its revolution 'in the street'. Durruti closed the meeting with a typically rousing conclusion: 'we have already talked for too long: it is the time for action....Seize what belongs to us....The world awaits our bulldozing revolution'.[31]

The rise in abstention in the November elections reflected the prevailing working-class dissatisfaction with the Republic as well as a pre-existing set of views about the incapability of elections and governments to change the lot of the dispossessed. Yet for the radicals, the news of the centre-right electoral victory and of the negligible turnout at the polls in anarchist strongholds was readily interpreted as evidence that a 'revolutionary situation' had arrived. In the days after the elections, the defence committees spearheaded a strategy of tension, launching a wave of gun and bomb attacks near several army barracks in the city. This coincided with a strike by CNT tram workers during which there were daily bomb attacks on tramlines and plant. The bombings, which occurred on and near busy streets, increasingly endangered civilians. One bomb was detonated at a tram station, seriously injuring a group of printers, one of whom was killed, as they left work. The following day, another huge bomb killed a soldier and injured eight workers.[32] Amid apocalyptic prophecies that a 'revolutionary hurricane' would unleash the 'final battle against fascism', posters appeared on the walls of the *barris* advising women and children to remain indoors as 'men of strong will' were about to embark upon the 'road to revolution'.[33]

When, on 8 December, the *faístas* made their move, as in January 1933, the authorities were prepared for the uprising.[34] Besides the fact that the anarchists had promised a rising if the Right won the elections, there had been

Figure 6.1 Reclaiming urban space: civil guards and members of the community observing a recently demolished barricade in l'Hospitalet, 1933

Source: Francesc Bonamusa, Pere Gabriel, Josep Lluís Martín Ramos and Josep Termes, *Història Gràfica del Moviment Obrer a Catalunya*, Barcelona, 1989, p.259

incessant rumours of an imminent insurrection from the moment that the results had been announced. Meanwhile, in response to bomb attacks, martial law had been introduced in Barcelona on 4 December, and the security forces flooded the streets. In the city centre, the Guardia Civil established machine-gun posts on key tram routes and at major intersections, and police cadets were mobilised to increase the presence of the security forces in the *barris*. With civil liberties suspended, the military authorities closed off the prole-tarian public sphere, banning all CNT unions and newspapers and arresting key activists, including Durruti, one of the main architects of the mobilisa-tion. In Terrassa, the main FAI stronghold in Barcelona province, the rising was effectively decapitated when seventy *faístas* were interned without trial. Nevertheless, the insurgents' ranks were swollen when anarchists and 'social' and 'common' criminals escaped from the Model Jail after members of the CNT Public Services Union excavated a tunnel running into the prison from the drains outside.[35]

This time the rising was accompanied by a general strike that was strongest in the industrial *barris* of Poblenou, Sant Martí and Sants. However, CNT pickets faced obvious difficulties imposing an exclusively anarchist-inspired stoppage in those factories in which dissident communists or anarcho-syndicalists accounted for the majority of the workforce, and there were reports of armed clashes between *faístas* and rival groups of workers. The frustration of the anarchists with those who rejected the liber-tarian revolution was reflected in a 'scorched earth' policy of bomb attacks at factories where the strike was resisted. On at least one occasion, *grupistas* bombed factories without warning, showing enormous contempt for the lives of non-CNT operatives.

The epicentre of the rising in the greater Barcelona area was the l'Hospitalet *barris* of La Torrassa, Collblanc and Santa Eulàlia, where local anarchists mobilised around the urban tensions and contradictions that had developed within these rapidly developed districts.[36] When, on 8 December, a general strike left the big factories empty, the *grupistas* took to the streets and the insurrectionaries had effective control of most of the city for four days. As one local anarchist reflected in his autobiography, the local commu-nity was drawn into the uprising: 'fathers, mothers, girlfriends, everyone, as soon as they knew what was going on went onto the streets to help in what-ever way they could'.[37] The 'l'Hospitalet Commune' promised a new social system. Bars and taverns that were deemed by anarchists to brutalise workers were closed down, and union committees and armed groups of workers requisitioned produce from shops, markets and warehouses, which was made available to the local community. Armed workers set out to dislo-cate the old structures of repression and punish those who were popularly viewed to have profited from the local networks of exploitation. Factories belonging to employers with a reputation for vindictiveness towards their workers were sabotaged or torched. At Santa Eulàlia market, where there had been persistent conflict between street vendors and market traders, dozens of stalls were attacked. Crowds occupied various official buildings. The municipal archive was destroyed. Offices belonging to urban property owners were seized, as was the local branch of the Radical Party, the party that had recently taken power in Madrid after the November elections. Nevertheless, the lives of the rich were respected. The only act of retribution was directed at a leading local member of the fascist party, the Falange Española, who was taken from his house and shot. As night fell on the first day of the rising, much of l'Hospitalet was left in darkness when members of Los Novatos (The Novices), one of the best-armed *grupos de afinidad* in the Barcelona area, blew up the central electricity terminal in La Torrassa. At this point, the *asaltos* stationed in l'Hospitalet withdrew to the relative safety of Barcelona. Electricity cables and telephone lines were also cut, and barricades were established at key places. Encouraged by the success of the 'l'Hospitalet Commune', an armed crowd set off towards Barcelona, although their march was halted after they clashed with security forces on the Sants – Collblanc border.[38]

While armed workers repelled the security forces sent from Barcelona to crush the rising from their barricades, the 'l'Hospitalet Commune' was effectively contained. Once the insurrection in Barcelona and beyond had been quelled, it could not survive in isolation. Faced with a growing number of incursions from the security forces, on 12 December the revolutionaries withdrew from the streets. Two days later, army units, backed by a force of 1,500 civil and assault guards and policemen, occupied the city and started to round up CNT militants.

It is difficult to draw up anything other than a critical balance of the 'cycle of insurrections'. First, the uprisings revealed the confused revolutionary perspectives of the anarchists, in particular the absence of a coherent spatial dimension. Not only were the objectives of the 'revolutionary gymnastics' unclear, but the insurgents did not possess the necessary arms and manpower to confront the security forces: even Los Novatos, one of the better-equipped *grupos de afinidad*, had nothing more substantial than Thompson sub-machine-guns.[39] Since their formation in 1931, the defence committees had been drilled in basic paramilitary techniques (principally the use of firearms and grenades), but they were little more than a streetfighting force and had not become a neighbourhood-based guerrilla army, as Nosotros had hoped.[40] Certainly, the *grupistas* provided evidence of their effectiveness as urban guerrillas in the *barris*, where they were relatively safe, protected by closely knit working-class communities, and where their well-developed supply and communication lines allowed them to move around with relative ease and launch lightning attacks on the security forces.[41] As one activist later observed: 'There was a great solidarity....Nobody reported us'.[42] However, the *grupos* were incapable of converting isolated local actions into a more offensive action that could lead to a powerful transformation at regional or state level. Although the risings increased the militancy of many activists and helped to forge a reliable corps

Figure 6.2 An Assault Guard protecting a tram during the 1933–34 Barcelona transport
strike

Source: Francesc Bonamusa, Pere Gabriel, Josep Lluís Martín Ramos and Josep Termes, *Història
Gràfica del Moviment Obrer a Catalunya*, Barcelona, 1989, p.256–7

of fighters in the heat of war, they tended to alienate the faint-hearted. Even
locally, the anarchists encountered problems mobilising communities, and it
was only during the 'l'Hospitalet Commune' in December 1933 that the
'revolutionary gymnastics' drew on community networks. This failure of the
anarchists to harness the solidarities of the *barris* was perhaps the greatest
shortcoming of the risings, which revealed that community solidarity was far
stronger than the organised solidarity of the CNT; the former, which was
based on a much smaller network of reciprocity (family, workplace and
barri) was more enduring and constant, little dependent on the wider political context, whereas the latter was conditional upon a more complex range
of political and institutional factors. This explains why the CNT's organised
solidarity was strong during 1931–32 due to the optimism following the
collapse of the monarchy and the birth of the Republic, whereas from early
1932 onwards it was eroded by state repression, which raised the potential
costs of mobilisation for many workers to unacceptable levels. Nor was there
a consistent attempt by the radicals to combine the risings with mass mobilisations or a revolutionary general strike. It is anyway unlikely that a
revolutionary general strike would have had any real chance of success,
given the decline in CNT power after the 1932 split and given that the 'cycle
of insurrections' began after the summer 1931 strike wave, when the masses
were already demobilised. Consequently, only limited numbers of workers

participated in the insurrections, and while more undoubtedly sympathised with this anti-state violence, given the relative secrecy that surrounded these vanguard actions, such support was invariably retrospective and passive. It is difficult to know exactly how many people participated in the risings, but it seems likely that there were between 200 and 300 *faístas* in Barcelona before the civil war, a minority of whom were opposed to violence of all forms. However, if we also consider members of the defence committees, we might conclude that there were, at most, 400 to 500 participants in the 'revolutionary gymnastics' out of 150,000 workers in the city.[43] For the most part, the insurrectionists were generally younger, unmarried and unskilled workers, who found it easier to bear the potential cost of a frontal clash with the state forces. There is also evidence that the *grupistas*, many of whom had been educated in *ateneus* and rationalist schools, had a higher level of learning and culture than that found in the average worker.[44]

Second, the 'revolutionary gymnastics' stimulated an ascendant repressive curve that enabled the state to assert its control over the *barris* and areas that were previously 'no-go zones' for the security forces. For instance, after the January 1933 rising, a Guardia Civil camp was established in the Santa Coloma *cases barates*.[45] Meanwhile, the December 1933 rising provided the authorities with a pretext to occupy La Torrassa and initiate a series of house searches in pursuit of 'wrongdoers'.[46] Yet while the repression could often be withstood due to local loyalties in the *barris*, the organised solidarity of the CNT was severely tested. Compared with the repression after the January 1932 rising, which was relatively short-lived and limited to Catalonia, that which followed the 1933 risings amounted to a comprehensive offensive against the CNT throughout Spain. By the time of the December 1933 rising, some of the major Barcelona unions had only recently reopened and then faced immediate closure. The l'Hospitalet CNT did not function openly until February 1936. Employers took advantage of the newly favourable circumstances to victimise workplace activists, cut wages and lay off workers.[47] All forms of working-class expression were persecuted: the workers' press was banned intermittently and fined capriciously by the authorities, while cultural institutions such as the *ateneus* and the rationalist schools were closed down for long periods. With hundreds of anarchists and *cenetistas* interned without trial and many more jailed for their involvement in strikes and insurrections, the prison population expanded vertiginously, prompting *Solidaridad Obrera* to declare that 'the whole of Spain is a prison'.[48] Repression also continued to affect revolutionary groups hostile to 'putschism', such as the BOC, which was sometimes banned; several of its activists were also interned without trial. With the authorities obsessed with 'anarcho-communist plots', the police tried to charge Andreu Nin, the communist intellectual and respected Catalan translator of Russian literary classics, with possession of explosives in an obvious frame-up that was eventually dropped after a number of high-ranking Catalan politicians intervened.[49]

Notwithstanding the nefarious consequences of the risings, and regardless of the fact that united proletarian action would increase the prospects of a successful revolution, the radicals persisted with their *politique de pire*, convinced that the worse things became the quicker their day would arrive. Indeed, shortly after the December 1933 action, the CNT National Committee resumed its attack on its 'fascist' enemies within the labour movement, boasting that the CNT–FAI was, 'as before, at the head of the revolution and in the front line against the fascist threat'; it also expressed its commitment to the 'revolutionary gymnastics', because 'these revolutions make the people ready'.[50]

6.2   Militarised syndicalism

The CNT did not entirely turn its back on its traditional trade union activities during the 'cycle of insurrections'; to do so would have brought the serious risk of losing its membership further. Nevertheless, there was a tendency for the *grupistas* to compensate for the CNT's lost collective power through small group violence and armed propaganda. For instance, with the unions incapable of halting redundancies, *grupos* threatened employers who sacked workers, either sending threatening letters (*anónimas*) or visiting factories and warning they would be 'dead men' if they did not hire workers from the CNT *bolsa de trabajo*. In one such case, Joseph Mitchell, the Scottish manager of the L'Escocesa textile factory, who had sacked several CNT activists, received a stamped note from a group called La mano que aprieta (The Arm Twisters) warning him that if the victimised *cenetistas* were not re-employed within fifteen days, they would bomb the factory: 'We will be very cruel, for it means nothing to us if the factory closes and the whole show ends up in the street....The vengeance will be terrible. There will be days of mourning in your home and in L'Escocesa'. The note ended with a pledge, which the *grupo* later honoured, to send Mitchell on 'a one-way trip from which there is no possible return'.[51] Nor was this an isolated case. In the tram sector, where 400 *cenetistas* had been victimised, *grupistas* launched a bombing campaign on plant and armed attacks on managers in a bid to achieve the re-employment of the sacked workers. In similar fashion, *grupistas* protested at prison conditions by shooting the director of the Model Jail. Two l'Hospitalet employers were also killed in the summer of 1933 in separate machine-gun attacks.[52]

The archetypal militarised conflict of this period was the builders' strike of 1933, an epic conflict that dominated city life for four months and which provides an insight into the multi-faceted nature of union practices and cultures of contestation in 1930s Barcelona: trade union divisions, the UGT's strategy of negotiation, the CNT's direct action, the anarchists' armed propaganda, and the commingling of traditional and modern (riots, strikes and demonstrations) protest repertoires.[53] Construction workers, the most deprecated section of the workforce, had been devastated by unemployment since the collapse of the dictatorship in 1930. A mainstay of *faísmo* since 1930, the Builders' Union sought to attain the six-hour day as a means of reducing unemployment, despite the fact that the employers in the sector had never even accepted the legal working day of eight hours.

When the dispute began, the UGT Construction Union immediately initiated a case in the *jurados mixtos* in an attempt to forestall a strike and channel the conflict into the institutional arena. However, since the CNT was, by a long way, the biggest union in this sector, a strike was inevitable. Although the CNT was careful to comply with legal stipulations prior to the stoppage, the authorities immediately started harassing the union, banning strike meetings at short notice in an attempt to demoralise the strikers. Determined to pursue their right to strike, the *cenetistas* were unbowed. If anything, the more the authorities clamped down on the union, the more violent became their response. This was epitomised by the 25,000-strong demonstration organised in June to protest against a series of bans on strike meetings. Despite the fact that the authorities had been informed of the march, the security forces blocked its path at Universitat Square, thereby preventing it from reaching nearby Catalunya Square. After a brief stand-off, during which the demonstrators refused to disperse, *asaltos* opened fire on the march, killing one striker and wounding many others. In the ensuing chaos, the march split up: part remained in Universitat Square, which was transformed into a battleground as builders armed themselves with bottles and chairs from nearby bars, tore up paving stones and clashed with the security forces. Unable to proceed to the city centre, another group of marchers veered off along Sant Antoni Avenue towards the Raval, although 'only after', in the words of *Solidaridad Obrera*, 'smashing to pieces all the windows of the shops and cafés of that bourgeois thoroughfare', causing thousands of pesetas worth of damage, requisitioning foodstuffs and registering their protest at the authorities by attacking the property of their middle-class supporters.[54] The following month, as the builders insisted upon their right to the streets, another protest march that was blocked by *asaltos* resulted in running battles as strikers attempted to regroup in the city centre. A section of the march entered the Raval, attacking businesses and seizing goods and food. Two later incidents highlighted the vicious social divisions in the city at this time. When the protesters entered Hospital Road, they were greeted by an armed group of shopkeepers, who opened fire, killing a bystander. Minutes later, some of the marchers identified a strike-breaking foreman, who was shot and killed.[55]

With the employers and the authorities holding firm in their opposition to any compromise, and with a blanket ban on demonstrations, the strike became protracted and the possibilities for mass mobilisation circumscribed. Increasingly, the defence committees intervened, launching a series of bomb attacks on building sites in the hope that the material damage would impel the employers to accept union demands.[56] By early August, explosions were occurring at a rate of nearly one a day, and *grupistas* started attacking Guardia Civil patrols escorting 'scabs' to building sites. *Tierra y Libertad* announced that the 'socialist assassins' who betrayed the struggles of the working class would be 'tried', and *grupistas* responded, killing seven leading *ugetistas* in Barcelona in the space of a few weeks. In the most grotesque case, an *ugetista* construction worker was murdered as he walked hand-in-hand with his young daughter in a Sants street.[57]

While some employers accepted union demands and sacked 'scabs' through fear of bomb attacks,[58] the constellation of forces – the authorities, employers, security forces and the socialists – allied against the CNT was such that the *grupistas* were unable to find a way out of the stalemate. Finally, the anarchist leadership of the Builders' Union put a motion to the rank-and-file in favour of returning to work with a 44-hour week, along with small wage rises and slightly improved working conditions, a settlement that differed little from the deal brokered by the UGT in the *jurados* months earlier and which had then been rejected by the CNT. Fearing a grassroots rebellion and in a clear break with CNT democratic traditions, the union leadership organised a secret ballot to vote on the deal. Indicative of the demoralisation among the rank and file, from a union membership of around 35,000, under 2,000 builders voted in the secret ballot, 1,227 of whom accepted the motion to return to work.[59]

We see then that the CNT had come to depend on a small core of militants for whom violence was the main form of politics. In many ways, this experience was comparable with the rise of *grupismo* after World War One, when the limitations placed on CNT syndical praxis allowed the most determined and committed militants to come to the fore. Thus, throughout 1934–35, the defence committees maintained a significant level of violence, even though, as was clear from the 1933 builders' strike, the vanguard militarism of the *grupistas* could not offset the CNT's waning collective strength.[60] Instead, individual and small-group terrorism increased repressive dynamics and further complicated trade union actions. On occasions, *grupista* terror provided employers with a convenient justification for closing workplaces and sacking workers.[61] The *grupistas* also displayed much disdain for union democracy: in 1934, during a dispute at a Barcelona textile factory, they pointedly ignored a branch union resolution rejecting 'individual terror' and killed the employer.[62] Nor did the *grupistas* tolerate the right of workers to affiliate to anti-CNT unions. As the CNT lost the importance it once held for the Barcelona working class, the *grupos* became increasingly sensitive to criticism from the growing number of anti-libertarian voices within the labour movement, the militaristic ethos of the *grupos* validating physical attacks on *bloquista* and *treintista* 'scum' (*canalla*) in the bid to 'persuade' workers to affiliate to the CNT for 'health reasons'.[63]

6.3   Funding the movement – the expropriators

The dependency of the CNT on the *grupos* was accentuated further by the financial crisis of the unions. At the start of the Republic, it had been agreed that branch unions would make monthly contributions to the local prisoners' support committee, the body that was responsible for the 'victims of the social struggle', helping those who were blacklisted after strikes, paying the legal costs of detainees and assisting the dependent relatives of jailed activists and the *perseguidos*, the militants forced to go 'on the run' to evade the authorities. Yet because it was common for many rank-and-file members and even militants to default on their union dues, contributions to the prisoners' support committee often went unpaid, the shortfall being made up by the regional and national committees and by local fundraising activities, benefit concerts and impromptu collections in workplaces and in the *barris*.[64]

However, once the CNT entered a new protest cycle in the summer of 1931 and became locked into battle with the state, official sanctions and repression severely disrupted the day-to-day fundraising activities of the unions. For instance, while in the spring of 1932 the Barcelona Prisoners' Support Committee met around one-third of its costs by organising benefits and collections, in the more repressive climate of 1933–34 the authorities were in no mood to tolerate such activities and CNT collections were criminalised, union fundraisers becoming liable to imprisonment under the Ley de Vagos.

During the same period, we also need to recall that the advent of the 'revolutionary gymnastics' placed additional demands on the CNT's resources as unions faced a barrage of legal bans and fines. The CNT press was a particular target for the authorities, and a combination of censorship, bans and fines meant that increasing amounts of union money was required to subsidise the press. By 1934, the editorial board of *Solidaridad Obrera* admitted that the paper was 'broke', on the verge of being 'killed' by the censor. The FAI press encountered similar problems: longstanding plans to create an anarchist daily had been shelved, and *Tierra y Libertad* was heavily in debt.[65]

Lastly, we need to consider the above in the context of the CNT's profound membership crisis after thousands of members departed the organisation during 1932–33. Worse still, the unions that left the CNT were, in general terms, based on more skilled sectors of the workforce and were thus better placed to fund the movement.[66] Meanwhile, as we have seen, the bulk of the unions that remained in the CNT, particularly in Barcelona, more often than not had larger numbers of unskilled and unemployed members, for whom non-payment of dues was the norm. By the start of 1934, therefore, the Barcelona local federation had a weekly deficit of 40,000 pesetas.[67]

Yet while the economic crisis of the CNT affected the entire organisation, its implications were greatest for those bodies that sustained the principles of active solidarity on which the Confederation was based. For instance, in September 1933 the Comité Pro-Perseguidos Internacionales (Exiles' Support Group), which assisted foreign anarchists fleeing repression, admitted that it was in a 'desperate state', its lack of economic resources leaving it 'embarrassed' and unable to help refugees with 'unwonted frequency'. The prisoners' support committees were, all too often, in a similarly parlous state. Matters became so bad that the Marseilles Prisoners' Support Committee, a pivotal body within the CNT support network that assisted activists smuggled out of Barcelona port, announced that it could no longer offer financial support to militants. Meanwhile, following restlessness among prisoners' families at the irregularity of welfare payments, a group of detainees in Barcelona issued a motion of censure against the local federation for tolerating the 'inefficiency' of the prisoners' support committee and the 'lack of attention' paid to those who had 'fallen in the struggle against capitalism and the state'.[68] The prisoners also proposed the formation of 'special committees' to collect what they obliquely described as 'extraordinary contributions'.[69]

In an attempt to save the organisation from collapse, the armed groups within the orbit of the CNT and the FAI initiated new forms of fundraising. It is not certain from where the instruction emanated. It has been suggested that the FAI Peninsular Committee issued an appeal to the defence committees and its own *grupos* for money.[70] Yet it is far from certain that the FAI had authority in such matters, and it is more likely that the order came from the Catalan CRT, which was ultimately responsible for the unions, press and prisoners' welfare in the region. However, what we can be sure about is the fact that the recourse to illegal funding strategies cannot be explained solely in terms of the economic crisis of the CNT, for many revolutionary groups faced economic limitations on their activities during the 1930s and did not follow this path. Rather, it was the rise of the radical anarchists, for whom armed actions were central to all social protest, which sealed the switch to illegal fundraising tactics. Indeed, in much the same way as the radicals justified the illegality of the unemployed, so also did they rationalise that which funded the movement, drawing a sharp distinction between the term 'robber' and those who requisitioned money for 'the cause'.[71] Thus, just as the armed *grupos* were called upon to fill the vacuum left by the decline in CNT syndical muscle, so too were they required to secure the internal funding of the Confederation.

There was no single funding mechanism. In some cases, a form of 'revolutionary tax' was levied against employers and companies, who were informed of the sum involved (which depended on company size and which might run into tens of thousands of pesetas for large enterprises), the method of payment and the sanctions for non-payment, which ranged from the threat of sabotage against plant to the murder of managers. Since the authorities discouraged employers from meeting these 'tax' demands, it is difficult to know how often it was paid. We can nevertheless get a sense of how the 'revolutionary tax' operated from anecdotal evidence in the memoirs of managers and activists and from the press following the killing of employers for non-payment. There is also evidence that the 'revolutionary tax' was imposed on businesses that had been involved in strikes with the CNT and

were thus held responsible for exhausting the resources of both the movement and their supporters.[72] In l'Hospitalet, the Comité libertario
pro-revolución social (Libertarian Committee for Social Revolution) levied
the 'tax' on high-profile businessmen, such as Salvador Gil i Gil, a local
councillor active in the repression of street traders.[73]

Yet the most common method of funding was armed expropriation,
normally involving attacks on banks and payrolls. As one militant explained,
'to raid a bank was an episode of the social war'.[74] Although, as we saw in
Chapter 2, this strategy was used by anarchist groups after World War One, it
was first utilised by CNT squads in the republican period during the wood
workers' strike (November 1932 to April 1933), when pickets punished
intransigent employers by expropriating their cash boxes and safes.[75]
Sometimes, businesses owned by right wingers were also deliberately
targeted.[76] This funding tactic became highly attractive because, as one
activist explained, 'one well prepared attack and you get away with a sum of
money equal to four weeks collections'.[77] By 1934, expropriations were a
recurring feature of urban life, sometimes bringing as much as 100,000
pesetas into union funds at a single stroke.[78]

The expropriations presented Companys, who replaced the recently
deceased Macià as president of the Generalitat at the end of 1933, with a
sharp dilemma. On 1 January 1934, in accordance with the devolution
programme specified by the Catalan Autonomy Statute, the Generalitat's
newly formed Comissaria d'Ordre Públic (Public Order Office) assumed
responsibility for policing.[79] Determined to demonstrate its competence in the
realm of public order to a suspicious centre-right government in Madrid and a
critical Lliga in Barcelona, the Generalitat increased 'the drive to persecute
robbers, murderers and wreckers', fearing that anything less would give the
impression that order had been lost.[80] Responsibility for the new autonomous
Catalan police rested with Josep Dencàs and Miquel Badia, Generalitat interior minister and Barcelona police chief, respectively. While apparently
Catalanising the security forces, Dencàs and Badia, both of whom had close
links with the quasi-fascist ERC youth movement, the escamots, politicised
policing in a way that had never been seen before. Along with his brother
Josep, Badia drafted the violently anti-CNT, anti-migrant escamots into the
Catalan police; the Sometent was also purged and replaced by escamots.[81]
Meanwhile, Jaume Vachier, an ERC councillor and businessman, took charge
of the Guàrdia Urbana.[82]

Because the expropriations were viewed as a deliberate attack on Catalan
institutions, the grupistas were now repressed without quarter. The legal sanctions applied against grupistas and expropriators were stern: anyone found in
possession of explosives could expect a prison term of up to twenty-two years;
armed robbery normally meant a sentence of between thirteen and seventeen
years, while the crime of firing at the police was normally punished with nine
years in jail.[83] Yet this did not deter the expropriators, who compromised the
key professional claim of the police – that the force detected crime – for if the

grupistas were not detained *in flagrante delicto* they proved difficult, near impossible, to apprehend.[84] In fact, when cornered, the expropriators, who were equipped with a range of weaponry, including pistols, sub-machine-guns and grenades, were a genuine match for the security forces. Following a payroll heist at a factory in central Barcelona, one *grupo* used guns and grenades to break through a police cordon and, when they were later intercepted by an *asalto* patrol in Santa Coloma, another gun battle ensued, after which the expropriators disappeared.[85]

The elimination of the 'cancer of banditry' was a key factor in the evolution of the new autonomous police.[86] Police Chief Badia, who was known to his admirers as Capità Collons (Captain Balls), took personal responsibility for the repression of the expropriators, regularly joining the front line during shoot-outs and picking up a number of gunshot wounds in the process. According to one Barcelona *faísta* who had connections in *catalaniste* circles, Badia planned to establish a special police unit dedicated to the extra-judicial killing of anarchists, an initiative that was blocked by the personal intervention of Companys, who feared the consequences of a return to the *pistolerisme* of the early 1920s.[87] Nevertheless, Badia succeeded in raising the stakes in the war against the expropriators and the *grupistas*, adding a new viciousness to the history of policing in Iberia. Independent doctors regularly confirmed that suspected *grupistas* leaving the Comissaria d'Ordre Públic had been brutally mistreated and, according to anarchists and communists who had experience with the police during the monarchy and the Republic, the autonomous Catalan security forces were the most vicious of all.[88] In one notorious case, following a shoot-out between police and an armed gang on the outskirts of the city, Badia left wounded 'murcianos' without medical treatment, and it was only after a heated argument with a Guardia Civil commander that an ambulance was called to the scene.[89] There is also evidence that the Generalitat police adopted a policy of selective assassination of 'FAI criminals'. The first suspicious death occurred in early 1934, when the body of a young *faísta* was found on wasteland on the outskirts of Barcelona. Although the deceased had apparently earlier participated in a gunfight with the police, the fact that he died from a single shot from a police-issue revolver suggested that he had been summarily executed. In a separate case, an unarmed *cenetista* was shot and killed in broad daylight by an off-duty policeman in a Les Corts street. Memories of 1920s police tactics were evoked again when an unarmed *grupista* was shot in the back after he allegedly 'attempted to escape'. Meanwhile, in mid-April, after a gunfight in which over 200 rounds were exchanged, Bruno Alpini, an Italian anarchist and expropriator, was killed on Paral.lel in what was regarded in anarchist circles as a classic act of Ley de Fugas.[90] The following month, two more expropriators were shot dead by police in the drive to 'clean up' Barcelona.[91]

Despite intense police pressure, the number of expropriations showed no sign of abating throughout 1934 and 1935, demonstrating that increased policing does not necessarily reduce illegality. This very point was recognised in a police report published in the press in April 1935: 'When a trial for robbery or an assassination occurs, immediately new robberies are committed…an established chain of punishable events.…It is this continuity that it is vital to break'.[92] There are several reasons for this 'continuity'. First, it was impossible for the authorities to provide a permanent guard for the numerous large sums of money transported around and concentrated within the city that were targeted by well-drilled and selective expropriators, who apparently launched attacks when they knew they had a good chance of escape. Moreover, since speed was one of the expropriators' main allies, they used cars, often hijacked taxis or stolen from the rich, that they knew were faster than police models. The expropriators also recognised that, if they were injured, they would be looked after by the organisation and could receive medical attention from doctors supportive of the CNT–FAI.[93]

Second, the expropriation squads were deeply rooted in the social formation and were virtually impossible for the police to infiltrate. Recruited from proven activists from the defence committees and the prisoners' support committee, as well as some of the more willing and capable members of the *grupos de afinidad*, the expropriators were trusted individuals, many of whom during earlier, less repressive times had organised union collections in workplaces and barris.[94] Some expropriators were 'professional revolutionaries' in the classic sense; they had experience of evading the police from the postwar years, possessed the necessary pseudonyms and false identities and tended to move around, staying with comrades and in 'safe houses'.[95] In a positive sense, this commitment to the movement explains the high level of probity among the expropriators, who also needed little reminder of the sanctions that would have been applied to anyone who attempted to abscond with the organisation's money.

In addition to the unity derived from a common ideology and shared objectives, the expropriators also relied on the affective ties of kinship and neighbouring. Many expropriators were recruited from local families with a history of anarchist and union activism. Moreover, the family structure, so often associated with the stability of the existing order, frequently gave considerable coherence to the high-risk activities of the expropriators. In one squad, a father and son worked together.[96] Meanwhile, Los Novatos, a *grupo de afinidad* active in funding initiatives, included five brothers from the Cano Ruiz family and two other sets of brothers, all of whom resided within a square kilometre of one another in the La Torrassa *barri*.[97]

The *esprit de corps* that so typifies such close-knit groups ensured that, when the security forces succeeded in detaining members of a squad, they stubbornly refused to betray their comrades by talking to the police or by passing information on to the authorities. Indeed, detained *grupistas* relied on a version of *omertà*, repeatedly informing police that they had occasioned upon their accomplices in a bar or cafe, that they could not remember anything about their appearance and that they had failed to ask their names. *Grupistas* also frequently told police that these same strangers had lent them any arms they had in their possession at the time of their arrest, a completely unbelievable story concocted not to appear credible but to frustrate police investigations. Meanwhile, anyone who gave in to police pressure ran the danger of being perceived as a traitor, a perfidy that was dealt with in summary fashion.[98]

A few other observations can be made about the expropriators. They were invariably male. Women rarely participated and, when they did, their involvement was almost exclusively of an auxiliary nature. The expropriators were also predominantly young and single. Even the more seasoned activists in the squads were normally under forty, while the most active expropriators of the 1930s were in their early twenties, such as Josep Martorell i Virgili, dubbed 'Public Enemy Number One' in the bourgeois press, who was only twenty when arrested, by which time he had launched a series of bank robberies for the CNT and for the anarchist movement.[99]

The expropriations provide yet another example of the readiness of the anarchists to mobilise beyond the factory proletariat and channel the rebellion of those deemed unmobilisable by other left-wing groups. This was perhaps epitomised by the presence of several former detainees from the Asil Durán borstal among the expropriators, such as the aforementioned Martorell.[100] The eclectic tactical repertoire of the anarchists, their continuing ability to combine 'modern' with older protest forms, increased the vitality of their resistance struggle, and, in equal measure, scandalised the 'men of order'. We will now address the implications of this in the cultural sphere.

7 Cultural battles

Class and criminality

The intense and variegated protest cycle of the republican years inspired an outpouring of moral panics from the social, economic and political elites. Indeed, it could be argued that the history of the Republic is the history of spiralling moral panics, which reached a crescendo in response to the expropriations. While there remained profound differences within and between these elites – the schism between monarchists and republicans to name just one – as we will see, there was much unity among the 'men of order', which now included the supporters of the 'republic of order', who clamoured for 'social peace' in the streets and who concurred that the CNT was the central problem of the Republic.

The first moral panics of the republican era developed around the direct action mobilisations of the summer of 1931 and formed part of a classic divide-and-rule strategy that tended towards splitting the working class along radical and non-radical lines. As we saw in Chapter 3, the republican authorities were obsessed with separating the bulk of the working class, the 'healthy elements' whose interests and objectives it was assumed could be satisfied within the new regime, from the 'subversives' and 'agitators', who allegedly 'coerced' workers to support strikes.[1] Accordingly, the moral panics can be seen as part of a project to integrate politically the 'good', in most cases skilled, workers, who were prepared to accept gradual change from above within the timescale set out by republican politicians, whereas the 'violent ones',[2] who represented a mortal danger to the future of reform, were to be isolated and repressed. This distinction was reiterated on a daily basis in the anti-*cenetista* press, principally *La Vanguardia*, *La Veu de Catalunya*, *L'Opinió* and *La Publicitat*, in whose pages the organised activities of the CNT (meetings and strikes, as well as the cultural and educational programmes in the *ateneus*) were systematically distorted. Indeed, it is striking that whereas mass meetings and rallies were rarely reported, isolated acts of picket violence or a gunfight between *grupistas* and the police gained wide coverage, thereby allowing the CNT to be depicted as a disorderly force.

The emphasis of the panics shifted and adapted to changing protest rhythms. As the more militant sections of the unemployed mobilised and insisted upon their right to the streets, they became the main target for the panics, being cast as 'undeserving poor', the under-socialised 'dangerous class' of nineteenth-century discourse. The problem with this 'underclass' of 'fraudsters' was not its poverty but its immorality, which made it a burden on society and a threat to attempts to help the rest of the poor. By placing the accent on the deviant nature of part of the unemployed, poverty was isolated from its social context and reduced to a moral issue.[3] There was a particular obsession with migrant youth, whom, it was claimed, were attracted by the reputation of Barcelona's 'dissolute life' (la mala vida). Completely unfettered by normal familial control, these 'runaway children' were a 'formidable danger' to public order.[4] This was the 'enemy within', a flexible grouping that could include street traders, petty criminals and pickets, consisting of 'outsiders', 'foreigners' and 'alien elements'.[5]

The moral panics had a pronounced spatial dimension; hence there were 'foci of immorality', such as the Raval. Although very much part of Barcelona's urbanisation process, the Raval was externalised and exoticised as 'Chinatown' and as 'the Andalusian Barcelona'.[6] It was a 'crime zone', a 'labyrinth' of 'infected streets', the 'catacombs of Barcelona': 'the veritable danger of the slums, where the disease and decay of its dark hovels create a climate favourable to the most vile germinations [and] legions of villains and swarms of parasites'.[7] Highlighting the continuity in the tone of the moral panics, the republicans denounced the Raval's bars and clubs as spaces of perversion, prostitution and drugs trade in tones that differed little from their monarchist predecessors.[8] For instance, one physician linked to Generalitat circles proposed a relationship between the high levels of disease in the Raval and the deficient mores of the area's inhabitants, many of whom 'lead a nocturnal life in the cabarets and other places of questionable morality'.[9]

Another continuity with the earlier moral panics was their hysteria. Indeed, in September 1931, a leader article in La Vanguardia on public disorder in Barcelona convinced the British and Italian governments to advise their subjects to avoid what was being portrayed as a lawless city. Aware of the damage that might be occasioned to the local economy and to hoteliers, restaurateurs and other groups that constituted an important source of its advertising revenue, La Vanguardia responded with a long editorial in which it explained that the security forces exercised complete control on the streets and that there was no breakdown of law-and-order in Barcelona, effectively contradicting the thrust of its coverage of public order before and after the birth of the Republic.[10] While successive civil governors actively fomented the moral panics, Ametlla, who occupied this office for part of 1933, correctly observed how, by overplaying the level of social conflict, the panics produced 'a psychosis of alarm and uncertainty' that sometimes upset the governance of the city.[11]

Yet the die was cast, and the panics spiralled alongside the militarisation of anarchism and the expropriations, La Vanguardia, L'Opinió and La Veu de Catalunya seemingly competing with one another to report the 'contagion' of crime in the most lurid and sensationalist terms possible.[12] *La Veu de Catalunya* devoted a page every day to 'Terrorism', which appeared as a huge banner headline. Since there was often not enough copy to fill the page, property crime and other everyday illegal acts were often included, as well as other news, some of which was mundane and completely unrelated to 'terrorism' but which nevertheless added to the impression that public order was constantly under attack.[13] Similarly, *L'Opinió* printed a section entitled 'The Robbery of the Day' in which minor non-violent thefts were described sensationally as if the streets were teeming with blood-crazed felons.[14]

The moral panics reached their height during 1933–35 in response to the expropriations. As far as the elites and the bourgeois republican press were concerned, the expropriations signified an ongoing assault on the urban order that exposed the failures of society's defences, and this caused far more anxiety than the revolutionary uprisings, which were little more than a short-term inconvenience, easily contained by the security forces. Typifying what Hall *et al.* have described as the 'mapping together' of diverse moral panics through 'signification spirals', a 'general panic' was produced by the press as a variety of fears were amalgamated and depicted as a unified, overarching offensive against the Republic and society as a whole.[15] The authors of the moral panics seized upon what they viewed as the 'best ingredients' for the gangs of 'professional gunmen and robbers' that comprised the CNT's 'Robbers' Union' (Sindicat d'atracadors): the primitive culture of the migrants ('the Murcians of the FAI'), 'born criminals', 'lumpenproletarian' detritus, 'bohemian youth' and young 'hobos' (*polissons*) fond of frequenting 'immoral establishments' in 'Chinatown'.[16] This characterisation was extended to the CNT, the FAI and the anarchist movement as a whole, which was described as 'a criminal group' of 'subhuman' and 'degenerate' individuals, 'underworld parasites', 'professional layabouts' and 'villains, thieves and bombers' led by *déclassé* 'down-and-outs' and 'a minority of adventurers of working-class origin'.[17] It was also suggested that the anarchists were 'anarcho-fascists', part of a wider conspiracy with the extreme Right, or, as one wit put it, the 'FAI-lange'.[18]

The moral panics reached their apotheosis in a series of articles published by Josep Planes in *La Publicitat*.[19] Interspersed with pseudo-anthropological digressions about pre-industrial brigands in Italy and Andalusia, Planes' articles were little more than moral panics about 'the anarchist problem' dressed up as investigative journalism. For Planes, political violence was submerged in a world of common criminality: anarchism and crime were synonymous, as all crime in Barcelona could, in one way or another, be traced to the anarchist movement, including prostitution rackets and the drugs trade, which he attributed to Italian, Argentinian and German anarchist refugees. However, his biggest concern was the expropriations. According to Planes, 'the characters who lead the various robbery gangs are the most prestigious figures from the anarchist movement', the 'gangsters of the labour movement'. This was an 'original type of criminality' that was 'typically Barcelonese': 'the anarchist-robbers or the robber-anarchists of Barcelona are nothing less than the Catalan equivalents of Al Capone....Today it is the fashion among all thieves, pickpockets and swindlers to pass themselves off as anarchists'. By collapsing the distinction between social protest and criminal behaviour, Planes revived an early theme of bourgeois criminology and one of the most basic premises of the first moral panics of the nineteenth century.

The aims of the moral panics were diverse. In the first instance, as we saw in Chapter 1, this was a language of power, a justification for a strong authority in the face of the 'disorder' of inherently 'uncontrollable' and unenlightened social sectors that generated so much anxiety among the political elite and their supporters about the future of the social, economic and political order. As such, the moral panics were a legitimising discursive tool. Their great attraction was their labelling and scapegoating function: they identified what were, from the perspective of the 'men of order', the sources of social problems and conflict that inspired their anxieties in the first place.[20] As David Sibley has observed, moral panics were an ideological mechanism through which 'exclusionary space' was extended.[21] From the start of the Republic, the specific patterns of security force activity, such as the fierce repression of street traders and unemployed activists, were legitimised and on occasion conditioned by the moral panics: they allowed the authorities to criminalise politically problematic communities and rebellious social groups, thereby reducing political differences to a matter of law-and-order. The major repressive policies of the republican era were also validated by the moral panics. For instance, the Ley de Vagos y Maleantes was introduced after a prolonged press campaign directed at a series of 'public enemies', such as pimps, drug pushers, the 'professional unemployed' and 'salaried subversives'.[22] Equally, urban reforms, such as the Plà Macià for slum clearance in the Raval, bore traces of the moral panics and the tirade against the 'crime zones' of 'Chinatown'. Meanwhile, the moral panics reinforced the application of exclusionary social policies and the denial of welfare to unemployed migrants. The daily press published a succession of stories about welfare abuse by 'tricksters' and 'con men' from 'Chinatown', 'the professionals of common crime, jail-birds, tramps, those who live outside the law and those who have never worked nor wish to', who spent unemployment benefit on expensive meats, patés and wines, thereby 'stealing' from 'the truly needy children of Barcelona'. Having depicted this 'underclass' as criminal and incapable of accepting its social responsibilities, the implication was clear: the small welfare budget could be cut, for the provision of relief would merely aggravate the dependent and deviant condition of the 'undeserving poor'.[23]

By identifying new social dangers and combining them with existing ones, the moral panics effectively demanded perpetual vigilance from the authorities and rising levels of repression. This is evidenced by the manner in which, during 1934–35, the panics focused on the *ateneus* and proletarian hiking clubs, which were accused of 'perverting' 'very young boys' and 'naive youngsters', who were 'forced to listen' to 'subversive' speeches amid orgiastic scenes of 'free love'. It was also alleged that the hiking clubs were a front for the organisation of expropriations, which were allegedly planned on organised trips out of the city, and that bombs were prepared inside the *ateneus*.[24] As was so often the case with the moral panics, press hysteria far surpassed the evidential basis of a set of stories designed to criminalise the last remaining legal activities of the anarchist movement and close off the libertarian public sphere altogether.

Figure 7.1 Anarchists on an excursion into the foothills around Barcelona during the Second Republic

Source: Francesc Bonamusa, Pere Gabriel, Josep Lluís Martín Ramos and Josep Termes, *Història Gràfica del Moviment Obrer a Catalunya*, Barcelona, 1989, p.248

As was the case during the monarchy, the moral panics nourished an overtly repressive mentality on Right and Left, which increasingly coincided in their desire for a 'strong government' to repress 'criminality' of all sorts'.[25] The left-wing republican newspaper *L'Opinió* advocated the autocratic formula of an 'armed democracy' to introduce 'extraordinary measures' to 'intimidate the gangsters' and eliminate 'the cancer of banditry', arguing that the 'complete extinction' of 'criminal groups', including the FAI and other 'criminal social dregs', was 'the most pressing problem and the most difficult to resolve of all those facing the Republic today'.[26] In similarly draconian fashion, the socialist USC declared that 'the first task that we must realise is the elimination of the FAI and all the *faístas* using all means possible, without hesitation, without pity and without reservations'.[27] This consensus flowed from the binary, Manichean divisions established by the panics: the contrast between 'insiders' and 'outsiders', 'deserving' and 'undeserving' poor, the 'constructive' versus the 'dangerous', the 'healthy' against the 'sick', all of which demanded the coming together of the 'men of good faith' (sic).[28] Thus the conservative La Veu de Catalunya and La Vanguardia concurred with the left-wing republican L'Opinió and La Humanitat and the socialist Justicia Social on the need for a complete ban of the CNT and the anarchist movement, a unity summed up in the Lliga's slogan: 'All united against the FAI!'[29] This is not to deny the distinctive political inflections of the moral panics expressed by the aforementioned newspapers; for example, La Vanguardia and La Veu de Catalunya suggested that crime had never existed under the monarchy, as if the departure of the king had stimulated a profound collapse in collective morality and respect for the law. Yet there was still a commonality between the traditionalist and republican moral panics: both were languages of anxiety, power and order that emphasised respectability and hierarchy and shared a set of ideological representations based on a conservative moral syntax.

Finally, in keeping with the republican objective of splitting the working class, the moral panics can be viewed as part of a cultural struggle for hearts and minds in the barris. There were several strands to this ideological project. First, the exaggerated nature of the moral panics was essential in order to generate broad concern about phenomena such as street trade and crime, which in reality threatened the narrow interests of a small proportion of the population. Yet by stressing an undifferentiated civic interest and the essential unity and harmony of the social system, the moral panics projected a consensual view of society and appealed to an imagined political community.[30] This explains why the moral panics were frequently couched in the language of disease borrowed from the discourse of nineteenth-century urban hygienists.[31] By describing social enemies as a 'plague' and 'infestation' and the migrants as moral 'pollution' and 'filth' that 'contaminated' the city, the authorities hoped to find popular support for a 'labour of hygiene' to eliminate 'scum'. Because this plague apparently threatened all citizens, regardless of social rank, it could not therefore be ignored and necessitated measures of social quarantine and a new surveillance of everyday life in order to 'cleanse' the city of germs and liberate it from the threats facing it.[32]

Second, the moral panics sought to disarm the anti-state struggle of the CNT and the anarchist movement by identifying them with the 'underclass' in an attempt to delegitimise the libertarian movement in the barris. The overriding message of the panics was that if the police could successfully deal with the 'recalcitrant' sectors of society, who endangered the 'common good', the authorities would have their hands free to bring felicity through reform to the barris. Press reports of criminal omniscience were thus used to justify the growing number of police intrusions in the barris in a bid to secure backing for the security forces in working-class communities that had traditionally been hostile to all forms of external authority. Not only would this rally part of the civilian population to the side of the state, it would also detach the radical anarchists from their supporters in the *barris*, breaking working-class resistance by undermining the solidarity and ties that made it possible in the first place.

7.1   'Criminal capitalism'

Despite the barrage of moral panics, the CNT and the FAI retained a profound influence as an organising structure in the *barris*. On one level, this was because the moral panics were a restatement of a dominant ideology that was poorly implanted in the *barris*. Yet, more than anything, CNT and FAI ideologues initiated a successful counter-cultural struggle in which they rebuffed the premises behind the moral panics and, in doing so, articulated a major restatement of the libertarian conception of crime, illegality and punishment. There were two aspects to this ideological struggle: first, a fierce defence of popular illegality; and second, a critique of the moral panics and the 'criminal' nature of capitalism.

As far as popular illegality was concerned, as we saw in Chapter 5, the anarchists provided ample justification for actions that conventional opinion defined as 'criminal'. In keeping with the libertarian orthodoxy that social behaviour was conditioned by circumstance and context, the anarchists emphasised the rational nature of illegality, contending that this phenomenon was intimately linked to existing social and political conditions, 'the product of a pernicious social organisation'. Thus, *Solidaridad Obrera* maintained, 'bourgeois society is responsible for all crime', since its distribution mechanism of 'privileges for the few and persecutions and privations for the rest establishes sharp differences in terms of material position, education and lifestyle, which shape both professional and occasional criminality'. Certain specific features of illegality in Barcelona were explained in terms of the peculiar characteristics of local capitalism. For instance, the question of youth illegality, which so preoccupied bourgeois republican social commentators, was viewed as a reaction to the limited opportunities facing young workers; thus, many of those who rebelled against the hyper-exploitation and sweated labour in Barcelona's factories were 'compelled' to live outside the law.[33] Illegality was also explained in terms of the acquisitive and proprietorial mentality generated by capitalist society. As 'Marianet', the Builders' Union leader, observed:

> In a society that legalises usury and has robbery as its basis, it is logical that there will be some who are prepared to risk their lives and achieve through their own audacity what others manage to do with the protection of coercive state forces.[34]

The economic crisis was identified as an important short-term determinant of the upsurge in illegality. Marín Civera, one of the most original thinkers on the revolutionary Left during the 1930s, explained the spread of illegality as a function of the haemorrhaging of the economic order. For Civera, illegality became a realistic and logical course of action for those workers denied the chance to survive from their labour.[35] Rejecting the problematic and ill-defined 'underclass' thesis,[36] the anarchists argued that most illegality was 'occasional criminality' perpetrated by the short-term unemployed, who had been barred from their rightful place at the 'banquet of life'. Illegality was then an alternative form of wealth distribution, part of a 'struggle for life' as the unemployed seized what was 'necessary to live' by defending their 'natural right to life'.[37]

In some respects, the anarchist rejection of the 'underclass' concept stemmed from a philosophical opposition to deterministic pseudo-Lombrosian concepts such as that of the 'pathology' of the 'born criminal', as well as other conservative notions of 'degeneration' and 'evil' that conditioned a considerable amount of republican thinking on law-and-order. As *Solidaridad Obrera* insisted, 'there is no such thing as "good" and "bad" people, only people who are "good" and "bad" at different times'. Certainly, the anarchists did not try to deny that there were recidivists, but they were created by the 'bourgeois judicial concept of punishment'. First the police and the courts labelled 'offenders' as 'criminals', whereupon they were isolated in jails, brutalised and dehumanised by a prison system that 'converted men into beasts'. Rather than rehabilitating detainees, the anarchists reasoned that the 'state revenge' of a 'perverse society' offered only 'pain and violence' and 'egoistic and punitive conceptions' that left many released prisoners marginalised and unemployable. *Solidaridad Obrera* concluded that 'Law is the enemy of real society', because 'nothing is solved with the jailing of the so-called common prisoners': only then, in the stateless, libertarian society, could the 'pinnacle of true justice' be attained, as crime would disappear through the emergence of truly stable communities capable of regulating themselves, without the intervention of the police or other extraneous forces.[38] On another level, given the anarchist defence of the 'outcast' and the 'underdog', the 'underclass' concept was rejected on affective grounds. In particular, the most deprecated sections of the working class – the predominantly working-class inhabitants of the Raval, the 'pariahs' of 'Chinatown' in elite imagination, and the migrants of La Torrassa, who were reviled as a 'lawless tribe' – were defended for being poor workers forced to lead 'an errant life outside the law'. For the anarchists, the 'mean streets' in these *barris* were spaces of hope, in which the banner of the cause of freedom had been raised and repressed; hence 'the streets were stained with so much proletarian blood'.[39]

The libertarian critique of the moral panics saw their agenda inverted. In keeping with their class war precepts, the anarchists dwelt on the 'felonies' committed against the working class, which 'has nothing and yet produces everything', by the 'criminal classes': the politicians and capitalists, the 'aristocracy of robbery', and the petite bourgeoisie, 'the traffickers in the misery of the people', 'the true racketeers of the human race'. These were the 'real thieves' who had the greatest opportunity to commit crime and the greatest chance of evading detection and who prospered within a 'criminal economy' rooted in 'speculation and robbery' and 'the sweat and blood spilt in fields, workshops, factories and mines'.[40] Accordingly, in the anarchist lexicon 'commerce replaces the word robbery', while 'trade' was a bourgeois euphemism for 'trickery', 'deceit', 'theft' and the 'scandalous businesses of the profiteers'. And yet 'the most vile of all criminals', the 'modern-day pirates and bandits [who] spend their lives in comfortable offices', were 'legal thieves', their 'respectable crimes' protected by bourgeois law and the police ('murderers' and 'criminals in the pay of the state'). Consequently, *Solidaridad Obrera* argued that:

> existing society is a society organised by robbers. From the small shop-keeper to the industrialist, right up to the most powerful capitalist consortiums, there is nothing but speculation, which, in plain language, means robbery....The whole of society rests on exploitation... there is no case of an employer who gives his workers the full value of the wealth that they produce.[41]

Postulating a rival set of proletarian moral panics, the anarchists attacked the 'plague' of evictions of the unemployed, which resulted in the 'repugnant crime' of homelessness, which left 'thousands and thousands of hungry, homeless people eat[ing] the filth from the streets and sleep[ing] on park benches'. The libertarian press also berated the 'false' bourgeois moralists who ignored certain types of violence. When a 14-year-old unemployed worker was violently assaulted by his former employer after demanding a statutory redundancy payment to which he was legally entitled, *Solidaridad Obrera* published the name and address of the aggressive capitalist and suggested that he should receive lessons in child welfare.[42] *Solidaridad Obrera* documented examples of the 'immorality' of 'capitalist civilisation' and its tolerance for pursuits like war and imperialism, which were far more destructive for human life than the expropriations. In this 'world of the superfluous' in which a tiny minority were 'swimming in opulence' and spending a small fortune on perfume, unsold foodstuffs were destroyed as millions of people across the globe faced starvation.[43]

Insisting that criminality was not the exclusive pursuit of the much-maligned proletarian class, the anarchist press publicised the activities of 'criminal fauna living at the expense of the people': the drunken violence of off-duty policemen, robberies by prison wardens, embezzlement by lawyers, tax evasion by landlords, corruption by republican politicians as well as violent business disagreements between shopkeepers.[44] Using an emotional tone that resembled the tenor of the moral panics, the CNT press repeatedly denounced the 'robberies' that were 'prejudicial to the sacred health of the people' committed by 'villainous' landlords who charged 'criminal' rents and 'stole' the deposits of outgoing tenants, bar owners who diluted drinks and shopkeepers who meddled with food and weights, and other 'bloodsuckers' (*chupasangres*) and 'vultures' 'trading in the physical necessities of humanity' and 'picking dry the ill-fated body of the worker'. According to *Solidaridad Obrera*:

> if [the authorities] analysed the foodstuffs sold daily to the public, all these people with private guards and security doors on their houses would go to jail....Every shop, warehouse [and] workshop is a den of villainy. The robbers are the owners...the 'honourable' folk who go to mass on Sunday morning and visit their lovers in the afternoon...the very gentlemen who are outraged when a poor, needy man steals a loaf of bread to feed his children, while they rob with weights and measures and steal even the air and the sun of the dispossessed.[45]

For the anarchists, crime and punishment revealed the class nature of 'the republic of rich layabouts (*chupópteros*)'. *Solidaridad Obrera* regularly exposed the prejudices of the penal system, pointing to the failure of the republicans to fulfil their pledge to submit all social classes to the law and how the crimes of the privileged and the powerful were frequently tolerated, uninvestigated or punished by small fines. An example of this was middle-class tax evasion, which, though first publicised by the CDE during the rent strike in 1931, was largely ignored by the authorities even though subsequent investigations, both in the anarchist and in the bourgeois press, revealed that some landlords owed thirteen years or more in tax arrears.[46] On the rare occasions when the police did punish middle-class crime, the misdemeanours were generally so extreme that the authorities had to act or see their credibility seriously compromised, such as when police detained a shopkeeper who adulterated flour with barium sulphate and lead carbonate, an act that left 800 consumers bedridden.[47] Yet middle-class detainees were never subjected to the same humiliating treatment that workers and the unemployed received from the police, prompting *Solidaridad Obrera* to declare that the hopes of justice in bourgeois society were as realistic as expectations of survival inside 'a third degree tuberculosis camp'.[48] The Ley de Vagos y Maleantes was cited as the most vivid example of the 'classist' nature of republican law, which, in the opinion of *Solidaridad Obrera*, meant that 'to be badly dressed' was a crime. Patterns of punishment also revealed the continuities with past regimes: 'all the coercive measures that surround the penal code of monarchies and republics are established to castigate the rebellion of the slaves'. Indeed, irrespective of the form of state, the law was, as *Tierra y Libertad* maintained, the 'historic caprice of a specific class' that was allowed to 'rob on a daily basis to increase its wealth'.[49]

Crime, then, from the perspective of the anarchists, was socially determined and historically conditioned by the prevailing relations between social classes. It followed, therefore, that what the law defined as 'murder' was not always treated as a criminal offence. Rather, anarchists maintained that the violent killing of an individual acquired the label of 'murder' only after the act had been interpreted and classified by a series of ideological and socio-legal agencies. To underline the socially determined nature of crime and killing, the anarchists cited as examples two hypothetical killings during an industrial dispute: the fatal shooting of a 'scab' by a picket and the killing of a picket by a member of the security forces. In the first instance, the judiciary would inevitably treat the death of a 'scab' as 'murder', whereas the second case was unlikely to reach the courts, let alone be defined as 'homicide' since, for a policeman, killing becomes 'a laudable act, in compliance with their duties'.[50]

7.2   The 'moral economy' of the Barcelona proletariat

The anarchist stance on illegality corresponded with the broad experiences and culture of the *barris* discussed in Chapter 2, a culture that was little affected by the dominant ideology and that contained a normative opposition to the law.[51] For instance, workers' experience of exploitation in the consumption sphere sat harmoniously with anarchist claims that proletarians were the victims of a series of robberies by the 'criminal classes' – employers, pawnbrokers, money lenders, landlords and shopkeepers – who submitted fundamental human needs like shelter, food and work to a ruthless business ethic.[52] Equally, Pich i Pon, Barcelona's leading property owner and the head of the COPUB, who so loudly denounced the 'illegality' of the rent strike, was known popularly as 'the leading pirate of Barcelona' because of his shady business interests, an image that was not dispelled by his involvement in the 1935 'Straperlo affair', the most important corruption scandal in the history of the Republic. Meanwhile, the Tayá brothers, shipping magnates and former owners of *La Publicitat*, one of the most sanctimonious vehicles for the 'moral panics', were notorious for fraudulently acquiring lucrative government franchises for their merchant fleets.[53]

If we explore the social reality of the *barris* in republican Barcelona, we see that one of the reasons why respectable fears about armed robbery failed to construct a consensus around a law-and-order agenda was because they constituted a form of imaginary violence for the overwhelming majority of the Barcelona working class, whose everyday insecurities were far removed from those of the 'men of order'. One of the biggest concerns for workers was the danger of disease, which was perhaps the most significant threat to order in the *barris* and which coincided with the anarchist description of bourgeois society as 'the society of death'.[54] For the most part, these were preventable diseases, such as typhoid, the incidence of which increased in the 1930s and which proved far deadlier in the *barris* than the expropriations and 'murderous robberies' that obsessed the bourgeois republican press. Tuberculosis was another serious problem: in 1935, a group of physicians estimated that 70 percent of all children in Barcelona displayed signs of this condition, which also presented a continual threat to adult proletarians.[55] These health problems were intimately linked to awful housing conditions. One pro-republican physician claimed that in some of the Raval's tenements, over three-quarters of all deaths could be attributed to poor housing stock. Meanwhile, according to *Tierra y Libertad*, 50 percent of all accommodation in Barcelona infringed 'the most elemental norms of safety'.[56] Even *La Veu de Catalunya* recognised that, in 1936, 'there are thousands and thousands of workers living in uncomfortable rented dwellings'.[57]

Another set of proletarian anxieties stemmed from the threat of unemployment, a specifically working-class problem that carried a series of catastrophic consequences, such as eviction and homelessness. An estimated 30,000 people were living on the streets, in shanty dwellings or in other short-term accommodation, a figure that was much lower than the number of unoccupied flats in Barcelona, which was estimated at around 40,000 in July 1936.[58] In the *barris*, where the distance between the unskilled working class and the urban poor was little more than the scant security provided by a badly paid job, the fate of the homeless was far more emotive than the sufferings of the victims of illegality. Underlining the gulf between the republican hierarchy and the 'dispossessed', while the Catalan political elite attended a lavish banquet to celebrate the third anniversary of the birth of the Republic, a homeless unemployed worker collapsed on the streets of Sant Andreu and died from malnutrition.[59] Such deaths of the homeless were often only reported in the trade union and left-wing press.[60] Working-class lives were also threatened by industrial accidents. As in the monarchy, the authorities failed to make the bourgeoisie comply with safety legislation. Moreover, owing to the economic recession, many employers offset the falling rate of profit by relaxing safety standards, which saw the number of industrial accidents in Barcelona grow by one-third during the Republic. After the funeral of three workers killed in a factory explosion, *Solidaridad Obrera* summed up the lot of 'the eternal victims of the capitalist machine' and the danger of being 'mutilated by capitalist economic life'.[61]

The anti-police culture of the CNT was another element that affirmed the collective social memory of the *barris*. The sense of the past of many workers was shaped by the fear of the security forces and their arbitrary violence. Pointing to the continuities with earlier struggles, the CNT compared Dencàs and Badia, the organisers of the Catalan police, with Arlegui and Martínez Anido, who spearheaded the anti-CNT repression during the 1920s, a period that remained the bloody yardstick for all anti-worker repression in Barcelona.[62] At the same time, the main target of the moral panics – the expropriators – were seen as 'insiders' who posed no threat to workers, for, while the expropriators sometimes killed members of the security forces, civilian injuries were extremely rare.[63] Not only did many workers appreciate that illegality was, during times of unemployment, central to survival in Barcelona's unstable low-wage economy, but there is also evidence that the expropriators, who generally targeted distant capitalist institutions such as banks and insurance companies, earned much admiration in the *barris*, where they were seen as evidence of the strength of working-class communities.[64] Even when the expropriators operated in the *barris*, their targets were on the other side of the fault line that separated the proletariat from the commercial middle classes.[65]

The principle vehicle for the moral panics, the bourgeois republican press, the 'mercenary press' in the view of *Solidaridad Obrera*, was also held in low regard in the *barris*, where it had long been perceived as being intimately tied to capitalist economic interests, which it defended as clearly as it opposed labour unions. Indeed, in the early 1920s, the partialities of the 'capitalist press' impelled CNT printers to impose 'red censorship' on many Barcelona newspapers. The anarchists skilfully encouraged scepticism towards the press in the *barris*, reminding workers that the enemies of the international revolutionary movement had always depicted its militants as 'bandits'. Ever fond of historical analogies, *Solidaridad Obrera* likened the denigration of the FAI by the Barcelona press to the insults hurled at Spartacus and his slave army by the Roman authorities.[66] Despite the veneer of press independence and the diversity of titles, it was common knowledge that most of Barcelona's newspapers were controlled by a narrow clique: Pich i Pon, the COPUB boss, owned *El Día Gráfico* and *La Noche*; *La Vanguardia* was the mouthpiece of the monarchist Conde de Godó, who hailed from one of the city's leading textile families; and *La Veu de Catalunya*, the organ of the Lliga, expressed the political interests of Catalan big business. This was fertile ground for anarchist allegations that the bourgeois press was 'the great prostitute of existing civilisation' staffed by 'hack' journalists 'on hire' to 'financial cliques'.[67] The situation with republican newspapers was little different. *La Publicitat*, which was purchased by the Tayá brothers, two freight entrepreneurs and vehement opponents of trade union rights who made their fortunes supplying the Allied war machine during World War One, was reputedly funded by the British consulate in Barcelona and was an energetic defender of Anglo-French imperialism. By the 1930s, *La Publicitat*, like *L'Opinió* and *L'Humanitat*, was closely identified with ruling factions inside the Generalitat, and all these papers advanced a view of social reality completely at variance with the experiences of the majority of workers.[68]

7.3   'Revolutionary constructivism': the end of the expropriations

The end of the 'cycle of insurrections', along with the expropriations that came in their wake, finally came about due to pressure from within the CNT and the FAI. The first criticism of the insurrectionary line came after the January 1933 rising, when a number of FAI *grupos* criticised the role of Nosotros, denouncing their minority revolutionary actions as pseudo-Bolshevism and arguing instead for a process of education and mass revolution. Most of the opposition concerned procedural irregularities and the lack of internal democracy within the CNT and the FAI following the spread of vanguard militarism. In the debate that followed the rising, many anarchists were horrified to learn that Nosotros and other *grupos* were invoking the name of the FAI while not actually belonging to the organisation. It was claimed that Nosotros, which relied on a largely unaccountable power base in the defence committees, had produced a democratic deficit within the unions that was at variance with the democratic traditions to which the CNT laid claim. To be sure, the members of Nosotros exploited their charismatic power and revolutionary reputation, constituting, in the opinion of one of their anarchist critics, a 'super-FAI' or a 'FAI within the FAI'.[69] Certainly, the rank-and-file was not consulted ahead of the January 1933 rising, and the level of internal discussion was negligible: no more than fifty delegates from the Catalan CRT defence committees voted for a rising that had huge ramifications for the CNT and the FAI. There was no further discussion, and the final details were outlined at a smaller gathering in a bar on Paral.lel.[70] While in times of repression it was common for small groups of dedicated activists to carry the rest of the organisation and take decisions in 'militants meetings', these still tended to be larger assemblies than the ones that sanctioned the insurrections, and their conclusions did not have the same import for the future of the CNT. Finally, after the December 1933 rising, when it seemed that the position of Nosotros was unassailable, several anarchist *grupos* left the FAI in protest.[71]

Concerns about internal democracy converged with growing disquiet about the elitism of the *grupistas* and the manifest failure of the CNT to make its own revolution.[72] The nefarious balance of the 'revolutionary gymnastics' was incontrovertible: the *grupistas* had, at times, attacked the PSOE and the dissident communists more than the bourgeoisie; the labour movement was more divided than ever; the CNT had split in Catalonia, and there were worrying fissures opening up between its different regional committees; and the collective energies of the CNT had been depleted in a series of futile clashes with the state, the result of which had been a fierce repression that jeopardised the future of the entire workers' movement, bringing Spain to the brink of fascism. Few were prepared to make a case for the continuation of the insurrectionary option. While during 1931–33 state repression had helped to justify the position of the more militant factions within the CNT, the insurrectionary tactic had only really triumphed among a small section of the middle and upper leadership of the unions and, although this position had been backed by important sections of the rank-and-file, outside Barcelona there were many in the CNT who did not support the putsches. Indeed, the Madrid and Asturian *cenetistas* reviled what they saw as the sterile revolutionary maximalism of the Barcelona anarchists. This was spelled out in *CNT*, the daily paper of the Confederation in central Spain, which observed that:

the lightning blow, the hasty gamble, are outmoded. Our revolution requires more than an attack on a Civil Guard barracks or an army post. That is not revolutionary. We will call an insurrectionary general strike when the situation is right; when we can seize the factories, mines, power plants, transportation, and all the means of production.[73]

There was also external pressure from the IWA (International Workers' Association), the international association of anarcho-syndicalist unions, for the CNT and the FAI to change tactics.[74]

In Barcelona, the growing opposition to the 'revolutionary gymnastics' culminated in the emergence of the Nervio ('Sinew') *grupo de afinidad*. The main intellectual figure within Nervio was Sinesio García Delgado, better known by the pseudonym Diego Abad de Santillán.[75] He was born in León, but his family emigrated to South America, where he became a leading figure in the Argentinian and the international anarcho-syndicalist movement. Expelled from Argentina in 1931, he moved to Barcelona, becoming editor of *Tierra y Libertad* in 1934 and secretary of the FAI in 1935. Another leading member of the group, Manuel Villar, took charge of *Solidaridad Obrera*.[76] Abad de Santillán and Nervio were determined to transform an insurrectionary movement into a more stable revolutionary union organisation without suffocating the spirit of radicalism at the base of the CNT and the FAI. By recuperating the 'constructive' concept of the revolution, which been banished from the Confederation since the departure of the moderate anarcho-syndicalists, Abad de Santillán's conception of social transformation left no scope for guerrilla actions and expropriations, a tactic he had opposed during his days in Buenos Aires, when Italo-Argentinian individualists murdered one of his close comrades.[77]

The final break with the expropriation tactic was sealed at a clandestine plenum of the local federation of anarchist groups held in the summer of 1935, just across from the Raval. Ironically, it fell to Durruti, previously one of the most enthusiastic advocates of 'economic attacks', to argue for an end to the expropriations. Although he relied on his credibility with the most radical sectors of the FAI to win the debate and vote on this issue, Durruti still faced stern opposition from a small group of Hispano-Argentinian 'men of action' and anarcho-individualists.[78] Nevertheless, there was a sharp decrease in the rate of expropriations, and by early 1936 the remaining armed robberies appeared to be the work of unemployed workers. Meanwhile, apart from a few missions in which 'scores were settled' with employers and individuals involved in state repression, the defence committees underwent a period of reorganisation during 1935–36.[79]

The shift from insurrectionism can also be explained in terms of the readiness of the CNT leadership to reincorporate the anarcho-syndicalists, who had formed the 'Opposition Unions' in an attempt to halt the membership haemorrhage of 1932–34. The marginalisation of the proponents of armed illegality and the new revolutionary organisational schema proposed by Abad de Santillán, which was framed in terms that were highly reminiscent of the *treintistas*, were essential preconditions for welcoming back the moderate anarcho-syndicalists.[80] As they announced in the 1931 'Treintista Manifesto', the anarcho-syndicalists favoured a disciplined union organisation funded by workers' contributions. The anarcho-syndicalists had opposed the expropriations from the immediate postwar period, and in 1926 Pestaña published a novel in which he narrated an armed robbery committed by common criminals posing as anarchists.[81] When armed fundraising tactics were employed again in the 1930s, the *treintistas* took it as further evidence of the CNT's subordination to an unaccountable, semi-clandestine insurrectionary body that, in the view of Peiró, one of the leading anarcho- syndicalists, had an 'Al Capone-style' approach to the revolution.[82]

The changing political context and the growing awareness on the Left that some kind of unity was needed to block the rise of fascism was a further circumstance that conditioned the tactical shift inside the CNT and the FAI.[83] In Asturias, in October 1934, the Alianza Obrera (Workers' Alliance), a coalition of anarchists, communists (dissident and orthodox) and socialists, launched the largest workers' insurrection in Europe since the 1871 Paris Commune, taking control of the means of production and holding the Spanish army at bay for two weeks.[84] The immediate cause of the rising was the news that the quasi-fascist CEDA was about to form a coalition government with the Radicals in Madrid, a move that many on the Left interpreted as a prelude to the conversion of the Republic into a corporate Catholic state. In Catalonia, however, the CNT leaders were locked into their local war against the Generalitat and the rest of the Catalan Left. So, while the ERC-controlled Generalitat was, for many republicans, the 'bulwark of the Republic', for Catalan anarchists devolution had resulted in 'a historic offensive' by the ERC-controlled police against the CNT.[85] The repression of the Catalan CNT – which far exceeded anything the organisation faced in areas under the jurisdiction of the Spanish Right – made it impossible for Barcelona *cenetistas* to support the Generalitat. Moreover, the earlier experience of state repression gave substance to claims that a CEDA government would be no worse than the 'Republican fascism' that Barcelona anarchists claimed had been in existence since 1931. However, the opposition of the CNT and the FAI to the development of the Aliança Obrera, the Catalan anti-fascist alliance, which it denounced as a coalition of its 'enemies' in the labour movement, was narrow-sighted sectarianism.[86] The introspective Catalan CNT, thus, opposed the October 1934 mobilisation on the grounds that it was a 'political' action designed to change the government of the day and not to make a genuine social revolution. Consequently, as Asturian workers fought for the survival of the 'Asturian Commune', Francisco Ascaso, Nosotros member and secretary of the Catalan CRT, issued a call to the Barcelona proletariat to return to work from a radio station controlled by the Spanish army.[87] And so the Catalan radicals remained aloof from the revolution that they had desired for so long, a rising infinitely more significant than the putsches of 1932–33.

The repressive dénouement to 'Red October' was ferocious and exceeded anything previously seen during the Republic. The spectre of Thiers haunted Spain. Martial law was declared under the terms of the Ley de Orden Público and was only finally lifted in September 1935. All liberal democratic spaces were closed: elected members of Barcelona Council and the Generalitat were dismissed, their powers revoked; armed robbers and pickets were tried in military courts as all civil liberties were rescinded.[88] Even the most basic trade union rights were abrogated, and independent syndical organisations, whether UGT, CNT or autonomous, were effectively banned as employers initiated a new offensive against working-class conditions, slashing wages and victimising thousands of militants.[89] With 40,000 workers jailed throughout Spain, there was a huge reduction in strikes: between April 1935 and January 1936 there were only thirteen strikes in Barcelona, and in October 1935, 280 political and trade union centres were closed in the city.[90] According to the British ambassador, Spain offered:

> the impression of a country under a dictatorship....The prisons are overflowing and provisional ones have to be found to contain the enormous number of people who have been arrested....With the unions in a powerless condition...the popular masses are likely to be in a state of sullen disaffection but at the mercy of the government for some time.[91]

After October 1934, Pich i Pon, the local Radical Party activist and COPUB president, and Anguera de Sojo, civil governor in 1931, two key figures in the divorce between the Republic and the local working class, controlled important political offices. Pich i Pon, who has been described by Bernat Muniesa as a 'dictator–mayor',[92] enjoyed sweeping executive power, serving as governor-general of Catalonia and Barcelona mayor. Meanwhile, having gravitated from the ranks of the republicans to the CEDA, Anguera de Sojo became labour minister, whereupon he resumed his battle with the CNT.[93] Among his measures to increase state control of the trade unions, Anguera de Sojo drafted a law banning all unions that had 'revolutionary aims'.[94] He also promulgated a series of employer-friendly decrees. Employers enjoyed new powers to close factories and to sack workers for alleged breaches of labour discipline or if they went on strike for 'political' reasons. Anguera de Sojo also set about redefining Catalonia's legal status, abolishing the autonomy statute and forming a commission to return powers to Madrid.[95]

While the centralisation of power during the *bienio negro* was a clear reversal of the devolution of 1931–34, it signified a further development of the 'law-and-order' state and the shift towards the coercive management of conflict that began with the 'republic of order' and the Ley de Defensa during 1931–33. So, although state control of the unions, internment under the Vagrancy Act and the reliance on martial law and military courts to deal with anyone who broke public order was much greater during the *bienio negro*, these were first deployed during 1931–33, and their use was made easier by legislation dating from this period, such as the Ley de Orden Público.

Unsurprisingly, the Catalan bourgeoisie enthused about the turn to the right. *La Vanguardia* praised 'the new Germany' of Hitler, which in less than two years had banished strikes. *La Veu de Catalunya* celebrated the use of martial law, while Cambó, always an accurate barometer of bourgeois opinion, acclaimed the Spanish army and welcomed the return of the death penalty to remove 'the black stain' of social protest 'from our beloved Barcelona'. Meanwhile, during a trip by CEDA leader José María Gil Robles to Barcelona, employers' groups feted the *jefe* (boss) of the resurgent Right in what was a victory parade through the centre of the city.[96]

The flirtation of the bourgeoisie with the Madrid Right and the army was comparable with the period immediately prior to Primo de Rivera's 1923 *pronunciamiento*. Also like in 1923, when the city's unions were unable to resist the coup, the Barcelona CNT was on a descending curve, its organisation buckling under the white heat of repression. Understandably, there was growing concern inside the CNT and the FAI, at both state level and in Barcelona, that the libertarian movement was peripheral to the march of socio-political developments.

Many anarchists were finally impelled to accept that the political situation had deteriorated since 1931 and that a major change in orientation was required to end the isolation of the Barcelona CNT. Moreover, since the key to the Asturian rising was the unity of the Left, the CNT leadership could not resist the groundswell of grassroots support for anti-fascist unity, a feeling that was encapsulated in the slogan 'Better Asturias than Catalonia', a clear critique of the Barcelona CNT's elitist *grupismo* of 1932–34.[97] As 'unity' became the new watchword of the Spanish Left, the conditions emerged for ending the rupture within the CNT: the *treintistas* expressed their desire to return to their 'libertarian home',[98] while Durruti, once a fervent advocate of separating from the moderate anarcho-syndicalists, was obliged to recognise in a 1935 prison letter that the split he once saw as a virtue had in fact made the CNT vulnerable and marginal.[99]

7.4   The discreet charm of the republicans

While there was no doubt on the Left that the political context demanded an anti-fascist alliance, questions remained about the nature of this unity. The dissident communists, along with some inside the CNT and the PSOE, favoured an exclusively proletarian Alianza Obrera (Workers' Alliance) based on the Asturian brand of revolutionary anti-fascism. However, in late 1935, following the announcement of elections for early 1936, the Popular Front (Frente Popular), which effectively revived the 1931 cross-class, republican-socialist electoral coalition, emerged as a rival pole of anti-fascist unity. (In Catalonia, the Popular Front was known as the Leftist Front (Front d'Esquerres)).[100] That the Popular Front should become the preferred choice of the anarchist leaders appears paradoxical at first sight, especially when we recall the anti-CNT policies enacted by the republican-socialist government during 1931–33 and the repression spearheaded by the Esquerra from the Generalitat during 1933–34. And yet, despite the common revolutionary objectives of the anarchists and the dissident communists, the CNT leaders rejected all proposals for an insurrectionary *entente* in the Workers' Alliance on the grounds that this would be a 'political' alliance.[101] This was a continuation of the sectarianism that the CNT leaders had displayed towards the dissident communists since 1931: any acceptance of the Alianza Obrera would have vindicated the politics of their dissident communist rivals, who had long been the main advocates of anti-fascist revolutionary unity.

In another sense, the seduction of the anarchists by the Popular Front reflected their traditional apoliticism. Because the CNT had no formal political representation, it periodically expressed itself through exogenous political forces, as we saw in 1930–31. This process was repeated during 1935–36, when the CNT and the FAI calculated that a Popular Front electoral victory would result in a new juridico-political opening that would allow for the reorganisation and expansion of the unions. (The Popular Front programme promised, among other things, the freedom of social and political prisoners, the revision of sentences passed under the Ley de Vagos against trade union activists and a purge of the police.[102]) Consequently, in the prelude to the elections, the revolutionary bluster of the preceding years was conspicuously absent from anarchist propaganda and, although the CNT–FAI did not publicly invite workers to vote in the 'electoral farce', there was nothing resembling the strident anti-republican rhetoric that accompanied the 1933 general elections, a course of action that threatened to hand power again to a rightist coalition apparently committed to a Hitlerian-style conquest of democracy from within and the destruction of the CNT. *La Revista Blanca*, the messenger of anarchist apoliticism, even referred to Companys' 'dignity' in much the same way as the anarchists had praised Macià four years earlier. Meanwhile, throughout the electoral period, paragons of anarchist virtue, including Durruti, tirelessly reiterated the need for an immediate amnesty, which, as one of the key policies of the Popular Front, was readily interpreted as an invitation to vote for the liberal–left coalition. Some were more candid: Peiró, on the eve of his return to the CNT, but still a member of the FAI, advised workers who normally abstained in elections to vote 'against fascism'.[103]

As in 1931, in February 1936 *cenetista* votes ensured the electoral victory of the middle-class republicans. Immediately, the jails were opened and thousands of the workers incarcerated after October 1934 were released. In Catalonia, the Generalitat regained the powers accorded to it under the autonomy statute. While the Popular Front government satisfied the CNT–FAI by restoring certain fundamental democratic protocols and providing a legal framework in which the unions could reorganise, there remained many points of friction between the two. In particular, the CNT–FAI criticised the reluctance of the government to ensure that workers who had been victimised after October 1934 got their jobs back. The CNT also attacked the government for ignoring the plight of its activists who had been victimised prior to October 1934. In response, the Confederation embarked on a series of mobilisations to ensure that its militants were re-employed. Interestingly, in the new political context after February 1936, mass syndical pressure succeeded where the *grupistas* had failed, the rejuvenated CNT unions securing the return of many of the workers victimised after the 'revolutionary gymnastics' to their former workplaces.[104]

Another source of contention between the authorities and the CNT was the issue of civil liberties. The CNT was furious that the new government continued to apply the Ley de Vagos against the unemployed. Although the promise of an amnesty for the thousands of 'political' prisoners jailed after October 1934 was fulfilled, this did not affect those the CNT described as 'social' prisoners, a category that included unemployed workers jailed for illegally 'procuring the means of subsistence', *cenetistas* and *faístas* interned under the Ley de Vagos, as well as the numerous 'expropriators' from the defence committees sentenced as 'common' criminals. In an attempt to usher in a new legality, the CNT–FAI initiated a campaign for the repeal of the 'repressive laws' of 1931–33, such as the Ley de Vagos and the Ley de Orden Público, and for a complete amnesty for all prisoners, including those jailed for 'crimes of hunger'. The frustration of the 'common' and 'social' prisoners and the agitation of the remaining *cenetistas* and *faístas* in the jails resulted in a series of prison uprisings.[105]

Despite encouraging protest inside the jails, the Barcelona CNT avoided unnecessary confrontations with the authorities, preferring to rebuild the syndical structures that had received such a battering during the clashes with the state between 1931 and 1935. In what was essentially a period of reorganisation, the *treintistas* were welcomed back to the 'libertarian family' at the May 1936 Zaragoza Congress, which mapped out the immediate trajectory of the CNT.[106] The membership figures of the reunified CNT could not conceal the relative decline of the union in Catalonia and, indeed, in Barcelona compared with 1931 (see Table 7.1).

Table 7.1 CNT Membership figures, 1931–1936, for Barcelona and Catalonia.

Date	Total Catalan membership	Barcelona CNT membership	Provincial catalan membership
June 1931	291,240	168,428	122,812
May 1936	186,152	87,860	98,292

Source: E. Vega, 'La CNT a les comarques (1931–1936)', *L'Avenç* 34, 1981, p. 57

In sharp contrast to the maximalism of the 'cycle of insurrections', the period from February to the start of the revolution and civil war in July was, then, largely a time of reflection and renewal for the Catalan CNT–FAI. There were only two significant actions by the *grupistas* in Barcelona during this time. The first came at the end of April, when the Badia brothers, Miquel and Josep, the former Barcelona police chief and organiser of the *escamots*, respectively, were assassinated in broad daylight in the city centre.[107] Anarchists could neither forget nor forgive the brothers' brutal contribution to the repression of the CNT in 1934; Miquel had already survived one assassination attempt and, like his brother, had ignored several assassination threats from FAI *grupos*, choosing to remain in Barcelona. According to sources inside the FAI, the Badia brothers were killed by Argentinian anarchist exiles who were friends of Alpini, the Italian expropriator killed by Catalan police in 1934.[108] The other *grupista* action was the assassination of Mitchell, the L'Escocesa manager whose life had been threatened in 1934 and who died in a drive-by shooting.[109]

Rather than signalling a new programme of *grupista* violence, these acts were a 'settling of accounts' from the struggles of 1933–34. Indeed, in the post-Asturias spirit of anti-fascism, the *grupistas* and the CNT leadership were loathe to present the authorities with serious difficulties, largely because it was common knowledge that the extreme Right and reactionary army officers had greeted the Popular Front electoral victory by conspiring to overthrow the Republic and institute an authoritarian regime. The CNT and the FAI therefore adopted an expectant attitude as they reorganised their cadres in anticipation of future struggles. This included the preparation of a *plano de defensa* (defence plan), the libertarian movement's blueprint for resistance to the military coup in Barcelona. As we will see, these preparations were timely, for the coup was not long in coming.

8 An 'apolitical' revolution

Anarchism, revolution and civil war

From early July, the CNT–FAI and its militants had been on a war footing in anticipation of a military coup. With activists deployed at the gates of the main barracks in the city and with informants recruited among conscript soldiers inside, the CNT leaders had ample intelligence that a coup was imminent. While the CNT leadership might have been correct in its claim that the workers were potentially the most valuable ally in the struggle against reaction, its demand that the central and Catalan authorities arm the supporters of a revolutionary syndicalist organisation was ultimately naive. Yet equally naive was the calculation of the authorities that loyal republican police units, whose combined forces then stood at 1,960, could counter a mobilisation of the 6,000 troops garrisoned in Barcelona.[1] Wary of offending the 'patriotic and loyal' army, the authorities censored warnings in *Solidaridad Obrera* that the military was about to rise against the Republic on the grounds that these were an 'insult' to the armed forces.[2] In mid-July, the CNT issued a call to its activists to concentrate in union centres and *ateneus* in preparation for the coming struggle. By night, small groups of militants requisitioned arms, disarming nightwatchmen and policemen.[3] Meanwhile, the few weapons possessed by the defence committees – mainly pistols and homemade grenades, along with a few rifles and a smaller number of sub-machine-guns – were distributed in the *barris*.

The tense wait came to an end between 4am and 5am on Sunday 19 July, when army units and their civilian fascist supporters set out from various garrisons around the city with the intention of seizing strategic locations (squares and traffic intersections), major public buildings (Generalitat departments and the civil governor's office) and the telephone exchange. The *grupistas* set their *plano de defensa* in motion. In what was a prearranged signal for the CNT defence committees to take to the streets, militants activated the factory sirens that normally called workers to work across the city. Besides rousing the people of Barcelona from their sleep, the shrill noise of the sirens doubtless had a psychological impact on the military rebels and their fascist supporters, who immediately encountered armed resistance from loyal police units and workers. As the morning wore on and more troops entered the streets, the fighting became ever more intense, particularly in the main squares in the city centre. The workers mobilised not to defend republican institutions but to protect their communities and the working-class public sphere, which were threatened by the military coup.[4] Barricades were erected across the city, especially around workers' centres and near the major thoroughfares, preventing the military from entering the *barris* and rendering their passage to the city centre perilous and problematic. By mid-afternoon, following intense fighting, the rebellion had clearly failed. CNT militants controlled hundreds of rifles, machine-guns and army cannons seized from the insurgents and were increasingly the protagonists in the street fighting. Popular forces occupied the radio station, while *cenetistas* seized the telephone exchange after a fierce gun battle.[5] The rebels, meanwhile, were desperately isolated in the Atarazanas barracks at the bottom of the Rambles and in the Carmelite church in the city centre and in the Sant Andreu barracks on Barcelona's northern outskirts.

While the military rising in Barcelona was badly organised (for instance, there was no attempt to seize the radio station), more than anything the supporters of the coup were overwhelmed by the armed response on the streets. Although only partially implemented, the principles of the *plano de defensa* proved quite effective. Premised on the reality that the *grupistas* lacked the firepower to prevent the rebels from leaving their barracks, the *plano* relied on guerrilla tactics designed to stretch the resources of the rebels and demoralise the enemy.[6] Yet it would be wrong to exaggerate the scale of coordination of what was effectively a series of local resistance actions by workers based around the barricades and organ-

Figure 8.1 Workers resisting the military coup, 19–20 July 1936

Source: Francesc Bonamusa, Pere Gabriel, Josep Lluís Martín Ramos and Josep Termes, *Història Gràfica del Moviment Obrer a Catalunya*, Barcelona, 1989, p.274

ised through community and union structures.[7] The knowledge that the *grupistas* had of the local area was an important factor. The army proved incapable of adapting to the local topography, while resisters adapted their fight to the built environment, using doorways, trees, roof tops and balconies to open up sudden new fronts in the struggle for the streets.[8] The Rambles, where the CNT defence committees established their headquarters, and the neighbouring Raval, for decades the site of popular insurrection in the city, became a key zone. The Builders' Union office, on Mercaders Street in the Raval, was another important operations centre, coordinating the efforts of various nearby barricades. Armed *cenetistas* massed in the myriad back streets of the Raval, where they organised flying squads that weaved their way to engage the military in the Atarazanas barracks and on the Paral.lel.[9]

Around midnight on the evening of 19 July, the Sant Andreu barracks was stormed by CNT activists, who seized 90,000 rifles. The following day, buoyed up by its new-found armed power, the CNT massed its forces on the Rambles for a final and successful assault on the Atarazanas barracks, the last stronghold of the rebels.[10] The *grupistas* and the CNT defence committees had finally triumphed over the military. However, the extent to which the elitist 'revolutionary gymnastics' were a suitable preparation for the July street fighting is debatable. Both the socialists and the dissident communists of the POUM (Partido Obrero de Unificación Marxista, or Workers' Party of Marxist Unification), the product of the fusion of the BOC with a small Trotskyist grouping, not to mention republican and *catalaniste* elements in the security forces, contributed greatly to the popular resistance to the rising.[11] However, what was beyond dispute was that on 20 July the CNT held the initiative: it was the biggest armed force, the *de facto* master of the streets of Barcelona and indeed of much of Catalonia, opening up a new revolutionary situation.[12] The July coup then created the revolutionary 'spark' that the anarchist radicals had long prophesied.

President Companys now faced something he had feared since 1931: the republican project was genuinely threatened by the armed power of the CNT. The republican state had fractured, its monopoly of armed power, the *sine qua non* for all state power, lost: part of the army had joined with the rebels, who controlled a significant amount of Spanish territory, while part of the security forces had lost its discipline and allied with the people. Importantly, although the state was displaced from the centre of political life, it had not been replaced by a new revolutionary power, and this gave Companys an opportunity to contain the revolutionary impulses emanating from the streets. On 20 July, with the street fighting over in Barcelona and with the Spanish Civil War underway, Companys invited the CNT–FAI leadership to the Generalitat in what constituted a risky but wily display of brinkmanship. Apparently overcome with emotion by the recent struggle, Companys flattered the CNT–FAI leaders on their role in the victory over the military, telling them:

Today you are the masters of the city and of Catalonia....You have conquered everything and everything is in your power. If you do not need me or want me as President of Catalonia...I shall become just another soldier in the struggle against fascism. If, on the other hand, you believe in this post...I and the men of my party...can be useful in this struggle.[13]

In effect, Companys invited the CNT–FAI to take power alone or join forces with the other Popular Front parties in the CCMA (Comité Central de Milicias Antifeixistes, or Central Committee of Anti-Fascist Militias), a new body composed of pro-republican political and trade union groups designed to organise the fight to recapture the areas where the coup had succeeded.[14]

The CNT–FAI leaders had no plan to seize state power or to organise revolutionary political structures and were unprepared to consolidate their victory on the streets by imposing a new political compact. Unlike the French and Russian revolutions, therefore, the Spanish revolution did not destroy the old state apparatus.[15] Instead, sensing that Companys and the republican order were impotent, the anarchists simply ignored the shell of the old state.

At an impromptu and hastily convened assembly, CNT–FAI activists committed the movement to 'democratic collaboration' with the republicans for the sake of unity in the war against fascism, thereby accepting Companys' offer to share power with the bourgeois republicans and other Popular Front groups. Among the CNT–FAI leaders, only García Oliver raised the call 'to go the whole way' (*ir a por el todo*) towards social trans-formation; however, he represented a tiny minority among his comrades, most of whom regarded him as an advocate of 'anarchist dictatorship'.[16] The inter-class CCMA was thus established on 21 July.[17] The CCMA, which had the appearance of a revolutionary body, was a trade union-domi-nated government and war ministry in all but name, and it allowed the anarchists to participate in power without compromising their anti-statist principles.[18] For the supporters of the republican state, meanwhile, the creation of the CCMA offered a respite from revolutionary political change: it preserved the legality of the bourgeois republican state and, as we will see, it provided an opportunity to outmanoeuvre the politically inexpert CNT–FAI leaders.

8.1   Urban revolution from below

While the anarchist leaders committed themselves to 'democratic collabora-tion' with the political representatives of the middle classes, the CNT–FAI grassroots made their revolution in the streets of Barcelona, reorganising production and taking over the factories and estates in what was the greatest revolutionary festival in the history of contemporary Europe. Throughout much of the area where the coup had been put down, the most revolutionary sections of the urban and rural working class had no interest in returning to the *status quo* as it stood before the failed coup: they interpreted the triumph over the military in the July days as an opportunity to fulfil their collective dreams of social and economic justice. In the case of Barcelona, these dreams were structured and inflected by the experience of direct action collective protests and by the sediments of culture that we discussed in Chapters 2 and 7. In this respect, the post-July urban transformation can be seen as the continuation of a much longer workers' struggle in defence of their 'right to the city'.[19]

The new working-class street power revolved around the barricades. On 24 July, *Solidaridad Obrera* reported that 'Barcelona consists of barricades populated by the defenders of proletarian liberties....Hundreds of barricades defend the proletarian city from its enemies'.[20] As one eye-witness observed, 'Barcelona was converted into a labyrinth of barricades', which signified the victory of the workers and their desire for a new order.[21] As a mobilising symbol, the barricades were an affirmation of the spirit of solidarity and community autonomy in the *barris*, while in practical terms they were central to the popular victory in the July street fighting: they impeded the movement of the military rebels and their civilian supporters and protected the *barris* from possible attack by the rebels.[22] The barricades also played a decisive role in the revolution: not only did they dislocate the rhythms and circuits of power within the old bourgeois city but, in the days of revolutionary euphoria and general strike that followed the defeat of the military coup, armed workers extended their power across Catalonia and into neighbouring Valencia and Aragon through a network of checkpoints.[23] Moreover, when, on 27 July, the Barcelona CNT issued a manifesto calling for a return to work, only those barricades that impeded the circulation of trams and buses were dismantled, the rest remaining as a signifier of the new power of the workers.[24]

The barricades were the spatial tool of a nascent power: the web of armed local or neighbourhood revolutionary committees who controlled movement to, from and within the city and that constituted the most fundamental cell of revolutionary power.[25] The committees were a grassroots response to the power vacuum that followed the fracturing of the republican state in July. During the early weeks of the revolution, nearly all power emanated from and filtered through the local committees, organs that, in the words of one union manifesto, wielded 'an authority [that] carried the stamp of the barricades'.[26] Catalan home rule within the Spanish state was superseded by revolutionary independence: workers' militias and their barricades controlled the French–Catalan border, and responsibility for defence rested in Barcelona, not Madrid. The authority of both the central government in Madrid and the Generalitat was eclipsed by that of the revolutionary committees. Notwithstanding the anti-statist sentiments of the anarchist leaders and their supporters, the committees functioned as a locally articulated executive power, imposing a kind of dictatorship of the proletariat on the streets of Barcelona.[27]

Figure 8.2 Armed workers, July 1936, accompanied by a uniformed but hatless
   member of the armed forces

Source: Ateneu Enciclopèdic Popular

Working-class power was exercised through a series of locally recruited
armed groups, such as the rearguard militias (*milicias de retaguardia*),
investigation and surveillance groups (*grupos de investigación y vigi-
lancia*), control patrols (*patrullas de control*) and the militias that set off to
fight the rebel-controlled zone. Formed by the local revolutionary committees for community defence, these armed squads imposed 'class justice' in
the *barris* and launched punitive raids into bourgeois residential areas,
frequently in cars requisitioned from the rich, in search of 'enemies of the
people': those who were perceived either to have supported the old urban
system and/or to have backed the military coup, whether actively or by
creating a political and social climate that favoured the military rebellion.[28]
In essence, the squads pursued the goal of community purity, of a neighbourhood purged of reactionaries and the construction of a revolutionary
city through the violent eradication of the social networks that perpetuated
the old city. When it came to determining the social and political loyalties
and past conduct of detainees, the local knowledge possessed by the armed
defenders of the revolution gave them a real and lethal advantage over a
distant bureaucracy.[29]

The armed revolutionary groups have often been criticised for the swift
and exemplary form of justice that they administered.[30] Many reports of
repression were grossly exaggerated at the time and afterwards, such as the
stories of revolutionaries raping nuns, and even pro-Francoists later recog-

nised that many accounts were pure fantasy aimed at winning the propaganda war.[31] It is also unfair to attribute all violence to the radical anarchists, for there was much 'revolutionary terror' in areas where anarchism was weak.[32] Moreover, we should not forget the immediate context for the violence in July and August: the insecurity and paranoia generated by 'fifth column' snipers and gunmen[33] and the anger at news of the systematic slaughter of CNT militants in Zaragoza by fascists and the military, which prompted *Solidaridad Obrera* to publish huge headlines promising 'An eye for an eye, a tooth for a tooth!'[34]

However, there was a qualitative and quantitative difference between violence in the fascist-controlled area, where it was used freely as a terroristic device to subdue potentially 'disloyal' masses and/or to crush the resistance of the civilian population, and that in the republican zone, where, as time went on, the various anti-fascist organisations and the authorities struggled to limit the extent of 'unofficial' or 'spontaneous' violence.[35] This is well illustrated in the case of some of the supporters of the expropriations. Following the July events, the 'social prisoners' – expropriators, 'men of action' and foreign anarchists who were classed as 'common criminals' and had therefore not been amnestied by the Popular Front government in February – were freed from Barcelona's Model Jail.[36] Upon their release, many joined the militias that set out to fight fascism, but some remained in Barcelona and joined the *patrullas* that policed the rearguard. Among the latter was Josep Gardenyes, who, along with other members of his *grupo de afinidad* and individual anarchists, remained devotees of the illegal deed. In the new circumstances after July, Gardenyes and *grupos* like his pursued once more the logic of their own illegalist agendas, giving rise to fears about the activities of *incontrolats* (uncontrollables) who were exploiting the new circumstances for personal gain. Fearing that illegalist practices could disgrace both the organisation and the revolutionary project, the CNT–FAI leaders issued a declaration warning that anyone who 'undertook house searches and committed acts contrary to the anarchist spirit' or that compromised the nascent 'revolutionary order' would be shot.[37] This threat was later implemented in the case of Gardenyes, who was detained by members of the *patrullas* and executed without trial, upsetting many radicals in the anarchist movement.[38]

Contrary to the Francoist/conservative view of 'Red Terror with a vengeance...a flood of murder and lawlessness',[39] most of the killings in Barcelona during the civil war were not carried out by newly formed militia groups; rather, they occurred in an organised manner under the tutelage of the republican authorities at the Montjuïc military fortress.[40] Doubtless the fact that workers were armed and that they were no longer contained by the old state apparatus encouraged many to take justice into their own hands, yet the 'terror' was anything but a 'wave of blind violence' by socially uprooted 'vandals', as has been suggested by some historians.[41] While there is no census or register of the members of the armed revolutionary groups, anecdotal and autobiographical evidence suggests that the groups included skilled workers in their number. They were also comprised of activists from the main anti-fascist organisations from before the civil war, who therefore had some level of political education and experience. Indeed, many of the district revolutionary committees were established through the transformation of organised working-class social and political spaces (the armed CNT defence groups responsible for picketing and security at meetings and marches, union workplace committees and community groups, such as the *ateneus*), the very autonomous proletarian para-society threatened by the July 1936 uprising. Moreover, the *patrullas*, the closest body there was to a revolutionary police force, were normally recruited from the districts they policed; and they drew strength from local networks of solidarity, friendship, kinship and neighbouring and assumed many of the functions of a community police force.[42] For instance, 'antisocial' elements such as pimps and drug pushers were killed by the *patrullas*.[43]

The violence was intimately linked to the cosmology of working-class society and the way people in the *barris* interpreted the world. It was directed at 'outsiders', who had been defined by CNT discourse as an immoral and parasitic 'other' surviving from the sweat of the labour of the workers and that had to be 'cleansed' for the 'good of public health', in other words, for the sake of the community.[44] Peiró, the moderate anarcho-syndicalist, summed up the prevailing structure of feeling when he wrote:

> Revolution is revolution, and it is therefore logical that the revolution brings in its wake bloodshed. The capitalist system, the temporal power of the Church and the rule of the *caciques* (bosses) over the centuries has all been sustained and fed by the pain and blood of the people. Logically, then, following the victory of the people, the blood of those who for many centuries maintained their power and privilege by means of organised violence, unnecessary pain and unhappiness and death, will be spilt.[45]

Perhaps surprisingly, then, although some industrialists perished after July, employers and senior managers accounted for a tiny proportion of those who were killed in the Barcelona area during the revolution and civil war.[46] There was no drive to eliminate the bourgeoisie as a class, and members of the *patrullas* and the district revolutionary committees often protected capitalists, even intervening to save the lives of some.[47] Industrialists, meanwhile, like the middle classes as a whole, enjoyed the political protection of republican groups and, increasingly, of the newly formed PSUC (Partit Socialista Unificat de Catalunya or Catalan Communist Party), the new champion of intermediate and petit bourgeois elements in the city. However, nearly all the industrialists who were murdered perished during the period from July to November, during what can best be described as 'revolutionary violence'. Targeting the traditional circuits of urban power, this violence was directed at the political and social enemies of the revolutionary city, particularly representatives of the organised Church, the main ideological structure of the old urban order, and members of the armed forces. Most of the dead were therefore regarded in the *barris* as the legitimate targets of repression or, as it was expressed in the *vox populi*, as the 'settling of scores'.[48] This was more than evident in the case of Planes, the *La Publicitat* journalist who contributed greatly to the 'moral panics' surrounding 'anarchist-robbers', whose body was found on the Arabassada highway, an isolated road on the outskirts of the city that became notorious as a destination point for the *paseos*, the one-way trips organised by armed workers for both suspected and proven counter-revolutionaries. Several policemen and other hated figures, such as Ramon Sales, the founder of the Sindicatos libres, were also killed.[49]

In political terms, the main organ of revolutionary power – the district committees, which were distinct from the CNT-organised district committees discussed in earlier chapters – were never as democratic as soviets: they did not practice genuine direct democracy, and delegates, who often attained their positions due to the respect they enjoyed among the community, were not subject to immediate recall. Nevertheless, while most of the members of the district committees were CNT members, they were nominally independent of the formal working-class organisations and often did not follow the orders of the Confederation.[50] Instead, the overwhelming majority of the committees practised a radical form of neighbourhood democracy that drew on Barcelona's working-class culture, with its emphasis on community self-reliance. The district committees formed the basis of the only genuinely revolutionary body established in July, the ephemeral Federación de barricadas (Federation of Barricades), which was founded by base activists in the heat of the struggle against the military.[51] Mirroring the district federations of the Paris Commune or the councils established during the other major urban working-class insurrections in Paris (1848 and 1871), Petrograd (1917), Berlin (1918–19) and Turin (1920), the Federación de barricadas represented, in embryonic form, a revolutionary alternative to state power. It surpassed the Paris Commune as an experiment in local power. Like the old state, the Federación de barricadas had an armed power, which was based in the 'Bakunin Barracks', formerly the Pedralbes Barracks, an important recruiting station for the anarchist militias. Yet the Federación de barricadas simultaneously highlighted one of the central shortcomings of the revolution: the absence of a new institutional form that could give expression to the popular desire for revolution and the objective need to prosecute a civil war. For while the Federación de barricadas employed revolutionary tactics in the battle for the streets in July, it had the essentially short-term aims of crushing the military uprising and of securing control of urban space. Moreover, no organisation argued that the Federación de barricadas or the local committees be transformed into a genuinely revolutionary government or assembly.[52]

While this unwillingness to create a coordinating revolutionary authority can, in part, be attributed to the ideology of the anarcho-syndicalist leadership, it also reflected the anti-power culture of the local working class. Indeed, the grassroots were largely concerned with power at street level and not with the creation of new structures. It is then difficult to talk of 'dual power', for there was a multiplicity of powers dispersed and located within discrete spatial scales, from the workplace and the neighbourhood to the city. Overall, there were three powers: the organs of the old state represented by the Generalitat, the CNT–FAI leadership, and the grassroots working-class power of the local revolutionary and factory committees.[53]

Yet from July onwards, the political limitations of the revolution were obscured by popular triumphalism, a feeling that workers as a class had finally seized control of their history.[54] As one shrewd activist commented: 'Groups of men and women revealed in an obvious, almost scandalous, form, the joy of victors; as if everything was done and completed, when in reality the most difficult and important work had not yet even begun'.[55] Triumphalism was exuded on the streets, where workers enjoyed new freedoms following the displacement of the state apparatus that had previously regulated access to public space. As one worker put it: 'the streets belonged to us'.[56] Activists, in particular, were intoxicated by their new feelings of power in the street, factory and working-class neighbourhoods, which they interpreted as the definitive victory over their enemies: they put faith in the invincibility of the 'people in arms', and they ostentatiously displayed their new-found weaponry, one of the most important symbols of working-class power, along with the cars confiscated from the well-to-do, in a carnival-like atmosphere that was fuelled by a popular feeling of liberation. Armed proletarian power appeared supreme, and many confused their victory over the military with the triumph of the revolution. Meanwhile, the introduction of compulsory unionisation allowed the CNT to regain the strength it had enjoyed in 1931 and more: by March 1937, membership had reached unprecedented levels, the Catalan organisation alone claiming 1.2 million members.[57] In these circumstances, one anarchist leader commented that 'To overpower the CNT in Barcelona could only be the dream of madmen'.[58]

The appearance of proletarian triumph was amplified at an everyday level because the dominant structures and collective symbols of bourgeois power and rank, such as money, ties and suits, were displaced by new working-class symbols and motifs. Amid a general proletarianisation of everyday life, hats and ties became far less evident on the streets as working-class dress was adopted by many prudent members of the elite and the middle classes, particularly those with something to hide, along with members of the clergy, who borrowed clothes from servants and sympathetic workers in an attempt to evade 'revolutionary justice'. In some extreme cases, the rich emulated the dress of radical anarchists and *milicianos*.[59] The red-and-black colours of the CNT–FAI, one of the new signifiers of urban power, were very much in evidence: they were on huge flags draped over occupied buildings; they hung from balconies; they were painted on collectivised trams and figured on the caps, scarves and badges sold on stalls on the Rambles.[60] The visual aspect of the city seemed to confirm the arrival of a new workers' democracy – buildings, palaces and hotels were adorned with banner slogans and the portraits of revolutionary leaders, and the walls became a popular tribune, decorated with propaganda, graffiti, fly-posters and manifestos, a democratic display of knowledge at street level.

Until May 1937, when the central republican state reasserted its authority, the district revolutionary committees allowed local communities to take control of the built environment and exercise new power over everyday life. As the committees set about addressing the immediate problems facing the *barris*, a new set of social relations and solidaristic practices was instituted. For instance, in the immediate aftermath of the coup, with the shops closed and with industry and commerce paralysed, the district revolutionary committees formed *comités de aprovisionamiento* (distribution committees) to organise food distribution in the *barris*. In practice, armed groups expropriated essential foodstuffs and clothes from shops and warehouses, which were then distributed in the *barris* by local revolutionary committees. In a further attempt to simplify food provision, and reflecting the same experience of neighbourhood democracy that underpinned the 1931 rent strike, a network of communal eating houses (*comedores populares*) was founded by the local committees and the city's unions, which distributed vouchers that entitled recipients to meals.

Ironically, the urban revolutionary fiesta started on the streets on 21 July, the same day that the anarchist leaders agreed to share power in the CCMA with the other Popular Front parties. Groups of workers, frequently organised through the local revolutionary committees, as well as union and political groups, occupied elite neighbourhoods, Church property, business offices, hotels and the palaces of the rich.[61] This pattern was repeated across the city, with anti-fascist groups and even small groups of anarchists occupying the houses of the well-to-do.[62] Consequently, at the very moment that the CNT–FAI leadership committed itself to collaborating with democratic forces, it was confronted by a revolution of its grassroots supporters.

The urban changes were most dramatic in the case of Laietana Way, the business avenue that had been the pride of the local bourgeoisie. Renamed Durruti Way following the death of the legendary Catalan anarchist leader in November 1936 on the Madrid front, this avenue became a signifier of the new power of the revolutionary organisations – the Banc d'Espanya building was occupied by the CNT[63], and Casa Cambó, formerly the head office of the Federació Patronal Catalana, the main Catalan employers' association, became known as Casa CNT–FAI, the nerve centre of the Barcelona anarchist and union movements; when the CNT Construction Union extended the Casa CNT–FAI and office space was given to the IWA, the international federation of anarcho-syndicalist unions, this building was converted into a centre for world revolution.[64] Laietana Way also reflected the changing nature of repressive power in Barcelona: before the revolution, the city's main police station was located there; after July, armed working-class bodies like the CNT's defence committee occupied an office block on this street, while the *servicios de investigación* (investigation services), a kind of workers' police, was based in the nearby Casa CNT–FAI. The July revolution therefore allowed for the reclamation and reoccupation by the working class of a space from which it had been expelled in the 1900s, in direct opposition to the bourgeois strategy of spatial marginalisation and exclusion.[65]

As far as the material and economic achievements of the revolutionary city, these dated from 27 July, when the CNT called for a return to work, prompting a second wave of occupations of factories and workplaces as workers seized control of the means of production.[66] Around 3,000 enterprises were collectivised in Barcelona alone.[67] No revolutionary group called for the expropriation of the bourgeoisie; rather, workers' control was a grassroots response in the many workplaces where managers and owners had either fled the city or been killed. At the same time, there were employers and senior managers, particularly those with technical knowledge and skills, who remained in many workplaces, earning salaries equivalent to those of the workers.[68]

The transformation of workplaces followed the anarchists' organic view of social relations, according to which the end of alienated labour presupposed transcending the artificial frontiers erected within the capitalist city between the social and the economic and between work and leisure. Prominent here were attempts to end the physical separation of work and community. Crèches were founded in big factories, allowing women to emerge from the domestic sphere and participate in the workplace. In some workplaces, ambitious educational programmes were introduced, including day classes in general education and foreign languages, which coincided with breaks in production. Libraries were also established in factories, permitting workers to broaden their intellectual horizons while at work and further harmonising the social and economic aspects of everyday life. However, as has been demonstrated by Michael Seidman, the demands of the civil war and the acceptance by the CNT–FAI leadership of a productivist ideology aimed at maximising war production seriously undermined these initiatives and resulted in continuing workplace alienation.[69]

Greater success was achieved with the expansion of the city's urban services after July, when the possibility arose of addressing longstanding demands for new forms of collective consumption by organising welfare, housing and urban social services more closely in line with the practical needs of communities. Even hostile sources acknowledged that the revolution brought an increase in social services.[70] Spaces constructed for the exclusive use of the bourgeoisie were collectivised and used for solidaristic ends. The social priorities of the revolutionary city were reflected in the changing function of hotels, such as the Barcelona Ritz, which became Hotel

Gastronómico no. 1, a communal eating house under union control providing meals for members of the militia, the urban dispossessed from poor inner-city *barris*, cabaret artists and factory workers.[71] In a further attempt to open up and humanise elite spaces, a canteen serving meals to members of the local community was established in a former office of the employers' association.[72] Private homes of members of the elite were also converted into public restaurants or into housing for the homeless, refugees and the aged, and for those who lived in overcrowded accommodation. Meanwhile, special committees were established at neighbourhood level to provide work opportunities for the unemployed, particularly in building programmes. For the remaining jobless, the new system of distribution in the revolutionary city entitled them to food from neighbourhood stores and to eat in public canteens. This assistance to the unemployed ensured that begging was largely eradicated after July.[73]

More ambitious still was the extension of medical services. One of the immediate concerns of the local revolutionary committees in July was the organisation of medical care for wounded street fighters. This was followed by a concerted drive to improve medical services in working-class districts in a bid to overcome the huge differentials between the *barris* and the elite neighbourhoods. By July 1937, therefore, in addition to the many local medical centres located in houses once owned by the rich, six new hospitals had been established.[74]

Figure 8.3 Hotel Gastronómico no. 1, formerly the Barcelona Ritz, one of the many communal eating houses established after July 1936

Source: Francesc Bonamusa, Pere Gabriel, Josep Lluís Martín Ramos and Josep Termes, *Història Gràfica del Moviment Obrer a Catalunya*, Barcelona, 1989, p.314

Another great success was the huge expansion of educational provision, a mission that was very much in keeping with the anarchist maxim that knowledge is an essential precondition for liberation. Barely a week after the suppression of the military rising, on 27 July, a Generalitat decree established the CENU (Consell de l'Escola Nova Unificada or Council for the New Unified School), a new educational authority that was greatly inspired by anarchist pedagogues. It was located in a former religious college in a huge building in central Barcelona, and the accent of its educational message was on class consciousness, on forging 'active agents' who could struggle consciously against oppression. In the first five months of revolution, the number of children in school in l'Hospitalet doubled to 8,000.[75] During the same period, over 20,000 new school places were established in Barcelona, creating a right to education that had never existed previously. By the spring of 1937, the CENU was coordinating the activities of 4,700 teachers in over 300 schools across Catalonia.[76]

While the CNT Construction Union built some new schools, most were located in confiscated buildings. Church schools and convents became places of secular learning: one former seminary became the Universidad Obrera (Workers' University), while some churches were adapted as schools by the Construction Union.[77] Public libraries and schools were founded in the houses of the rich, their private book collections routinely socialised and amalgamated to form new public or school libraries. Reflecting the moral stance of the CNT, one school was established in a former dance hall.[78] In what was a continuation of the pre-civil war cultural initiatives of the CNT–FAI, the anarchists extended their adult education classes in the neighbourhood *ateneus*, many of which were able to increase their activities and reach growing numbers of people by either moving to buildings once owned by the rich or the Church or by expanding their former premises.

The urban revolution also entailed the creative destruction of the old markers of power, rank and privilege in what constituted both an assertion of revolutionary power over the cityscape and an attempt to establish a non-hierarchical landscape. On a symbolic level, urban reference points, such as the street names that previously honoured aristocrats, bankers, monarchs, virgins and saints, were changed to acknowledge revolutionary heroes such as Engels, Kropotkin, the Chicago and the Montjuïc martyrs and Spartacus, popular literary figures like Dostoyevsky, or, in the case of Social Revolution Street, simply as a tribute to the revolution. Other spaces were named after those who fell in the fight against fascism, such as 'The Square of the Unknown Militiaman'.[79] Other symbolic reference points of the old urban order, such as bourgeois monumentalism, were similarly destroyed in a radical reform of the built environment. In the days following the July street fighting, the monument to Count Güell, one of the most illustrious members of the Barcelona bourgeoisie, was redecorated with paint and given a new graffiti dedication 'To the victims of the military rising' (*Victimes 19 Juliol*).[80] Other statues with elite significance were removed, such as the monument to the monarchist General

Prim, which was taken by members of the anarchist youth movement and melted down for use in the war industries.[81]

The motor car was one bourgeois status symbol that was joyfully appropriated by revolutionaries. In what was the first revolution in the motor age, nearly all of the hostile accounts of the revolutionary period emphasise the irrationality of those workers who seized the cars of the rich, crudely daubing the vehicles with the initials CNT–FAI before destroying them – and occasionally the lives of the occupants – in traffic accidents caused either by the dangerous driving of 'mad' or 'crazy' men or by lack of driving experience.[82] But revolutionary motoring possessed its own logic. In the first instance, the destruction of cars reflected a desire to usher in a new set of spatial relations as well as resistance to the attempts by the local and central republican authorities to impose a new urban order of controlled consumption, consisting of new rules of circulation and traffic lights designed to improve the flow of capital and goods. That many sets of traffic lights were destroyed during the July street fighting, along with the readiness of revolutionaries to ignore the remaining ones, can be interpreted as a protest against the changing rhythms of the capitalist city, a defiance anchored in a working-class culture that had long defined itself in terms of its hostility towards mechanised and capitalised forms of transport such as trams and cars, which threatened the intimate social geography of the *barris*. Indeed, in contrast to members of the elite, workers had a more direct relationship with the streets, and they experienced urban life very differently, as we saw in Chapter 2.

On another level, once news of the rising broke, it was rational that armed workers should seize cars, for not only did this enhance their mobility in the struggle against the insurgents, it also simultaneously prevented the same cars from being used by counter-revolutionaries.[83] It seems most likely that cars were marked with the initials CNT–FAI not for purposes of identification at barricades, since it would be easy for counter-revolutionaries to do the same, but as a symbol of the workers' victory over the old order and their conquest of the icons of bourgeois privilege. For revolutionary motorists, cars were a thrilling demonstration of their new power over their everyday lives, and it was inevitable that some would derive pleasure from that power through play. It was these games that, in the words of one observer of revolutionary urban behaviour, converted Barcelona into an 'improvised driving school', 'a cemetery for cars'.[84] Equally, the destruction of cars can be viewed as just one example of the ascetic thrust of the Spanish revolution, a proletarian anti-consumerist iconoclasm directed at an important element in the nascent system of consumer capitalism. Meanwhile, even though there may have been much reckless driving during the revolution, traffic accidents were hardly new, and before and after the revolution motoring skills and road safety in the city were the cause of much concern. Yet perhaps more than anything, the condemnations of revolutionary motoring underscored the sense of anguish of the elite at the demise of bourgeois control of the city.[85] In this respect, the trepidation caused by 'the cars of fear and death'[86] used to transport many former car owners on *paseos* is utterly comprehensible.[87]

The urban revolution presupposed the destruction of certain elements of the architecture of state repression. One poignant example was the women's prison on Amàlia Street, in the Raval. Previously the city's main jail and the site of executions in the nineteenth century, a substantial part of its population consisted of poor female workers who, through economic misfortune, had turned to prostitution. Staffed by nuns with a reputation for brutality and inquisitorial practices, for many workers the women's prison was a particularly despised symbol of the tyranny and obscurantism of the old order. Inevitably, then, on 19 July, when the street fighting had barely ended, the prison was stormed by a crowd that led the detainees to freedom. Once empty, members of the local community demolished part of the jail. In an attempt to humanise the building, the red-and-black CNT flag was flown over the jail and a sign outside announced: 'This torture house was closed by the people, July 1936'.[88] Later, at an assembly of the anarcho-feminist group Mujeres Libres (Free Women), a decision was taken to demolish the jail; this was acted upon by members of the Construction Union on 21 August.[89]

Other spaces that contained memories of the repression of yesteryear were closed down, such as the Asil Durán, a church-run borstal synonymous in the *barris* with the torture and abuse, sometimes sexual, of its working-class male internees.[90] Also, in what was both an affirmation of proletarian memory and an attack on official memory, armed groups destroyed the court archives and the management records of the Barcelona Tram Company, where a few hundred workers had been victimised after a long and bitter strike that ended just a few months before the revolution.[91]

Consistent with the culture of working class resistance to the spatial logic of bourgeois control in the city and betraying signs of earlier protest repertoires, those deemed responsible for the military coup were punished through the destruction of their property.[92] There are numerous reports of crowds sacking and destroying the homes of the rich and right-wing politicians, as well as Italian and German economic interests.[93] Reliable sources, including several hostile eye-witness accounts, attest to the orderly nature of these protests.[94] There was also a normative element to these actions. For instance, following an attack on the offices of an Italian shipping company on the Rambles, property and furniture was emptied onto the street along with a sign that read: 'This furniture is the property of foreigners who disgraced themselves. Don't you disgrace yourselves by taking it'.[95]

Perhaps the most controversial example of creative destruction was directed at Church property. The repression of the Church was a unique aspect of the Spanish revolution. In most parts of Barcelona, the local revolutionary committees organised the initial offensive against the Church during 'days of smoky justice'.[96] A succession of observers, both foreign and native, have,

Figure 8.4 Workers burning property, July 1936. One of the many horses to perish in the street fighting can also be seen here.

Source: Ateneu Enciclopèdic Popular

from diverse political perspectives, highlighted the deliberate nature of the crowds that transformed religious spaces. Thus the Austrian sociologist Franz Borkenau described a church burning in central Barcelona as 'an administrative business', with the fire brigade on hand to prevent fire spreading to adjoining buildings.[97] There was a strong politico-moral element to the assault on the organised Church: a member of an anti-clerical crowd invited Stansbury Pearse, a Barcelona-based English businessmen, to join an attack on a church in the name of the 'humanity of the people'.[98] That crowds were not motivated by personal gain was borne out by their disregard for money and valuable items, which were frequently burned or discarded. We can also assume that the crowds were fully conscious of their actions, since on 21 July the CNT forbade the sale of alcohol.[99] Furthermore, the fate of some churches was decided at community assemblies.[100] Equally, once it had been agreed that churches were to be protected, efforts were taken on the ground to ensure that they were not attacked.[101] Few church buildings were therefore destroyed (a 1937 republican government report concluded that only thirteen of 236 ecclesiastical structures had been demolished in Barcelona).[102]

Most of the destructive activity focused on collective symbols of worship. Many of the fires organised by anti-clerical crowds took place outside churches and saw the burning of these church symbols, along with paintings and furniture, such as pews. Although some treasures were destroyed, the desecration of church murals and art reflected the overwhelming popular desire to eliminate what were perceived as collective symbols of the oppressive old order. Meanwhile, there is evidence that revolutionary groups made a concerted effort to save items of artistic value, and 'technical commissions' were formed to assess the contents of churches.[103] Religious art previously confined to the catacombs was placed in museums and exhibited, while the libraries of Catholic settlements were dispatched to schools and other educational establishments. Although confiscated Church gold was used to fund the republican war effort, and church bells were melted down by the war industries, efforts were taken to preserve items of cultural or historical value.[104]

The invasion of the churches was frequently accompanied by a popular sacrophobic fiesta. In what might be described as a set of anti-clerical counter-rituals, workers donned vestments and robes and carried liturgical objects to burlesque religious practices in mock masses, ceremonies and processions, all of which caused much hilarity among the crowds that gathered to view such spectacles.[105] Holy statues were a particular target for derision; some were decked out in militia uniforms, while others were publicly destroyed, decapitated and even executed by firing squads. On a more macabre level, tombs were frequently profaned. Mummified bodies were displayed outside churches for public scrutiny and ridicule, and skulls were used to adorn altars and for games of street football.[106] There was also an effort to eliminate references to religion in everyday life, the farewell 'adios' being replaced by 'salut'.[107]

Despite the attention that has been devoted to church burning and desecration, most church property was expropriated by local revolutionary committees, trade unions and political parties and then designated for new uses. In what constituted a radical resumption of the process of the disentitlement and civil utilisation of church property that started in the first part of the nineteenth century, many religious buildings were used for a variety of secular purposes, such as public canteens, schools, community and refugee centres, warehouses, workshops, militia recruiting stations, and detention and interrogation centres.[108] The reallocation of Church property was eminently rational: it responded to a plan to overcome deficits in the built environment by converting what anti-clericals regarded as spaces of darkness and obscurantism into spaces of light and reason. Thus in one *barri* the local church was converted into a cinema. Elsewhere, confession boxes were used as newspaper kiosks, market stalls and bus shelters, while later in the civil war, church crypts were converted into air raid shelters in response to the real danger of air attack.[109]

The assault on the Church was governed by an overarching project: to launch a mortal blow against the bourgeois traditionalist public sphere by collapsing the foundations of the principle transmitter of elite ideology.[110] For revolutionaries, the 'religious problem' required emphatic action to 'purify' society of the 'plague of religion' by 'destroying the Church as a social institution'.[111] In this way, apparently petty or vindictive acts of profanity, such as the ridiculing of icons and the radical subversion of the ecclesiastical ritual on which Catholic practice was based, demonstrated that the Church had been conquered by a new power and that human beings could take control of their lives and destroy the alienating force of religion. Similarly, the storming of churches signified the popular triumph over one of the key elements of the landscape of power. Even the most extreme sacrophobic violence, such as the mass elimination of priests, can be viewed in terms of this conscious project to extinguish organised religion, thereby freeing city space from corrupting clerical influences and forging a new space without religion.

There is a consensus among specialists on anti-clericalism that no single factor can explain the scale of the violence after July 1936.[112] Certainly, short-term political factors played a part: the willingness to punish the Church for its support of the old regime and its later contribution to political instability during the Republic. Then, once the civil war began, Church support for the insurgents led the clergy to be regarded as a military enemy. Yet the iconoclasm of the war was part of a long history of popular blasphemy in Spain, which had reportedly found an echo in the *vox populi*.[113] Equally, the burning of churches and other subversive practices had figured in the protest repertoire of the Barcelona working class since the 1830s and, right up until the civil war, were nourished by the liberal proletarian secular culture propagated by republicans, socialists and anarchists.[114]

One explanatory factor that has generally been overlooked in any analysis of anti-clericalism is the cultural frames of local workers.[115] In the popular mind, as we saw in Chapter 2, the Church, which had long justified the *status quo* and called on the lowly to accept as divine will the suffering that accompanied their social position, was synonymous with reactionary causes. Furthermore, as in the 1909 anti-clerical riots, as a major landowner and financial power, the Church was closely identified with the state and the urban and agrarian elites, a vision that was not dispelled by the vociferous opposition of the clergy to trade unions, both in their publications and from the pulpit.[116] Moreover, many workers, as we saw in Chapter 1, had direct experience of the 'persecutory religiosity'[117] of the clergy in a range of institutions, such as schools, hospitals, workhouses, orphanages and borstals, in which the inefficient central state allowed the Church to play a prominent role.[118] For many workers, therefore, the attack on the Church after July 1936 signalled an end to the intrusive presence of the clergy in their everyday lives and a blow against a hated structure of oppression.

Yet in some areas of everyday life the effects of the revolution were more muted. The survival and accommodation of some urban rhythms and cultural traditions within the new city caused consternation among the more puritanical revolutionaries. Take, for instance, the inability of the revolution to completely overturn gender relations. Although Spain's first female cabinet minister, the anarcho-feminist Montseny, ensured that women attained formal legal equality with men, as well as the right to divorce and abortion on demand, male attitudes were slow to change. Many of the daily impediments to the full participation of women in social and political life continued during the revolution: cafes and bars remained male spaces; even by day women faced sexual harassment on the streets and on public transport, and many young women still went chaperoned in public.[119] In part, this reflected the logic of Popular Frontism, which relegated profound social transformation to an indeterminate date in the future. Yet equally relevant was the adherence to traditional gender values by many within the democratic camp, such as the Generalitat, which employed sexualised images of women to mobilise men for the militias.[120] Similar criticisms can be levelled against the main – male-led – revolutionary groups. A foreign female revolutionary noted the sexual segregation at POUM meetings as well as a residual level of *machismo* among *poumistas*, who openly mocked militia women.[121] For all their efforts to break with the culture of the 'old Spain', anarchists were not averse to rallying women to the anti-fascist cause in ways that reaffirmed traditional female roles, such as 'making socks, scarves and winter clothes for our militiamen'.[122] Meanwhile, Montseny, often seen as the doyenne of anarcho-feminism, justified the flirtatious remarks (*piropos*) made by the militiamen guarding Casa CNT–FAI to passing women, even suggesting that women might find them pleasant![123] This ambivalence is further witnessed in the failure of the anarchist movement to close Barcelona's brothels after the July revolution, something that was easily within its power. While the more radical sections of the anarchist movement insisted that the revolution lacked all meaning if prostitution was allowed to continue, other anarchists, including some of the CNT–FAI leadership, who were known to visit prostitutes, appreciated the importance of an outlet for the sexual energies of male factory workers and militiamen on leave. A similar pragmatism prevailed among the CNT–FAI rank and file, and anarchist militiamen were regularly spotted in the large queues that formed outside the city's remaining brothels.[124]

8.2   The end of the revolution

Notwithstanding the profound revolutionary energies and impulses of the *barris*, the revolution was an incomplete revolution. Central to the weaknesses of the revolution, both in Catalonia and indeed elsewhere in the Republican zone, was its failure to generate an overarching institutional structure capable of coordinating the war effort and simultaneously harmonising the activities of the myriad workers' collectives. In political terms, the revolution was underdeveloped and inchoate. Apart from the ephemeral Federación de barricadas, the revolution in Barcelona failed to generate any revolutionary institution. As we have seen, the anarchists had a doctrinal opposition to the state, and they baulked at fashioning new organs of political power in July, while the POUM – the only party to raise the slogan of a 'revolutionary state' – was weakened by its limited influence and its political ambivalence and contradictions.[125] This unresolved question of political power created an inherently unstable situation; it also signified the political limits, and indeed the limitations, of the revolution in Catalonia and in Spain. Consequently, the initial revolutionary push of July–August 1936 was not built upon; it represented the apogee of the revolution, as workers' power remained fragmented and atomised on the streets, dispersed among a multitude of *comités* without any coordination at regional or national level.

It is frequently noted that the collectivist project was undermined by the dilemmas of 'war versus revolution' that dominated the republican camp during the civil war.[126] Yet in the classic debate of war versus revolution, the revolution side of the equation was always in a position of weakness. Perforce the logic of the war dictated the creation of some kind of centralised authority geared towards directing the struggle against the anti-republican generals and their Italian fascist and German Nazi backers.[127] In the absence of a revolutionary political structure, it was the bourgeois republican state that increasingly played a coordinating role during the civil war. Although eclipsed by the power of the proletarian-dominated CCMA during July and August, the Generalitat and the republican state survived the revolution and continued to enjoy a legal existence. Remarkably, the anarchist hierarchy consented to and connived at the reconstruction of the bourgeois state 'from above' for *raisons de guerre*. Having committed the CNT–FAI to a Popular Front policy of 'democratic collaboration' in July, the anarchist leadership was drawn ineluctably into an accommodation with existing political forces. This resulted in a series of compromises that facilitated the emergence of counter-revolutionary poles of power, culminating in the reconstitution of the old state and, simultaneously, in the erosion of the power of the local committees. In this respect, the period of the CCMA (July–September), when revolutionary fervour was at its height, constituted a breathing space for the supporters of republican authority during which the collapsed authority of the state was gradually strengthened to the detriment of the new grassroots forms of revolutionary power. Thus, in what was the first step towards the centralisation of power, the CCMA institutionalised new bodies like the distribution committees, assuming overall responsibility for food supply and the administration of justice, law and order and military defence, areas that had briefly fallen under the jurisdiction of the local revolutionary committees. While the local committees retained much importance and power, bodies such as the workers' *patrullas* lost their autonomy.[128]

The next major compromise by the anarchist leaders came at the end of September. Following pressure from the ERC for the CCMA to be replaced by a reconstituted Generalitat, the CNT–FAI hierarchy embraced Companys' offer of three cabinet posts within a new Popular Front-style government. When, on 26 September, the incumbent anarchist ministers took their posts in the Catalan government, they became bound through collective responsibility to the other Popular Front parties, including the middle-class republicans.[129] While for internal reasons the CNT–FAI leaders dressed up their governmental role with a maximalist discourse, even portraying the Generalitat as a revolutionary body to the rank-and-file, they nevertheless fully accepted the collaborationist logic of the Popular Front, which involved containing the revolution in order to preserve wartime cabinet unity, or what one anarchist later described as the 'anti-fascist pact'.[130]

Constrained by their ministerial commitments, the anarchist ministers became passive spectators as the revolutionary changes were eroded by the other Popular Front parties. In October 1936, the Generalitat issued two decrees that, on paper at least, affirmed the formal power of the state over the revolution. The first decree disbanded the anarchist-dominated local revolutionary committees that emerged after July, replacing them with municipal councils (consells municipals) made up of all Popular Front parties.[131] Meanwhile, a second decree 'legalised' the large revolutionary collectives, effectively bolstering the power of the Generalitat over the economy. While these centralising decrees were ignored in areas of revolutionary strength and/or where republican groups and the Popular Front parties were weak, they nevertheless guaranteed that 'normality was re-established' in the political sphere, as was noted by one leading republican.[132] Having grasped the political nettle by joining the Generalitat, there was now nothing to stop the CNT–FAI entering central government in November. Solidaridad Obrera summed up the prevailing mood of reformism among the anarchist leaders, commenting that a government with anarchist ministers had 'ceased to be a force for the oppression of the working class just as the state [was] no longer an organism that divides society into classes'.[133] As the CNT–FAI hierachy became obsessed with high politics, it stood by as the POUM, the left-wing of the Generalitat, was expelled from the cabinet in December 1936. In return for an increase in CNT–FAI representation in government, the anarchist cabinet members accepted the exclusion of the POUM.[134]

The passivity of the anarchist hierarchy stood in sharp contrast to the aggression with which the most fervent supporters of the Popular Front pursued the reconstruction of the republican state. With the ERC discredited by its failure to prevent the July revolution and Companys' apparent accommodation of the CNT–FAI, the PSUC emerged as 'the champion of social conservatism' and galvanised the opposition to the revolution.[135] In contrast to the ERC, which relied on quiet diplomacy to curb the anarchists, the Stalinist PSUC possessed the political will to confront the revolutionary Left. Through their vociferous denunciations of the 'disorder' of revolution, the Stalinists articulated a new ideology of order and acquired a social constituency among the same intermediate urban sectors – small capitalists, shopkeepers and the Catalan police – that had been attracted to the 'republic of order' after 1931 and that had felt defenceless since the July revolution.[136] Another major area of PSUC growth was among the rabassaires, the Catalan tenant farmers and small rural property owners, who were, ironically, the closest local equivalent to the kulaks. Thus, by the end of 1937, nearly 10,000 Catalan peasants were paid-up Communist Party members, accounting for over one-quarter of PSUC members.[137] In order to coordinate the anti-revolutionary energies of their supporters, the *psuquistes* formed the GEPCI (Gremis i Entitats de Petits Comerciants i Industrials, or Federation of Small Traders and Manufacturers), a conservative pressure group made up of 18,000 shopkeepers and small traders, who petitioned for a return to free trade.[138] While the social constituency of the PSUC made it a unique formation among the Comintern parties, given that the immense majority of Catalan workers were already organised by the CNT by the time of its creation, the middle classes and other intermediate strata organised within the GEPCI represented the only potential growth area for the new party. Moreover, because the propertied strata that entered the PSUC lacked any mobilising power in the streets and were accustomed to expressing themselves politically through conventional governmental channels, they were attracted to the Stalinist strategy for reconstructing the apparatus of the republican state.

In the first part of 1937, the CNT–FAI rank-and-file responded to the growing attacks on the revolution. The opposition to the Popular Front coagulated among the surviving local revolutionary committees, the CNT defence committees and the *patrullas*. It also acquired organised expression from sections of the anarchist and POUM youth movements, which organised a rally of 14,000 young revolutionaries in Barcelona in February 1937, prompting calls for a 'Revolutionary Youth Front' (*Frente Revolucionario Juvenil*).[139] This upsurge of revolutionary feeling reflected the popular frustration that the socio-economic and political concessions made by the CNT–FAI leaders since July 1936 had not been converted into either significant foreign aid for the Republic or Soviet military aid to the revolutionary Catalan militias. There was also a material basis to this revolutionary opposition. The nascent protest movement galvanised around soaring inflation, which had pushed up the cost of certain basic foodstuffs by 100 percent in the six months of the civil war, much to the detriment of the poorest sectors of urban society. The revolutionaries attributed inflation to the avarice of the small capitalist interests organised in the GEPCI and protected by the PSUC, which, it was alleged, and not entirely without justification, were hoarding crops in an attempt to raise prices. Testifying to the rupture between the urban and the rural economies, armed workers' groups from Barcelona, including members of the *patrullas*, initiated raids from the city to requisition crops from the countryside.[140] Given the PSUC sponsorship of the rights of agrarian property holders, such activities inflamed tensions between the state security forces and armed workers' groups.

Despite arguments for a 'second revolution',[141] the revolutionary opposition never became more than a defensive movement, primarily concerned with checking the assault by a reconstituted republican state on the power of the local committees and the *patrullas*. However, even as a defensive alliance, the revolutionary opposition signified an open challenge to the reconstruction of state power. Thus, throughout the spring, the PSUC and republicans increased their political campaign against the local committees and the *patrullas* and for the right of the state to wield a monopoly of armed power and to control the working-class public sphere. In February, the Stalinists maintained the momentum of their campaign in favour of a 'single authority' by organising a protest by policemen against the *patrullas*.[142] On the streets, meanwhile, the clashes between the *patrullas* and the Generalitat police became increasingly frequent as intermittent warfare erupted in Catalonia between the reorganised state forces and the dispersed revolutionary powers.[143] Finally, at the end of April, the Generalitat decreed that the *patrullas* be disarmed, a measure that prompted a series of isolated gunfights between the members of the *patrullas* and the security forces as each of the two armed powers moved to disarm the other. According to the Generalitat, the level of tension in Barcelona was so great that it proved necessary to ban the May Day commemorations scheduled for the first weekend in May, a decision that, given the city's proud working-class traditions, can equally be interpreted as a provocation by the government. Certainly, the prohibition of May Day rallies did nothing to dampen the conflicts on the streets between the rival armed powers as two days later the 'civil war within the civil war' erupted in Barcelona, on 3 May 1937.

The spark for the so-called 'May Days' was the attempt by the Catalan police to seize the telephone exchange, a move that brought to a head all the latent tensions between the two powers in Barcelona, sparking off four days of street fighting between the state police on the one hand and the *patrullas*, the POUM and anarchist militants from the local revolutionary committees on the other. Barcelona was divided: the *barris* were sealed off from the rest of the city by a network of barricades guarded by armed workers, while 2,000 policemen and armed PSUC units enjoyed an unstable grip over the main civic and administrative buildings in the city centre, such as the Generalitat Palace. Although the revolutionaries had the upper hand in Barcelona and in most of Catalonia, their mobilisations lacked coordination, so, while anarchist radicals and *poumistas* seized the streets and controlled working-class neighbourhoods, there was no organ capable of channelling the revolutionary energies against the state.[144] In effect, then, the May 1937 struggles were a leaderless, spontaneous protest movement against the erosion of revolutionary power, which, like the popular uprising against the military coup the previous July, lacked a clear political focus. Meanwhile, the CNT–FAI leaders, who remained trapped within the logic of Popular Front collaborationism, adopted a conciliatory stance from the start of the fighting, eventually brokering a negotiated compromise designed to end the conflict and bring down the barricades.[145]

Companys' assurances that there would be 'neither victors nor vanquished' after the 'May Days' proved empty.[146] Afterwards, we see the definitive eradication of revolutionary power. With the remnants of the barricades still on the streets, the anarchist leaders were pushed onto the defensive when, much to their surprise, they were ejected from the Generalitat, just as the POUM had been six months earlier. The Catalan authorities no longer saw the need to consult the anarchist chiefs, who quickly appreciated that they had not extracted adequate political guarantees when brokering the truce that ended the May conflict. By calling for the barricades to be dismantled, the CNT–FAI leaders effectively negotiated away their main sources of power, which was in the streets. The remaining revolutionary committees were subsequently disbanded, their arms confiscated, by governmental decree and, when necessary, with violence. The power of the *barris*, like the revolution, was at an end. Lastly, the POUM was banned and repressed, legally and extra-judicially, as reflected by the fate of its leader, Andreu Nin, who was brutally tortured and murdered.

Revolution now became a distant dream, completely superseded by the war. This did not stop the city from being punished for its revolutionary 'heresy'. During 1937–39, fascist air raids killed 2,428 people and destroyed around 1,500 buildings in the 'city of evil'.[147] Tellingly, the air raids were not entirely random or indiscriminate attacks on the urban fabric. Rather, terror from the skies focused on the *barris*, especially the Raval, Barceloneta and Poble Sec, regardless of whether these areas possessed any targets of military significance. Bourgeois neighbourhoods, by comparison, were largely unaffected.[148] This targeted repression reached its height during the Franco dictatorship, when the working class bore the brunt of repressive state policies and when it became the policy of the regime to humiliate the proletarian city. While the city of the workers survived the long night of Francoism, the labour movement culture that emerged in the full light of day in the 1970s was markedly distinct from that which prevailed in the 1930s.

Notes

Introduction

1 E.P. Thompson, *The Making of the English Working Classes*, London, 1963.
2 For a pioneering exception to this trend, see J.M. Roberts, 'Spatial governance and working class public sphere: the case of a chartist demonstration at Hyde Park', *Journal of Historical Sociology* 14 (3), 2001, pp.308–36.
3 J.L. Oyón, 'Spain', in R. Roger (ed.), *European Urban History*, Leicester, 1993, p.38.
4 P. López Sánchez, *Un verano con mil julios y otras estaciones. Barcelona: de la Reforma Interior a la Revolución de Julio de 1909*, Madrid, 1993.
5 J.I. Bueno Madurga, *Zaragoza, 1917–1936. De la movilización popular y obrera a la reacción conservadora*, Zaragoza, 2000; C. Gil Andrés, *Echarse a la calle. Amotinados, huelguistas y revolucionarios (La Rioja, 1890–1936)*, Zaragoza, 2000; E. Cabezas Ávila, *«Los de siempre». Poder, familia y ciudad (Ávila, 1875–1923)*, Madrid, 2000; P. Radcliff, *From Mobilization to Civil War: the Politics of Polarization in the Spanish City of Gijon, 1900–1937*, Cambridge, 1996.
6 G. Jackson, *The Spanish Republic and the Civil War*, Princeton, 1965.
7 A. Elorza, *La utopía anarquista bajo la Segunda República*, Madrid, 1973, p.447.
8 J. Scott, *Weapons of the Weak. Everyday Forms of Peasant Resistance*, New Haven, Conn., 1985.
9 A. Paz, *Durruti, El proletariado en armas*, Barcelona, 1978.
10 E. Comin Colomer, *Historia del anarquismo español*, 2 vols, Barcelona, 1956.

Chapter 1

1 J. Nadal and J. Malaquer, 'Catalunya, la fàbrica d'Espanya', in various authors, *Catalunya, fàbrica d'Espanya. Un segle d'industrialització catalana*, Barcelona, 1985.
2 Central government had previously relied upon the walls to limit the growth of this potentially disloyal city.
3 See P.F. Monlau, *Abajo las murallas!!!*, Barcelona, 1841, and J. Font, *Consideraciones sobre los inconvenientes que irrogan a la salud de los jornaleros y a la pública de Barcelona*, Barcelona, 1852.
4 Cerdà was a parliamentary deputy for Barcelona during the ephemeral First Republic (1868–1874). See M. Nieto, *La I República española en Barcelona*, Barcelona, 1974.
5 Laboratori d'Urbanisme, *Treballs sobre Cerdà i Barcelona*, Barcelona, 1992.
6 The Eixample finally took shape in the 1920s and 1930s, although, contrary to Cerdà's vision, it evolved with a far higher concentration of buildings and hardly any open or green spaces.

7   D. Harvey, *Consciousness and the Urban Experience*, Oxford, 1985, pp.63–220.

8   S. García, 'Urbanization, working class organization and political movements in Barcelona', unpublished PhD thesis, University of Hull, 1983.

9   For the crisis of the Restoration monarchy, see M. Tuñón de Lara *et al.*, *Revolución burguesa, oligarquía y constitucionalismo (1834–1923)*, Barcelona, 1981.

10   However, it is noteworthy that the foundations of the Restoration state were always weak in Catalonia. See A. Jutglar, *Historia crítica de la burguesía en Cataluña*, Barcelona, 1984, pp.275–9.

11   I. Molas, *Lliga Catalana. Un estudi d'Estasiologia*, Barcelona, 1972, 2 vols.

12   *La Veu de Catalunya* (hereafter *Veu*), 18 February 1905.

13   See *Veu*, 18 January 1902, 8 September and 11 October 1905, 18 February 1906, 1 March and 26 April 1914. For Prat's vision, see *Veu*, 24 April 1909.

14   M. Perau *et al.*, *Noucentisme i ciutat*, Barcelona, 1994.

15   *Veu*, 11 October 1905.

16   See J. Culla i Clarà, *El republicanisme lerrouxista a Catalunya (1901–1923)*, Barcelona, 1986.

17   *Veu*, 17 March 1902.

18   *Veu*, 11 December 1908.

19   J. Grau, 'Vers la "Ciutat immensa": l'acció municipalista de la Mancomunitat de Catalunya, 1914–1923', in J. Roca (ed.), *El municipi de Barcelona i els combats pel govern de la ciutat*, Barcelona, 1997, pp.213–20.

20   The period 1876–88 has been described as one of 'gold fever' (*febre d'or*). To quote Walter Benjamin, the Exhibitions were 'places of pilgrimage to the fetish Commodity' (*Charles Baudelaire. A Lyric Poet in the Era of High Capitalism*, London, 1973, p.165).

21   The novelist Josep María de Sagarra reflected that World War One 'brought the nineteenth century to a close in Barcelona' (*Memòries*, Barcelona, 1981, Vol. 2, p.290).

22   I. Solà-Morales, 'L'Exposició Internacional de Barcelona (1914–1929) com a instrument de política urbana', *Recerques* 6, 1976, pp.137–45; M. Tatjer Mir, 'Els barris obrers del centre històric de Barcelona', in J.L. Oyón (ed.), *Vida obrera en la Barcelona de entreguerras*, Barcelona, 1998, p.28.

23   A myriad of small workshops were scattered across the city. In 1927, around 50 percent of the workforce was employed in small-scale enterprises (P. Gabriel, 'La Barcelona obrera y proletaria', in A. Sánchez (ed.), *Barcelona, 1888–1929. Modernidad, ambición y conflictos de una ciudad soñada*, Madrid, 1994, p.104). In 1931, the average company's capital in Catalonia was 1.17 million pesetas, under half that of the Basque country (3.6 million pesetas) (A. Balcells, *Crisis económica y agitación social en Cataluña (1930–1936)*, Barcelona, 1971, p.162, n.14).

24   Jutglar, *Historia*, pp.319–40.

25   C. Massana, *Indústria, ciutat i propietat. Política econòmica i propietat urbana a l'Àrea de Barcelona (1901–1939)*, Barcelona, 1985, pp.20–1, 120–9.

26   During the 1920s, the population of working-class neighbourhoods like Sants, Sant Martí and Sant Andreu grew by over 30, 40 and 45 percent, respectively, and by 1930 Barcelona's main industrial districts had more inhabitants than many big Spanish towns and cities (A. Cabré and I. Pujades, 'La població de Barcelona i el seu entorn al segle XX', *L'Avenç* 88, 1985, pp.33–7).

27   J. Peirats, *Figuras del movimiento libertario español*, Barcelona, 1978, p.89; J.M. Ainaud de Lasarte *et al.*, *Barcelona contemporánea 1856–1999*, Barcelona, 1996, pp.38–9.

28   J. Vandellós, *La immigració a Catalunya*, Barcelona, 1935; J. Termes, *L'Immigració a Catalunya i altres estudis d'història del nacionalisme català*, Barcelona, 1984.

29   M. Castells, *The Urban Question. A Marxist Approach*, London, 1977, p.146.

30 I. Terrades, 'Towards a comparative approach to the study of industrial and urban politics: the case of Spain', in M. Harloe (ed.), *New Perspectives in Urban Change and Conflict*, London, 1981, p.179. An outbreak of bubonic plague in the Can Tunis district in 1905, which claimed twenty-three lives, underlined the shortcomings of urban welfare networks (J. Fabre and J. M. Huertas, *Tots els barris de Barcelona*, Barcelona, 1976, Vol. 4, pp.201–2; J. Busquets, *Barcelona. Evolución urbanística de una capital compacta*, Madrid, 1992, p.216). See also A. Carsi, *El abastecimiento de aguas de Barcelona*, Barcelona, 1911, and P. Garcia Fària, *Insalubridad en las viviendas de Barcelona*, Barcelona, 1890).

31 Despite the appalling levels of typhoid in Barcelona, several planned improvements in the city's water supply foundered on corruption (E. Masjuan, *La ecología humana en el anarquismo ibérico*, Barcelona, 2000, pp.66–80).

32 For instance, nuns and priests served as nurses in hospitals and as schoolteachers. The clergy was also entrusted with running institutions such as orphanages, borstals, psychiatric hospitals and workhouses. In all these institutions, the Church played a highly abusive and repressive role, singling out non-worshippers and atheists for punishment.

33 E. Salut, *Vivers de revolucionaris. Apunts històrics del Districte Cinqué*, Barcelona, 1938, p.26.

34 J. Aiguader, 'La solució de la casa higiènica i a bon preu', *Ateneu Enciclopèdic Popular Noticiari* 17, 1922, p.67.

35 N. Rider, 'Anarchism, urbanisation and social conflict in Barcelona, 1900–1932', unpublished PhD thesis, University of Lancaster, 1987, pp.99–100.

36 *Ibid.*, pp.113–217; X. Tafunell, 'La construcción en Barcelona, 1860–1935: continuidad y cambio', in J.L. García Delgado (ed.), *Las ciudades en la modernización de España. Los decenios interseculares*, Madrid, 1992, pp.5–9, n.10.

37 N. Rider, 'Anarquisme i lluita popular: la vaga dels lloguers de 1931', *L'Avenç* 89, 1986, p.8, and 'Anarchism', p.22.

38 The population of the Raval grew from 192,828 in 1900 to 230,107 in 1930: Tatjer in Oyón (ed.), p.16.

39 There were six outbreaks of bubonic plague between 1919 and 1930. Barcelona workers were also thirty-eight times more likely than London workers to contract typhoid: Dr L. Claramunt i Furest, *La pesta en el pla de Barcelona*, Barcelona, 1933, pp.6–8 and *La Lluita contra la Fibra Tifòidea a Catalunya*, Barcelona, 1933, pp.189–206; V. Alba and M. Casasús, *Diàlegs a Barcelona*, Barcelona, 1990, p.15; Rider, 'Anarchism', p.152.

40 Rider, 'Anarquisme', p.8; L. Claramunt, *Problemes d'urbanisme*, Barcelona, 1934, pp.14–18; Massana, *Indústria*, pp.22, 126–30; J. Aiguader, *El problema de l'habitació obrera a Barcelona*, Barcelona, 1932, p.14; *Solidaridad Obrera* (hereafter *SO*), 14 May 1931.

41 One flop house was known locally as 'the three eights' after the number of daily shifts in the beds (R. Vidiella, *Los de ayer*, Barcelona, 1938, p.33).

42 M. Gil Maestre, *La criminalidad en Barcelona y en las grandes poblaciones*, Barcelona, 1886, pp.147–57; P. Villar, *Historia y leyenda del Barrio Chino (1900–1992). Crónica y documentos de los bajos fondos de Barcelona*, Barcelona, 1996, pp.37–41; Busquets, *Barcelona*, p.213; Tatjer in Oyón (ed.), p.29.

43 In the Raval, where no land was available for construction, *barracas* were built on the roofs of tenement slums (J. Artigues, F. Mas and X. Sunyol, *The Raval. Història d'un barri servidor d'una ciutat*, Barcelona, 1980, pp.53–4).

44 During the 1920s, when the average monthly wage for an unskilled labourer was 130–150 pesetas, a 25-square-metre *barraca* might command a monthly rent of between 15 and 75 pesetas.

45 It has been claimed that the 'shanty dwellers' consisted of 'social groups belonging to the lumpenproletariat and the least skilled sectors of the proletariat' (T. García Castro

de la Peña, 'Barrios barceloneses de la dictadura de Primo de Rivera', *Revista de Geografía* 7 (1–2), 1974, p.83). Unfortunately, besides not defining what is signified by the term 'lumpenproletariat', García also concedes that 'in their majority they [i.e. the *barraquistes*] were workers employed as unskilled labourers'. Moreover, according to figures cited by the same author (pp.82–3), in the early 1920s, 49 percent of *barraquistes* were Catalan, 28 percent of whom were natives of Barcelona. This would therefore seem to suggest that the 'shanty dwellers' were not marginal, déclassé migrants but local workers rendered homeless by housing shortages.

46 See the series of articles in *Justicia Social* (hereafter *JS*) between 24 November 1923 and 23 August 1924. There are no accurate statistics for the total number of *barracas*, and the figures in Table 1.1 are no more than a general indicator.

Table 1.1 Numbers of shanty houses and dwellers in Barcelona, 1914–27

Year	Number of shanty dwellings	Number of Shanty dwellers
1914	1,218	4,950
1922	3,859	19,984
1924	n.a	25,000
1927	6,000	n.a.

In 1929, during the hey-day of barraquisme immediately prior to the Exhibition, there were an estimated 6,478 *barracas* on Montjuïc alone. Figures from J. L. Oyón, 'Las segundas periferias, 1918–1936: una geografía preliminar', in Oyón (ed.), p.62, n.15; Massana, *Indústria*, p.405; C. Massana and F. Roca, 'Vicis privats, iniciativa pública. Barcelona 1901–39', *L'Avenç* 88, 1985, p.41; Fabre and Huertas, *Barris*, Vol. 4, p.159.

47 M. Domingo and F. Sagarra, *Barcelona: Les Cases Barates*, Barcelona, 1999.

48 García, 'Barrios', p.84; Fabre and Huertas, *Barris*, Vol. 5, p.158–9.

49 See López, *Verano*, *passim*.

50 One immigrant worker claimed that the *Cases Barates* 'could be described as *barracas*' (interview with 'Juan', November 1997).

51 García, 'Barrios', p.84; Rider, 'Anarchism', p.197; S. Cánovas Cervantes, *Apuntes históricos de 'Solidaridad Obrera'. Proceso histórico de la revolución española*, Barcelona, 1937, p.233; Massana and Roca, 'Vicis', p.40; *L'Opinió*, 8 May 1932; *SO*, 9 May 1931.

52 *L'Opinió*, 8 May 1932.

53 García, 'Barrios', p.84.

54 A. Merrifield and E. Swyngedouw (eds), *The Urbanization of Injustice*, London, 1996.

55 C. Canyellas and R. Toran, 'L'Ajuntament de Barcelona i el règim restauracionista (1875–1901)', *L'Avenç*, 116, 1988, pp.9–15. By 1928, the wealthiest 3.5 percent of Barcelona's landlords controlled over 50–60 percent of all housing stock (Massana, *Indústria*, pp.7, 176–84).

56 M. Vilanova, 'Intransigència de classe, alfabetització i gènere. Les fronteres interiors de la societat de Barcelona, 1900–75', in J. Roca (ed.), *L'articulació social de la Barcelona contemporània*, Barcelona, 1997, p.71; López, *Verano*, pp.49–98.

57 Tatjer, in Oyón (ed.), pp.14, 19.

58 Tatjer, in Oyón (ed.), p.16; Fabre and Huertas, *Barris*, Vol. 5, pp.157–8.

59 J.L. Oyón, 'Obreros en la ciudad: líneas de un proyecto de investigación en historia urbana', *Historia Contemporánea* 18, 1999, pp.317–45. Perched high above the city, Sarrià and Pedralbes were the most isolated of all these bourgeois settlements, 'as far from Barcelona as one could get while still being part of the city' (R. Hughes, *Barcelona*, London, 1992, p.343).

60 J. Estivill and G. Barbat, 'L'anticlericalisme en la revolta popular del 1909', *L'Avenç* 2, 1977, p.32.

61 Castells, *Urban Question*, p.169.

62 C. Ealham, 'Class and the city: spatial memories of pleasure and danger in Barcelona, 1914–23', *Oral History* 29 (1), 2001, pp.33–47.

63 R. Núñez Florencio, *El terrorismo anarquista, 1888–1909*, Madrid, 1983.

64 López, *Verano*, pp.215–41; J. Connelly Ullman, *The Tragic Week. A Study of Anticlericalism in Spain, 1875–1912*, Cambridge, Mass., 1968, pp.167–304; J. Romero Maura, *'La rosa de fuego'. El obrerismo barcelonés de 1899 a 1909*, Madrid, 1989.

65 M. Pérez Ledesma, 'El miedo de los acomodados y la moral de los obreros', in P. Folguera (ed.), *Otras visiones de España*, Madrid, 1993, pp.27–64; *Veu*, 10 August 1905, 24 April 1909; P. López Sánchez, 'El desordre de l'ordre. Al.legats de la ciutat disciplinària en el somni de la Gran Barcelona', *Acàcia* 3, 1993, p.103. This conservative project was reflected in the work of the city's most imaginative architect, Antoni Gaudí, a highly anti-democratic thinker, who was closely linked to bourgeois circles. Gaudí's famous church, La Sagrada Família, can be viewed as part of a project to 'Christianise' Barcelona's godless proletariat (Hughes, *Barcelona*, pp.474–5, 498).

66 The classic study of moral panics is S. Cohen, *Folk Devils and Moral Panics*, London, 1972.

67 F. Alvarez-Uría, *Miserables y locos. Medicina mental y Orden social en la España del siglo XIX*, Barcelona, 1983, pp.308–64.

68 See C. de Andrés, *La clase obrera o breve descripción de lo que debe ser un buen obrero*, Madrid, 1900; M. Bembo, *La mala vida en Barcelona*, Barcelona, 1912; G. López, *Barcelona sucia. Artículos de malas costumbres. Registro de higiene*, Barcelona, n.d.; A. Masriera, *Los buenos barceloneses. Hombres, costumbres y anécdotas de la Barcelona ochocentista*, Barcelona, 1924; T. Caballé *La criminalidad en Barcelona*, Barcelona, 1945.

69 Villar, *Historia*, *passim*; Vidiella, *Ayer*, p.133. Liberal-left journalists such as Paco Madrid added to the rising sense of panic surrounding 'Chinatown'. See his articles in *El Escándalo* and his sensationalist study *Sangre en Atarazanas*, Barcelona, 1926.

70 A. Avel.li Artís (Sempronio), *Aquella entremaliada Barcelona*, Barcelona, 1978; D. de Bellmunt, *Les Catacumbes de Barcelona*, Barcelona, 1930; J. Planes, *Nits de Barcelona*, Barcelona, 1931.

71 J. Alvarez Junco, *El Emperador del Paralelo. Lerroux y la demagogía populista*, Madrid, 1990, p.399; J. del Castillo and S. Alvarez, Barcelona, *Objetivo* Cubierto, Barcelona, 1958, p.31.

72 Middle-class children tended not to spend time in the streets, as according to certain prejudices 'only hooligans play in the street' (J. Ballester, *Memòries d'un noi de Gràcia*, Barcelona, 1999, p.52).

73 According to Church sources, there were between 8,000 and 10,000 gang members in Barcelona at the start of the twentieth century (Romero, 'Rosa', p.130, n.50; J. Juderías, *La juventud delincuente. Leyes e instituciones que tienden a su regeneración*, Madrid, 1912, p.8; J. Elías, *La obrera en Cataluña, en la ciudad y en el campo*, Barcelona, 1915, p.53; J. Vallmitjana, *Criminalitat típica local*, Barcelona, 1910, p.8).

74 *El Diluvio* (hereafter *Diluvio*), 27 November 1920; *Veu*, 10 June 1931. Much of this journalism, including that which appeared in liberal-left newspapers, was steeped in middle-class sexual obsessions and anxieties.

75 See especially Juderías, *Juventud*, and Vallmitjana, *Criminalitat*.

76 Salut, *Vivers*, pp.147–8.

77 For an insider's view of the immigrant world, see F. Candel, *Els altres catalans*, Barcelona, 1963.

78 Fabre and Huertas, *Barris*, Vol. 4, pp.124, 202.

79 F. Barangó-Solís, *Reportajes Pintorescos*, Barcelona, 1934, pp.107–15; Avel.li, *Barcelona*, pp.171–2; de Bellmunt, *Catacumbes, passim*.

80 L. Almeric, *El hostal, la fonda, la taverna y el café en la vida Barcelonesa*, Barcelona, 1945, p.67. Interestingly, the spread of flamenco in Barcelona after World War One can be attributed to Raval bar owners, who created the myth of 'little Andalusia' (*Andalusia chica*) in order to attract foreign tourism to the city (A. Bueso, *Recuerdos de un cenetista*, Barcelona, 1978, Vol. 2, pp.74–5.

81 P. Garcia Fària, *Medios de aminorar las enfermedades y mortalidad en Barcelona*, Barcelona, 1893; A. Farreras, *De la Setmana Tràgica a la Implantació del Franquisme*, Barcelona, 1977, p.39.

82 A. Rovira, *La nacionalització de Catalunya*, Barcelona, 1914. The *españolista* right rivalled these criticisms with their own attacks on the migrants as 'the detritus of the city'; see, for example, *La Voz de Hospitalet*, 16 March 1929.

83 P. Rossell, *La raça*, Barcelona, 1930.

84 *El Correo Catalán*, 7 August 1909; Fabre and Huertas, *Barris*, Vol. 4, p.202.

85 *Veu*, 20 August 1901.

86 *Veu*, 14 February 1904; J. Solé-Tura, *Catalanismo y revolución burguesa. La síntesis de Prat de la Riba*, Madrid, 1970, pp.255–8. For an example of this literature, see A. Masriera, *Barcelona isabelina y revolucionaria*, Barcelona, 1930.

87 F. de Xercavins, *¿Cabe una institución entre la escuela y la cárcel'*, Barcelona, 1889; B. Porcel, *La revuelta permanente*, Barcelona, 1978, p.54; Salut, *Vivers*, pp.147–8; Avel.li, *Barcelona*, p.172; Gil, *Criminalidad*, pp.ix–x, 39.

88 A. Pulido, *El cáncer comunista. Degeneración del socialismo y del sindicalismo*, Valencia, n.d., p.10; *El País*, 21 January and 17 February 1894; *Veu*, 14 February 1904.

89 Anarchism was identified with a lack of culture; for references to its 'horrifying uncouthness', 'unpredictability', 'irresponsibility' and 'lack of control', see *Veu*, 23 February 1902 and 21 October 1930.

90 See M. Berman, *All That Is Solid Melts Into Air. The Experience of Modernity*, London, 1983, pp.98–105.

91 In the words of David Sibley, the aim here was the establishment of 'moral barricades' that close space, exclude and set limits to what is acceptable, thereby 'demarcat[ing] the boundaries of society, beyond which lie those who do not belong' (*Geographies of Exclusion. Society and Difference in the West*, London, 1995, pp.42, 49).

92 Jutglar, *Historia*, pp.224–6. Vilanova in Roca (ed.), *L'articulació*, p.81, emphasises the militant nature of the bourgeoisie, which, 'despite the evident moderation of the masses…was most in favour of acting violently against the world of work rather than accepting negotiations, because from its point of view profit was more decisive than agreement, co-existence and social understanding'.

93 S. Hall, C. Critcher, T. Jefferson, J. Clarke and B. Roberts, *Policing the Crisis: Mugging, the State and Law and Order*, London, 1978, p.221; Sibley, *Geographies*, p.14; M. Foucault, *Discipline and Punish. The Birth of the Prison*, Harmondsworth, 1991, pp.101, 286.

94 V. Gay, *Constitución y vida del pueblo español. Estudio sobre la etnografía y psicología de las razas de la España contemporánea*, Madrid, 1905; G. Sergi, *La decadencia de las naciones latinas*, Barcelona, 1901; P. Garcia Fària, *Anarquía o caciquismo*, Barcelona, 1902.

95 The Asil Durán, the city's main borstal, was opened in 1890; in 1904 the Model jail was established; at the end of 1907 the council-funded Guàrdia Urbana was founded; and in 1916 the Asil de Port was created for the incarceration of the poor in the waterfront area. A. Pomares and V. Valentí, 'Notas per a un estudi sobre el control social a la Barcelona del segle XIX: la instrucció pública', *Acàcia* 3, 1993, p.135; *El Escándolo* (hereafter *Escándolo*), 16 September 1926.

96 This involved supervising popular leisure, censoring the content of plays or songs of any material deemed seditious, blasphemous or politically unacceptable, and regulating potentially autonomous political spaces, such as meetings and demonstrations.

97 *SO*, 8 June 1918; Núñez, *Terrorismo*, pp.99–103. According to one Barcelona police chief, work in the force was viewed as 'the quick solution to a family catastrophe' (E. Mola, *Memorias de mi paso por la dirección general de seguridad. Lo que yo supe...*, Madrid, n.d., Vol. 1, p.28).

98 M. Ballbé, *Orden público y militarismo en la España constitucional (1812–1983)*, Madrid, 1985, pp.300–1; R. Núñez Florencio, 'El ejército ante la agitación social en España (1875–1914)', in J. Alvarado and R. Maria Pérez (eds), *Estudios sobre ejército, política y derecho en España (siglos XII–XX)*, Madrid, 1996, p.324.

99 Núñez, *Terrorismo*, pp.93–8.

100 This allowed for the detention of police suspects on the order of the civil governor as 'governmental prisoners' (*presos gubernativos*) for two weeks, during which time agents could 'work' to obtain a 'confession'; if necessary, the period of internment could be extended by the civil governor. It was often alleged that the police used this form of detention to recruit informants.

101 F. Madrid, *Ocho meses y un día en el gobierno civil de Barcelona*, Barcelona, 1932, p.199, n.1; Porcel, *Revuelta*, pp.107, 117, 128; A. Pestaña, *Terrorismo en Barcelona (Memorias inéditas)*, Barcelona, 1979, pp.80–2.

102 Basically, 'shot while trying to escape'.

103 This concept of 'moral guilt' served as the pretext for the execution of anarchist educationalist Francesc Ferrer, whose rationalist philosophy was deemed to have been responsible for the urban riots of 1909.

104 J. Peiró, *Juan Peiró. Teórico y militante de anarcosindicalismo español*, Barcelona, 1978, pp.12, 21, 26, 28; Porcel, *Revuelta*, pp.107, 117.

105 A law of 1879 gave the army ultimate responsibility for public order.

106 M. Turrado Vidal, *La policia en la historia contemporánea de España (1766–1986)*, Madrid, 1995, pp.144, 162; Ballbé, *Orden*, pp.247–303; J. Lleixá, *Cien años de militarismo en España. Funciones estatales confiadas al Ejército en la Restauración y el Franquismo*, Barcelona, 1986, pp.57–95.

107 D. López Garrido, *La Guardia Civil y los orígenes del Estado centralista*, Barcelona, 1982, *passim*; Ballbé, *Orden*, pp.250–71.

108 J.M. Jover, *Política, diplomacia y humanismo popular en la España del siglo XIX*, Madrid, 1976, p.53; P. Gual Villalbí, *Memorias de un industrial de nuestro tiempo*, Barcelona, n.d., pp.162–4, 194.

109 Letters from the civil governor of Barcelona to the minister of the interior and the director-general of security, 1, 11 and 29 March, 1 December 1919, 17 May 1922, 7 August 1923, Legajo 54a (AHN/MG).

110 F. del Rey Reguillo, *Propietarios y patronos. La política de las organizaciones económicas en la España de la Restauración*, Madrid, 1992, p.464.

111 *Veu*, 28 February 1902; Romero, '*Rosa*', p.511.

112 Romero, '*Rosa*', p.519.

113 Prat de la Riba once wrote that 'The Spanish police, like all state organs, is incapable of operating in lands of intense civilisation: it is a primitive body, a useless fossil' (*Veu*, 27 December 1906). The Lliga also claimed that the central

authorities tolerated a 'criminal population' in Barcelona, since it would drain the local economy and limit the future prosperity of Catalonia. It even asserted that the government sponsored provocateurs to come to Catalonia to create conflicts in order to divide Catalans (G. Graell, *La cuestión catalana*, Barcelona, 1902, *passim*, and Solé-Tura, *Catalanismo*, pp.249, 255–8). Not without reason was Cambó, the Lliga leader, described as 'the politician of the great panics' (J. Maurín, *Los hombres de la Dictadura*, Barcelona, 1977 [1930], p. 138).

114 It is significant that both the *catalaniste* and *españolista* wings of the bourgeoisie concurred that Barcelona was a 'lawless city' (del Castillo and Alvarez, *Barcelona*, p.32).

115 This project was articulated by the 'national poet' of Catalonia, Joan Maragall, who wrote of the need 'to purify (*depurar*) the mass, expelling bad people, rendering them incapable of committing evil, watching them, also impeding criminal propaganda' (cited in López, *Verano*, p.85).

116 See Gual, *Memorias, passim*; S. Bengoechea, *Organització patronal i conflictivitat social a Catalunya; tradició i corporativisme entre finals de segle i la Dictadura de Primo de Rivera*, Barcelona, 1994, pp.175–283. According to Léon-Ignacio, the 'new' employers imposed social relations 'like those in the colonies between the natives and the white minority. The bourgeoisie considered its operatives as an inferior and separate race' ('El pistolerisme dels anys vint', *L'Avenç*, 52, 1982, p.24).

117 See E. González Calleja and F. del Rey Reguillo, *La defensa armada contra la revolución. Una historia de la guardias cívicas en la España del siglo XX*, Madrid, 1995.

118 del Rey, *Propietarios*, pp.628–50. Shopkeepers joined the militia in their droves, particularly in neighbourhoods where the workers' movement was a force to be reckoned with. It is also significant that, despite the ultra-conservative *españolismo* of the Sometent, many leading figures from the nationalist Lliga joined the ranks of the militia.

119 Sometent membership in Catalonia grew dramatically, from 43,891 in 1918 to 65,735 in 1923. This expansion was based on Barcelona, where the militia grew from 17,685 in 1918 (when it accounted for 40 percent of all *sometentistes*) to 34,740 in 1923 (52.85 percent) (del Rey, *Propietarios*, pp.639–40, n.232).

120 Gun licences were easily obtained by the 'good citizens of Barcelona', who were free to arm themselves and their bodyguards.

121 A. Pestaña, *Lo qué aprendí en la vida*, Bilbao, 1973 (2nd edn), Vol. 2, pp.68–71.

122 His real identity remains a mystery. His original surname is believed to have been 'Colman' or 'Kölmann'. To add to the confusion, his *nom de guerre* is frequently cited as 'de Koening' or 'de König'. Besides working for the German secret service, it has also been claimed that the 'Baron' was employed by either British or French intelligence. He was deported in May 1920 when it emerged that the 'Baron' was operating a protection racket and intimidating employers. He apparently settled in Paris, where he dedicated himself to extortion and blackmail before changing his identity and disappearing without trace. (J. Subirato Centura, 'La verdadera personalidad del "Barón de Koenig"', *Cuadernos de Historia Económica de Cataluña*, 1971, pp.103–18).

123 The Sindicatos Libres were formed in December 1919 from the fusion of several small Catholic trade unions. Léon-Ignacio, *Los años del pistolerismo*, Barcelona, 1981, *passim*; Pestaña, *Terrorismo*, pp.122–80.

124 For instance, Bravo Portillo and the 'Barón de Koenig' were personal friends of General Joaquín Milans del Bosch, the captain-general of the Barcelona garrison from 1918 to 1920.

125 He later occupied ministerial positions in the dictatorships of General Primo de Rivera and General Franco. During the civil war, he was responsible for much of the repression in the Francoist zone.

126 See P. Foix, *Los archivos del terrorismo blanco. El fichero Lasarte, 1910–1930*, Madrid, 1978 [Barcelona, 1931].

127 J.M. Huertas, *Obrers a Catalunya. Manual d'història del moviment obrer (1840–1975)*, Barcelona, 1994, p.189; J. Peirats, *La CNT en la revolución española*, Madrid, 1978, Vol. 1, pp.33–6. A. Balcells, *El sindicalismo en Barcelona, 1916–1923*, Barcelona, 1965, p.137; Foix, *Archivos*, p.73.

128 *Las Noticias* (hereafter *LasN*), 2 September 1923; *Comercio y Navegación* (hereafter *CyN*), August–October 1923.

129 F. Cambó, *Les dictadures*, Barcelona, 1929, p.206.

130 E. Mola, *Memorias. El derrumbamiento de la monarquía*, Madrid n.d., Vol. 3, pp.127–35.

131 *L'Opinió*, 18 July 1930.

132 Letter from the president of el Gremio de Ultramarinos y Similares de l'Hospitalet to the mayor of l'Hospitalet, April 1930, and letter from the presidents of la Cambra Oficial de la Propietat, la Asociación de Propietarios, el Gremio de Ultramarinos y Similares, el Gremio de Líquidos, el Centro Gremial de Carboneros and la Sociedad de Maestros Peluqueros y Barberos to the mayor of l'Hospitalet, 30 September 1930 (AHl'HL/AM).

Chapter 2

1   D. Harvey, *Spaces of Hope*, Edinburgh, 2000.

2   Bourdieu, *Outline*, p.80; A. Giddens, *The Class Structure of Advanced Societies*, London, 1981, pp.111–13; D. Harvey, 'Labour, capital, and class struggle around the built environment in advanced capitalist societies', *Politics and Society* 6, 1976, p.271.

3   Tatjer, in Oyón (ed.), pp.22, 30.

4   Oyón, in Oyón (ed.), pp.81–2. This is not to suggest that the *barris* were populated exclusively and entirely by workers, but we need to avoid exaggerating the degree of coexistence between social classes in neighbourhoods.

5   J. Roca and E. Díaz, 'La Torrassa. Un antecedent de barri-dormitori', *L'Avenç* 28, 1980, pp.62–9; Rider, 'Anarchism', pp.1120–1.

6   D. Marín, 'Una primera aproximació a la vida quotidiana dels Hospitalencs: 1920–1929. Les històries de vida com a font històrica', *Identitats* 4–5, 1990, p.30; Roca and Díaz, 'Torrassa', pp.63, 69.

7   C. Sentís, *Viatge en Transmiserià. Crònica viscuda de la primera gran emigració a Catalunya*, Barcelona, 1994, pp.65–8.

8   D. Marin, 'De la llibertat per conèixer, al coneixement de la llibertat', unpublished PhD thesis, University of Barcelona, 1995, p.289.

9   M.J. Sirera Oliag, 'Obreros en Barcelona, 1900–1910', unpublished PhD thesis, University of Barcelona, 1959.

10 According to the 1934 electoral register, two-thirds of male voters were 'day labourers, unskilled workmen or hands', while 12 percent were 'skilled' workers (C. Boix and M. Vilanova, 'Participación y elecciones en Barcelona de 1934 a 1936', *Historia y Fuente Oral* 7, 1992, p.66).

11 A. Soto Carmona, *El trabajo industrial en la España contemporánea*, Barcelona, 1989, pp.633–4, 662.

12 Ministerio de Trabajo y Previsión, *Estadística de los accidentes de trabajo*, Madrid, 1930, pp.114–47.

13 *LaV*, 15 August 1931.

14 Oyón, 'Obreros', p.324.

15 According to one worker, rents 'were beyond the reach of immigrants' (interview with 'Juan', November 1997).

16 J. L. Martín Ramos, 'Consequències socials: la resposta obrera', *L'Avenç* 69, 1984, p.46.

17 Rider claims that prices were 'at around 170 per cent of their 1914 level for most of the twenties', while wages decreased in real terms ('Anarchism', pp.65, 159).

18 Figures from García, 'Urbanization', pp.201, 210–12.

19 J. Llarch, *Los días rojinegros. Memorias de un niño obrero – 1936*, Barcelona, 1975, p.22; R. Sanz, *Los hijos de trabajo. El sindicalismo español antes de la guerra civil*, Barcelona, 1976, p.72–7; P. Eyre, *Quico Sabaté, el último guerrillero*, Barcelona, 2000, pp.33, 36; J. Ferrer and S. Piera, *Simó Piera: Perfil d'un sindicalista. Records i experiències d'un dirigent de la CNT*, Barcelona, 1975, pp.17–25; A. Pestaña, *Lo que aprendí en la vida*, Bilbao, 1973, Vol. 1, p.13.

20 R. Williams, *The Country and the City*, London, 1973, p.104.

21 D. Harvey, *Social Justice and the City*, London, 1973, pp.281–2.

22 A. Etzioni, *The Spirit of Community: Rights, Responsibilities and the Communitarian Agenda*, London, 1995, p.ix.

23 R. Liebman, *Structures of Solidarity. Class, Kin, Community and Collective Action in Nineteenth-Century Lyon*, Michigan, 1988.

24 Interview with 'Juan', November 1997.

25 J. Oliva, *Recuerdos de un libre pensador nacido en Gràcia*, n.p., n.d., p.4.

26 Interview with Helenio Molina, recorded for *Vivir la utopia*, Televisión Española, 1996.

27 Interview with Arcos, *Vivir*; interview with 'Juan', November 1997.

28 Oyón, 'Obreros', pp.341–3. Around three-quarters of Barcelona's workers walked to work, a far higher number when compared with similar-sized European cities (C. Miralles and J.L. Oyón, 'De casa a la fábrica. Movilidad obrera y transporte en la Barcelona de entreguerras, 1914–1939', in Oyón (ed.), pp.160–1).

29 X. Roigé, 'Família burgesa, família obrera. Evolució dels models de parentiu i industrialització a Barcelona, s.XIX–1930', in Roca (ed.), *L'articulació*, p.167.

30 Oyón, in Oyón (ed.), p.88; A. Paz, *Chumberas y alacranes (1921–1936)*, Barcelona, 1994, p.67.

31 M. Vilanova, 'Fuentes orales y vida cotidiana en la Barcelona de entreguerras', in Oyón (ed.), p.135.

32 Tatjer, in Oyón (ed.), p.21.

33 D. Stark, 'Class struggle and the transformation of the labour process', *Theory and Society* 9, 1980, pp.89–130.

34 R. Williams, *Resources of Hope: Culture, Democracy, Socialism*, London, 1989, pp.4, 21–2; N. Thrift, 'Flies and germs: a geography of knowledge', in D. Gregory and J. Urry (eds), *Social Relations and Spatial Structures*, London, 1985, pp.366–403.

35 A. Merrifield, 'Situated knowledge through exploration: reflections on Bunge's "Geographical Explorations"', *Antipode* 27 (1), 1995, pp.49–70.

36 Ealham, 'Class', pp.33–47.

37 Giddens, *Class*, pp.111–13.

38 Willis, *Learning*, pp.26, 34, 124–5; Abercrombie *et al.*, *Ideology*, p.118.

39 A. Leeds, *Cities, Classes, and the Social Order*, Ithaca, NY, 1994, pp.224–31.

40 Romero 'Rosa', p.130; Fabre and Huertas, *Barris*, Vol. 5, p.216.

41 García, 'Barrios', p.83; J. Giménez, *De la Unión a Banet. Itinerario de una rebeldía*, Madrid, 1996, p.38; Paz, *Chumberas*, p.109.

42 Sentís, *Viatge*, p.78; Domingo and Sagarra, *Barcelona*, p.106.

43 On the survival of so-called 'traditional' forms of protest, see M. Pérez Ledesma, *Estabilidad y conflicto social: España, de los íberos al 14-D.*, Madrid, 1990, pp.165–202'

44 *El Diario de Barcelona* and *El Liberal*, 4–6, May 1903.

45 L. Golden, 'Les dones com avantguarda: el rebombori del pa del gener de 1918', *L'Avenç* 45, 1981, pp.45–50.

46 Circular from the Ministro de la Gobernación a los Gobernadores Civiles de todas las provincias, 4 September 1926, and letter from the civil governor of Barcelona to the minister of the interior, 25 June 1929, Legajo 54a (AHN/MG); Paz, *Chumberas*, p.122.

47 Eyre, 'Sabaté', p.36.

48 In European terms, the rate of crime against individuals in Barcelona was very low indeed, whereas the city led the way in 'property crimes' (Romero, '*Rosa*', p.133).

49 Interview with 'Juan', November 1997.

50 Castells, *Urban Question*, p.169.

51 Sentís, *Viatge*, pp.58–60.

52 D. Beriain, *Prat de Llobregat, ayer: un pueblo sin estado (relatos y semblanzas)*, n.p., n.d, p.28; Sentís, *Viatge*, p.63.

53 Paz, *Chumberas*, pp.79–80.

54 Interview with 'Juan', November 1997.

55 Civil governor of Barcelona to the minister of the interior, 25 June 1929, Legajo 54a (AHN/MG).

56 Porcel, *Revuelta*, p.139; López, *Verano*, pp.99–103; Pestaña, *Terrorismo*, pp.138–43; Villar, *Historia*, p.115.

57 Porcel, *Revuelta*, p.103; Salut, *Vivers*, pp.9–11, 52–7, 114, 123–4, 147–8.

58 To borrow an expression coined by Ira Katznelson, these *barris* were 'relatively autonomous communities' (*Marxism and the City*, Oxford, 1992, p. 237).

59 From its creation in 1870 until its repression in 1874, the city was an important centre of the Bakuninist Federación Regional Española de la Asociación Internacional de Trabajadores (Spanish Regional Federation of the International Working Men's Association).

60 G. Esenwein, *Anarchist Ideology and the Working-Class Movement in Spain, 1868–1898*, Berkeley, Calif., 1989, pp.220–9; Eyre, 'Sabaté', pp.45–6; Porcel, *Revuelta*, p.54; Salut, *Vivers*, pp.147–8.

61 J. Mir y Miró (ed.), *Dinamita cerebral*, Barcelona, 1980.

62 Golden, 'Dones', p.50.

63 C. Tilly, *From Mobilisation to Revolution*, Reading, Mass., 1978, pp.151–66.

64 R. Vidiella, *Los de ayer*, Barcelona, 1938, pp.43–4; *La Huelga General*, 5 February 1903.

65 *SO*, 31 March 1931.

66 *Frente Libertario*, March 1975.

67 Romero, '*Rosa*', pp.210–1; A. Duarte, 'Entre el mito y la realidad. Barcelona 1902', *Ayer* 4, 1991, p.166.

68 Romero, '*Rosa*', pp.502, 519.

69 E. Hobsbawm, *Labouring Men*, London, 1964, p.7.

70 Various unions complained of this to government agencies, see Legajo 59a (AHN/MG).

71 D. Cosgrove, 'Towards a radical cultural geography: problems of theory', *Antipode* 15 (1), 1983, p.6.

72 J. Peirats, 'Una experiencia histórica del pensamiento libertario. Memorias y selección de artículos breves', *Anthropos Suplementos* 18, 1990, p.9.

73 M. Lladonosa, *El Congrès de Sants*, Barcelona, 1975.

74 J. Peiró, *Ideas sobre sindicalismo y anarquismo*, Madrid, 1979, pp.124–7.

75 A. Monjo, 'La CNT durant la II República a Barcelona: líders, militants, afiliats', unpublished PhD thesis, University of Barcelona, 1993, p.175.

76 J. Peirats, *Mecanismo organico de la Confederación Nacional del Trabajo*, Santa María de Barberá, 1979, p.117.

77 Interview with 'Antonio'.

78 A. Andreassi, *Libertad también se escribe en minúscula. Anarcosindicalismo en Sant Adrià del Besòs, 1925–1939*, Barcelona, 1996, pp.39–44.

79 A. Monjo, 'Barrio y militancia en los años treinta', in Oyón (ed.), pp.148–9.
80 Interview with 'Antonio'.
81 Interview with Manuel Vicente Alcón, cited in Monjo, in Oyón (ed.), p.149.
82 Interview with 'Antonio'.
83 Interview with Manuel Vicente Alcón, cited in Monjo, 'CNT', p.293.
84 *Acción*, 6 July 1930.
85 Massana, *Indústria*, p.401.
86 E. Masjuan, 'El pensament anarquista i la ciutat', in Oyón (ed.), p.252.
87 E.P. Thompson, 'The moral economy of the crowd in the eighteenth century', *Past and Present* 50, 1971, pp.71–136.
88 Interview with Josep Costa Font, cited in Monjo, 'CNT', p.238.
89 See S. Lash and J. Urry, 'The new Marxism of collective action', *Sociology* 18 (1), 1984, pp.36–41.
90 Peirats, unpublished memoirs, p.1; A. Figuerola, *Memòries d'un taxista barceloní*, Barcelona, 1976, pp.68–9, 242–3.
91 Giménez, *Itinerario*, p.43.
92 E. Martín, *Recuerdos de un militante de la CNT*, Barcelona, 1979, p.93.
93 'It was the "older ones" – normally older brothers, workmates even parents, or older friends – who provided orientation' (Marin, 'Llibertat', p.562).
94 Paz, *Chumberas*, p.88; interviews with 'Antonio', 'Francisco' and 'Enric', recorded by Alejandro Andreassi, 9 March 1992, 30 October 1991, 14 September 1992; Federico Arcos in P. Avrich (ed.), *Anarchist Voices: An Oral History of Anarchism in America*, Princeton, NJ, 1996, p. 402; Marin, 'Llibertat', p.461.
95 Paz, *Chumberas*, p.121.
96 Marin, 'Llibertat', p.129.
97 *Ibid.*, pp.117–8.
98 P. Solà, *Els ateneus obrers i la cultura popular a Catalunya (1900–1939): L'Ateneu Enciclopèdic Popular*, Barcelona, 1978.
99 Monjo, in Oyón (ed.), p.151.
100 Two works by Fola Igúbide (*El Cristo moderno* ('The Modern Christ') and *El Sol de la Humanidad* ('The Sun of Humanity') were particular favourites in the ateneus.
101 Paz, *Chumberas*, pp.117–18; Masjuan, in Oyón (ed.), pp.252–3.
102 *Veu*, 11 April 1913.
103 *La Huelga General*, 5 January 1902.
104 Monjo, 'CNT', pp.296–7, 381.
105 Marin, 'Llibertat', p.416, n. 24; Monjo, in Oyón (ed.), p.151.
106 Paz, *Chumberas*, p.88.
107 F. Carrasquer, 'Autopercepción intelectual de un proceso histórico', in F. Carrasquer *et al.* (eds), 'Félix Carrasquer. Proyecto de una sociedad libertaria: experiencias históricas y actualidad', *Anthropos* 90, 1988, p.24.
108 Francisco Manzanares, cited in Marin, 'Llibertat', p.485, n.65.
109 Interview with 'Antonio', 9 March 1992; J. Termes, 'Els ateneus populars: un intent de cultura obrera', *L'Avenç* 104, 1987, pp.8–12; Andreassi, *Libertad*, pp.42–3.
110 Rider, 'Anarchism', pp.214–22; Antonio Turón, cited in Monjo in Oyón (ed.), p.148.
111 Marin, 'Llibertat', pp.125–7, 501–2.
112 It has also been described as a proletarian 'para-society' or 'counter-society' (López, *Verano*, p.40).
113 V. García, 'José Peirats Valls: una bibliografía biografiada', in I. de Llorens *et al.* (eds), 'José Peirats Valls: Historia contemporánea del Movimiento Libertario. Visión crítica de un compromiso anarquista: la Revolución Social', *Anthropos* 102, 1989, p.14.
114 A. Durgan, *BOC, 1930–1936: El Bloque Obrero y Campesino*, Barcelona, 1996.

115 See M. Amàlia Pradas, 'Pistoles i pistolers. El mapa de la violència a la Barcelona dels anys 1920', *L'Avenç* 285, 2003, pp.13–20.

116 *Boletín de información de la CNT–FAI*, 24 July 1936.

117 See R. Ferrer, *Durruti, 1896–1936*, Barcelona, 1985, pp.48–68; Paz, *Durruti*, *passim*; J. García Oliver, *El eco de los pasos. El anarcosindicalismo...en la calle...en el Comité de Milicias...en el gobierno...en el exilio*, Barcelona, 1978, *passim*; R. Sanz, *El sindicalismo y la política. Los 'solidarios' y 'nosotros'*, Toulouse, 1966, *passim*; and *Hijos*, *passim*.

118 Marin, 'Llibertat', p.144.

119 V. Alba, *Dos revolucionarios:* Joaquán Maurán, Andreu Nin, Madrid 1975, p.77; Pestaña, *Vida*, Vol. 1, pp.40, 45; Paz, *Durruti*, pp.29–33; Sanz, *Hijos*, p.111.

120 Paz, *Durruti*, pp.17–22, 67; Sanz, *Hijos*, pp.51–77, 95–118; *La Revista Blanca* (hereafter *LaRB*), 1 April 1924.

121 Huertas, *Obrers*, p.187.

122 Peirats, 'Experiencia', p.16.

123 Paz, *Chumberas*, p.88.

124 Alba, *Cataluña*, pp.186–7; Vinyes i Ribes, 'Bohemis, marxistes, bolxevics', *L'Avenç* 77, 1984, pp.48–54; Salut, *Vivers*, p.135; V. Serge, *The Birth of Our Power*, London, 1977, pp.29–30; Cruells, *Seguí*, p.162; Peiró, *Peiró*, pp.33–4; A. Pèrez Baró, *Els 'feliços' anys vint. Memories d'un militant obrer, 1918–1926*, Palma de Mallorca, 1974, p.163.

125 J. Peiró, *Trayectoria de la CNT*, Madrid, 1979 [Barcelona, 1925], pp.85–98.

126 *SO*, 3 January 1932.

127 Interview with 'Antonio', 9 March 1992.

128 Andreassi, *Libertad*, pp.42–3.

129 Andreassi, *Libertad*, pp.42–4.

130 Cited in D. Berenguer, *De la Dictadura a la República*, Madrid, 1931, p.204.

Chapter 3

1 F. Cambó, *Les dictadures*, Barcelona, 1929, p.206.

2 B. Muniesa, *La burguesía catalana ante la II República española. 'Il Trovatore' frente a Wotan*, Barcelona, 1985, Vol. 1, pp.125–71.

3 *La Batalla* (hereafter *LaB*), 20 June 1930; *CyN*, July 1931; J. Hernández Andreu, *España y la crisis de 1929*, Madrid, 1986, pp.115–18.

4 *LasN*, 3, 6, 14–20 and 31 January, 8 February, 7 and 21 March, 4–5 and 9–11 April 1931.

5 *SO*, 28 February 1931.

6 For republican discourse, see P. Radcliff, 'Política y cultura republicana en el Gijón de fin de siglo', in N. Townson (ed.), *El republicanismo en España*, pp.373–94, and D. Castro Alfín, 'Jacobinos y populistas. El republicanismo español a mediados del siglo XIX', in J. Alvarez Junco (ed.), *Populismo, caudillaje y discurso demagógico*, Madrid, 1987, pp.181–217.

7 P. Gabriel, 'El marginament del republicanisme i l'obrerisme', *L'Avenç* 85, 1985, pp.34–8.

8 See E. de Guzmán, *1930: Historia política de un año decisivo*, Madrid, 1976.

9 Peirats, *CNT*, Vol. 1, pp.43–50.

10 *SO*, 10 April 1931.

11 M. Ivern i Salvà, *Esquerra Republicana de Catalunya (1931–1936)*, Montserrat, 1988–1989, 2 vols.

12 M. Cruells, *Francesc Macià*, Barcelona, 1971, pp.17–32.

13 J. Aiguader, *Catalunya i la Revolució*, Barcelona, 1931, pp.148–9; *L'Opinió*, 30 January and 13 February 1931.

14 *Llibertat*, 20 February and 20 March 1931; *L'Opinió*, 27 March 1931.

15 This would be achieved by making 'the economic exploitation of man by man impossible' through 'the progressive transformation of the existing system of private property' (*L'Opinió*, 29 August, 2 April and 13 March 1931).

16 *L'Opinió*, 13 February, 13 March and 29 August 1931.

17 *L'Opinió*, 13 March, 29 August, 3 and 11 December 1931.

18 A. Maserons, *La República Catalana*, Barcelona, 1931, pp.46–50.

19 Alba, *Cataluña*, p.147; Cruells, *Macià*, p.159; N. M. Rubió, *La caseta i l'hortet*, Barcelona, n.d.; *El Mirador*, 12 November 1931.

20 *L'Opinió*, 2 April, 13 March and 29 August 1931; *Escándolo*, 15 July 1926.

21 *L'Opinió*, 8 April, 30 October and 26 June 1931; decree of the Comité Revolucionari de l'Hospitalet, 14 April 1931 (AHl'HL/AM).

22 Maserons, *República*, pp.46–50.

23 Busquets, *Barcelona*, p.204; *L'Opinió*, 13 March 1931.

24 Cruells, *Seguí*, pp.141–4; J. Ferrer, *Un líder socialista: Layret (1880–1920)*, Barcelona, 1973, pp.199–226; M. Buenacasa, *El movimiento obrero español, 1886–1926. Historia y crítica* (2nd edn), Madrid, 1977, pp.78–81.

25 *SO*, 2 July 1931; *García*, Eco, p.98; Aiguader, *Catalunya*, p.41; Mola, *Memorias*, Vol. 1, pp.177–8.

26 *L'Opinió*, 13 March 1931.

27 *SO*, 26 March 1931.

28 *SO*, 11 and 19–20 March, 25–26 April 1931.

29 *Acción*, 5 July 1930; *SO*, 11–12, 19– 21 and 26 March, 1 and 25–26 April, 22 May 1931.

30 *SO*, 20 and 26–27 February, 18 and 25–27 March 1931.

31 *SO*, 22 January and 18 March 1931; B. Pou and J. Magriñá, *Un año de conspiración (antes de la República)*, Barcelona, 1933, pp.159–62; E. Vega i Massana, *El trentisme a Catalunya. Divergències ideòlogiques en la CNT (1930–1933)*, Barcelona, 1980, pp.54–62.

32 Bueso, *Recuerdos*, Vol. 1, p.329; Alba, *Cataluña*, p.234; *SO* and *LasN*, 14 April 1931.

33 *El Combate Sindicalista*, 6 September 1935.

34 Molas, *Lliga*, Vol. 1, pp.269–70.

35 Paz, *Chumberas*, p.69; R. Liarte, *El camino de la libertad*, Barcelona, 1983, p.62; Aiguader, *Catalunya*, p.28; Ferrer and Piera, *Piera*, pp.132–3; J. del Pi, *Interpretació llibertari del moviment obrer català*, Bordeaux, 1946, p.29.

36 Marin, 'Aproximació', p.37.

37 C. Ametllà, *Memòries polítiques (1918–1936), Barcelona*, 1979, Vol. 2, p.69; F. Madrid, *El 14 d'Abril*, Barcelona, 1977; F. Soldevila, *Història de la proclamació de la Republica a Catalunya*, Barcelona, 1977, *passim*; J.B. Culla, 'L'altra cara del 14 d'Abril', *L'Avenç* 26, 1980, pp.56–61; Bueso, *Recuerdos*, Vol. 1, p.344.

38 A. Cirici, *Els temps barats*, Barcelona, [1973] 1977, p.181.

39 Cucurull, *Catalunya*, p.53.

40 S. Cánovas Cervantes, *Apuntes históricos de 'Solidaridad Obrera'. Proceso histórico de la revolución española*, Barcelona, 1937, pp.78–82; M. Maura, *Así cayó Alfonso XIII*, Mexico, 1962, pp.165–6; F. Largo Caballero, *Mis recuerdos*, Mexico, 1976, p.108.

41 *SO*, 15 April 1931.

42 Sanz, *Sindicalismo*, pp.197–8.

43 Bueso, *Recuerdos*, Vol. 1, p.345; Cirici, *Temps*, p.182.

44 Accounts of the events concerning April 14–15 include Bueso, *Recuerdos*, Vol. 1, pp.330–50; A.M. de Lera, *Angel Pestaña: Retrato de un anarquista*, Barcelona, 1978, pp.263–76; *La Nau* (hereafter *Nau*), 15 April 1931; *SO*, 16 April 1931.

45 Cries of 'We are thieves, but we want freedom too' incited a crowd to attempt to storm the jails: *LasN*, 16 April 1931; *Nau*, 15 April 1931; *La Noche* (hereafter *Noche*), 15 April 1931.

46 de Lera, *Pestaña*, pp.263–8; *SO*, 16 April 1931.
47 R. Alcaraz, *La Unió Socialista de Catalunya*, Barcelona, 1987; M. Caminal, *Joan Comorera. Catalanisme i Socialisme (1913–1936)*, Barcelona, 1984, 2 vols.
48 Cucurull, *Catalunya*, pp.58–9; Alba, *Cataluña*, p.239. For the development of the autonomous authority of the Generalitat, see I.E. Pitarch, *L'estructura del Parlament de Catalunya i les seves funcions polítiques (1932–1939)*, Barcelona, 1977.
49 Cánovas, *Apuntes*, pp.152–8, 171–5; M. Cabrera, *La patronal ante la II República. Organizaciones y estrategia, 1931–1936*, Madrid, 1983, p.137; E. de Guzmán, *La Segunda República fue así*, Barcelona, 1977, p.76.
50 C. Cañellas and R. Toran, 'Dels regionalistes de la Lliga a la Dictadura de Primo de Rivera', *L'Avenç* 58, 1983, pp.42–9; *L'Opinió*, 13 March, 8 April and 5–6 June 1931; J. Alzina, *L'Economia de la Catalunya Autònoma*, Barcelona, 1933, p.89; *LaV*, 8 July 1931; Balcells, *Crisis*, pp.72–6, 91–2; Poblet, *Aiguader*, p.203; Cruells, *Macià*, p.131.
51 Soto, *Trabajo*, pp.359–60.
52 J. Casassas, 'La República y la guerra civil, 1931–1939', in B. de Sala (ed.), p.70; Huertas, *Obrers*, p.236.
53 Balcells, *Crisis*, p.127.
54 *L'Opinió*, 13, 24 and 26 June 1931.
55 *L'Opinió*, 21 June, 12 July, 13 and 21 August 1931; *LasN*, 26 April and 6 June 1931; *Nau*, 27 April 1931; Fabre and Huertas, *Barris*, Vol. 4, p.171.
56 *La Calle* (hereafter *Calle*), 11 February 1931.
57 P. Coromines, *Diaris i Records de Pere Coromines. La República i la Guerra Civil*, Barcelona, 1975, Vol. 3, p.14.
58 cited in Maseras, *República*, p.60.
59 Quoted in C. Cañellas and R. Toran, 'El domini hegemònic d'Esquerra Republicana', *L'Avenç* 58, 1983, p.51.
60 Madrid, *Ocho*, pp.136, 138, 143–5, 171–214, 250, 266; *Nau*, 2 May 1931; *LasN*, 1 and 3 May 1931; *Diluvio*, 30 May 1931.
61 Cánovas, *Apuntes*, pp.17–8, 87–8; Maura, *Así*, pp.48, 182–3.
62 Azaña, *Obras*, Vol. 4, pp.36, 93; Jackson, *Republic*, p.43.
63 *L'Opinió*, 13 March 1931.
64 E. Montero, 'Reform idealized: the intellectual and ideological origins of the Second Republic', in H. Graham and J. Labanyi (eds), *Spanish Cultural Studies: An Introduction*, Oxford, 1995, pp.124–7.
65 *L'Opinió*, 9 June 1928, 14 November 1930 and 27 August 1931; *JS*, 16 and 30 January, 6 and 20 February 1926.
66 Aiguader, *Problema, passim*.
67 Ucelay, *Catalunya, passim*, and Ivern, who claims that the Esquerra 'did not defend any single social class nor any specific social interests' (*Esquerra*, Vol. 2, p.299).
68 M. Lladonosa and J. Ferrer, 'Nacionalisme català i reformisme social en els treballadors mercantils a Barcelona entre 1903 i 1939. El CADCI', in A. Balcells (ed.), *Teoría y práctica del movimiento obrero en España (1900–1936)*, Valencia, 1977, pp.283–329.
69 Fabre and Huertas, *Barris*, Vol. 5, p.115.
70 See, for example, *Butlletí del Ateneu Obrer d'ERC del Districte V*, August–September 1934.
71 Molas, *Lliga*, Vol. 1, p.348. The data provided by Ivern on the social background of the ERC leaders (*Esquerra*, Vol. 1, pp.78–80 and Vol. 2, pp.288, 291–4) confirms my view.
72 J. Malaquer, *Mis primeros años de trabajo, 1910–1939*, Barcelona, 1970, p.90.
73 *L'Opinió*, 9 August 1931.
74 *L'Opinió*, 1 August 1931; *Fortitud*, 1 July 1933; Poblet, *Aiguader*, pp.42–3.

75 *L'Opinió*, 26 August 1931.
76 *Calle*, 8 January 1932.
77 *El Sol* (hereafter *Sol*), 19 December 1931.
78 Maura, *Así*, pp.281–6.
79 *L'Opinió*, 13, 24 and 26 June 1931.
80 *L'Opinió*, 17 July 1931.
81 *Nau*, 20, 22 and 30 April, 2 May 1931; *L'Opinió*, 16 July 1931, *LasN*, 1 and 3 May 1931.
82 *L'Opinió*, 21 June and 10 July 1931.
83 *L'Opinió*, 10 July 1931; J. Termes, *Federalismo, anarcosindicalismo, catalanismo*, Barcelona, 1976, p.143.
84 This divisive strategy was not attempted elsewhere. See Gil, *La Rioja*, p.188.
85 Sentís, *Viatge*, p.78.
86 Interview with Juan Giménez, *Vivir*; Sentís, *Viatge*, p.33.
87 *L'Opinió*, 10 July 1931 and 7 April 1934; *Nau*, 27 April 1931.
88 *L'Opinió*, 13 March and 29 August 1931.
89 *L'Opinió*, 10 and 19 July, 29 August, 2 December 1931; *Nau*, 22 and 27–28 April, 3 May 1931.
90 The ERC condemned 'Japanese imperialism' as 'the yellow peril'! *L'Opinió*, 18 May 1932.
91 11 percent of the migrant population in Barcelona came from Murcia (Tatjer, 'La inmigración...', p.135), which accounted for about 5 percent of the entire population of the city (Ainaud de Lasarte *et al.*, *Barcelona*, pp.100–1).
92 *L'Opinió*, 7 August and 20 September 1931; Sentís, *Viatge*, pp.72, 87–88.
93 Sentís, *Viatge*, pp.73–74, 83–95.
94 *L'Opinió*, 10 July, 13 August, 5 November and 2 December 1931, 17 May, 26 October and 2 December 1932; *Diluvio*, 6 May 1931; *Llibertat*, 5 August, 5 October and 20 December 1933.
95 P. Hall, *Cities of Tomorrow. An Intellectual History of Urban Planning and Design in the Twentieth Century*, Oxford, 1988 p.364.
96 *Matí*, 4 June 1931; Madrid, *Ocho*, pp.137–8; *LaV*, 13 August 1931.
97 See J. Serna, 'La desocupació i el control social', *Batlia* 8, 1988, pp.9–23; *L'Opinió*, 21 August and 2 December 1931.
98 *Matí*, 21 June 1931; *L'Opinió*, 4 August 1932.
99 *SO*, 9 October 1932 and 20 September 1933; *Sembrar*, 19 November 1932.
100 Sentís, *Viatge*, p.56.
101 *SO*, 9 October 1932 and 20 September 1933; *Sembrar*, 19 November 1932.
102 *L'Opinió*, 19 and 25 July, 13 and 29 August 1931; *Nau*, 27 April 1931.
103 Balcells, *Crisis*, p.19; Soto, *Trabajo*, pp.359–60; *LaV*, 13 August 1931; *L'Opinió*, 21 June 1931; Hernández, *España*, p.97; *SO*, 25 March and 1 November 1931.
104 *L'Opinió*, 10 and 16 July, 13 August 1931; *Diluvio*, 30 May 1931; *LasN*, 1 and 3 May 1931; *SO*, 25 September 1931; *Noche*, 17 November 1931.
105 Telegram from Barcelona civil governor (Anguera de Sojo) to interior minister (Maura), 2 September 1931, Legajo 7a (AHN/MG).
106 *L'Opinió*, 14 and 17 July, 16 August, 23 October 1931, 29 April, 31 May 1932; *Llibertat*, 6 June 1931; *L'Obra*, 12 September 1931; *LasN*, 7 March, 29 April, 3 May and 8 November 1931, 11 May 1934.
107 *L'Opinió*, 6 May, 24 June, 10 and 17 July, 13, 16 and 27 August, 22 September, 23 October, 19 November 1931; *Llibertat*, 6 June 1931; Madrid, *Ocho*, pp.145, 158; Minutes of l'Hospitalet Council meeting, 10 January 1933 (AHl'HL/AM); *LasN*, 4 and 27 June 1931.
108 *CyN*, May 1931.
109 Cabrera, *Patronal*, p.255.

110 *LaV*, 9 July, 12 August, 23 September, 29 October and 2 December 1931, 4 March 1932; *LasN*, 14 May and 5 December 1931; Fomento del Trabajo Nacional (hereafter FTN), *Memoria de la Junta Directiva Correspondiente al Ejercicio de 1931*, Barcelona, 1932, p.201.

111 *CyN*, November 1931.

112 La *Nau*, 24 April 1931; FTN, Memoria...1931, pp.119, 122, 135–6, 140, 201–2; COPUB, Memoria de los trabajos realizados durante el ejercicio de 1931, Barcelona, 1932, p.488; *CyN*, April, May 1931; El Trabajo Nacional, April–December 1931; *Veu*, 18 April 1931.

113 FTN, Memoria...1931, pp.135–40, 201–6.

114 *Veu*, 19 June 1931.

115 *LaV*, 19, 23–24 July, 13 August 1931, 9–10 April 1932.

116 Letters from La Sociedad de Patronos Cultivadores to the mayor of l'Hospitalet, 30 October and 12 November 1931 (AHl'HL/AM); letter from the presidents of la COPUB, la Associación de Propietarios, el Gremio de Ultramarinos y Similares, el Centro Gremial de Carboneros and la Sociedad de Maestros Peluqueros y Barberos to the mayor of l'Hospitalet, 30 September 1931 (AHl'HL/AM).

117 *LasN*, 20 May, 3 and 31 October, 2 and 21 November 1931; *Noche*, 3, 7 and 10 November 1931; *LaV*, 21 August and 13 September 1931, 4 July 1932; *SO*, 28 April and 24 December 1931.

118 A. Farreras, *El turisme a Catalunya del 1931 al 1936*, Barcelona 1973. In early 1932, the Generalitat formed the Federació de Turisme de Catalunya i Balears (*Veu*, 11 February 1932).

119 *Matí*, 14 June 1931; *LaV*, 12 August, 13, 18 and 23 September 1931; *L'Opinió*, 7 August and 20 September 1931; *LasN*, 22 May, 2 October and 17 December 1931; minutes from l'Hospitalet council meeting, 28 August 1934 (AHl'HL/AM); letter from la Unió de Venedors del Mercat de Collblanc to the mayor of l'Hospitalet, 4 September 1935, (AHl'HL/AM).

120 *SO*, 9 May 1931; *L'Opinió*, 9, 13 and 26 June, 14 July 1931; Poblet, *Aiguader*, p.179; *LasN*, 12 May and 18 December 1931.

121 Telegram from Barcelona civil governor (Anguera de Sojo) to Interior Ministry, 24 October 1931, Legajo 7a (AHN/MG); COPUB, Memoria...1931, pp.20, 488, 497–8; and *Memoria de los trabajos realizados durante el ejercicio de 1932*, Barcelona, 1933, pp.39–40; Ametlla, *Memòries*, Vol. 2, p.214.

122 Maura, *Así*, pp.274–5; J.S. Vidarte, *Las Cortes Constituyentes de 1931–1933. Testimonio del primer secretario del Congreso de los Diputados*, Barcelona, 1976, p.293; Turrado, *Policia*, pp.198–9.

123 Maura, *Así*, pp.274–5; Ballbé, *Orden*, p.339.

124 Azaña, *Diarios completos*, Barcelona, 2000, p.425; Maura, *Así*, p.206.

125 *LaB*, 15 April and 1 May 1931; *SO*, 15 April and 1 May 1931.

126 Madrid, *Ocho*, pp.156–7; Manuel Azaña, *Obras completas. El transito de un mundo histórico*, Mexico, 1967, Vol. 3, p.294; Maura, *Así*, p.206; Borrás, *España*, pp.109–10.

127 *LasN*, 31 December 1931.

128 *SO*, 16, 25 and 29 April 1931.

129 *SO*, 21 September 1932, 6 April and 20 August 1933.

130 Barcelona civil governor (Companys) to interior minister (Maura), 14 May 1931, Legajo 60a (AHN/MG); Turrado, *Policía*, p.192; Ballbé, *Orden*, p.336; *LasN*, 23 May 1931; Madrid, *Ocho*, pp.156–8; Manuel Azaña, *Obras completas. Memorias Políticas y de Guerra*, Mexico, 1968, Vol. 4, p.284.

131 *SO*, 28 May,1–2, 7–9 and 26 August 1931; *LasN*, 8 May 1931; *LaV*, 16 July 1931.

132 Telegrams from Barcelona civil governor (Anguera de Sojo) to Interior Ministry, 16, 24 and 28 October 1931, Legajo 7a and 39a (AHN/MG); Ametlla, *Memòries*, Vol. 2, p.211.

133 *SO*, 16 September 1931.

134 *SO*, 5 and 12 September 1931.

135 *SO*, 4 November 1931.

136 *SO*, 30 June, 6 and 21–31 July, 29 August, 7 September 1934; *Adelante*, 22 and 30 January 1934.

137 See, for example, *SO*, 17–19 July 1934.

138 *SO*, 21 October 1932 and 19 July 1934; *LaV*, 31 March and 5 September 1934.

139 *SO*, 21 September 1932, 6 April and 20 August 1933.

140 *SO*, 15 November 1933.

141 *LaV*, 11 September 1931; communiqué from the Guàrdia Urbana to the mayor of l'Hospitalet, 22 June 1934 (AHl'HL/AM).

142 F. Miró, *Una vida intensa y revolucionaria. Juventud, amor, sueños y esperanzas*, Mexico, 1989, pp.137–9.

143 *SO*, 25 December 1932; *El Luchador* (hereafter *Luchador*), 27 November 1931.

144 *LaRB*, 11 May 1934; *SO*, 23 September 1934.

145 See H. Becker, *Outsiders*, New York, 1963, *passim*; I. Janovic, 'Labour market and imprisonment', *Crime and Social Justice*, 1977, pp.17–31; Richard Quinney, *Class, State and Crime*, New York, 1977, pp.131–40.

146 *LasN*, 6 October 1931; *L'Opinió*, 11, 13 and 16 August 1931.

147 *SO*, 11, 12, 14 and 28–31 July, 1 August 1931; *L'Opinió*, 29 July 1931; *LaV*, 16 and 30 July, 5, 21, 26 and 29–30 August, 30 September 1931.

148 *L'Opinió*, 29 July 1931; communiqué from the Guàrdia Urbana to the mayor of l'Hospitalet, 26 April 1936 (AHl'HL/AM); *SO*, 19 June 1931, 30 June, 6 and 21–31 July, 29 August, 7 September 1934; *Adelante*, 22 and 30 January 1934.

149 Telegram from Barcelona civil governor (Esplà) to the interior minister (Maura), 15 July 1931, Legajo 7a (AHN/MG).

150 *SO*, 11, 12, 14 and 28–31 July, 1 August 1931, 21 October 1932, 1 July 1933; *LasN*, 9 May 1931; *L'Opinió*, 29 July 1931; *LaV*, 16 and 30 July, 5, 21, 26 and 29–30 August, 30 September 1931; *TyL*, 7 and 24 October 1932.

151 Ametlla, *Memòries*, Vol. 2, pp.93–4. Anguera de Sojo's strong clerical views prompted suggestions that he had 'escaped from an altar during the Inquisition' (*Adelante*, 2 March 1934).

152 Telegram from Barcelona civil governor (Anguera de Sojo) to Interior Ministry, 2 September 1931, Legajo 7a (AHN/MG).

153 See, for instance, Ametlla, *Memòries*, Vol. 2 pp.215–6.

154 Interview with Antonio Zapata, *Vivir la utopia*; Ametlla, *Memòries*, p.214.

155 *SO*, 30 June, 6 and 21–31 July, 29 August, 7 September 1934; *Adelante*, 22 and 30 January 1934.

156 Sentís, *Viatge*, p.80; Miró, *Vida*, p.123.

157 Azaña, *Obras*, Vol. 2, pp.106–7.

158 Azaña, *Obras*, Vol. 2, p.65 and Vol. 4, pp.93, 185, 260–2; *L'Opinió*, 24 July, 11 August and 23 October 1931; *LaB*, 31 December 1931 and 14 January 1932.

159 M. Rosa Abad Amorós, 'Limitación jurídica de las libertades públicas en la II República', *Cuadernos Republicanos*, 1993, 16, pp.107–16.

160 M.C. García-Nieto, *La Segunda República. Economía y aparato del estado. 1931–1936*, Madrid, 1974, Vol. 1, pp.256–7; Ballbé, *Orden*, pp.323–35.

161 Ballbé, *Orden*, pp.318, 337, n.35.

162 Civil governor (Anguera de Sojo) to Interior Ministry, December 1931, Legajo 7a (AHN/MG).

163 Ballbé, *Orden*, pp.359–63.

164 Martín, *Recuerdos*, pp.77–8.

165 Ametlla, *Memòries*, Vol. 2, p.187.

166 FTN, *Memoria*...;1931, pp.203–4; Barcelona civil governor to interior minister, 2 September 1931, Legago 7a (AHN/MG).

167 FTN, Memoria...de 1933, p.140.

168 *LaV*, 23 February, 15 August 1933.

169 *L'Opinió*, 3 February, 7 March, 7–8 April, 25 June, 11 and 25–29 August 1933.

170 *JS*, 25 November 1933, 14 March 1936; *LaB*, 3 August 1933.

171 *LasN*, 17 June 1931; *L'Opinió*, 17 and 19 July 1931.

172 *SO*, 23 September 1933, 21 September 1935; *LaV*, 9 August, 5, 9 and 19 September, 3 October 1934, 10 February and 11 December 1935; *LasN*, 30 May 1934; *La Humanitat*, 15 January 1936.

173 *L'Opinió*, 30 September and 5 November 1933; *SO*, 5, 8 and 14 October 1933, 28 August and 3 October 1934; *LasN*, 31 January 1936; *Catalunya Roja*, 23 September 1933; *LaV*, 5 and 26 September 1933, 19 May and 7 June 1935.

174 Martín, *Recuerdos*, pp.77–8; *LaB*, 22 June 1933; *SO*, 2 August, 1, 13 and 15 September, 7 October 1933, 24 October and 31 December 1935, 11 and 30 January 1936; *LasN*, 4 May 1934 and 31 January 1936; *TyL*, 31 January 1936.

175 Massana and Roca, 'Vicis', p.40; Tatjer, in Oyón (ed.), p.38; Massana, *Indústria*, p.220.

176 Aiguader, *Problema*, p.6.

177 *La Publicitat* (hereafter *LaP*), 15 October 1931.

178 García, 'Barrios...', p.85.

179 F. Madrid, *Sangre en Atarazanas*, Barcelona, 1926, *passim*; *Escándolo*, 22 and 29 October 1925, 6 and 20 May, 15 July, 7 and 14 October 1926; Madrid, *Ocho*, pp.156–7, 175; Villar, *Leyenda*, p.149.

180 *LaV*, 21 September and 22 October 1933; *SO*, 13 September and 3 October 1933; Villar, *Leyenda*, p.151.

181 Villar, *Leyenda*, p.152.

182 N. Rubió i Tudurí, *Pla de distribució en zones del territori català*, Barcelona, 1932.

183 Evidence of Le Corbusiers's increasingly authoritarian stance and his faith in the 'strong idea' was his decision to dedicate his 1935 work, *La ville radieuse*, 'To authority' (R. Fishman, *Bourgeois Utopias*, New York, 1987, pp.236–7).

184 Fishman, *Utopias*, p.187.

185 *A.C.*, June 1937.

186 Fabre and Huertas, *Barris*, Vol. 5 p.65.

187 See C. Cirici, 'Madrid–Barcelona. El nacimiento de dos metropolis modernas', in B. de Sala (ed.), *Barcelona–Madrid, 1898–1998: sintonías y distancias*, Barcelona, 1997, pp.147–8; O. Bohigas, 'Una arquitectura a la Catalunya republicana i autònomia', in B. de Sala (ed.), pp.85–93; and J.M. Rovira, 'Los orígines del Plan Macià: entre la ciudad radiante y la ciudad funcional', in Oyón (ed.), pp.263–86.

188 Harvey, *Consciousness*, pp.63–220.

189 Fishman, *Utopias*, pp.9–10, 13, 163–263.

190 L. Casassas i Simó, *Barcelona i l'Espai Català*, Barcelona, 1977, pp.208–17.

191 *Ibid.*, p.217.

192 Cited in S. Tarragó, 'El "Pla Macià" o "La Nova Barcelona"', *Cuadernos de Arquitectura y Urbanismo* 90, July–August 1972, p.29.

193 *L'Opinió*, 16 March 1933; F. Roca, *El Pla Macià*, Barcelona, 1977; Artigues *et al.*, *Raval*, pp.55–6; *LaP*, 16 August 1933.

194 Le Corbusier, cited in Berman, p.168.

195 B. Fine, 'Law and class', in B. Fine, R. Kinsey, J. Lea, S. Picciotto and J. Young (eds), *Capitalism and the Rule of Law. From Deviancy Theory to Marxism*, London, 1973, p.32.

196 *Estampa*, 9 July 1932; F. Lacruz, *El alzamiento, la revolución y el terror en Barcelona (19 julio 1936 – 26 enero 1939)*, Barcelona, 1943, p.107.
197 L. Jiménez de Asúa, *Ley de vagos y maleantes. Un ensayo sobre peligrosidad sin delito*, Madrid, 1934; *Orden Público y Vagos y Maleantes*, Barcelona, pp.65–82.

Chapter 4

1 Sanz, *Sindicalismo*, pp.197–9.
2 J. Berruezo, *Por el sendero de mis recuerdos (1920–1939)*, Santa Coloma de Gramanet, 1987, p.42.
3 A few days later, the central government ratified the choice of Companys as civil governor. Bueso, *Recuerdos*, Vol. 1, pp.345–8; Vega, *Trentisme*, p.64.
4 *SO*, 14–15 April 1931.
5 Cucurull, *Catalunya*, p.58; *SO*, 16 April 1931.
6 *SO*, 16 April 1931.
7 *SO*, 14–23 April 1931.
8 *SO*, 14–15 April 1931.
9 *SO*, 16 April 1931.
10 Marín, 'Aproximació', pp.32–5; Ferrer and Piera, *Piera*, pp.22–5; *SO*, 28 August 1931.
11 Vega, *Trentisme*, p.105, n.1; CRT, *Memorias de los comicios de la regional catalana celebrados los días 31 de mayo y 1 de junio, y 2, 3 y 4 de agosto de 1931*, Barcelona 1931, pp.50–6; Balcells, *Crisis*, p.192.
12 CNT, *Memoria del Congreso Extraordinario celebrado en Madrid los días 11 al 16 de junio de 1931*, Barcelona 1932, pp.119–20.
13 *SO*, 8 January 1931.
14 Monjo in Oyón (ed.), pp.146–7.
15 *Acción*, 12 July 1930; *SO*, 5 September 1930.
16 *SO*, 3 January 1932.
17 Paz, *Chumberas*, pp.91–7, 106–8, 123.
18 Marín, 'Aproximació', pp.32–5; Ferrer and Piera, *Piera*, pp.22–5.
19 Paz, *Chumberas*, p.100.
20 Marin, 'Llibertat', pp.408–16, 453–4, 469, 480–5.
21 J. Peirats, unpublished memoirs, p.32.
22 Miró, *Vida*, pp.70, 82, 313.
23 Peiró, *Peiró, passim*; J. Peiró, *Escrits, 1917–1939*, Barcelona, 1975; Pestaña, *Vida*, *passim*; A.M. de Lera, *Ángel Pestaña: retrato de un anarquista*, Barcelona, 1978, *passim*.
24 Peiró, *Trayectoria*, pp.105–84.
25 Sanz, *Sindicalismo*, pp.197–9.
26 *Luchador*, 1 and 15 May, 12 June, 3 July 1931; *SO*, 25 April 1931.
27 García, *Eco*, p.115.
28 For Nosotros, see García, *Eco*; Sanz, *Sindicalismo*; Paz, *Durruti*.
29 *SO*, 25 April 1931.
30 Miró, *Vida*, p.127.
31 J.J. Gallardo Romero and J.M. Márquez Rodríguez, *Ortiz: General sin dios ni amo*, Santa Coloma de Gramanet, 1999, p.79.
32 *La Tierra*, 2 September 1931.
33 Marin, 'Llibertat', p.410.
34 *LaB*, 12 March, 18 April and 14 May 1931.
35 *LaV*, 19, 21 and 24 July, 1–29 August 1931; *CyN*, August–September 1931; E. Vega i Massana, 'La Confederació Nacional del Treball i els Sindicats d'Oposició a Catalunya i el País Valencià (1930–1936)', unpublished PhD thesis, Barcelona University, 1986, pp.522, 1060.

36 *LaV*, 16 July and 23 August 1931.

37 *SO*, 13–15 January and 26–28 March 1931.

38 Miralles and Oyón, 'De casa', in Oyón (ed.), p.162; Poblet, *Aiguader*, pp.203–4; *SO*, 22 May, 23 June and 30 July 1931; *L'Opinió*, 10 September, 3 and 11 December 1931.

39 Report of Consul-General King, 8 July 1931, FO371/15774/W8199/46/41 (PRO).

40 *SO*, 8 July 1931; *Trabajo*, 15 June 1931; *LaV*, 13 and 30 August 1931.

41 *LaB*, 20 June 1930 and 12 March 1931.

42 *SO*, 13 January, 26 March and 13 August 1931; *LasN*, 11 December 1931; *Trabajo*, 15 and 30 June, 31 July 1931.

43 S. Tarrow, *Power in Movement. Social Movements, Collective Action and Politics*, Cambridge, 1994, pp.153–69; M. Pérez Ledesma, *Estabilidad y conflicto social. España, de los iberos al 14-D*, Madrid, 1990, pp.203–5.

44 *La Tierra*, 8 July 1931; Cánovas, *Apuntes*, pp.171–5.

45 Soto, *Trabajo*, p.592; *Trabajo*, 15 September 1931; *SO*, 17 June and 23 July 1931; Martín, *Recuerdos*, p.51; *CyN*, May 1931.

46 *El Trabajo Nacional*, November–December 1931; *CyN*, November 1931; *LaV*, 19 and 23–24 July, 13 August 1931; FTN, *Memoria...1931*, p.122.

47 *Luchador*, 14 August 1931.

48 García, 'Urbanization', pp.144–5.

49 *SO*, 8–9, 22 and 30 May, 13 June, 4 and 10 July 1931.

50 Maura, *Así*, pp.281–6.

51 *LaV*, 7 and 24 July 1931; *SO*, 5, 10 and 24 July 1931; *El Socialista* (hereafter *Socialista*), 3 and 11 July 1931; Azaña, *Obras*, Vol. 4, p.36; *LasN*, 2 and 10 July 1931.

52 Jackson, *Republic*, p.43; *SO*, 21 July 1931; *Crisol*, 11 June 1931; *Socialista*, 9 and 13 June 1931; *La Internacional*, 18 July 1931; *Sol*, 14 June and 21 July 1931.

53 *LasN* and *Matí*, 10 June 1931; *L'Opinió*, 11 June 1931; *SO*, 10–12 June 1931.

54 *SO*, 1–2 and 10 July 1931.

55 Bueso, *Recuerdos*, Vol. 1, pp.103–9; Rider, 'Anarchism', chapter 11; *SO*, 4–6 June 1931.

56 *SO*, 11 June 1931.

57 *SO*, 28 April, 19 June, 3, 5, 10 and 23–29 July, 20 August, 2 September 1931.

58 *SO*, 28 May 1931.

59 *SO*, 7, 19 and 27–30 May, 9 June, 3, 16 and 19 July 1931; *LaV*, 4 July and 9–15 August 1931.

60 *SO*, 30 May 1931.

61 *SO*, 27 May, 3 and 8 July 1931; *Trabajo*, 15 June 1931.

62 Martín, *Recuerdos*, pp.86–7, 91–2.

63 *SO*, 30 July and 20 August 1931.

64 *SO*, 7 and 28 May 1931; *LaV*, 19 and 22 July, 5 and 16 August 1931; *LasN*, 29 May, 16 June, 27–28 November 1931; *El Día Gráfico* (herein *ElDG*), 27 November 1931; *Trabajo*, 15 August 1931.

65 *SO*, 28 May, 1–2, 7–9 and 26 August 1931; *LasN*, 8 May 1931; *LaV*, 16 July 1931.

66 *LaV*, 7, 9 and 24 July, 1931; *Sol*, 4 June 1931; *LasN*, 14 and 25 June 1931; *L'Opinió*, 9 August 1931; *SO*, 19 July 1931; Maura, *Así*, pp.281–6; *La Tierra*, 8 July 1931.

67 Paz, *Chumberas*, p.184.

68 *SO*, 7–25 July, 11, 20 and 22 August 1931; *LaV*, 23 and 31 July, 5 and 30 August, 1–2 September 1931.

69 *SO*, 25 July 1931.

70 *LaV*, 24–25 July 1931; *SO*, 25 July 1931; Bueso, *Recuerdos*, Vol. 2, pp.58–60.

71 Interior minister to Barcelona civil governor (Anguera de Sojo), 27 August 1931, Legajo 39a (AHN/MG).
72 Barcelona civil governor (Anguera de Sojo) to interior minister, 4 September 1931, Legajo 39a (AHN/MG).
73 Interior minister to Barcelona civil governor (Anguera de Sojo), 4, 13 and 24 September 1931, Legajo 39a (AHN/MG).
74 *LaV*, 9, 19, 24 and 27 July, 11, 13 and 19–20 August 1931; *L'Opinió*, 10 July 1931; Soto, *Trabajo*, p.494; *SO*, 10–13 June, 10–11 and 20 July 1931.
75 *SO*, 16, 25 and 29 April 1931.
76 Barcelona civil governor (Anguera de Sojo) to interior minister, 1 September 1931, Legajo 7a (AHN/MG).
77 *Estampa*, 9 July 1932; *SO*, 21 March 1933.
78 *LaV*, 1 September 1931.
79 *SO*, 21 September 1932, 6 April and 20 August 1933.
80 *SO*, 13 August 1931.
81 *SO*, 9, 14, 23 and 30 July, 6–14 and 23 August 1931.
82 Minutes of the plenum of the Barcelona CNT Local Federation, 24 October 1931 (AHN/SGC).
83 J. Casassas, 'Barcelona, baluard de la República', in S. Sanquet and A. Chinarro (coords), *Madrid–Barcelona, 1930–1936: la tradició d'allò que és nou*, Barcelona, 1997, p.38.
84 Huertas, *Obrers*, p.243.
85 Marin, 'Llibertat', p.408, n.15.
86 *SO*, 6, 18 and 22 July, 4–26 August, 6 September 1934; D. Abad de Somtillán, *Memorias 1897–1936*, Barcelona 1977, p.229.
87 Martín, *Recuerdos*, p.26; García, *Eco*, p.123; *TyL*, 4 July and 1 August 1931.

Chapter 5

1 Martín, *Recuerdos*, pp.91–2.
2 *LasN*, 16 June 1931 and 2 January 1936; communiqué from the Guàrdia Urbana to the mayor of l'Hospitalet, 11 March 1936 (AHI'HL/AM); *LaV*, 15 March and 11 August 1933.
3 *LasN*, 1 October, 4, 8 and 27 November, 26 December 1931, 4 February and 3 May 1932; communiqués from the Guàrdia Urbana to the mayor of l'Hospitalet, 13 May, 19 and 21 June 1933 (AHI'HL/AM).
4 *LasN*, 30 April, 5 November and 8 December 1931; *LaV*, 11 September 1931; interview with 'Juan', November 1997.
5 *LaV*, 5, 28 July, 19, 21 August, 20 September 1931, 29 July 1932; *LasN*, 4 April, 18 May, 5 and 27 June 1931, 8 January 1932; *Matí*, 4 and 6 June 1931; *SO*, 25 July 1931.
6 Letters from La Sociedad de Patronos Cultivadores to the mayor of l'Hospitalet, 30 October and 12 November 1931 (AHI'HL/AM); interview with 'Juan', November 1997.
7 *LaV*, 4 March 1932; *LasN*, 20 May and 5 December 1931, 24 February 1932; interview with 'Juan', November 1997; communiqués from the Guàrdia Urbana to the mayor of l'Hospitalet, 5 October, 6–20 November 1932, 12 May 1933, 4, 12–19, 22 and 28 June, 10 July, 4 August, 25 September 1934, 11 March, 21 May, 21 June, 6 July 1936 (AHI'HL/AM).
8 *LasN*, 6 January, 18 April, 3, 6, 10, 16–17 and 23 May, 5, 13, 17 and 26 June, 25 August, 19 September, 12 November, 16 and 22 December 1931, 2, 7 and 25 February 1932; communiqué from the Guàrdia Urbana to the mayor of l'Hospitalet, 19 June 1936 (AHI'HL/AM).
9 *LasN*, 7 May, 12 and 19 June, 9 October, 20 November, 16 and 18 December 1931; *L'Opinió*, 19 November 1931; *LaV*, 6–13 March and 7 April 1932; commu-

niqué from the Guàrdia Urbana to the mayor of l'Hospitalet, 2 April 1933 (AHl'HL/AM).

10 *CyN*, February–March and June 1933; *LasN*, 2–4 February and 1–13 May 1934; *LaV*, 31 October 1933, 24 February, 10 March, 30 June, 2 September 1934; *L'Opinió*, 10 March and 21 June 1934; *LaP*, 11 April 1934; *Veu*, 8 April 1934.

11 *LasN*, 11 and 20 January, 1 February, 1 and 31 March, 9 and 11 April, 8 May, 16, 19 and 25 June, 1, 24 and 29–30 October, 3–6, 20 and 27 November, 1, 19–24 and 30 December 1931, 8 January 1932; *LaV*, 25 July, 1, 4–5 and 28 August, 1 September 1931, 6 March 1932; *L'Opinió*, 16 June, 30 August and 24 July 1931.

12 *LaV*, 6–13 March and 7 April 1932.

13 Sentís, *Viatge*, p.78.

14 F. Candel, *Ser obrero no es ninguna ganga*, Barcelona, 1976 (2nd edn), pp. 82–3.

15 See *SO*, 16 June 1931.

16 *LasN*, 2–3 May 1931; *SO*, 16 June 1931.

17 Sentís, *Viatge*, p.78.

18 *SO*, 15 February 1932 and 9 April 1936; minutes of council meeting, 1 June 1933 (AHl'HL/AM).

19 Rider, 'Anarquisme', p.9.

20 See N. Rider, 'The practice of direct action: the Barcelona rent strike of 1931', in D. Goodway (ed.), *For Anarchism. History, Theory and Practice*, London, 1989, pp.79–105 and *SO*, 3 September 1931.

21 J. Hinton, 'Self-help and socialism. The Squatters' Movement of 1946', *History Workshop Journal* 25, 1985, pp.100–26.

22 *L'Opinió*, 13 and 27 March 1931; *Calle*, 15 May and 16 October 1931.

23 A. Bueso, *Como fundamos la CNT*, Barcelona, 1976, pp.53–4; *SO*, 13 January, 26–28 March, 13 May, 15 August and 3 September 1931; *TyL*, 5 September 1931.

24 *SO*, 25 March and 1 November 1931.

25 *SO*, 16, 18 and 25 April, 23 June, 1 and 25 November 1931.

26 *SO*, 26 and 30 April, 7, 21 and 24 June, 18 July, 15 August, 3 September, 6 November 1931.

27 *SO*, 8 July 1931.

28 *Nau*, 20 April 1931; *SO*, 21 April 1931.

29 *Diluvio*, *LaV* and *LasN*, 1 May 1931; report from Consul-General King, 5 May 1931, FO371/15772/W5305/46/41 (PRO).

30 *LasN* and *LaV*, 3 May 1931.

31 Petition from the CNT to the mayor of l'Hospitalet, 1 May 1931 (AHl'HL/AM); *LasN* and *LaV*, 3 May 1931; *SO*, 1 May 1931.

32 *SO*, 3 May 1931.

33 *LasN* and *SO*, 3 May 1931; Madrid, *Ocho*, p.140; García, *Eco*, pp.115–16.

34 *LasN* and *SO*, 3 May 1931.

35 In his *Eco*, pp.115–17, García Oliver overplays the role of armed *faístas*, claiming that well-drilled *faístas* controlled 'all four corners' of Republic Square. This is not confirmed by other sources: *SO*, *LasN* and *Nau*, 2–5 May 1931; *Luchador*, 8 May 1931; *TyL*, 8 May 1931; Madrid, *Ocho*, pp.138–44.

36 Fabre and Huertas, *Barris*, Vol. 4, p.171.

37 *SO*, 4 June 1931.

38 *SO*, 27 June 1931.

39 *LasN* and *SO*, 27 June 1931.

40 *SO*, 11 June 1931; *LasN*, 11–12 June 1931.

41 *SO*, 14 June and 4 July 1931.

42 *LaV*, 9 July 1931.

43 *LaV*, 15 and 28 July 1931.

44 *LaV*, 5 July 1931; *LasN*, 21 June 1931.

45 *LaV* and *SO*, 21 July 1931.
46 *SO*, 19 June 1931; *L'Opinió*, 29 July 1931; *LaV*, 31 July 1931.
47 *LasN*, 9 and 16 May, 24 December 1931.
48 *LaV*, 9 September 1931.
49 Communiqués from the Guàrdia Urbana to the mayor of l'Hospitalet, 14 June 1936 (AHl'HL/AM).
50 *SO*, 13–15 May, 5 June, 4 and 21 July, 5, 14–15 and 26 August 1931; *LaV*, 8 July and 24 September 1931; *LasN*, 26 June 1931. Perhaps the best measure of the strike was the increasingly fierce complaints of the landlords (Rider, in Goodway (ed.), p.95).
51 *SO*, 24 June, 2, 12 and 19 August, 1–3 September 1931; *Luchador*, 4 September 1931; *TyL*, 11 July 1931.
52 *LasN*, 3 May 1931; *SO*, 12 August 1931.
53 *TyL*, 11 July and 1 August 1931.
54 *SO*, 28 June and 3 July 1931.
55 F. Fox Piven and R.A. Cloward, *Poor People's Movements. Why They Succeed, How They Fail*, New York, 1977, p.x.
56 *SO*, 9 and 31 May, 4, 8 and 18, July, 3 September 1931; *TyL*, 8 August 1931.
57 Interview with 'Juan', November 1997.
58 *ElDG*, 5 August 1931; *SO*, 20 September 1931.
59 *SO*, 20 May 1931.
60 *SO*, 15 August 1931.
61 Rider, 'Anarquisme', p.14.
62 *SO*, 15–19 and 28 August 1931, 17 September 1935; *LasN*, 30 June, 11 and 22 October, 29 November 1931; *ElDG*, 2 October 1931.
63 Paz, *Chumberas*, p.87.
64 *SO*, 3 September 1931.
65 *Nau*, 24 April 1931; *LaV*, 27 and 30 August 1931; letter from La Unió de Venedors del Mercat de Collblanc to the mayor of l'Hospitalet, 4 September 1935 (AHl'HL/AM).
66 Aiguader, *Catalunya*, pp.12–14; *Correspondència de l'Ajuntament de l'Hospitalet, 1931–1936*, and minutes of l'Hospitalet Council meetings, 1931–1936 (AHl'HL/AM).
67 Ivern, *Esquerra*, Vol. 1, p.78.
68 Rider, 'Anarquisme', p.17.
69 *LaV*, 26 September 1931; COPUB, *Memoria...1932*, p.91.
70 COPUB, *Memoria...1931*, pp.93, 255–67, 440; *LasN*, 1 May and 7 October 1931; *LaV*, 7 and 18–21 July, 16 August 1931.
71 Letter from Pich i Pon, president of the COPUB to the Interior Ministry, 30 July 1931, Legajo 7a (AHN/MG).
72 *L'Opinió*, 7 August and 20 September, 19 November, 2 December 1931, 14 January 1932; *Calle*, 1 January 1932; *Diluvio*, 16 May 1931; *LasN*, 22 May 1931; Madrid, *Ocho*, pp.145, 156–7.
73 *LasN*, 1 May, 4 and 27 June, 13 December 1931; *L'Opinió*, 6 May, 24 June, 10 and 17 July, 13 and 20–21 August, 23 October, 5 and 19 November 1931; Madrid, *Ocho*, pp.145, 158; *LaV*, 1 May, 15 July and 19–20 August 1931; Azaña, *Obras*, Vol. 2, pp.67–8; *Diluvio*, 1 May 1931; *Matí*, 4 June 1931; *Calle*, 1 January, 7 and 29 April 1932.
74 *L'Opinió*, 6 May 1931.
75 *LasN*, 1 May 1931; *L'Opinió*, 17 July 1931; *LaV*, 13 August 1931.
76 *L'Opinió*, 10 July 1931.
77 *Calle*, 1–8 January 1932.
78 *L'Opinió*, 20 August 1931; *LaV*, 19 and 21 August 1931.

79 *LaV*, 13 August 1931 and 3 March 1932; *L'Opinió*, 1 June 1932; *SO*, 13 September 1932; communiqués from the Guàrdia Urbana to the mayor of l'Hospitalet, 8 and 13 September 1934; minutes from l'Hospitalet Council meetings, 10 January 1933 and 28 August 1934 (AHl'HL/AM); letter from the mayor of l'Hospitalet to the commander of the Guàrdia Civil post, 7 March 1936 (AHl'HL/AM); *LasN*, 12 November and 16 December 1931.

80 Legajo 7a (AHN/MG).

81 COPUB, *Memoria...1931*, pp.263, 479.

82 *SO*, 31 July 1931.

83 COPUB, *Memoria...1931*, pp.44, 255–7, 440, 492; COPUB, *Memoria...1932*, p.65; *SO*, 5 June, 30–31 July, 5, 12, 15 and 26 August, 10 October 1931; *ElDG*, 13 October 1931; *LasN*, 14 October 1931; Juzgado Municipal to the mayor of l'Hospitalet, 28 August 1931 (AHl'HL/AM).

84 *SO*, 14, 18 and 27 August, 9 September 1931; *LasN*, 11 October 1931; *TyL*, 5 September 1931; *LaV*, 19 and 27 August 1931.

85 Telephone conversation between Barcelona civil governor (Anguera de Sojo) and Interior Ministry subsecretary, 11am, 4 September 1931, and telegrams and letters between interior minister (Maura) and Barcelona civil governor (Anguera de Sojo), 4 and 9 September 1931, Legajo 7a (AHN/MG).

86 M. Bookchin, *The Spanish Anarchists: The Heroic Years, 1868–1936*, Edinburgh, 1997, pp.182, 187, n.12.

87 *LaV* and *L'Opinió*, 3–9 September 1931; *Calle*, 11 and 25 September 1931; *SO*, 3, 6 and 12 September 1931; *TyL*, 5, 12 and 19 September 1931; *Luchador*, 25 September, 2 and 9 October 1931; *LaB*, 10 and 17 September 1931; Madrid, *Ocho*, p.227; letters from Sir G. Grahame, 5, 7 and 11 September 1931, FO371/ 15775/W10124/46/41, FO371/15775/W10194/46/41, FO371/15775/W10335/ 46/41 and FO371/15775/W10541/46/41 (PRO).

88 *LasN*, 1–2 December 1931; communiqué from the Guàrdia Urbana to the mayor of l'Hospitalet, 26 April 1936 (AHl'HL/AM).

89 *LasN*, 2 and 7 October 1931; *LaV*, 19 September 1931; *L'Opinió*, 20 September 1931.

90 *LasN*, 24 December 1931; COPUB, *Memoria...1931*, pp.20, 488, 497–8, and *Memoria...1932*, pp.39–40.

91 Ballbé, *Orden*, p.331; *SO*, 22 October, 1–10 November, 4 December 1931; *TyL*, 22 August 1931; *Noche*, 13 November 1931.

92 *LasN*, 10 November and 18 December 1931, 29 August 1935; *LaV*, 23 August 1935; minutes of the l'Hospitalet Council meeting, 1 June 1933, and communiqués from the Guàrdia Urbana to the mayor of l'Hospitalet, 17 July, 7 October 1932 and 10 April 1936 (AHl'HL/AM).

93 *Estampa*, 9 July 1932.

94 *ElDG*, 24–25 September 1931; *LasN*, 1 and 21 October 1931; *LaV*, 24 September 1931; *SO*, 30 October 1931. See also C. Ealham, 'La lluita pel carrer, els venedors ambulants durant la II República', *L'Avenç* 230, 1998, pp.21–6.

95 Sentís, *Viatge*, p.78.

96 *SO*, 17 September 1935; *LasN*, 11 and 22 October, 29 November 1931; *Adelante*, 7 January 1934.

97 Sentís, *Viatge*, p.68.

98 Paz, *Chumberas*, pp.87, 123.

99 *L'Opinió*, 19 July 1931..

100 *SO*, 24 December 1931; communiqués from the Guàrdia Urbana to the mayor of l'Hospitalet, 17 July 1932, 18 March and 14 June 1936 (AHl'HL/AM).

101 Madrid, *Ocho*, p.145; *Veu*, 15 December 1932; Cánovas, *Apuntes*, p.162; *La Colmena Obrera* (hereafter *Colmena*), 6 December 1931.

102   Communiqués from the Guàrdia Urbana to the mayor of l'Hospitalet, 10 October 1932 (AHl'HL/AM).

103   Jefatura Superior de Policia de Barcelona to the Juzgado Municipal de l'Hospitalet, 28 September and 25 October 1931, and Gobierno Civil de Barcelona to the mayor of l'Hospitalet, 20 April, 1 May and 1 June 1932 (AHl'HL/AM).

104   Communiqués from the Guàrdia Urbana to the mayor of l'Hospitalet, 10 June 1933 and 10 April 1936 (AHl'HL/AM); *SO*, 7 July 1933 and 1 February 1936.

105   See Vega, *Trentisme, passim*.

106   Bueso, *Recuerdos*, Vol. 2, pp.349–53; *L'Opinió*, 30 August 1931.

107   Telegram from Barcelona civil governor (Anguera de Sojo) to Interior Ministry, 20 October 1931, Legajo 7a (AHN/MG).

108   *SO*, 6–10 November 1931.

109   *SO*, 23 August, 1–2, 9, 17 and 29 September, 6 October, 3–10 and 26–28 November 1931; *TyL*, 13 and 27 June, 5 December 1931; *Luchador*, 9 October and 20 November 1931.

110   *SO*, 1–7 November and 8 December 1931; *TyL*, 26 September–31 October 1931.

111   *TyL*, 31 October 1931; *SO*, 3 November, 3–5 and 8 December 1931; *L'Opinió*, 3 December 1931; *LaP*, 6 December 1931; *LaB*, 10 December 1931.

112   *SO*, 22–24 September, 14 and 21 October 1931; *Luchador*, 23 October 1931; García, *Eco*, p.216.

113   *SO*, 14–15 September 1933.

114   *SO*, 14 January, 13, 19, 26 and 30 May, 19 and 24 June 1931.

115   *SO*, 22 April, 5, 10, 22 and 29 May, 2 June, 11 and 14 July, 2 and 11 August 1931; minutes of the plenum of the Barcelona CNT local federation, 29 November 1931 (AHN/SGC); *LasN*, 1 May 1931.

116   *Calle*, 14 April and 8 July 1932.

117   Sentís, *Viatge*, pp.80–1; interview with 'Antonio', November 1997.

118   *SO*, 24 September and 2 October 1930.

119   *SO*, 20 May 1931, 13 and 22 July 1934.

120   *SO*, 31 October 1931.

121   *SO*, 3 September 1931.

122   *SO*, 20 October 1932, 29 October 1933, 24 April 1934.

123   Oyón, in Oyón (ed.), p.88.

124   *SO*, 9 September 1932.

125   Giménez, *Itinerario*, p.49.

126   R. Vidiella, 'Psicología del anarquismo español', *Leviatán*, May 1934, pp. 50–8.

127   *SO*, 27 February, 2 April, 12 and 29 May, 4 and 21 July, 7–8, 15, 18 and 20 August 1931.

128   Minutes of the plenum of the Barcelona CNT local federation, 24 October 1931 (AHN/SGC).

129   *SO*, 12–15 May 1931.

130   *TyL*, 5 September 1931; *SO*, 6–8 and 18 August 1931; communiqués from the Guàrdia Urbana to the mayor of l'Hospitalet, 10 April 1936 (AHl'HL/AM); *LaV*, 13 and 25 August, 29 September 1931, 31 March 1932; *Noche*, 9 November 1931; *LasN*, 18 November and 13 December 1931; Giménez, *Itinerario*, pp.43ff; Marin, 'Llibertat', p.469.

131   Communiqué from the Guàrdia Urbana to the mayor of l'Hospitalet, 10 April 1936 (AHl'HL/AM).

132   *SO*, 10 August and 7 December 1932, 4 and 16 April 1933, 20 February and 15 September 1935.

133   *TyL*, 24 June 1932; *SO*, 22 March and 9 November 1932, 18 and 25 March 1933, 1 March 1935.

134   *TyL*, 26 April and 8 May 1931, 9 June 1933.

135 García, *Eco*, p.188; *SO*, 23 June, 26 August, 16 September and 13 October 1932, 12 January and 11 February 1933, 15 April 1934, 15 September 1935.

136 *Iniciales*, November 1934; *FAI*, 8 January 1935.

137 J. Llarch, *La muerte de Durruti*, Barcelona, 1985, pp.44–5.

138 *SO*, 26 April 1934; *Luchador*, 7 July 1933; *FAI*, 8 January 1935.

139 *SO*, 20 April and 16 September 1932, 15 April 1934.

140 *TyL*, 13 January and 17 March 1933; *SO*, 21 February, 14 March, 4 and 15 April 1933; *CyN*, February–July 1933; *LaV*, 5 January, 14 and 18 February, 14–15 March 1933; *Catalunya Roja*, 26 February 1933.

141 *LaV*, 17 January, 26 February, 10, 12 and 30 March 1933.

142 *LaV*, 27 September 1933 and 9 September 1934; *L'Opinió*, 21 June 1934; Legajo 54a (AHN/MG).

143 *LaV*, 23 July, 20 August and 6 September 1931, 17 March, 19 July, 25–26 October and 8 November 1932, 11 and 24 January, 19 February, 15 and 31 March, 2 April, 14, 23 and 31 May, 1–2 and 20 June, 18 and 27 July, 2, 8 and 11 August, 15 and 24 October, 15 December 1933, 14 February, 3 April, 1 and 6 June, 19 and 25 July, 5 August, 26 September, 22 November, 4 and 7 December 1934, 5 and 16 March, 10 April, 15 and 31 May, 4 June, 22 August, 26 October, 25 December 1935; *LasN*, 1 February, 11 April, 8 and 31 May, 4 June, 3 November–1 December 1931, 19 January, 16 February and 17 August 1932, 14 April, 8–9 May, 4 and 26–27 September 1934, 24 January 1935; *Noche*, 2 November 1931; *LaP*, 31 May 1933 and 10–12 April 1934; *Veu*, 5 January and 31 May 1933, 8, 12 and 21 April 1934; *SO*, 9 August 1923; *Matí*, 4 June 1931; *L'Opinió*, 8 October 1933.

144 *TyL*, 19 November 1935; Abad, *Memorias*, p.188. According to police estimates, in 1935 there were around 16,000 'illegal' immigrants in Barcelona: 5,500 Germans, 1,500 Italians, 600 Argentinians, and 130 Portuguese (*LaP*, 2 January 1935).

145 *LasN*, 7 March, 17 May, 5 June and 29 November 1931, 4 May 1934; *LaV*, 8 and 17 September 1931, 5 July and 13–15 December 1932, 7 May, 8 and 11 August, 27 September and 15 October 1933, 4 December 1934; *Nau*, 24 April 1931; *L'Opinió*, 26 October 1933; Abad, *Memorias*, pp.182, 220–1.

146 *LaV*, 6 January, 18 and 24 March, 4 and 7 April, 31 May, 18 July 1933, 27 December 1934, 4 and 28 January 1935; Revista Anarchica, *Red Years, Black Years. Anarchist Resistance to Fascism in Italy*, London, 1989, pp.7, 37–8, 43; *TyL*, 19 September 1931; *SO*, 29 September 1934; *LasN*, 17 May and 5 June 1931, 4 October 1934, 5 February, 16 May and 4 July 1936; A. Téllez Solá, *Sabaté;. Guerrilla urbana en España (1945–1960)*, Barcelona, 1992, p.42; *Veu*, 6 January 1933, 18 and 21 April 1934; García, *Eco*, p.230.

147 *SO*, 26 August 1932.

148 *LaV*, 20 August 1931; *Veu*, 24 December 1933.

149 C. Ealham, ' "From the summit to the abyss": the contradictions of individualism and collectivism in Spanish anarchism', in P. Preston and A. MacKenzie (eds), *The Republic Besieged: Civil War in Spain, 1936–39*, Edinburgh, 1996, pp.135–62.

150 *LasN*, 11 April, 3 November and 21 December 1931, 17 August 1932, 21 April 1934, 2 July 1936; *LaV*, 16 December 1932, 13 August, 27 September and 19–20 October 1933, 31 March and 3 April 1934, 13 January 1935; *Iniciales*, December 1935–February 1936; *LaP*, 11 April 1934; *L'Opinió*, 8 and 19–20 October 1933; *Veu*, 21 April 1934; Llarch, *Muerte*, pp.23–4; *SO*, 3 December 1935 and 7 February 1936.

151 *LasN*, 4 September 1934.

152 *LaV*, 27 December 1934.

153 M. Muñoz Diez, *Marianet, semblanza de un hombre*, Mexico, 1960, pp.25–30.

154 *TyL*, 11 July 1931.
155 Minutes of the plenum of the Barcelona CNT local federation, 10 January 1932 (AHN/SGC); *LaB*, 7 January, 6 June and 29 September 1932.
156 *Unidad sindical*, 31 March and 21 April 1932.
157 *Fam*, 10 February 1933.

Chapter 6

1 My analysis is based on the following sources: *LasN*, *L'Opinió*, *Veu* and *LaV*, 20–30 January 1932; *TyL*, 23 January–26 February 1932; *Luchador*, 5–26 February 1932; *SO*, 20 January and 3–6 March 1932; *Cultura Libertaria*, 5 February 1932; *LaB*, 29 January–11 February 1932; minutes of the plenum of the Barcelona CNT local federation, 5 February, 7 and 10 March 1932 (AHN/SGC); C. Borderias, 'La insurrección del Alt Llobregat. Enero 1932. Un estudio de historia oral', MA thesis, University of Barcelona, 1977.

2 Gobernador Civil de Barcelona al Ministro de la Gobernación, 29 December 1931, Legajo 7a (AHN/MG).

3 *SO*, 17 January 1932.

4 Paz, *Chumberas*, p.119.

5 Azaña, *Obras*, Vol. 2, pp.139–41, Vol. 3, pp.311–12; Ballbé, *Orden*, p.342.

6 Madrid, *Ocho*, pp.171–2; Azaña, *Obras*, Vol. 3, pp.326–39; *Calle*, 19 February 1932; *LasN*, 11 February 1932; *TyL*, 26 February and 4 March 1932; *LaB*, 9 and 30 June 1932.

7 Minutes of the plenum of the Barcelona CNT local federation, 8 February 1932 (AHN/SGC); *LasN*, 2 and 17 February 1932; *TyL* and *Cultura Libertaria*, 1 April 1932.

8 *TyL*, 8 April 1932; *LasN*, 16–21 February 1932; *LaV*, 5 April 1932; Peirats, *CNT*, Vol. 1, pp.65–6.

9 *Cultura Libertaria*, 5 February 1932; *LaB*, 29 January, 4 and 11 February 1932.

10 *Luchador*, 5 and 12 February 1932.

11 Thus, Jover, of the 'Nosotros' group, claimed that the revolution 'would have triumphed in Spain and even in Barcelona had the Regional Committee not sabotaged it'. Minutes of the plenum of the Barcelona CNT local federation, 5 and 7 February, 7 and 10 March 1932 (AHN/SGC).

12 Minutes of the plenum of the Barcelona CNT local federation, 29 November 1931, 10 February and 25 March 1932 (AHN/SGC).

13 *LaB*, 25 February, 3 March, 7 July, 15 September, 13 and 27 October, 10 and 17 November 1932.

14 *TyL*, 1 and 22 April 1932; *Luchador*, 5, 12, 19 February, 8, 15 April 1932; *SO*, 15 March 1932.

15 *SO*, 18 March, 3 May, 17 June, 30 September 1932; *Cultura Libertaria*, 20 May, 17 June, 15 July, 16 and 23 September, 7 and 21 October, 3, 10 and 17 November, 14 and 21 December 1932, 3 January and 3 March 1933; *Sindicalismo*, 14 February, 14 and 21 April 1933; *TyL*, 14 April 1933.

16 *SO*, 26 April 1932; *LaB*, 21 April and 1 May 1932.

17 Report from Consul-General King, 30 May 1932, FO371/16505/W6457/12/41 (PRO).

18 *SO*, 1 January 1933.

19 This analysis is based on *CyN*, January 1933; *LaV*, *Veu* and *L'Opinió*, 1–23 January 1933; *SO*, 1–26 January, 5 February 1933; García, *Eco*, pp.130–3; Paz, *Durruti*, pp.244–9; letter from Sir G. Grahame, 10 January 1933, FO371/17426/W472/116/41 and reports from Consul-General King, 10–11 January 1933, FO371/17426/W576 /116/41 and FO371/17426/W577/116/41 (PRO).

20 García, *Eco*, p.172.

21 Elorza, *Utopía*, p.455; Bookchin, *Anarchists*, p.227.

22 *SO*, 13–14, 28 and 31 January, 2–4 February 1933; *Luchador*, 10 February 1933; *TyL*, 27 January and 17 March 1933.

23 The promotion of Menéndez from a position in Barcelona to one in central government highlighted the way in which an experience of public order in the Catalan capital was viewed in official circles as a suitable apprenticeship for a senior position in the state apparatus.

24 F. Urales, *La barbarie gubernamental: España 1933*, Barcelona, 1933; J. Mintz, *The Anarchists of Casas Viejas*, Chicago, 1982, pp.186–200.

25 CRT, *Memoria...1933*, pp.5–9.

26 Paz, *Durruti*, pp.248–9; *SO*, 10 February 1933.

27 P. Preston, *The Coming of the Spanish Civil War. Reform, Reaction and Revolution in the Second Republic*, London, 1978, pp.92–130.

28 *SO*, 15–17, 28 and 31 January 1933, 15 June, 2, 16 and 28 August 1934; *TyL*, 1 August and 20 October 1933.

29 *Luchador*, 28 July 1933; *SO*, 21 July, 4 August, 29 October and 15 November 1933.

30 *SO*, 1 and 10 February, 1 March, 22 September, 12, 15 and 17 October, 23 November 1933; *LaRB*, 15 November 1933.

31 *SO*, 22 October, 1, 7–10, 17 and 23 November, 1–2 December 1933; *TyL*, 24 November and 1 December 1933; *LaRB*, 30 November 1933.

32 *Adelante*, 19, 23–24 and 28 November, 2–3 December 1933; *LaV*, 19, 21, 23, 28 and 30 November, 3 and 5 December 1933; *SO*, 3 December 1933.

33 *SO*, 11, 16 and 18 November 1933; *Adelante*, 23 November 1933; *Fortitud*, 31 December 1933; *TyL*, 24 November 1933.

34 See *La Humanitat*, *LaV*, *Veu*, *Adelante* and *L'Opinió*, 5–22 December 1933; *JS*,16 December 1933; *CyN*, December 1933; report from Sir G. Grahame, 12 December 1933, FO371/17427/W14410/116/41 and report from Consul-General King, 12 December 1933, FO371/17427/W14776/116/41 (PRO).

35 Peirats, unpublished memoirs, pp.38–9.

36 Communiqués from the Guàrdia Urbana to the mayor of l'Hospitalet, 8–10 December 1933, and report from the mayor of l'Hospitalet to Lluís Companys, president of the Generalitat, 29 December 1933 (AHl'HL/AM); Peirats, unpublished memoirs, pp.37–9; D. Marin, *Clandestinos*, Barcelona, 2002, pp.196–201.

37 Miguel Grau, cited in Marin 'Llibertat', p.124, n.48.

38 *SO*, 24 April 1934.

39 Eyre, *Sabaté*, p.66.

40 Abad, *Memorias*, pp.216–7, 246; Ortiz, p.86.

41 *LaV*, 31 October and 1 November 1934; *Adelante*, 17 February 1934; *LasN*, 12 May 1934; Malaquer, *Años*, p.114.

42 J. Camós, 'Testimoniatges de Francesc Pedra i Marià Corominas. L'activitat política a l'Hospitalet de Llobregat (1923–46)', *L'Avenç* 60, 1983, p.13.

43 Balcells, *Crisis*, p.196, n.22; Huertas, *Obrers*, p.243; Miró, *Cataluña*, p.49.

44 *LaP*, 10 April 1934 and 8–9 January 1935.

45 *Veu*, 19 January 1933; *LaV*, 11–14 January 1933; *SO*, 12 and 26–31 January, 16 and 30 August, 20 September 1933.

46 *Adelante*, 5 January 1934.

47 *SO*, 28 January 1933.

48 Sanz, *Sindicalismo*, p.245; *LaB*, 9 February 1933; Urales, *Barbarie*, p.23; *SO*, 5–8 February and 10 March 1933.

49 M. Sánchez, *La Segona República i la Guerra Civil a Cerdanyola (1931–1939)*, Barcelona, 1993, p.59; *LaB*, 12 January–2 February, 27 April,

8 June, 27 July 1933; Azaña, *Obras*, Vol. 3, pp.505, 512; *L'Opinió*, 1–8 April 1933.

50 *Adelante*, 19 and 30 December 1933; *LaRB*, 28 December 1933.

51 *LaV*, 11 and 16 January, 22 February, 13 September 1934; *L'Opinió*, 19 January 1934.

52 *LaV*, 5 January, 17 May and 20 July 1933; *CyN*, June–July and November 1933.

53 For the 1933 builders' strike, see *CyN*, April–September 1933; *SO*, 5 March–15 August 1933; *TyL*, 28 April 1933; *LaB*, 20 April–24 August 1933; *LaV* and *L'Opinió*, 18 March–17 August 1933; *JS*, 29 April, 27 May, 19 August and 21 October 1933; *Sindicalismo*, 1–15 September 1933.

54 *SO*, *LaP*, *LaV*, 13 June 1933; *TyL*, 16 June 1933; *CyN*, June 1933; *Luchador*, 23 June 1933.

55 *LaV*, 11 July 1933; *SO*, 12 July 1933; *CyN*, July 1933.

56 Interview with 'Juan', November 1997.

57 *CyN*, May–August 1933; *TyL*, 2 June 1933; *L'Opinió*, 9 July 1933; *Sindicalismo*, 14 July 1933; *JS*, 15 and 22 July, 4 November 1933; *LaV*, 21 July 1933.

58 Martín, *Recuerdos*, p.87.

59 *TyL*, 11 August 1933; *SO*, 12 and 15 August 1933; *Correspondencia Sindical Internacional*, 20 June and 18 July 1933.

60 *SO*, 7 July and 3–18 August 1934; *LaV*, 24–27 November 1934 and 23 July 1935; *LasN*, 11 December 1935 and 2 February 1936.

61 *LaV*, 28 April, 4–17 August, 31 October, 1 November and 26 December 1934, 27 June 1935; *LasN*, 16–17 January 1936; *Adelante*, 8 March 1934.

62 *Adelante*, 9–11 and 21 February 1934; *LaV*, 22 February and 4–5 December 1934.

63 *LasN*, 26–27 May 1934; *SO*, 1–5 and 23–24 September, 1–10 October, 4 November 1933, 5 August 1934; *Sindicalismo*, 14 July, 1–4 and 25 August, 15 September, 27 October, 3 November 1933; *El Transporte*, 18 June 1934; *Cataluña Obrera*, 26 May 1933; *CyN*, March–November 1933; *Catalunya Roja*, 19 October 1933; *TyL*, 2 June 1933; *Luchador*, 31 March, 9–23 June and 28 July 1933; *LaB*, 31 August, 7–21 September and 19 October 1933; *Adelante*, 17–20 October, 1–7 and 19 November 1933; *Mall*, 4 November 1933.

64 Monjo, 'CNT', pp.155, 225.

65 *SO*, 9 December 1931, 5 and 17 January, 9 March 1932, 15 January, 24 June, 10 August, 7 October 1933, 13 July 1934; minutes of the Barcelona CNT local federation, 28 December 1931 (AHN/SGC); CRT, *Informe que el director de 'Soli', Liberto Callejas, presenta al pleno de Sindicatos de Cataluña, que se celebrará en Terrassa los días 24 y siguientes de diciembre de 1932*, Barcelona, n.d., *passim*; CRT, *Memoria...1933*, *passim*; Peirats, *Figuras*, p.44; *LaP*, 8 April 1934; *TyL*, 17 and 24 October 1931; *Iniciales*, January–June 1935.

66 Take, for instance, the *treintista*-inclined Sabadell unions, which were among the wealthiest and best organised in Catalonia.

67 *SO*, 20 September 1933; *LaP*, 5–11 April 1934.

68 Minutes of the plenums of the Barcelona CNT local federation, 7 and 29 November 1931 (AHN/SGC); *LaP*, 5–11 April 1934; *SO*, 11 December 1931, 18 and 24 March, 29 May 1932, 17 and 19 September 1933; *TyL*, 19 November 1935.

69 *SO*, 19 September 1933; *LaP*, 8 April 1934.

70 J.L. Gutiérrez Molina, *La Idea revolucionaria. El anarquismo organizado en Andalucía y Cádiz durante los años treinta*, Madrid, 1993, p.73.

71 Paz, *Chumberas*, p.113.

72 Malaquer, *Trabajo*, p.114; *Veu*, 16 May 1933; *LaV*, 19 May 1933; communiqué from the Guàrdia Urbana to the mayor of l'Hospitalet, 20 March 1936 (AHl'HL/AM); L.

Massaguer, *Mauthausen: fin de trayecto. Un anarquista en los campos de la muerte*, Madrid, 1997, p.14.

73 The committee was described as the 'Committee for Social Revolutionary Terrorism' in the daily press. *LaV*, 19 May 1933, 27 March and 19 July 1934; *LasN*, 4 October 1934; *Veu*, 16 May 1933; Marin, *Clandestinos*, p.184.

74 Porcel, *Revuelta*, pp.118–21.

75 García, *Eco*, p.208; *CyN*, February–March and June 1933; *LaV*, January–March, 15 June and 31 October 1933.

76 Eyre, *Sabaté*, pp. 42–4.

77 Porcel, *Revuelta*, pp.118–21.

78 See the daily press for 1934, especially *L'Opinió*, 2 January and 30 March 1934; *LasN*, 1–31 May and 4 October 1934; *LaV*, 27 March, 19 July, 2 August and 5–9 September 1934; *LaP*, 5–12 April 1934.

79 A. Balcells, *Historia Contemporánea de Cataluña*, Barcelona, 1983, p.256.

80 *Veu*, 12 July 1933; *L'Opinió*, 24 and 28 March, 3 and 13 April 1934; *LaV*, 14 July 1934.

81 *Veu*, 17 February and 24 May 1934; *Butlletí Oficial de la Generalitat*, 21 June 1934.

82 *LaV*, 28 March 1934; *L'Opinió*, 24 March 1934; *Adelante*, 2 March 1934.

83 *LaV*, 3 April and 2 September 1934; *Veu*, 18–28 April 1934; *SO*, 6 July 1934.

84 *LaV*, 30 April 1935.

85 *LaV*, 18 September 1932, 25 June 1933, 15 and 23 February, 31 March and 15–18 April 1934, 2 July 1935; *LaP*, 1–12 April 1934, 2 July 1935; *TyL*, 29 August 1931; *LasN*, 18 September 1932 and 4 September 1934; *Adelante*, 9–13 January 1934; García, *Eco*, p.94.

86 *L'Opinió*, 24 and 28 March, 3 April, 9 August 1934.

87 J. Balius, *Octubre catalán*, Barcelona, n.d, p.11.

88 *SO*, 6–7 and 31 July 1934; Balius, *Octubre*, p.10; García, *Eco*, p.225; *LaP*, 10 April 1934.

89 *SO*, 24 August 1934; Alba and Casasús, *Diàlegs*, p.28; *LaV*, 19 and 25 July 1934; *LasN*, 15–18 May 1934; Balius, *Octubre*, p.11.

90 *LaV*, 23 February, 15–18 April and 17–19 July 1934; *SO*, 17–20 and 25 July, 9 September 1934; *Veu*, 15 April 1934; *L'Opinió*, 17 April 1934; *El Noticiero Universal*, 16 April 1934; Paz, *Chumberas*, p.142.

91 *L'Opinió*, 7 March and 17 April 1934; *LaP*, 18 April 1934; *LasN*, 20 April 1933 and 17–18 May 1934; *SO*, 9 September 1934.

92 *Iniciales*, November 1934; *FAI*, 8 January 1935; *LaV*, 22–25 December 1934 and 30 April 1935.

93 *LaP*, 1–6 April 1934.

94 *TyL*, 18 July 1931, 23 January 1932, 24 February and 23 September 1933; *LaP*, 8–9 January 1935; *LaV*, 25 July 1931, 27 December 1932, 19–20 October and 6 December 1933, 27 December 1934, 3, 8–9, 16 and 27 January, 2 February, 10 April, 29 July 1935; *LasN*, 6 and 16 February 1932, 4 September 1935; *Matí*, 14 November 1935; *SO*, 6 September 1934 and 28 April 1936; *L'Opinió*, 19–20 October 1933.

95 Massaguer, *Mauthausen*, p.14.

96 García, *Eco*, pp.30, 61, 469; *LaV*, 6 January, 4 and 21 April, 3, 6 and 23 June, 18 August, 31 October, 13–14 December 1933, 2 January, 22 February, 5 August, 7, 22 and 27 December 1934, 4–9 January, 14 and 31 May 1935; *L'Opinió*, 2 January 1934; *LasN*, 14–20 January, 16–17 May 1931, 6–8 and 23 May 1934, 4–5 February 1936; *La Humanitat*, 5 June 1933; *Veu*, 6 January 1933 and 6 March 1934; *LaP*, 1 April and 11 May 1934, 4 and 8–9 January 1935; *SO*, 27 August 1932 and 25 April 1936; Léon-Ignacio, *Años*, p.298; Monjo, 'CNT', p.191.

97 Marin, 'Llibertat', pp.480–5.

98 *LaP*, 11 April 1934; *LaV*, 15 February, 11 December 1934 and 11–12 December 1935; *LasN*, 4 September 1934.

99 *LaV*, 29 April, 6 and 23 June, 13 December 1933, 30 January, 1 and 15 February, 31 March 1934; *TyL*, 29 August 1931 and 14 July 1933; *LaP*, 1–10 April 1934 and 8–9 January 1935; Peiró, *Peiró*, pp.32–3; *LasN*, 16 February 1932; García, *Eco*, pp.210–11; *La Humanitat*, 5 June 1933; *L'Opinió*, 30 March 1934.

100 *LaP*, 4 January 1935; Téllez, *Sabaté*, p.24; *Veu*, 27 April 1934.

Chapter 7

1 Gobernador Civil de Barcelona (Anguera de Sojo) al Ministro de la Gobernación, 2 September 1931, Legajo 7a (AHN/MG).

2 *LaV*, 6 September 1931.

3 *SO*, 13 October 1931; *LaV*, 13 August 1931; *LaP*, 8 and 12 June 1931; L'Opinió, 17–19 and 24–25 July, 29 August, 2 December 1931.

4 *Veu*, 27 April 1934.

5 FTN, *Memoria...1931*, pp.203–4; L'Opinió, 17, 19 and 25 July, 2 December 1931, 26 October 1932; *LaP*, 10 July 1931.

6 *LaP*, 11 April 1934; *JS*, 28 November 1931; *L'Opinió*, 22 September 1933, 7 April and 9 August 1934.

7 *LaV*, 26 April 1934 and 10 November 1935; de Bellmunt, *Catacumbes*, pp.73–82; *L'Opinió*, 26 March and 22 September 1933; *LaP*, 16 August 1933, 11 and 18 April 1934.

8 *L'Opinió*, 22 September 1933 and 9 August 1934; *LaP*, 11 April 1934.

9 Claramunt, *Problemes*, p.14.

10 *LaV*, 13 and 25 September 1931.

11 Ametlla, *Memòries*, Vol. 2 p.219.

12 *LaV*, 1, 9 and 25 September 1931.

13 *Veu*, 15 April, 3 and 22 November 1931, 7 January 1932.

14 *L'Opinió*, 26 March and 5 November 1933, 15 May and 9 August 1934.

15 Hall *et al.*, *Policing*, pp.218–27.

16 *JS*, 22 July, 7 and 14 October, 11 November 1933; Paz, *Chumberas*, p.113; *Veu*, 27 April 1934.

17 *La Victòria*, 28 May, 11 June and 31 December 1932; *LaV*, 26 April and 29 July 1934; *L'Opinió*, 26 March and 5 November 1933, 7 March, 19 April, 1 May and 15 August 1934; *JS*, 1 August 1931, 29 April, 22 July and 11 November 1933; *Cataluña Obrera*, 26 May and 9 June 1933; *LaP*, 18 April 1934.

18 Aurora Bertrana, *Memòries del 1935 fins al retorn a Catalunya*, Barcelona, 1975, p.787.

19 *LaP*, 6 and 10–12 April 1934.

20 Hall *et al.*, *Policing*, p.157.

21 Sibley, *Geographies*, p.77.

22 *LasN*, 17 June 1931; L'Opinió, 17 and 19 July 1931.

23 *SO*, 13 October 1931; *LaV*, 13 August 1931; *LaP*, 8 and 12 June 1931; *L'Opinió*, 17–19 and 24–25 July, 29 August, 2 December 1931.

24 *LaP*, 12 April 1934; *LaV*, 31 March 1934; *Veu*, 4 and 26 April 1934; Berruezo, *Sendero*, p.62.

25 *LaV*, 31 January, 14–16 and 25–26 March 1933, 2 and 28 January, 20 and 22 February, 10 and 27–28 March, 29 April, 18 July, 5 and 7 August, 7 September 1934; *Veu*, 11 April 1934; *Foc*, 5 January 1933.

26 *L'Opinió*, 6 April and 12 July 1933, 21 January, 7, 11, 13, 24 and 28–29 March, 3, 7 and 13 April, 9 August 1934.

27 *JS*, 16 December 1933.
28 See, for instance, *LaV*, 6 September 1931; *L'Opinió*, 23 October 1931 and 12 December 1933; *JS*, 1 August 1931.
29 *Veu*, 12 December 1933.
30 Hall *et al.*, *Policing*, pp.53–77.
31 G. Pearson, *The Deviant Imagination. Psychiatry, Social Work and Social Change*, London, 1975, pp.160–7.
32 See FTN, *Memoria…1934*, pp.7–8, 212, 219, 222.
33 *SO*, 24 July, 9 September and 16 December 1932, 15 January, 25 March and 18 August 1933, 6 December 1935; *TyL*, 24 December 1935.
34 *SO*, 26 April 1934.
35 *Orto*, May 1932.
36 E. Mingione, 'Polarización, fragmentación y marginalidad en las ciudades industriales', in A. Alabart, S. García and S. Giner (eds), *Clase, poder y ciudadanía*, Madrid, 1994, pp.97–122.
37 *TyL*, 26 April 1932; *SO*, 14 February 1935.
38 *SO*, 26 August and 16 September 1932, 14 March 1933, 15 April 1934; *Tiempos Nuevos*, 21 and 28 March 1935.
39 *SO*, 9 April 1933, 20 March 1934 and 15 September 1935; *LaRB*, 19 April 1935.
40 A. Carrasco, *Barcelona con el puño en alto! Estampas de la revolución*, Barcelona, 1936, p.30.
41 *SO*, 22 March, 30 July, 23 September, 23 November and 7 December 1932, 8 and 14 March, 1 and 18 April, 23 June, 8 August 1933, 24 April 1934; *Colmena*, 30 October 1931; *TyL*, 16 September and 8 December 1932, 9 June and 25 August 1933.
42 *SO*, 15 January, 24 May, 24 and 30 July, 2 August, 8 December 1932.
43 *SO*, 28 August and 4 September 1932, 16 and 18 April 1934, 3 December 1935; *TyL*, 7 November and 5 December 1931, 1 July, 9 September and 30 December 1932.
44 *TyL*, 4 July 1931 and 7 October 1932; *SO*, 31 June and 15 August 1931, 30 July, 21–23 and 29 October, 20–27 December 1932, 1 and 8 January, 30 September 1933, 14 March and 5 April 1936; *LaB*, 1 September and 27 October 1932, 8 January, 8, 19 and 24 February, 27 April 1933; *Adelante*, 28 October 1933; *LaRB*, 6 July 1934; Tuñón, *Movimiento*, p.824.
45 *SO*, 15 January, 23 June, 8, 15 and 27 October, 20 December 1932, 24 April and 26 August 1934, 26 November 1935; *Luchador*, 7 July 1933.
46 Landlords also often lied about the size of their properties and the number of tenants occupying them (Sentís, *Viatge*, p.65).
47 *SO*, 26 November 1935.
48 *LaP*, 10 January 1932; *SO*, 4 November 1932, 1 August 1933 and 6 March 1936.
49 *SO*, 2 August 1932, 26 February and 23 June 1933, 8 July, 1934; *TyL*, 7 November 1931 and 16 September 1932.
50 *TyL*, 26 April 1931; *SO*, 23 June 1932 and 7 April 1934.
51 H.F. Moorhouse and C.W. Chamberlain, 'Lower class attitudes to property: aspects of the counter-ideology', *Sociology* 8 (3), 1974, p.388.
52 *SO*, 15 August 1931, 1 and 20 April 1932; *TyL*, 19 July 1936.
53 *SO*, 23 November 1932 and 3 January 1936; *Iniciales*, March 1932; *La Voz Confederal*, 25 May 1935; *The Times*, 28–29 October 1935; J. M. Fernández, 'Los "affaires" Straperlo y Tay. Dos escándalos de la II República', *Tiempo de Historia* 38, 1978, pp.18–28.
54 'The Society of Death' was chapter 1 of José Prat's, *La sociedad burguesa*, Barcelona, 1934.
55 *L'Opinió*, 30 September 1933; Claramunt, *Lluita*, pp.193, 200–9, 215–16, 219–29; *SO*, 23 July 1931; *Boletín Oficial del Ministerio de Trabajo y Previsión* 67, February

1936, pp.43–58, 183–4; Aiguader, *Problema*, p.6; *Luchador*, 5 June 1931; *Tiempos Nuevos*, 28 February 1935; Alba and Casasús, *Diàlegs*, p.15.

56 *TyL*, 2 August 1935; Claramunt, *Problemes*, p.18; *SO*, 9 April 1933 and 20 March 1934; *Guerra di Classe*, 17 October 1936.

57 *Veu*, 13 February 1936.

58 *Adelante*, 7 January 1934; *SO*, 15 January and 26 July 1932, 20 April, 8 June and 7 July 1933, 4 July 1936; *L'Opinió*, 30 September 1933; *Iniciales*, January 1934; *LaB*, 5 May 1932; *LasN*, 2 January 1936; COPUB, *Memoria...1935*, pp.49, 488; *TyL*, 30 August 1934 and 18 November 1932.

59 *SO*, 14 April 1934.

60 *LasN*, 17 November and 8 December 1931; *L'Opinió*, 17 December 1931; *SO*, 2 August and 4 September 1932, 10 February, 16 and 18 August 1933, 8 July and 4 August 1934, 3 December 1935; *Luchador*, 3 and 10 March 1933; *LaB*, 5 January 1933; *Adelante*, 17 February 1934.

61 *SO*, 17 June and 24 December 1931, 4 August 1934, 24 June 1936; *Tiempos Nuevos*, 28 February 1935; Soto, *Trabajo*, pp.659–63; *Colmena*, 9 January 1932.

62 *SO*, 6–11 July, 3 August and 8 September 1934.

63 *LaV*, 19 May 1933, 27 March and 19 July 1934; *LasN*, 4 October 1934; *Veu*, 16 May 1933.

64 *LaV*, 31 March 1934 and 11 August 1935; García, *Eco*, p.616; Porcel, *Revuelta*, pp.118–21. Barcelona novelist Juan Marsé, born in the Guinardó *barri*, demonstrated in his novel *Si te dicen que caí* how children admired the *grupistas*.

65 *SO*, 9 January and 30 July 1932, 15 February 1933; Liarte, *Camino*, p.201; *TyL*, 17 October 1931.

66 Paz, *Durruti*, p.260; *SO*, 20 June and 1 August 1933, 18 and 24 April, 2 August 1934; *Matí*, 6 September 1935.

67 *SO*, 14 July 1932; *TyL*, 27 April 1934.

68 Bueso, *Recuerdos*, Vol. 1, p.69; Fernández, 'Affaires', pp.18–33.

69 Miró, *Cataluña*, p.66.

70 Miró, *Vida*, p.126; García, *Eco*, pp.123–4, 172; *LaP*, 30 June 1933.

71 Peirats, unpublished memoirs, p.31; Gutiérrez, *Idea*, p.77.

72 *CNT*, 9 January 1933; Gutiérrez, *Idea*, p.77.

73 *CNT*, 9 January 1933.

74 *Tiempos Nuevos*, 18 April 1935; Pestaña, *Terrorismo*, pp.100–2; *SO*, 29 June 1934.

75 For Diego Abad de Santillán's ideas, see A. Elorza (ed.), *El anarquismo y la revolución en España. Escritos, 1930–1938*, Madrid, 1976, *passim* and A. Cappelletti *et al.*, 'Diego Abad de Santillán. Un anarquismo sin adjetivos. Una visión crítica y actual de la revolución social' *Anthropos*, 138, 1992.

76 Miró, *Cataluña*, pp.48–9, 51, 54, 61–2.

77 O. Bayer, *Anarchism and Violence. Severino di Giovanni in Argentina, 1923–1931*, London, 1986, *passim*; Llarch, *Muerte*, pp.57–9; various authors, 'Anarquismo', *Anthropos*, p.12, 30, 38; *Nervio*, July 1934; *SO*, 23 September 1932.

78 Paz, *Durruti*, pp.311–14.

79 *Ibid.*, p.314; *LasN*, 1 January–18 July 1936; *CyN*, January–July 1936; Eslava, *Verdugos*, p.307; Abad, *Memorias*, p.201.

80 Elorza, *Utopia*, pp.464–5. In a letter from jail, dated September 1935 and reprinted in *SO*, November 1990, Durruti emphasised the need to introduce certain tactical changes that would allow the anarcho-syndicalists to rejoin the CNT.

81 A. Pestaña, *Inocentes*, Barcelona, 1926.

82 *Sindicalismo*, 10 November 1933; J. Peiró, *Perill a la reraguarda*, Mataró, 1936, pp.xvii–xviii; J. Manent i Pesas, *Records d'un sindicalista llibertari català, 1916–1943*, Paris, 1976, pp.178–84.

83 V. Alba, *La Alianza Obrera. Historia y análisis de una táctica de unidad*, Madrid, 1978, pp.191–200; A. Barrio, *Anarquismo y anarcosindicalismo en Asturias (1890–1936)*, Madrid, 1988, pp.390–409; J.M. Macarro, 'La autovaloración anar- quista: un principio de análisis y acción. Sevilla, 1931–1936', *Estudios de Historia Social* 31, 1984, pp.135–49.

84 For the Asturian events, see N. Molins, *UHP. La revolució proletari d'Asturies*, Barcelona, 1935; 'Ignotus' (Manuel Villar), *El anarquismo en la insurrección de Asturias (La CNT y la FAI en octubre de 1934)*, Valencia, 1935; D. Ruiz, *Insurrección defensiva y revolución obrera. El octubre español de 1934*, Barcelona, 1988.

85 Peirats, unpublished memoirs, p.44.

86 *TyL*, 16 February–11 October 1934; Solidaridad, 13 February–3 May 1934; *SO*, 16 February–19 September 1934; *Sindicalismo*, 4 April 1934.

87 Sanz, *Sindicalismo*, pp.258–9; Peirats, *Figuras*, pp.262–3; CNT, *El Congreso Confederal de Zaragoza 1936*, Bilbao, 1978, pp.154–68.

88 See C. Ealham, 'Crime and punishment in 1930s Barcelona', *History Today*, October 1993, pp.31–7.

89 R. Vinyes, 'Sis d'octubre, repressió i represaliats', *L'Avenç* 30, 1980, p.52; Balcells, *Crisis*, p.227.

90 *CyN*, May 1935–February 1936.

91 Reports from Sir G. Grahame, 25 October and 6 December 1934, FO371/ 18597/W9526/27/41, FO371/18597/W10704/27/41 and FO371/18599/W9522/ 325/41 (PRO).

92 B. Muniesa, *La burguesía catalana ante la II República*, Barcelona, 1985–86, Vol. 2, p.242.

93 *Veu*, 5 October 1934.

94 Elorza, *Utopia*, pp.315–18.

95 Muniesa, *Burguesía*, Vol. 2, pp.226–9.

96 *LaV*, 9–27 October and 4 November 1934; *Veu*, 7 November 1934; FTN, *Memoria...1934*, pp.5–8, 215, 218–31.

97 *SO*, 11 October 1934; *LaB*, 13 September 1935; *LaRB*, 26 April–31 May, 14 June–19 July 1935.

98 *Sindicalismo*, 30 May and 7 August 1935.

99 Letter reprinted in *SO*, November 1990.

100 P. Preston, 'The creation of the Popular Front in Spain', in H. Graham and P. Preston (eds), *The Popular Front in Europe*, London, 1987, pp.84–105; R. Vinyes, *La Catalunya Internacional. El frontpopulisme en l'exemple català*, Barcelona, 1983.

101 *LaB*, 15 November and 27 December 1935, 24 January 1936; *Front*, 7 February 1936.

102 Muniesa, Burguesiâ , Vol. 2, p.254.

103 *LaRB*, 7 June 1935 and 3 January 1936; *SO*, 8, 17 and 24 January 1936; J. Peirats, *Examen crítico-constructivo del movimiento libertario español*, Mexico, 1967, pp.26–27; J.M. Molina, *Consideraciones sobre la posición de la CNT de España*, Buenos Aires, 1949, p.13; *LasN*, 5 February 1936; Peiró quoted in B. Martin, *The Agony of Modernization. Labor and Industrialization in Spain*, Ithaca, NY, 1990, p.363; D. Abad de Santillán, *Por qué perdimos la guerra*, Buenos Aires, 1940, p.37.

104 *SO*, 17 February–15 July 1936.

105 *LasN*, 5 February and 19 May 1936; *TyL*, 17 April 1936; *SO*, 22 and 31 January, 20–22 and 26 February, 3–7 March 1936; Azaña, *Obras*, Vol. 4, p.570.

106 CNT, *El Congreso Confederal de Zaragoza 1936*, Bilbao, 1978.

107 Letter from C.G. King, 5 June 1936, FO371/20522/W5256/62/41 (PRO); García, *Eco*, p.580; Liarte, *Camino*, pp.221–5; Sanz, *Sindicalismo*, p.248; Abad, *Memorias*, p.259.

108 Paz, *Chumberas*, p.197.
109 *LasN*, 3–4 and 10–11 July 1936; letters from C.G. Vaughan, 26 June and 2 July 1936, FO371/20522/W5989/62/41, FO371/20522/W6059/62/41 and FO371/ 20522/ W5990/62/41 (PRO).

Chapter 8

1   A. Paz, *Durruti en la Revolución española*, Madrid, 1996, pp.462–4.
2   *SO*, 17 July 1936.
3   Miró, *Vida*, p.168.
4   A. Paz, *Viaje al pasado (1936–1939)*, Barcelona, 1995, p.19.
5   On the streetfighting, see Llarch, *Rojinegros*, pp.87–103 and Juan García Oliver, 'Ce que fut le 19 de Juillet', *Le Libertaire*, 18 August 1938.
6   *Le Libertaire*, 18 August 1938.
7   Llarch, *Rojinegros*, p.96.
8   A. Paz, *19 de Juliol del '36' à Barcelona*, Barcelona, 1988, pp.76, 78, 85.
9   *Le Libertaire*, 18 August 1938.
10 *Diluvio*, 22 July 1936.
11 Paz, *Juliol*, pp.69–115; M. Cruells, *La revolta del 1936 à Barcelona*, Barcelona, 1976, pp.155–214; Bueso, *Recuerdos*, Vol. 2, pp.144–95; García, *Eco*, pp.171–7.
12 C. Ametlla, *Catalunya, paradís perdut (la guerra civil i la revolució anarco-comunista)*, Barcelona, 1984, p.92.
13 Cited in H. Graham, *The Spanish Republic at War, 1936–1939*, Cambridge, 2002, p.218.
14 J.E. Adsuar, 'El Comitè Central de Milícies Antifeixistes', *L'Avenç*, 14, 1979, pp.50–6.
15 F. Borkenau, 'State and revolution in the Paris Commune, the Russian Revolution, and the Spanish Civil War', *The Sociological Review* 29 (1), 1937, pp.41–75.
16 García, *Eco*, pp.177–94.
17 *LaV*, 22 July 1936.
18 C. Lorenzo, *Los anarquistas españoles y el poder*, Paris, 1972, 81–8; García, *Eco*, pp.153–293. The CCMA also had jurisdiction over the economy, the war industries and policing.
19 H. Lefebvre, *Le droit à la ville*, Paris, 1968.
20 *SO*, 24 July 1936.
21 Paz, *Viaje*, pp.23–4.
22 For instance, a huge barricade prevented entry into the Raval from Paral.lel.
23 Ametlla, *Catalunya*, p.41.
24 Letter from Benjamin Péret to André Breton, Barcelona, 11 August 1936, in B. Péret, *Death to the Pigs: Selected Writings*, London, 1988, p.182; F. Borkenau, *The Spanish Cockpit. An Eyewitness Account of the Political and Social Conflicts of the Spanish Civil War*, London, 1937, p.175; J. Langdon-Davies, *Behind the Spanish Barricades*, New York, 1936, pp.119, 126.
25 Paz, *Juliol*, p.87. For an analysis of the nature of popular power, see G. Munis, *Jalones de derrota, promesa de victoria. Crítica y teoría de la Revolución Española*, Bilbao, 1977, pp.286–359.
26 'Al pueblo de Barcelona', joint CNT–UGT manifesto, September 1936.
27 They were described as 'governing committees' (Comités Gobierno) (Lorenzo, *Anarquistas*), a point appreciated by elite commentators, who recognised their 'unlimited power' on the streets (A. Guardiola, *Barcelona en poder del Soviet (el infierno rojo). Relato de un testigo*, Barcelona, 1939, pp.30, 47). Meanwhile, according to German sociologist, Franz Borkenau, Barcelona 'overwhelmed me by

the suddenness with which it revealed the real character of a workers' dictatorship' (*Cockpit*, p.175).

28 Bueso, *Recuerdos*, Vol. 2, p.191.
29 Paz, *Viaje*, pp.71–2.
30 Guardiola, *Barcelona*, p.67; F. Lacruz, *El alzamiento, la revolución y el terror en Barcelona (19 julio 1936 – 26 enero 1939)*, Barcelona, 1943, p.138; C. Salter, *Try-Out in Spain*, New York, 1943, p.18.
31 J.M. Sánchez, *The Spanish Civil War as a Religious Tragedy*, Notre Dame, IN, 1987, p.57; Borkenau, *Cockpit*, p.75.
32 J. Miravitlles, *Gent que he conegut*, Barcelona, 1980, p.82.
33 *Noticiero*, 27 July 1936; Lacruz, *Alzamiento*, p.97; Paz, *Viaje*, p.44.
34 *SO*, 24 July 1936.
35 M. Richards, *A Time of Silence: Civil War and the Culture of Repression in Franco's Spain, 1936–1945*, Cambridge, 1998, pp.31–2.
36 *Treball*, 8 August 1936; Peirats, *CNT*, Vol. 1, pp.211, 215; Abad, *Memorias*, pp.220–1; Paz, *Juliol*, pp.101–3.
37 *SO*, 30 July 1936.
38 García, *Eco*, pp.229–30.
39 Salter, *Try-Out*, p.18.
40 J.M. Solé i Sabaté and J. Villarroya i Font, *La repressió a la reraguarda de Catalunya (1936–1939)*, Barcelona, 1989, Vol. 1, p.12.
41 Solé and Villarroya, *Repressió*, Vol. 1, pp.172, 450; J. de la Cueva, 'Religious persecution, anticlerical tradition and revolution: on atrocities against the clergy during the Spanish Civil War', *Journal of Contemporary History* 33, 1998, p.358.
42 J. Casanovas i Codina, 'El testimoniatge d'un membre de les patrulles de control de Sants', in *La guerra i la revolució a Catalunya. II Col.loqui Internacional sobre la Guerra Civil Espanyola (1936–1939)*, Barcelona, 1986, pp.51–9. Following complaints about a shopkeeper who was profiteering from food shortages, members of the militia and locals joined forces to destroy the shop of the offending trader (*Noticiero*, 27 July 1936).
43 H. Kaminski, *Los de Barcelona*, Barcelona, 1976 [1937], p.66.
44 *SO*, 6 September 1936.
45 Peiró, *Perill*, pp.39–40.
46 Solé and Villarroya, *Repressió*, Vol. 1, p.347.
47 Llarch, *Rojinegros*, pp.126, 150–1; A. Monjo and C. Vega, *Els treballadors i la guerra civil. Història d'una indústria catalana col.lectivitzada*, Barcelona, 1986, pp.68–9.
48 Beriain, *Prat*, pp.52–3.
49 T. Caballé y Clos, *Barcelona roja. Dietario de la revolución (julio 1936 – enero 1939)*, Barcelona, 1939, pp.50–62.
50 According to Paz, 8,000–10,000 activists in Barcelona followed neither the orders of the Central Committee of Anti-fascist Militias nor those of the 'higher committees' of the CNT–FAI (*Viaje*, p.64).
51 Paz, *Viaje*, p.28.
52 According to Paz, *Viaje*, p.64, the barricades 'lacked a precise objective'. Only when the power of the revolution had faded did radical anarchists appreciate that the district revolutionary committees might have served as the focal point for local politics; see *Ruta*, 14 May 1937.
53 Paz, *Viaje* p.51.
54 P. Broué, R. Fraser and P. Vilar, *Metodología histórica de la Guerra y Revolución españolas*, Barcelona, 1980, p 39.
55 Beriain, *Prat*, p.86; Carrasco, *Barcelona*, p.13.
56 Antonio Turón interviewed in *Vivir*.

57 CRT, *Memoria del Congreso Extraordinario de la Confederación Regional del Trabajo de Cataluña celebrado en Barcelona los días 25 de febrero al 3 de marzo de 1937*, Barcelona, 1937.

58 Sanz, *Sindicalismo*, p.306.

59 Kaminski, *Barcelona*, p.37; Lacruz, *Alzamiento*, p.129; Salter, *Try-Out*, p.29; Llarch, *Rojinegros*, pp.127–8, 152.

60 Borkenau, *Cockpit*, pp.69–70; J. McNair, *Spanish Diary*, Manchester, n.d., p.6. M. Low and J. Brea, *Red Spanish Notebook*, San Francisco, 1979 [1937], p.21.

61 In the city centre, the POUM occupied the Hotel Falcón, the Lyon d'Or cafe and the Virreina Palace on the Rambles; the anarchist youth established its HQ in the palace of an aristocrat who had fled to France (Bueso, *Recuerdos*, p.190; Paz, *Viaje*, pp.28, 76; Carrasco, *Barcelona*, p.15).

62 Paz, *Viaje*, p.56.

63 Solé and Villarroya, *Repressió*, Vol. 1, p.290.

64 Information provided by Manel Aisa Pàmpols.

65 See López Sánchez, *Verano*, pp.49–73.

66 Paz, *Viaje*, p.48.

67 A. Castells Durán, *Les col.lectivitzacions a Barcelona, 1936–1939*, Barcelona, 1993.

68 Perhaps as much as 50 percent of the bourgeoisie fled Barcelona (A. Souchy and P. Folgare, *Colectivizaciones: la obra constructiva de la revolución española*, Barcelona, 1977, p.75).

69 M. Seidman, *Workers against Work. Labor in Paris and Barcelona during the Popular Fronts*, Berkeley, Calif., 1991, *passim*.

70 J. Palou Garí, *Treinta y dos meses de esclavitud en la que fue zona roja de España*, Barcelona, 1939, p.30.

71 Langdon-Davies, *Barricades*, pp.119, 142. The Right was scandalised by the transformation of the Ritz; see 'Schmit', *5 meses con los rojos en Barcelona*, Palma de Mallorca, 1937, p.26.

72 Paz, *Juliol*, p.114.

73 Low and Brea, *Notebook*, p.19; Borkenau, *Cockpit*, p.115; C. Santacana i Torres, *Victoriosos i derrotats: el franquisme a l'Hospitalet, 1939–1951*, Barcelona, 1994, p.52.

74 G. Leval, *Collectives in the Spanish Revolution*, London, 1975, pp.269–70. Before the revolution, infant mortality rates in proletarian Raval were twice as high as in bourgeois parts of the city.

75 *Ideas*, 29 December 1936.

76 Miró, *Vida*, p.287.

77 *Noticiero*, 27 July 1936.

78 Llarch, *Rojinegros*, pp.121–2.

79 Paz, *Viaje* pp.56, 115; Caballé, *Barcelona*, pp.85–6.

80 Langdon-Davies, *Barricades*, plate 2.

81 Paz, *Viaje*, p.58; Caballé, *Barcelona*, p.71.

82 M. Laird, 'A diary of revolution', *The Atlantic Monthly*, November 1936, p.524; Langdon-Davies, *Barricades*, pp.119, 145; C. Pi Sunyer, *La República y la guerra. Memorias de un político catalán*, Mexico, 1975, p.390; Salter, *Try-Out*, pp.9–11; Guardiola, *Barcelona*, p.39; Lacruz, *Alzamiento*, pp.117–18; H.E. Knoblaugh, *Correspondent in Spain*, London, 1937, p.33; Caballé, *Barcelona*, p.11; Pérez, *Terror*, p.9; 'Schmit', *Barcelona*, pp.5–6.

83 Salter, *Try-Out*, pp.9–11.

84 The Arenas bullring in the working-class *barri* of Sants was the resting place for wrecked cars in the days after the revolution (Carrasco, *Barcelona* pp.21–2).

85 Laird, 'Diary', pp.524–6; Lacruz, *Alzamiento*, p.129; Ametlla, *Catalunya*, p.86.

86   Llarch, *Rojinegros*, p.120.
87   Pi, *Republica*, p.390; Guardiola, *Barcelona*, pp.36, 39; Caballé, *Barcelona*, p.11.
88   Langdon-Davies, *Barricades*, p.141.
89   *SO*, 13 August 1936; Caballé, *Barcelona*, p.44. Additional information provided by Manel Aisa Pàmpols.
90   *SO*, 6 December 1932 and 8 August 1933.
91   *SO*, 26 July 1936.
92   On the survival of so-called 'traditional' forms of protest, see Pérez Ledesma, *Estabilidad y conflicto social*, pp.165–202.
93   The house of Pich i Pon, the COPUB president, was attacked, while property belonging to Emiliano Iglesias, the Radical Party leader in the city, and Cambó, leader of the bourgeois Lliga, was destroyed (*SO*, 26 July 1936; Caballé, *Barcelona*, pp.32–4).
94   Laird, 'Diary', p.522; Borkenau, *Cockpit*, p.74; Pi, *República*, p.393; Lacruz, *Alzamiento*, p.121; Palou, *Esclavitud*, pp.143–4.
95   P. O'Donnell, *Salud! An Irishman in Spain*, London, 1937, p.100.
96   Paz, *Viaje*, p.42; Carrasco, *Barcelona*, p.29.
97   *The Times*, 23–24 July 1936; O'Donnell, *Salud!*, pp.97–9, 151; E.A. Peers, *Catalonia Infelix*, London, 1937, pp.258–9; Borkenau, *Cockpit*, p.74.
98   Stansbury Pearse declined the invitation 'on the grounds that he was an Englishman'! ('Spain: the truth', *The Tablet*, 15 August 1936, pp.203–4).
99   Carrasco, *Barcelona*, p.15.
100 P. O'Donnell, 'An Irishman in Spain', *The Nineteenth Century*, December 1936, p.704.
101 On the walls of some churches was written: 'Respect this building! It belongs to the people!' (I. Griful, *A los veinte años de aquello, julio-diciembre de 1936*, Barcelona, 1956, p.33).
102 A. Balcells, 'El destí dels edificis eclesiàstics de Barcelona durant la guerra civil espanyola', in A. Balcells (ed.), *Violència social i poder polític. Sis estudis històrics sobre la Catalunya contemporània*, Barcelona, 2001, pp.202–9.
103 Langdon-Davis, *Barricades*, pp.177–8.
104 Balcells, 'Edificis', p.191.
105 O'Donnell, 'Irishman', pp.701, 704–5.
106 Between 23 and 25 July, 40,000 people filed past the Iglesia de la Enseñanza on Aragó Street to inspect the disinterred and partly mummified bodies of clerics (Pérez, Terror, pp.18–21).
107 G. Orwell, *Homage to Catalonia*, London, 1938, p.3.
108 Beriain, *Prat,* p.55; Solé and Villarroya, *Repressió*, Vol. 1, pp.102, 289; Balcells, 'Edificis', p.191.
109 Balcells, 'Edificis', pp.202, 207, 209.
110 *SO*, 15 August 1936.
111 Carrasco, *Barcelona*, pp.13, 27; *SO*, 30 July and 20 August 1936; *LaB*, 19 August 1936; *LaV*, 2 August 1936.
112 M. Pérez Ledesma, 'Studies on anticlericalism in contemporary Spain', *International Review of Social History* 46, 2001, pp.227–55; Sánchez, *Tragedy*, pp.23–4.
113 M. Delgado, *La ira sagrada: anticlericalismo, iconoclastia y antirritualismo en la España contemporánea*, Barcelona, 1992, pp.71–9.
114 Alvarez Junco, *Emperador*, pp.397–418.
115 D. Castro Alfín, 'Cultura, política y cultura política en la violencia anticlerical', in R. Cruz and M. Pérez Ledesma (eds), *Cultura y movilización en la España contemporánea*, Madrid, 1997, p.70.

116 J. Estivill and G. Barbat, 'L'anticlericalisme en la revolta popular del 1909', *L'Avenç* 2, 1977, p.35.

117 G. Ranzato, 'Dies Irae. La persecuzione religiosa nella zona repubblicana durante la Guerra civile spagnola (1936–1939)', *Movimento operaio e socialista* 2, 1988, p.195.

118 J. Estivill and G. Barbat, 'Anticléricalisme populaire en Catalogne au début du siècle', *Social Compass* 28, 1980, pp.219, 225.

119 Miró, *Vida*, p.195; Kaminski, *Barcelona*, p.61; Borkenau, *Cockpit*, p.73; Low and Brea, *Notebook*, p.61.

120 One recruiting poster carried an image of a woman in tight-fitting dungarees uttering the slogan 'Les milicies us necessiten!' ('The militias need you!'), representing, in the words of one British observer, 'the hiring of Aphrodite to help the work of Ares, which I had always felt to be hitting below the belt' (Langdon-Davies, *Barricades*, p.156).

121 Low and Brea, *Notebook*, pp.47, 181, 186–7.

122 Carrasco, *Barcelona*, p.81.

123 Kaminski, *Barcelona*, pp.36, 63.

124 *Ruta*, 28 November 1936; Low and Brea, *Notebook*, pp.196–7.

125 *LaB*, 6 August and 17 September 1936, 1 May 1937.

126 C. Ealham, 'The Spanish Revolution: 60 Years On', *Tesserae. Journal of Iberian and Latin American Studies* 2, 1996, pp.209–34.

127 In his oral history of the civil war, Ronald Fraser observed that 'power, like nature, abhors a vacuum. Even more so in the crucible of a civil war which is the politics of class struggle risen to the extreme of armed conflict': *Blood of Spain. The Experience of Civil War, 1936–1939*, London, 1979, p.180.

128 Casanovas i Codina, 'Testimoniatge', pp. 51–9.

129 P. Pagès, *Andreu Nin: su evolución política (1911–1937)*, Madrid, 1975, pp.223– 66; F. Bonamusa, *Andreu Nin y el movimiento comunista en España (1930–1937)*, Barcelona, 1977, pp.289–96, 305–13.

130 *LaB*, 23 September, 1 and 24 October 1936; *SO*, 27–29 September 1936; Josep Costas, cited in M. Sánchez *et al.*, *Los sucesos de mayo de 1937, una revolución en la República*, Barcelona, 1988, p.48.

131 *Butlletí Oficial de la Generalitat*, 17 October 1936.

132 A. Ossorio y Gallardo, *Vida y sacrificio de Lluís Companys*, Buenos Aires, 1943, p.172.

133 *SO*, 4 November 1936.

134 *SO*, 16–17 December 1936; *Diari de Barcelona*, 9 and 16 December 1936; *La Humanitat*, 13 December 1936.

135 Martin, *Agony*, p.399.

136 M. Benavides, *Guerra y revolución en Cataluña*, Mexico, 1978, p.220.

137 A. Mayayo i Artal, 'Els militants: els senyals lluminosos de l'organització', *L'Avenç* 95, 1986, p.46; V. Alba, *História del Marxisme a Catalunya, 1919–1939*, Barcelona, 1974, Vol. 2, p.287.

138 Munis, *Jalones*, p.298; B. Bolloten, *The Spanish Civil War. Revolution and Counter-revolution*, Hemel Hempstead, 1991, pp.84, 396–7. According to the semi-offical history of the CNT, 'in Catalonia, communism converted itself into the receptacle of the demands of the small bourgeoisie, little artesans and shopkeepers and especially, the little landowners of the Catalan countryside': Peirats, *CNT*, Vol. 2, p.127.

139 *Ruta*, 16 February–9 March 1937; *Nosotros*, 9 and 14 April 1937; *Acracia*, 10 and 28 April 1937; *Ideas*, 7 January and 11 March 1937.

140 *Diari de Barcelona*, 8 January and 9 February 1937; *LaB*, 1 and 5 January 1937.

141 Agrupación Amigos de Durruti, *Hacia la segunda revolución*, n.p., n.d.

142 *Diari de Barcelona*, 9 February 1937; Cruells, *Societat*, p.233.

143 H. Graham, '"Against the state": a genealogy of the Barcelona May Days (1937)', *European History Quarterly* 29 (1), 1999, pp.485–542.

144 Los Amigos de Durruti, a dissident anarchist group, issued a number of slogans from the barricades, but it lacked the influence to challenge the conciliatory stance of the CNT–FAI hierarchy. See Frank Mintz and Miguel Peciña, *Los amigos de durruti, los trotsquistas y los sucesos de mayo*, Madrid, 1978, and Agustín Guillamón, 'Los Amigos de Durruti, 1937–1939', *Balance* 3, 1994.

145 There are no reliable figures for the casualties of the 'May events', and estimates vary from 235 to 1,000 deaths and 1,000 to 4,500 wounded: Huertas, *Obrers*, p.273; Alba, *Marxisme*, Vol. 2, p.227; D. Abad de Santillán, *Por qué perdimos la guerra*, Buenos Aires, 1940, p.138. The lower estimate seems more accurate.

146 Cited in P. Broué, *La revolución española*, Barcelona, 1977, p.135.

147 J. Villarroya i Font, *Els bombardeigs de Barcelona durant la guerra civil (1936–1939)*, Barcelona, 1981; J. Langdon-Davies, 'Bombs over Barcelona', *The Spectator*, 14 July 1938.

148 J. Gomis, *Testigo de poca edad (1936–1943)*, Barcelona, 1968, pp.40, 77, 96–7.

Bibliography

Archives

Archivo Histórico Nacional, Madrid, Ministerio de Gobernación (Interior), Serie-A (AHN/MG).
Archivo Histórico Nacional, Salamanca, Sección Guerra Civil (AHN/SGC).
Arxiu Històric de l'Hospitalet de Llobregat – Arxiu Municipal, 1931–36 (AHl'HL/ AM).
Public Records Office, Kew, London (FO371: Foreign Office General Correspondence).

Press

Barcelona-based unless otherwise indicated.

Acció, 1931–33.
Acción, Paris 1925–27.
Acción, 1930–31.
Acción, 1934–35.
Acracia, Lleida, 1937.
Adelante, 1933–34.
La Batalla, 1923, 1930–37.
El Be Negre, 1932–34.
Boletín de información de la CNT–FAI, 1936.
Butlletí de l'Ateneu Obrer d'Esquerra Republicana de Catalunya del Districte V, 1934.
Butlletí de l'Avenç Obrer Català de l'Esquerra Republicana de Catalunya, 1933.
La Calle, 1931–32.
Cataluña Obrera, 1933.
La Catalunya Insurgent, 1935.
Catalunya Roja, 1932–34.
CNT, Madrid, 1933.
La Colmena Obrera, Badalona, 1931–32.
Combate, 1934.
El Combate Sindicalista, 1935.
Comercio y Navegación, 1920–24, 1931–36.
Comunismo, Madrid, 1931–34.
El Correo Catalán, 1909.

Correspondencia Sindical Internacional, 1933–34.
Cultura Libertaria, 1932–33.
El Detective, 1934.
El Detective de Cataluña, 1933.
El Día Gráfico, 1931.
El Diari de Barcelona, 1936–37.
El Diario de Barcelona, 1903.
El Diluvio, 1920, 1931, 1936.
El Escándolo, 1925–26.
Estampa, 1932.
FAI, 1934–35.
Fam, 1933.
FOC, 1932–33.
Fortitud, l'Hospitalet de Llobregat, 1932–33.
Frente Libertario, Paris, 1975.
Frente Único, 1931.
Front, 1932, 1935–36.
GATCPAC, 1937.
Guerra di Classe, 1936–37.
L'Hora, 1930–31, 1934–35.
La Huelga General, 1902–03.
La Humanitat, 1933–36.
Ideas, l'Hospitalet de Llobregat, 1936–7.
Iniciales, 1929–36.
La Internacional, 1931.
La Internacional Comunista, 1932–33.
La Internacional Sindical Roja, 1933.
Justicia Social, 1923–24, 1931–36.
Justicia Social–Octubre, 1936.
Leviatán, Madrid, 1934–36.
¡Liberación!, 1935–36.
El Liberal, 1903.
Llibertat, l'Hospitalet de Llobregat, 1930–31, 1933–36.
El Luchador, 1931–33.
Lucha Social, 1922.
Mall, 1933.
Mañana, 1930–31.
El Matí, 1931, 1935.
La Nau, 1931.
Nervio, Buenos Aires, 1934.
La Noche, 1931.
Nosotros, 1937.
Las Noticias, 1923, 1931–36.
El Noticiero Universal, 1934, 1936.
La Nueva Era, 1930–31, 1933–34, 1936.
L'Obra, l'Hospitalet de Llobregat, 1931.
L'Opinió, 1930–34.

Orto, Valencia, 1932.
El País, 1894.
La Publicitat, 1931–36.
¡Rebelión!, 1934.
La Revista Blanca, 1930–36.
Ruta, 1936–37.
Sembrar, Manresa, 1932–33.
Sindicalismo, 1933–34.
El Sindicalista, 1934–35.
El Sol, Madrid, 1931.
Solidaridad, 1934.
Solidaridad Obrera, 1918–23, 1930–36.
Solidaridad Proletaria, 1924–25.
El Soviet, 1931–32.
The Times, 1935–36.
Tiempos Nuevos, 1934–35.
La Tierra, Madrid, 1931.
Tierra y Libertad, 1930–36.
Trabajo, 1931.
El Trabajo Nacional, 1931.
El Transporte, 1933–34.
Treball, 1936–37.
Unidad Sindical, 1931–32.
La Vanguardia, 1923, 1931–36.
La Veu de Catalunya, 1901–09, 1930–36.
La Victòria, 1932–33.
La Voz Confederal, 1934–35.

Official publications

This also includes reports, congress minutes, etc. of public bodies and political and social organisations.

Boletín Oficial del Ministerio de Trabajo y Previsión, Madrid, 1932, 1935–36.
Butlletí Oficial de la Generalitat, 1933–36.
CNT, *Memoria del Congreso Extraordinario celebrado en Madrid los días 11 al 16 de junio de 1931*, Barcelona, 1931.
CNT, *Congreso de constitución de la Confederación Nacional del Trabajo*, Barcelona, 1976.
CNT, *El Congreso Confederal de Zaragoza 1936*, Bilbao, 1978.
COPUB, *Memoria de los trabajos realizados durante el ejercicio de 1931*, Barcelona, 1932.
COPUB, *Memoria de los trabajos realizados durante el ejercicio de 1932*, Barcelona, 1933.
COPUB, *Memoria de los trabajos realizados durante el ejercicio de 1933*, Barcelona, 1934.
COPUB, *Memoria de los trabajos realizados durante el ejercicio de 1934*, Barcelona, 1935.

COPUB, *Memoria de los trabajos realizados durante el ejercicio de 1935*, Barcelona, 1936.

CRT de Cataluña, *Memorias de los Comicios de la Regional Catalana celebrados los días 31 de mayo y 1 de junio, y 2, 3 y 4 de agosto de 1931*, Barcelona, 1931.

CRT de Cataluña, *Informe que el director de 'Solidaridad Obrera', Liberto Callejas, presenta al pleno de Sindicatos de Cataluña, que se celebrará en Terrassa los días 24 y siguientes de diciembre de 1932*, Barcelona, n.d.

CRT de Cataluña, *Memoria del Pleno Regional de Sindicatos Únicos de Cataluña. Celebrado en Barcelona del 5 al 13 de marzo de 1933*, Barcelona, 1933.

CRT de Cataluña,*Memorias de la Conferencia Regional Extraordinaria celebrada en Barcelona durante los días 25, 26 y 27 de enero de 1936*, Barcelona, 1936.

CRT de Cataluña, *Memoria del Congreso Extraordinario de la Confederación Regional del Trabajo de Cataluña celebrado en Barcelona los días 25 de febrero al 3 de marzo de 1937*, Barcelona, 1937.

FAI, *Memoria del Pleno Peninsular de Regionales, celebrado en Madrid los días 28, 29 y 30 de octubre de 1933*, Barcelona, 1933.

FAI, *Memoria del Pleno Peninsular, celebrado los días 30 de enero y 1 de febrero de 1936*, Barcelona, 1936.

FTN, *Memoria de la Junta Directiva Correspondiente al Ejercicio de 1931*, Barcelona, 1932.

FTN, *Memoria de la Junta Directiva Correspondiente al Ejercicio de 1932*, Barcelona, 1933.

FTN, *Memoria de la Junta Directiva Correspondiente al Ejercicio de 1933*, Barcelona, 1934.

FTN, *Memoria de la Junta Directiva Correspondiente al Ejercicio de 1934*, Barcelona, 1935.

Ministerio de Trabajo y Previsión, *Estadística de los accidentes de trabajo*, Madrid, 1930.

Ministerio de Trabajo y Previsión Social, *Labor realizada desde la proclamación de la República hasta el 8 de septiembre de 1932*, Madrid, n.d.

Memoirs, eye-witness accounts, contemporary sources and theoretical works by protagonists

Abad de Santillán, Diego, *Por qué perdimos la guerra*, Buenos Aires, 1940.

——— *El anarquismo y la revolución en España. Escritos 1930–1938*, Madrid, 1976.

——— Diego, *Memorias, 1897–1936*, Barcelona, 1977.

Agrupación Amigos de Durruti, *Hacia la segunda revolución*, n.p., n.d.

Aiguader i Miró, Jaume, 'La solució de la casa higiènica i a bon preu', *Ateneu Enciclopèdic Popular Noticiari*, 17, 1922.

Aiguader i Miró, Jaume, *Catalunya i la Revolució*, Barcelona, 1931.

Aiguader i Miró, Jaume, *El problema de l'habitació obrera a Barcelona*, Barcelona, 1932.

Alaiz, Félipe, *Azaña: combatiente en la paz, pacifista en la guerra*, Toulouse, n.d.

Ametlla, Claudi, *Memòries polítiques*, 2 vols, Barcelona, 1963 and 1979.

Ametlla, Claudi, *Catalunya, paradís perdut (la guerra civil i la revolució anarco-comunista)*, Barcelona, 1984.

Azaña, Manuel, *Obras completas*, 4 vols, Mexico, 1966–68.

Balius, Jaume, *Octubre catalán*, Barcelona, n.d.

Ballester, Joan, *Memòries d'un noi de Gràcia*, Barcelona, 1999.

Barangó-Solís, Fernando, *Reportajes Pintorescos*, Barcelona, 1934.

Bellmunt, Domenec de, *Les Catacumbes de Barcelona*, Barcelona, 1930.

Berenguer, Dámaso, *De la Dictadura a la República*, Madrid, 1931.

Beriain Azqueta, Demetrio, *Prat de Llobregat, ayer: un pueblo sin estado (relatos y semblanzas)*, n.p., n.d.

Berruezo Silvente, José, *Por el sendero de mis recuerdos (1920–1939)*, Santa Coloma de Gramanet, 1987.

Bertrana, Aurora, *Memòries del 1935 fins al retorn a Catalunya*, Barcelona, 1975.

Borkenau, Franz, *The Spanish Cockpit. An eyewitness account of the political and social conflicts of the Spanish Civil War*, London, 1937.

Buenacasa, Manuel, *La CNT, los 'treinta' y la FAI*, Barcelona, 1933.

Bueso, Adolfo, *Recuerdos de un cenetista*, 2 vols, l'Esplugues de Llobregat, 1976–78.

Caballé y Clos, Tomás, *Barcelona roja. Dietario de la revolución (julio 1936–enero 1939)*, Barcelona, 1939.

Cambó, Francesc, *Memòries (1876–1936)*, 2 vols, Barcelona, 1981.

Cánovas Cervantes, Salvador, *Apuntes históricos de 'Solidaridad Obrera'. Proceso histórico de la revolución española*, Barcelona, 1937.

Carrasco, Alfonso, *¡Barcelona con el puño en alto! Estampas de la revolución*, Barcelona, 1936.

Carsi, Alberto, *El abastecimiento de aguas de Barcelona*, Barcelona, 1911.

Cirici, Alexandre, *Els temps barats*, Barcelona, 1977 [1973].

Claramunt i Furest, Lluís, *La lluita contra la febre tifòide a Catalunya*, Barcelona, 1933.

—— Lluís, *La pesta en el pla de Barcelona*, Barcelona, 1933.

—— Lluís, *Problemes d'urbanisme*, Barcelona, 1934.

Coromines, Pere, *Diaris i Records de Pere Coromines. La República i la Guerra Civil*, Barcelona, 1975.

Dencàs, Josep, *El 6 d'octubre des del Palau de Governació*, Barcelona, 1979 [1935].

Díaz Sandino, Felipe, *De la Conspiración a la Revolución, 1929–1937*, Madrid, 1990.

Farreras, Antoni, *De la Setmana Tràgica a la Implantació del Franquisme*, Barcelona, 1977.

Fernández Jurado, Ramon, *Memòries d'un militant obrer (1930–1942)*, Barcelona, 1987.

Figuerola, Albert, *Memòries d'un taxista barceloní*, Barcelona, 1976.

Foix, Pere, *Los archivos del terrorismo blanco. El fichero Lasarte, 1910–1930*, Madrid, 1978 [1931].

García Faria, Pedro, *Insalubridad en las viviendas de Barcelona*, Barcelona, 1890.

García Oliver, Juan, 'Ce que fut le 19 de juillet', *Le Libertaire*, 18 August 1938.

—— *El eco de los pasos. El anarcosindicalismo...en la calle...en el Comité de Milicias...en el gobierno...en el exilio*, Barcelona, 1978.

Gil Maestre, Manuel, *La criminalidad en Barcelona y en las grandes poblaciones*, Barcelona, 1886.

Giménez Arenas, Juan, *De la Unión a Banet. Itinerario de una rebeldía*, Madrid, 1996.

Gomis, Juan, *Testigo de poca edad (1936–1943)*, Barcelona, 1968.

Gríful, Isidre, *A los veinte anos de aquello, julio–diciembre de 1936*, Barcelona, 1956.

Gual Villalbí, Pere, *Memorias de un industrial de nuestro tiempo*, Barcelona, n.d.

Guardia Coca, Francesc de la, *Formulari práctic professional de la Policia*, Barcelona, 1934.

Guardiola, Antonio, *Barcelona en poder del Soviet (el infierno rojo). Relato de un testigo*, Barcelona, 1939.

Juderías, Julián, *La juventud delincuente. Leyes e instituciones que tienden a su regeneración*, Madrid, 1912.

Jiménez de Asúa, Luis, *El estado peligroso. Nuevo fórmula para el tratamiento penal y preventivo*, Madrid, 1922.

—— Luis, *Ley de Vagos y Maleantes. Un ensayo legislativo sobre peligrosidad sin delito*, Madrid, 1934.

Kaminski, Hanns, *Los de Barcelona*, Barcelona, 1976 [1937].

Knoblaugh, H. Edward, *Correspondent in Spain*, London, 1937.

Lacruz, Francisco, *El alzamiento, la revolución y el terror en Barcelona (19 julio 1936 – 26 enero 1939)*, Barcelona, 1943.

Laird, Megan, 'A diary of revolution', *The Atlantic Monthly*, November 1936.

Langdon-Davies, John, *Behind the Spanish Barricades*, New York, 1936.

—— 'Bombs over Barcelona', *The Spectator*, 14 July 1938.

Liarte, Ramón, *El camino de la libertad*, l'Hospitalet de Llobregat, 1983.

Llarch, Joan, *Los días rojinegros. Memorias de un niño obrero, 1936*, Barcelona, 1975.

López Arango, Emilio, and Diego Abad de Santillán, *El anarquismo en el movimiento obrero*, Buenos Aires, 1925.

López, Guillermo, *Barcelona sucia. Artículos de malas costumbres. Registro de higiene*, Barcelona, n.d.

López Rodríguez, Waldo, *Proyecto de Reorganizacion de la Policia de España*, Zaragoza, 1899.

Low, Mary, and Juan Brea, *Red Spanish Notebook*, San Francisco, 1979 [1937].

Madrid, Francesc, *Sangre en Atarazanas*, Barcelona, n.d.

Madrid, Francesc, *Ocho meses y un día en el gobierno civil de Barcelona*, Barcelona, 1932.

Malaquer Nicolau, Jordi, *Mis primeros años de trabajo, 1910–1939*, Barcelona, 1970.

Manent i Pesas, Joan, *Records d'un sindicalista llibertari català, 1916–1943*, Paris, 1976.

Martín, Enrique, *Recuerdos de un militante de la CNT*, Barcelona, 1979.

Maura, Miguel, *Así cayó Alfonso XIII...*, Barcelona, 1966.

Maurín, Joaquim, *El sindicalismo a la luz de la Revolución Rusa (Problemas que plantea la revolución social)*, Lleida, n.d.

—— *L'anarcosyndicalisme en Espagne*, Paris, 1924.

—— *El Bloque Obrero y Campesino: origen, actividad, perspectivas*, Barcelona, 1932.

—— *El fracaso del anarcosindicalismo. La crisis de la CNT*, Barcelona, 1932.

—— *Revolución y contrarrevolución en españa*, Paris, 1966 [1935].

—— *Los hombres de la Dictadura*, Barcelona, 1977 [1930].

—— *La Revolución Española*, Barcelona, 1977 [1932].

McNair, John, *Spanish Diary*, Manchester, n.d.

Miravitlles, Jaume, *Los obreros y la política*, Barcelona, 1932.

—— *Ha traït Macià?*, Barcelona, 1932.

Miró, Fidel, *Una vida intensa y revolucionaria. Juventud, amor, sueños y esperanzas*, Mexico City, 1989.

Mola Vidal, Emilio, *Memorias de mi paso por la Dirección General de Seguridad*, 3 vols, Madrid, 1933.

Molina, Juan Manuel, *Consideraciones sobre la posición de la CNT de España*, Buenos Aires, 1949.

Montseny, Frederica, *Escrits politics*, Barcelona, 1979.

—— *Mis primeros cuarenta años*, Barcelona, 1987.

Nin, Andreu, *Los problemas de la revolución española*, Barcelona, 1977.

O'Donnell, Peadar, 'An Irishman in Spain', *The Nineteenth Century*, December 1936.

—— *Salud! An Irishman in Spain*, London, 1937.

Oliva, Joan, *Recuerdos de un libre pensador nacido en Gràcia,* n.p., n.d.

Orwell, George, *Homage to Catalonia*, London, 1938.

Palou Garí, José, *Treinta y dos meses de esclavitud en la que fue zona roja de España*, Barcelona, 1939.

Paz, Abel, *Chumberas y alacranes (1921–1936)*, Barcelona, 1994.

—— *Viaje al pasado (1936–1939)*, Barcelona, 1995.

Pearse, Stansbury, 'Spain: the truth', *The Tablet*, 15 August 1936.

Peirats Valls, José, 'Una experiencia histórica del pensamiento libertario. Memorias y selección de artículos breves', *Suplementos Anthropos*, 18, 1990.

—— José, unpublished memoirs.

Peiró, Joan, *Perill a la reraguarda*, Mataró, 1936.

—— *Trayectoria de la CNT*, Mexico, 1959 [1925].

—— *Escrits, 1917–1939*, Barcelona, 1975.

Péret, Benjamin, *Death to the Pigs: Selected Writings*, London, 1988.

Pèrez Baró, Albert, *Els "Feliços" anys vint. Memòries d'un militant obrer, 1918–1926*, Palma de Mallorca, 1974.

Pestaña, Alice, *El protectorado del niño delincuente. Un ensayo de educación correcional*, Madrid, 1935.

Pestaña, Ángel, *Lo que aprendí en la vida*, 2 vols, Bilbao, 1973 [1933].

—— *Trayectoria sindicalista*, Madrid, 1974.

—— *Terrorismo en Barcelona (Memorias inéditas)*, Barcelona, 1979.

Pi Sunyer, Carles, *La República y la guerra. Memorias de un político catalán*, Mexico, 1975.

Planes, Josep Maria, *Nits de Barcelona*, Barcelona, 1931.

Porcel, Baltasar, *La revuelta permanente*, Barcelona, 1978.

Pou, Bernat, and Jaume, Magriñá, *Un año de conspiración (antes de la República)*, Barcelona, 1933.

Prat, José, *La sociedad burguesa*, Barcelona, 1934.

'Pueblo Español, Juan del', *FAI*, Madrid, n.d.

Pulido, A., *El cáncer comunista. Degeneración del socialismo y del sindicalismo*, Valencia, n.d.

Rossell i Vilar, M., *La raça*, Barcelona, 1930.

Rubió i Tudurí, Nicolau Maria, *La caseta i l'hortet*, Barcelona, n.d.

—— *Regional Planning. El Pla de distribució de zones del territori català*, Barcelona, 1932.

Salter, Cedric, *Try-Out in Spain*, New York, 1943.

Salut, Emili, *Vivers de revolucionaris. Apunts històrics del Districte Cinqué*, Barcelona, 1938.

Sanz, Ricardo, *El sindicalismo y la política. Los 'Solidarios' y 'Nosotros'*, Toulouse, 1966.

—— *Los hijos de trabajo. El sindicalismo español antes de la guerra civil*, Barcelona, 1976.

Seguí, Salvador, *Escrits*, Barcelona, 1972.

Sentís, Carles, *Viatge en Transmiserià. Crònica viscuda de la primera gran emigració a Catalunya*, Barcelona, 1994.

Serge, Victor, *Memoirs of a Revolutionary*, London, 1984 [1963].

Urales, Federico, *La barbarie gubernamental: España 1933*, Barcelona, 1933.

Vandellós, Jordi, *La immigració a Catalunya*, Barcelona, 1935.

—— *Catalunya, poble decadent*, Barcelona, 1935.

Vallmitjana, Juli, *Criminalitat tipica local*, Barcelona, 1910.

Vidiella, Rafael, *Los de ayer*, Barcelona, 1938.

Xercavins, Francisco de, *¿Cabe una institución entre la escuela y la cárcel?*, Barcelona, 1889.

Secondary sources

Abad Amorós, Maria Rosa, 'Limitación jurídica de las libertades públicas en la II República', *Cuadernos Republicanos* 16, 1993.

Abercrombie, Nicholas, Stephen Hill and Bryan S. Turner, *The Dominant Ideology Thesis*, London, 1980.

Adsuar, Josep Eduard, 'El Comité Central de Milícies Antifeixistes', *L'Avenç*, 14, 1979.

Ainaud de Lasarte, Josep Maria *et al.*, *Barcelona Contemporánea 1856–1999*, Barcelona, 1996.

Alba, Victor, *Historia de la Segunda República española*, Mexico, 1960.

—— *Història del Marxisme a Catalunya, 1919–1939*, 4 vols, Barcelona, 1974–75.

—— *Cataluña de tamaño natural*, Barcelona, 1975.

—— *Els problemes del moviment obrer català*, Barcelona, 1976.

—— *La Alianza Obrera. Historia y análisis de una táctica de unidad*, Madrid, 1978.

Alba, Victor, and Marià Casasús, *Diàlegs a Barcelona*, Barcelona, 1991.

Alcaraz i Gonzàlez, Ricard, *La Unió Socialista de Catalunya*, Barcelona, 1987.

Almeric, Lluís (Clovis Eiméric), *El hostal, la fonda, la taberna y el café en la vida Barcelonesa*, Barcelona, 1945.

—— *La Rambla de Barcelona, su historia urbana y sentimental*, Barcelona, 1945.

Alquézar, Ramón, *L'Ajuntament de Barcelona en el Marc del Front d'Esquerrres*, Barcelona, 1986.

Alvarez Junco, José, *La ideología política del anarquismo español (1868–1910)*, Madrid, 1991 [1976].

—— *El Emperador del Paralelo. Lerroux y la demagogia populista*, Madrid, 1990.

Alvarez Junco, José, and Manuel Pérez Ledesma, 'Historia del movimiento obrero. ¿Una segunda ruptura?', *Revista de Occidente*, 1982, 12.

Álvarez-Uría, Fernando, *Miserables y locos. Medicina mental y Orden social en la España del siglo XIX*, Barcelona, 1983.

—— 'Vells i nous pobres. Rodamons i pobres vàlids a la llum de les ciències socials i polítiques', *Acàcia* 3, 1993.

Amàlia Pradas, Maria, 'Pistoles i pistolers. El mapa de la violència a la Barcelona dels anys 1920', *L'Avenç* 285, 2003.

Andreassi Cieri, Alejandro, *Libertad también se escribe en minúscula. Anarcosindicalismo en Sant Adrià del Besòs, 1925–1939*, Barcelona, 1996.

Arias Velasco, José, *La Hacienda de la Generalidad, 1931–1938*, Barcelona, 1977.

Arranz, Manel, Camps, Nicasi *et al.*, *El Poblenou: 150 anys d'història*, Barcelona, 1991.

Artal, Francesc, Emili Gasch, Carme Massana and Francesc Roca, *El pensament econòmic català durant la República i la guerra civil (1931–1939)*, Barcelona, 1976.

Artigas i Vidal, Jaume *et al.*, *El Raval. Història d'un barri servidor d'una ciutat*, Barcelona, 1980.

Artís i Tomás, Andreu Avel.li (Sempronio), *Aquella entremaliada Barcelona*, Barcelona, 1978.

Balcells, Albert, *El sindicalismo en Barcelona, 1916–1923*, Barcelona, 1965.

—— *Crisis económica y agitación social en Cataluña (1930–1936)*, Barcelona, 1971.

Balcells, Albert (ed.), *El arraigo del anarquismo en Cataluña. Textos de 1926–1932*, Madrid, 1973.

—— *Marxismo y catalanismo, 1930–1936*, Barcelona, 1977.

—— *Historia Contemporánea de Cataluña*, Barcelona, 1983.

Balcells Albert (ed.), *Violència social i poder polític. Sis estudis històrics sobre la Catalunya contemporània*, Barcelona, 2001.

Ballbé y Rama, Manuel, *Orden público y militarismo en la España constitucional (1812–1983)*, Madrid, 1985.

Bayer, Osvaldo, *Anarchism and Violence. Severino di Giovanni in Argentina, 1923–1931*, London, 1986.

Bengoechea, Soledad, *Organització patronal i conflictivitat social a Catalunya; tradició i corporativisme entre finals de segle i la Dictadura de Primo de Rivera*, Barcelona, 1994.

Berman, Marshall, *All That Is Solid Melts Into Air. The Experience of Modernity*, London, 1983.

Bolloten, Burnett, *The Spanish Civil War. Revolution and Counter-revolution*, Hemel Hempstead, 1991.

Bonamusa, Francesc, *El Bloc Obrer i Camperol: Els primers anys, 1930–1932*, Barcelona, 1974.

Bonamusa, Francesc, Pere Gabriel, Josep Lluís Martín Ramos and Josep Termes, *Història Gràfica del Moviment Obrer a Catalunya*, Barcelona, 1989.

Bookchin, Murray, *The Spanish Anarchists: The Heroic Years, 1868–1936*, Edinburgh, 1997 (second, revised edition).

Borderias, Cristina, 'La insurrección del Alto Llobregat. Enero 1932. Un estudio de historia oral', unpublished MA thesis, Barcelona University, 1977.

Borkenau, Franz, 'State and revolution in the Paris Commune, the Russian Revolution, and the Spanish Civil War', *The Sociological Review* 29 (1), 1937.

Brademas, John, *Anarcosindicalismo y revolución en España (1930–1937)*, l'Esplugues de Llobregat, 1974.

Broué, Pierre, *La revolución española*, Barcelona, 1977.

Broué, Pierre, Ronald Fraser and Pierre Vilar, *Metodología histórica de la Guerra y Revolución españolas*, Barcelona, 1980.

Broué, Pierre, and Emile Témime, *The Revolution and the Civil War in Spain*, London, 1972.

Bru de Sala, Xavier (ed.), *Barcelona–Madrid, 1898–1998: sintonías y distancias*, Barcelona, 1997.

Bueso, Adolfo, *Como fundamos la CNT*, Barcelona, 1976.

Busquets Grau, Joan, *Barcelona. Evolución urbanística de una capital compacta*, Madrid, 1992.

Caballé y Clos, Tomás, *La criminalidad en Barcelona*, Barcelona, 1945.

Cabré, Anna and Isabel Pujades, 'La població de Barcelona i el seu entorn al segle XX', *L'Avenç* 88, 1985.

Cabrera, Mercedes, *La patronal ante la Segunda República. Organizaciones y estrategia, 1931–1936*, Madrid, 1983.

Calhoun, Craig, 'Class, place and industrial revolution', in Nigel Thrift and Peter Williams (eds), *Class and Space. The Making of Urban Society*, London, 1987.

Camós i Cabecerón, Joan, 'Testimoniatges de Francesc Pedra i Marià Corominas. L'activitat política a l'Hospitalet de Llobregat (1923–46)', *L'Avenç* 60, 1983.

——— *L'Hospitalet: la història de tots nosaltres, 1930–1936*, Barcelona, 1986.

Cañellas, Cèlia, and Rosa Toran, 'Dels regionalistes de la Lliga a la Dictadura de Primo de Rivera', *L'Avenç* 58, 1983.

——— 'El domini hegemònic d'Esquerra Republicana (1931–1939)', *L'Avenç* 58, 1983.

——— 'L'Ajuntament de Barcelona i el règim restauracionista (1875–1901)', *L'Avenç* 116, 1988.

Cappelletti, Angel, *et al.*, 'Diego Abad de Santillán. Un anarquismo sin adjetivos. Una visión crítica y actual de la revolución social', *Anthropos* 138, 1992.

Carrasquer, Félix, *et al.*, 'Félix Carrasquer. Proyecto de una sociedad libertaria: experiencias históricas y actualidad', *Anthropos* 90, 1988.

Casanovas i Codina, Joan, 'El testimoniatge d'un membre de les patrulles de control de Sants', in *La guerra i la revolucio a Catalunya. II Col.loqui Internacional sobre la Guerra Civil Espanyola (1936–1939)*, Barcelona, 1986.

Casassas i Simó, Lluís, *Barcelona i l'Esplai Català*, Barcelona, 1977.

Castells Durán, Antoni, *Les col.lectivitzacions a Barcelona, 1936–1939*, Barcelona, 1993.

Castells, Manuel, *The Urban Question. A Marxist Approach*, London, 1977.

Castillo, José del, and Santiago Alvarez, *Barcelona, Objetivo Cubierto*, Barcelona, 1958.

Castro Alfín, Demetrio, 'Cultura, política y cultura política en la violencia anticlerical', in Rafael Cruz and Manuel Pérez Ledesma (eds), *Cultura y movilización en la España contemporánea*, Madrid, 1997.

Connelly Ullman, Joan, *The Tragic Week. A Study of Anticlericalism in Spain, 1875–1912*, Cambridge, Mass., 1968.

Correa López, Marcos José, *La ideología de la CNT a través de sus Congresos*, Cádiz, 1993.

Cruells, Manuel, *Francesc Macià*, Barcelona, 1971.

——— *La revolta del 1936 à Barcelona*, Barcelona, 1976.

Cuadernos de Ruedo Ibérico, *El movimiento libertario español*, Paris, 1974.

Cucurull, Félix, *Catalunya, republicana i autònoma (1931–1936)*, Barcelona, 1984.

Culla i Clarà, Joan B., *El Catalanisme d'Esquerra (1928–1936). Del grup de L'Opinió al Partit Nacionalista Republica d'Esquerra*, Barcelona, 1977.

Delgado, Manuel, *La ira sagrada: anticlericalismo, iconoclastia y antirritualismo en la España contemporánea*, Barcelona, 1992.

Durgan, Andrew, *BOC, 1930–1936: El Bloque Obrero y Campesino*, Barcelona, 1996.

Durgan, Andrew, 'Els comunistes dissidentes i els sindicats a la Catalunya Republicana', *L'Avenç* 142, 1990.

Ealham, Chris, 'Crime and punishment in 1930s Barcelona', *History Today*, October 1993.

—— 'Anarchism and illegality in Barcelona, 1931–1937', *Contemporary European History* 4 (2), 1995.

—— '"From the summit to the abyss": the contradictions of individualism and collectivism in Spanish anarchism', in Paul Preston and Ann MacKenzie (eds), *The Republic Besieged: Civil War in Spain, 1936–39*, Edinburgh, 1996.

—— 'La lluita pel carrer, els vendedors ambulants durant la II República', *L'Avenç* 230, 1998.

—— '"Revolutionary gymnastics" and the unemployed: the limits of the anarchist revolutionary utopia in Spain, 1931–1937', in Keith Flett and David Renton (eds), *The Twentieth Century: A Century of Progress?*, London, 2000.

—— 'Class and the city: spatial memories of pleasure and danger in Barcelona, 1914–23', *Oral History* 29 (1), 2001.

—— 'The crisis of organised labour: the battle for hegemony in the Barcelona workers' movement, 1930–1936', in Angel Smith (ed.), *Red Barcelona*, London, 2002.

Elorza, Antonio, *La utopía anarquista bajo la Segunda República*, Madrid, 1973.

Enzensberger, Hans Magnus, *El corto verano de la anarquía. Vida y muerte de Buenaventura Durruti*, Barcelona, 1977.

Estivill, Jordi, and Gustau Barbat, 'L'anticlericalisme en la revolta popular del 1909', *L'Avenç* 2, 1977.

—— 'Anticléricalisme populaire en Catalogne au début du siècle', *Social Compass* 27, 2–3, 1980.

Eyre, Pilar, *Quico Sabaté, el último guerrillero*, Barcelona, 2000.

Fabre, Jaume, and Josep Maria Huertas, *Tots els barris de Barcelona*, 8 vols, Barcelona, 1976.

—— 'Amb Hermós Plaja. El pare de dues acràcies', *L'Avenç* 28, 1980.

—— 'Juanel i Lola Iturbe, una vida d'amor i d'anarquia', *L'Avenç* 39, 1981.

Ferrer, Joaquim and Simó Piera, *Simó Piera: Perfil d'un sindicalista. Records i experiències d'un dirigent de la CNT*, Barcelona, 1975.

Ferrer, Rai, *Durruti, 1896–1936*, Barcelona, 1985.

Fishman, Robert, *Bourgeois Utopias*, New York, 1987.

Foix, Pere, *Apòstols i Mercaders. Quaranta anys de lluita social a Catalunya*, Barcelona, 1976 [1957].

Fraser, Ronald, *Blood of Spain. The Experience of Civil War, 1936–1939*, London, 1979.

Gabriel, Pere, *et al.*, 'Joan Peiró: Sindicalismo y anarquismo. Actualidad de una historia', *Anthropos* 114, 1990.

Gallardo Romero, Juan José, and José Manuel Márquez Rodríguez, *Revolución y guerra en Gramenet de Besòs (1936–1939)*, Santa Coloma de Gramenet, 1997.

Gallardo Romero, Juan José, and José Manuel Márquez Rodríguez, *Ortiz: General sin dios ni amo*, Santa Coloma de Gramanet, 1999.

García, Soledad, 'Urbanization, working class organization and political movements in Barcelona', unpublished PhD thesis, University of Hull, 1983.

García Castro de la Peña, Teresa, 'Barrios barceloneses de la dictadura de Primo de Rivera', *Revista de Geografía*, 7 (1–2), 1974.

García Delgado, José Luis (ed.), *Las ciudades en la modernizaci¢n de España. Los decenios interseculares*, Madrid, 1992.

Gil, Carlos, *Echarse a la calle. Amotinados, huelguistas y revolucionarios (La Rioja, 1890–1936)*, Zaragoza, 2000.

Golden, Lester, 'Les dones com avantguarda: el rebombori del pa del gener de 1918', *L'Avenç* 45, 1981.

Gómez Casas, Juan, *Historia del anarcosindicalismo español*, Madrid, 1969.

—— *Historia de la FAI. Aproximación a la historia de la organización específica del anarquismo y sus antecedentes de la Alianza de la Democracia Socialista*, Madrid, 1977.

González Calleja, Eduardo, and Fernando del Rey Reguillo, *La defensa armada contra la revolución. Una historia de las «guardias cívicas» en la España del siglo XX*, Madrid, 1995.

González Casanova, José Antonio, *Elecciones en Barcelona, 1931–1936*, Madrid, 1969.

—— *Federalismo y Autonomia en Cataluña (1868–1938)*, Barcelona, 1979.

González Urién, Miguel, and Fidel Revilla González, *La CNT a través de sus Congresos*, Mexico City, 1981.

Graham, Helen, ' "Against the state": a genealogy of the Barcelona May Days (1937)', *European History Quarterly* 29 (1), 1999.

—— *The Spanish Republic at War, 1936–1939*, Cambridge, 2002.

Gregory, Derek, and John Urry (eds), *Social Relations and Spatial Structures*, London, 1985.

Guillamón, Agustín, 'Los amigos de Durruti, 1937–1939', *Balance* 3, 1994.

Gutiérrez Molina, José Luis, *La Idea revolucionaria. El anarquismo organizado en Andalucía y Cádiz durante los años treinta*, Madrid, 1993.

Hall, Stuart, Chas Critcher, Tony Jefferson, John Clarke and Brian Roberts, *Policing the Crisis: Mugging, the State and Law and Order*, London, 1978.

Harris, Richard, 'Residential segregation and class formation in the capitalist city', *Progress in Human Geography* 8 (1), 1984.

Harvey, David, *Consciousness and the Urban Experience: Studies in the History and Theory of Capitalist Urbanisation*, Baltimore, 1985.

—— *Spaces of Hope*, Edinburgh, 2000.

Hernández Andreu, Juan, *La depresión económica en España*, Madrid, 1980.

Heywood, Paul, *Marxism and the Failure of Organised Socialism in Spain, 1879–1936*, Cambridge, 1990.

Huertas, Josep Maria, *Obrers a Catalunya. Manual d'història del moviment obrer (1840–1975)*, Barcelona, 1994.

Humphries, Stephen, 'Steal to survive: the social crime of working class children, 1890–1940', *Oral History* 9 (1), 1981.

Ivern i Salvà, Maria Dolors, *Esquerra Republicana de Catalunya (1931–1936)*, 2 vols, Montserrat, 1988–89.

Jackson, Peter, *Maps of Meaning*, London, 1992.

Jutglar, Antoni, *Historía crítica de la burguesía catalana*, Barcelona, 1984.

Katznelson, Ira, 'Community, capitalist development, and the emergence of class', *Politics and Society* 9 (2), 1979.

—— *Marxism and the City*, Oxford, 1992.

Lefebvre, Henri, *Le droit à la ville*, Paris, 1968.

—— *Writings on Cities*, Oxford, 1996.

Lera, Angel Maria de, *Angel Pestaña: Retrato de un anarquista*, Barcelona, 1978.

Léon-Ignacio, *Los años del pistolerismo*, Barcelona, 1981.

—— 'El pistolerisme dels anys vint', *L'Avenç* 52, 1982.

Leval, Gaston, *Collectives in the Spanish Revolution*, London, 1975.

Lladonosa, Manuel, *El Congrés de Sants*, Barcelona, 1975.

—— *Sindicalistes i llibertaris. L'experiència de Camil Piñón*, Barcelona, 1989.

Llarch, Joan, *Obreros mártires de la libertad*, Barcelona, 1978.

—— *La muerte de Durruti*, Barcelona, 1985.

Lleixà, Joaquim, *Cien años de militarismo en España. Funciones estatales confiadas al Ejército en la Restauración y el Franquismo*, Barcelona, 1986.

Llorens, Ignacio de, *et al.*, 'José Peirats Valls: Historia contemporánea del Movimiento Libertario. Visión crítica de un compromiso anarquista: la Revolución Social', *Anthropos* 102, 1989.

López Garrido, Diego, *La Guardia Civil y los orígenes del Estado centralista*, Barcelona, 1982.

López Sánchez, Pere, *Un verano con mil julios y otras estaciones. Barcelona: de la Reforma Interior a la Revolución de Julio de 1909*, Madrid, 1993.

—— 'El desorde de l'ordre. Al.legats de la ciutat disciplinària en el somni de la Gran Barcelona', *Acàcia* 3, 1993.

Lorenzo, César, *Los anarquistas y el poder, 1868–1969*, Paris, 1972.

Macarro Vera, José Manuel, 'La disolución de la utopía en el movimiento anarcosindicalista español', *Historia Social* 15, 1993.

Marcet, Xavier, and Josep Puy, 'Francesc Sàbat: anarcosindicalista, batlle i exiliat', *L'Avenç* 45, 1982.

Marin, Dolors, 'Una primera aproximació a la vida quotidiana dels Hospitalencs: 1920–1929. Les històries de vida com a font històrica', *Identitats* 4–5, 1990.

—— 'De la llibertat per conèixer, al coneixement de la llibertat. L'adquisició de cultura durant la dictadura de Primo de Rivera i la Segona República Espanyola', unpublished PhD thesis, Barcelona University, 1995.

—— *Clandestinos. El Maquis contra el franquismo, 1934–1975*, Barcelona, 2002.

Martin, Benjamin, *The Agony of Modernization. Labor and Industrialization in Spain*, Ithaca, NY, 1990.

Masjuan Bracons, Eduard, *Urbanismo y ecología en Cataluña*, Madrid, 1992.

—— *La ecología humana en el anarquismo ibérico*, Barcelona, 2000.

Massana, Carme, and Francesc Roca, 'Vicis privats, iniciativa pública. Barcelona 1901–1939', *L'Avenç* 88, 1985.

Massana, Carme, *Indústria, ciutat i propietat. Política econòmica i propietat urbana a l'Área de Barcelona (1901–1939)*, Barcelona, 1985.

Mintz, Frank, and Miguel Peciña, *Los amigos de Durruti, los trotsquistas y los sucesos de mayo*, Madrid, 1978.

Miravitlles, Jaume, *Gent que he conegut*, Barcelona, 1980.

Miró, Fidel, *Cataluña, los trabajadores y el problema de las nacionalidades*, Mexico City, 1967.

Molas, Isidre, *Lliga Catalana. Un estudi d'Estasiologia*, 2 vols, Barcelona, 1972.

—— *El sistema de partidos políticos en Cataluña, 1931–1936*, Barcelona, 1973.

Monjo, Anna, and Carme Vega, *Els treballadors i la guerra civil. Història d'una indústria catalana col.lectivitzada*, Barcelona, 1986.

Monjo, Anna, 'La CNT durant la II República a Barcelona: líders, militants, afiliats', unpublished PhD thesis, Universitat de Barcelona, 1993.

Monreal, Antonio, *El pensamiento político de Joaquim Maurín*, Barcelona, 1984.

Montero, Enrique, 'Reform idealized: the intellectual and ideological origins of the Second Republic', in Helen Graham and Jo Labanyi (eds), *Spanish Cultural Studies: An Introduction*, Oxford, 1995.

Moorhouse, Bert and Chris Chamberlain, 'Lower class atittudes to property: aspects of the counter-ideology', *Sociology* 8 (3), 1974.

Muniesa, Bernat, *La burguesía catalana ante la II República*, 2 vols, Barcelona, 1985–86.

Munis, Gregorio, *Jalones de derrota, promesa de victoria. Crítica y teoría de la Revolución Española*, Bilbao, 1977.

Muñoz Diez, Manuel, *Marianet, semblanza de un hombre*, Mexico, 1960.

Núñez Florencio, Rafael, *El terrorismo anarquista, 1888–1909*, Madrid, 1983.

—— 'El ejército ante la agitación social en España (1875–1914)', in J. Alvarado and R. Maria Pérez (eds), *Estudios sobre ejército, política y derecho en España (siglos XII–XX)*, Madrid, 1996.

Ossorio y Gallardo, Angel, *Vida y sacrificio de Lluís Companys*, Buenos Aires, 1943.

Oyón, José Luis (ed.), *Vida obrera en la Barcelona de entreguerras*, Barcelona, 1998.

Oyón, José Luis, 'Obreros en la ciudad: líneas de un proyecto de investigación en historia urbana', *Historia Contemporánea* 18, 1999.

Pagès, Pelai, *Andreu Nin: su evolución política (1911–1937)*, Madrid, 1975.

Paniagua, Xavier, *La sociedad libertaria. Agrarismo e industrialización en el anarquismo español (1930–1939)*, Barcelona, 1982.

—— 'Una gran pregunta y varias respuestas. El anarquismo español: desde la política a la historiografía', *Historia Social* 12, 1992.

Paz, Abel, *Durruti, El proletariado en armas*, Barcelona, 1978.

—— *19 de Juliol del '36' à Barcelona*, Barcelona, 1988.

—— *Durruti en la Revolución española*, Madrid, 1996.

Pearson, Geoffrey, *Hooligan. A History of Respectable Fears*, London, 1983.

Peirats, José, *Examen crítico-constructivo del movimiento libertario español*, Mexico, 1967.

—— *Figuras del movimiento libertario español*, Barcelona, 1978.

—— *La CNT en la revolución española*, 3 vols, Madrid, 1978.

—— *Mecanismo orgánico de la Confederación Nacional del Trabajo*, Barcelona, 1979.

Peiró, Josep, *Juan Peiró. Teórico y militante de anarcosindicalismo español*, Barcelona, 1978.

Perau, Martí, *et al.*, *Noucentisme i ciutat*, Barcelona, 1994.

Pérez Ledesma, Manuel, *Estabilidad y conflicto social: España, de los íberos al 14-D*, Madrid, 1990.

—— 'Studies on anticlericalism in contemporary Spain', *International Review of Social History* 46, 2001.

Pi, Joan del, *Interpretació llibertari del moviment obrer català*, Bordeaux, 1946.

Pile, Steve, and Michael Keith (eds), *Geographies of Resistance*, London, 1997.

Pile, Steve, Christopher Brook and Gerry Mooney (eds), *Unruly Cities*, London, 1999.

Piven, Frances Fox, and Richard A. Cloward, *Poor People's Movements. Why They Succeed, How They Fail*, New York, 1977.

Poblet, Josep Maria, *Jaume Aiguader: una vida 'amb Catalunya i per Catalunya'*, Barcelona, 1977.

Pomares, Assumpció, and Vicenç Valentí, 'Notas per a un estudi sobre el control social a la Barcelona del segle XIX: la instrucció pública', *Acàcia* 3, 1993.

Preston, Paul, *The Coming of the Spanish Civil War. Reform, Reaction and Revolution in the Second Republic*, London, 1978.

Preston, Paul (ed.), *Revolution and War in Spain, 1931–1939*, London, 1986.

Rama, Carlos M., *La crisis española del siglo XX*, Mexico, 1976.

Ranzato, Gabriele, 'Dies Irae. La persecuzione religiosa nella zona repubblicana durante la Guerra civile spagnola (1936–1939)', *Movimento operaio e socialista* 2, 1988.

Rey Reguillo, Fernando del, *Propietarios y patronos. La política de las organizaciones económicas en la España de la Restauración*, Madrid, 1992.

Rider, Nick, 'Anarquisme i lluita popular: la vaga dels lloguers de 1931', *L'Avenç* 89, 1986.

—— 'Anarchism, urbanisation and social conflict in Barcelona, 1900–1932', unpublished PhD thesis, University of Lancaster, 1987.

—— 'The practice of direct action: the Barcelona rent strike of 1931', in David Goodway (ed.), *For Anarchism: History, Theory, Practice*, London, 1989.

Roca, Francesc, *El Pla Macià*, Barcelona, 1977.

—— *Política econòmica i territori a Catalunya (1901–1939)*, Barcelona 1979.

Roca, Joan (ed.), *L'articulació social de la Barcelona contemporània*, Barcelona, 1997.

—— *El municipi de Barcelona i els combats pel govern de la ciutat*, Barcelona, 1997.

Roca Cladera, Josep, and Enriqueta Díaz Perera, 'La Torrassa. Un antecedent de barri-dormitori', *L'Avenç* 28, 1980.

Romero Maura, Joaquín, *'La Rosa del Fuego'. Republicanos y anarquistas: la política de los obreros barceloneses entre el desastre colonial y la Semana Trágica, 1899–1909*, Madrid, 1989.

Rosenhaft, Eve, *Beating the Fascists? The German Communists and Political Violence, 1929–1933*, Cambridge, 1983.

Ruipérez, María, 'Federica Montseny: cultura y anarquía', *Tiempo de Historia* 52, 1979.

Sánchez, Alejandro (ed.), *Barcelona, 1888–1929. Modernidad, ambición y conflictos de una ciudad soñada*, Madrid, 1994.

Sánchez, José M., *The Spanish Civil War as a Religious Tragedy*, Notre Dame, Indiana, 1987.

Sánchez, Mariano, *et al.*, *Los sucesos de mayo de 1937, una revolución en la República*, Barcelona, 1988.

Santacana i Torres, Carles, *Victoriosos i derrotats: el franquisme a l'Hospitalet, 1939–1951*, Barcelona, 1994.

Scott, James C., *Weapons of the Weak. Everyday Forms of Peasant Resistance*, New Haven, Conn., 1985.

Seidman, Michael, *Workers against Work. Labor in Paris and Barcelona during the Popular Fronts*, Berkeley, Calif., 1991.

Sibley, David, *Geographies of Exclusion. Society and Difference in the West*, London, 1995.

Siguán, Marisa, *et al.*, 'Federico Urales: Una cultura de la acracia, ejercicio de un proyecto de libertad solidaria', *Anthropos* 78, 1987.

Sirera Oliag, Maria José, 'Obreros en Barcelona, 1900–1910', unpublished PhD thesis, Universitat de Barcelona, 1959.

Soja, Edward, *Postmodern Geographies. The Reassertion of Space in Critical Social Theory*, London, 1989.

Solá, Lluís, *El Be Negre (1931–1936)*, Barcelona, 1967.

Solà i Gussinyer, Pere, *Els Ateneus Obrers i la cultura popular a Catalunya (1900–1936): l'Ateneu Enciclopèdic Popular*, Barcelona, 1978.

—— L'ateneísme àcrata durant la segona república', *L'Avenç* 11, 1978.

Solà–Morales, Ignasi, 'L'Exposició Internacional de Barcelona (1914–1929) com a instrument de política urbana', *Recerques* 6, 1976.

Solé i Sabat, Josep Maria, and Joan Villarroya i Font, *La repressió a la reraguarda de Catalunya (1936–1939)*, 2 vols, Barcelona, 1989.

Solé-Tura, Jordi, *Catalanismo y revolución burguesa. La síntesis de Prat de la Riba*, Madrid, 1970.

Soto Carmona, Álvaro, *El trabajo industrial en la España contemporánea (1874–1936)*, Barcelona, 1989.

Souchy, Agustín, and Paul Folgare, *Colectivizaciones: la obra constructiva de la revolución española*, Barcelona, 1977.

Tatjer Mir, Mercè, 'La inmigración en Barcelona en 1930: los andaluces en la Barceloneta', *Estudios Geográficos* 159, 1980.

Taylor, Ian, Paul Walton and Jock Young, *The New Criminology. For a Social Theory of Deviance*, London, 1973.

Taylor, Ian, Paul Walton and Jock Young (eds), *Critical Criminology*, London, 1975.

Taylor, Michael, *Community, Anarchy and Liberty*, Cambridge, 1982.

Termes, Josep, *Federalismo, anarcosindicalismo, catalanismo*, Barcelona, 1976.

—— *La immigració a Catalunya i altres estudis d'història del nacionalisme català*, Barcelona, 1984.

—— 'Els ateneus populars: un intent de cultura obrera', L'Avenç 105, 1987.

Terrades, Ignasi, 'Towards a comparative approach to the study of industrial and urban politics: the case of Spain', in Michael Harloe (ed.), *New Perspectives in Urban Change and Conflict*, London, 1981.

Topalov, Christian, 'Social policies from below: a call for comparative historical studies', *International Journal of Urban and Regional Research* 9 (2), 1985.

Trinidad Fernández, Pedro, 'La configuració històrica del subjecte delinqüent', *Acàcia* 3, 1993.

Tuñón de Lara, Manuel, *El movimiento obrero en la historia de España*, Madrid, 1972.

Turrado Vidal, Martín, *La policía en la historia contemporánea de España (1766–1986)*, Madrid, 1995.

Ucelay da Cal, Enric, *La Catalunya Populista. Imatge, cultura i política en l'etapa republicana (1931–1939)*, Barcelona 1982.

Vega i Massana, Eulàlia, *El trentisme a Catalunya. Divergéncies ideològiques en la CNT (1930–1933)*, Barcelona, 1980.

—— 'La CNT a les comarques catalanes (1931–1936)', *L'Avenç* 34, 1981.

—— 'La Confederació Nacional del Treball i els Sindicats d'Oposició a Catalunya i el País Valencià (1930–1936)', unpublished PhD thesis, Barcelona University, 1986, 3 vols.

—— *Anarquistas y sindicalistas, 1931–1936*, Valencia, 1987.

Villar, Paco, *Historia y leyenda del Barrio Chino (1900–1992). Crónica y documentos de los bajos fondos de Barcelona*, Barcelona, 1996.

Villarroya i Font, Joan, *Els bombardeigs de Barcelona durant la guerra civil (1936–1939)*, Barcelona, 1981.

Vinyes i Ribes, Ricard, *La Catalunya Internacional. El frontpopulisme en l'exemple català*, Barcelona, 1983.

—— 'Bohemis, marxistes, bolxevics. De la indigència a la revolució', *L'Avenç* 77, 1984.

—— *La presència ignorada: la cultura comunista a Catalunya (1840–1931)*, Barcelona, 1989.

Williams, Raymond, *The Country and the City*, London, 1973.

Willis, Paul, *Learning to Labour: How Working Class Kids Get Working Class Jobs*, Farnborough, 1977.

Index

Support AK Press!

AK Press is one of the world's largest and most productive

anarchist publishing houses. We're entirely worker-run and democratically managed. We operate without a corporate structure—no boss, no managers, no bullshit. We publish close to twenty books every year, and distribute thousands of other titles published by other like-minded independent presses from around the globe.

The Friends of AK program is a way that you can directly contribute to the continued existence of AK Press, and ensure that we're able to keep publishing great books just like this one! Friends pay a minimum of $25 per month, for a minimum three month period, into our publishing account. In return, Friends automatically receive (for the duration of their membership), as they appear, one free copy of every new AK Press title. They're also entitled to a 20% discount on everything featured in the AK Press Distribution catalog and on the website, on any and every order. You or your organization can even sponsor an entire book if you should so choose!

There's great stuff in the works—so sign up now to become a Friend of AK Press, and let the presses roll!

Won't you be our friend? Email friendsofak@akpress.org for more info, or visit the Friends of AK Press website: http://www.akpress.org/programs/friendsofak

Printed in the USA
CPSIA information can be obtained
at www.ICGtesting.com
JSHW011059290824
69014JS00013B/238